To Mom and Dad
To Tutdé and Tutnang
And to all new life and new creation born of love, courage, faith,
and a little bit of luck

Sing whenever you want to
And if they say you're out of tune don't stop
It's your voice, and that's who you are

Music of Death and New Creation

Music of Death and New Creation

Experiences in the World of Balinese Gamelan Beleganjur

Michael B. Bakan

The University of Chicago Press
Chicago and London

MICHAEL B. BAKAN is assistant professor of ethnomusicology in the School of Music at Florida State University, where he directs the Sekaa Gong Hanuman Agung Balinese gamelan. He has composed numerous original works for gamelan and is a professional percussionist.

The University of Chicago Press, Chicago 60637
The University of Chicago Press, Ltd., London
© 1999 by The University of Chicago
All rights reserved. Published 1999

08 07 06 05 04 03 02 01 00 99 1 2 3 4 5
ISBN: 0-226-03487-9 (cloth)
ISBN: 0-226-03488-7 (paper)

Library of Congress Cataloging-in-Publication Data

Bakan, Michael B.
    Music of death and new creation : experiences in the world of Balinese gamelan beleganjur /
Michael B. Bakan.
        p.   cm. — (Chicago studies in ethnomusicology)
    Discography: p.
    Includes bibliographical references and index.
        ISBN 0-226-03487-9 (cloth : alk. paper). — ISBN 0-226-03488-7 (paperback : alk. paper)
            1. Music—Indonesia—Bali Island—History and criticism.
    2. Gamelan.   3. Gamelan music—History and criticism.   I. Title.
    II. Series.
    ML345.I5B35 1999
    784.2′09598′6—dc21   98-42727
                                                                                     CIP
                                                                                      MN

Contents

Plates, Figures, and Musical Examples

Musical Excerpts on the Compact Disc

1. Batel colotomy (p. 42)   1:02
   Recorded in 1995 by Michael Bakan at a temple festival (*oda-lan*) in Kesiman, Denpasar. Performed by Seka Gong Sandya of Banjar Kebun Kuri Tengah, Kesiman.

2. Gamelan Adi Merdangga (p. 43)   1:30
   Recorded in 1995 by Michael Bakan at the grand opening cere-mony of a McDonald's restaurant in Denpasar. Performed by Adi Merdangga STSI.

3. "Traditional" beleganjur style, ngaben
   procession (pp. 47, 71)   2:27
   Recorded in 1995 by Michael Bakan in Denpasar. Performed by the beleganjur group of Banjar Belaluan Sadmerta, Denpasar. (Note: neither ponggang nor reyong was used in this performance.)

4. Malpal, ngaben procession (pp. 47, 73)   1:15
   Recorded in 1995 by Michael Bakan in Denpasar. Performed by the beleganjur group of Banjar Belaluan Sadmerta, Denpasar.

5. Kreasi-influenced beleganjur style,
   ngaben procession (pp. 48, 71, 81)   9:06
   Recorded in 1995 by Michael Bakan in Denpasar. Performed by Sekaha Beleganjur Jaya Kusuma of Banjar Geladag Pedungan, Denpasar.

6. Gilak colotomy (p. 49)   0:24
   From the digital master recording of "Beleganjur Angga Yo-wana," originally released on the commercial cassette *Kreasi Beleganjur* (Bali Record B 720). Performed by Seka Gong Ka-lingga Jaya of Banjar Kaliungu Kaja, Denpasar. Used by permission.

7. Reverse gilak colotomy (p. 338, n. 18) 0:34

From the digital master recording of "Beleganjur Angga Yo-wana," originally released on the commercial cassette *Kreasi Beleganjur* (Bali Record B 720). Performed by Seka Gong Ka-lingga Jaya of Banjar Kaliungu Kaja, Denpasar. Used by permission.

8. Bendé part as "colotomic counterpoint" (p. 50) 0:24

Recorded in 1995 by Michael Bakan in Denpasar. Performed by Sekehe Beleganjur Adnyana Dharma of Banjar Belong, Sanur Kaja, Denpasar.

9. Inverted pyramid of rhythmic activity (p. 50) 0:48

Recorded in 1995 by Michael Bakan in Denpasar. Performed by Sekehe Beleganjur Adnyana Dharma of Banjar Belong, Sanur Kaja, Denpasar.

10. Reyong figurations (reyongan): noltol (p. 55), ngubit (long) (p. 56), lambé in "unison" texture (pp. 55, 60), ngubit (short) (p. 56) 1:16

From the digital master recording of "Beleganjur Angga Yo-wana," originally released on the commercial cassette *Kreasi Beleganjur* (Bali Record B 720). Performed by Seka Gong Ka-lingga Jaya of Banjar Kaliungu Kaja, Denpasar. Used by permission.

11. Angsel bawak (p. 61) 0:17

Recorded in 1995 by Michael Bakan in Denpasar. Performed by Sekehe Beleganjur Adnyana Dharma of Banjar Belong, Sanur Kaja, Denpasar.

12. Angsel lantang (variant) (p. 62) 0:20

Recorded in 1995 by Michael Bakan at a kite-flying competi-tion in Ketewel, Denpasar. Performed by Sekehe Beleganjur Panga Kumara of Banjar Tatasan Kaja, Denpasar.

13. Batu-batu (p. 63) 0:34

Recorded in 1995 by Michael Bakan in Denpasar. Performed by the beleganjur group of Banjar Belaluan Sadmerta, Denpasar.

14. Kilitan cengceng (pp. 66, 67) 0:23

Recorded in 1995 by Michael Bakan in Denpasar. Performed by

22. "Tabuh Pat Jagul" (arranged by I Wayan
    Beratha) (p. 136)   1:04
    From the CD *Music of the Gamelan Gong Kebyar,* vol. 1 (Vital
    Records 401). Recorded by Wayne Vitale, 1991. Performed by
    musicians from STSI Denpasar. Used by permission.

23. "Jagul" drumming, kreasi beleganjur
    (p. 136)   0:40
    From the digital master recording of "Beleganjur Angga Yo-
    wana," originally released on the commercial cassette *Kreasi
    Beleganjur* (Bali Record B 720). Performed by Seka Gong Ka-
    lingga Jaya of Banjar Kaliungu Kaja, Denpasar. Used by
    permission.

24. Lagu pengawak of "Beleganjur Angga
    Yowana" (Asnawa) (p. 140)   0:35
    From the digital master recording of "Beleganjur Angga Yo-
    wana," originally released on the commercial cassette *Kreasi
    Beleganjur* (Bali Record B 720). Performed by Seka Gong Ka-
    lingga Jaya of Banjar Kaliungu Kaja, Denpasar. Used by
    permission.

25. Pengawak, "Beleganjur Angga Yowana"
    (Asnawa) (p. 142)   2:29
    From the digital master recording of "Beleganjur Angga Yo-
    wana," originally released on the commercial cassette *Kreasi
    Beleganjur* (Bali Record B 720). Performed by Seka Gong Ka-
    lingga Jaya of Banjar Kaliungu Kaja, Denpasar. Used by
    permission.

26. "Double-time" cymbal patterns in the
    Pengawak of "Beleganjur Angga Yo-
    wana" (Asnawa) (p. 147)   0:29
    From the digital master recording of "Beleganjur Angga Yo-
    wana," originally released on the commercial cassette *Kreasi
    Beleganjur* (Bali Record B 720). Performed by Seka Gong Ka-
    lingga Jaya of Banjar Kaliungu Kaja, Denpasar. Used by
    permission.

27. Cymbal patterns in the Kawitan of "Bele-
    ganjur Angga Yowana" (Asnawa)
    (p. 147)   0:21
    From the digital master recording of "Beleganjur Angga Yo-
    wana," originally released on the commercial cassette *Kreasi*

Beleganjur (Bali Record B 720). Performed by Seka Gong Ka-
lingga Jaya of Banjar Kaliungu Kaja, Denpasar. Used by
permission.

28. "Wira Ghorava Cakti '95" (I Ketut Suan-
    dita) (pp. 150, 151)   6:18
    Recorded in 1995 by Michael Bakan during a beleganjur parade
    at the Bali Arts Festival. Performed by Sekehe Beleganjur Yu-
    wana Dharma Laksana of Banjar Meranggi, Kesiman Petilan,
    Denpasar.

29. Kecak-inspired cymbal interplay (Suan-
    dita) (p. 151)   0:21
    From the digital master recording of "Wira Ghorava Cakti"
    (1992), originally released on the commercial cassette *Balagan-
    jur: Juara I Lomba '92–'93* (Maharani/Rick's Records; no cata-
    logue number). Performed by Sekehe Beleganjur Yuwana
    Dharma Laksana of Banjar Meranggi, Kesiman Petilan, Denpa-
    sar. Used by permission.

30. Jejagulan (Sukarata) (p. 152)   1:16
    Recorded in 1992 by Michael Bakan in Denpasar. Performed by
    Sekehe Beleganjur Panga Kumara of Banjar Tatasan Kaja, Den-
    pasar. (Drummers: Sukarata and Bakan.)

31. Foreign influences: Pengecet, "Belegan-
    jur Padma Mudra" (Sukarata) (p. 156)   3:02
    Recorded in 1992 by Michael Bakan in Denpasar. Performed by
    Sekehe Beleganjur Panga Kumara of Banjar Tatasan Kaja, Den-
    pasar. (Drummers: Sukarata and Bakan.)

32. Beleganjur contest demonstration perfor-
    mance, complete (Sukarata) (p. 178)   7:51
    Recorded in 1995 by Michael Bakan in Denpasar. Performed by
    Sekehe Beleganjur Adnyana Dharma of Banjar Belong, Sanur
    Kaja, Denpasar.

33. Conclusion of "Beleganjur Angga Yo-
    wana" (Asnawa), including unconven-
    tional cymbal techniques (p. 202)   5:07
    From the digital master recording of "Beleganjur Angga Yo-
    wana," originally released on the commercial cassette *Kreasi
    Beleganjur* (Bali Record B 720). Performed by Seka Gong Ka-
    lingga Jaya of Banjar Kaliungu Kaja, Denpasar. Used by
    permission.

Acknowledgments

This book has been ten years in the making. I am grateful to many people who have helped me along the way to its completion. First, my thanks to the organizations and agencies who funded this project: the Florida State University Council on Research and Creativity, for a grant to conduct fieldwork in Bali in 1995; the University of California, Los Angeles, for a 1992–93 Laffin Dissertation Year Fellowship; the Social Science Research Council, Asian Cultural Council, and Institute for Intercultural Studies, for grants and fellowships in support of 1992 dissertation field research in Bali; and the Social Sciences and Humanities Research Council of Canada, which provided support for my 1989 and 1990 Bali fieldwork.

Some of the material in this book has appeared in other publications. Chapter 6 is a modified version of an article in *Asian Music* (Bakan 1997–98); chapter 7 is an abridged and revised version of a paper in *College Music Symposium* (Bakan 1993–94); and parts of chapters 1, 2, and 5 are found in a recent article in *Ethnomusicology* (Bakan 1998b). My thanks to the journal editors (James Cowdery, Martin Hatch, Lee Riggins, and Sean Williams) and anonymous readers of these articles for their insights and suggestions, which have been of great assistance to me in writing this book as well.

I extend my deepest gratitude to my two *gurus,* I Ketut Gedé Asnawa and I Ketut Sukarata, without whom this book would not have been possible. Their kindness and generosity, and their dedication to the development of the project, have been immeasurable. I can never thank them enough, nor their families, who so graciously welcomed me into their homes and into their lives. Let me take this opportunity to comment briefly on the different ways in which Asnawa and Sukarata are "represented" in this book. While Sukarata is accorded considerably more explicit attention than Asnawa, I must emphasize that this reflects the book's particular scholarly and narrative agendas and nothing more.

Asnawa's contributions and importance to this study were equal to Sukarata's; chapters 1–3 are as much a reflection of my work with him as chapters 7–9 are of my work with Sukarata.

Besides Asnawa and Sukarata, I am indebted to several other master Balinese musicians with whom I have studied gamelan over the years, in Bali, the United States, and Canada: I Wayan Beratha, I Wayan Dibia, I Wayan Jaya, I Nengah Jejel, I Wayan Suweca, and I Nyoman Wenten especially. Asnawa, Wenten, and Dibia, as well as I Nyoman Sedana and I Madé Lila Arsana, assisted me greatly as "technical consultants" in a variety of capacities, including reading versions (or portions) of the work at various stages of its development, assisting with translations, setting up field interviews, and patiently responding to my endless (and likely often annoying) questions. Rucina Ballinger, Judith Becker, Paul Berliner, Benjamin Brinner, Lisa Gold, David Harnish, Edward Herbst, Mantle Hood, Margaret Kartomi, Charles Keil, Andrew McGraw, Bruno Nettl, Sumarsam, Emiko Susilo, Michael Tenzer, Andrew Toth, Wayne Vitale, Richard Wallis, Sarah Willner, and others in the Balinese studies and ethnomusicology communities were also extremely generous in sharing their expertise on a variety of matters. At the dissertation stage and beyond, the members of my committee—Jacqueline Dje Dje, Colin Quigley, Philip Newman, and most especially Elaine Barkin, Sue Carole DeVale, and Timothy Rice—provided direction and guidance that have continued to be of great benefit throughout the evolution of this book.

Numerous individuals and institutions in Bali have assisted me in this project in ways too numerous to detail here, among them I Komang Astita and his family, I Madé Bandem, Guru Citawati, I Wayan Dira, I Madé Ebuh, I Wayan Gunawan (of Kintamani), I Nyoman Kartiasa, I Wayan Karya, Ni Nanik Kormaniati, I Madé Lasmawan, I Madé Murna, Pandé Gedé Mustika, I Nyoman Pasek, Ni Madé Puspawati, I Wayan Rai, I Nyoman Rembang, I Wayan Sinti, I Ketut Suandita, I Wayan Suharta, Ni Nanik Sujati, I Wayan Sumendra, Luh Tirta Wardani, I Wayan Widya, I Wayan Wira, the STSI and SMKI conservatories, the Badung Ministry of Education and Culture, I Yong Sagita Swastika and the staff of Maharani Records, I Ricky Yulianto and the staff of Bali Record, and the many gamelan performance organizations with whom I worked and studied during the course of my research, most especially those of Tatasan Kaja, Kaliungu Kaja, Belaluan Sadmerta, Padang Tegal Kaja, Belong Sanur, Kehen, Meranggi, Batur Tengah,

Seminyak, the Printing Mas company, and the Kartika Plaza Hotel (Kuta), and also groups in Bebaran, Wanasari, Kebun Kuri Tengah, Geladag Pedungan, and Kesiman.

My colleagues and students at Florida State University have been unfailingly supportive and helpful. Special thanks to my colleagues in the Musicology area—Charles Brewer, Jeffery Kite-Powell, Dale Olsen, and Douglass Seaton—for their various forms of assistance and their consistent encouragement, and to Jane Clendinning, Brian Gaber, Clifford Madsen, and Jon Piersol for their input and support. Thanks to Ian Daly for his important contributions in the preparation of the manuscript; to John Banks for mastering the compact disc; to the students of my 1996 doctoral seminar—Jennifer Ladkani, Laurie Semmes, and Robin Wildstein—for their careful readings of the first complete draft of the work; and to Ama Aduonum, Lawrence App, Karla Brandt, John Coggiola, Christopher Corley, Josh Cummings, Ashleigh D'Aunoy, Ronald Dunn, Craig Filar, Dave Maynard, David Pruett, Bama Roberts, the members of Sekaa Gong Hanuman Agung, and the many other students who helped out in one way or another.

The people at the University of Chicago Press have been wonderful. To David Brent and Philip Bohlman I am especially grateful. David, thank you for your continued faith in this book and in me; Phil, thanks for the support, guidance, and encouragement that have meant so much. Special thanks also, to Nancy Trotic for her excellent work copyediting the manuscript, to Erik Carlson for his consummate professionalism and endless patience, and to the press's two anonymous readers for their insightful criticisms and many helpful suggestions.

This book would never have happened without the love and support of my friends and family. Thanks to Pam and David and Charles and Mary and Wayne and Julie and Mary Ann and Larry for being there; to Dr. Fred and Otuomé for saving my neck (literally); to Marina and Nancy for keeping my stomach full; to my aforementioned FSU Musicology cronies and their families for their friendship; and to Marilyn, for inspiring and being a part of so much of what this book is about, and for continuing to be a true friend "in spite of it all."

To my beloved parents, Rita and Paul, I owe you everything and more. Thank you for all of your love and understanding, and thank you also, Mom, for being one heck of a good unofficial editor. Laura and Joel, you are the best big sister and brother an ethnomusicologist could ever hope to have. Your love and support have really meant a lot, and yours too, Marlee. Myim, you can't read yet, but when you are able to I hope you will enjoy this book. It's about drumming and it's by your Uncle Boom Boom; that ought to be enough.

Megan, you are the love of my life. Here's to our new life and perhaps to a new creation or two of our own.

Kajar, I suspect you will never read this, but if you ever do I just want you to know that you are my best and dearest friend, and that Bali will never be the same without you.

Note

In Indonesian and Balinese, the letter *a* is pronounced as in the English word *bar* if located in the middle of a word, as in the French *le* if at the end of a word; the letter *e* (with no accent) is also pronounced as in *le*. The letter *c* is pronounced "ch" (*cak* equals "chak"); *i* is pronounced "ee" (*gilak* equals "geelak"); *ai* is pronounced as a long *i* (*main* equals "mine"); *u* is pronounced "oo" (*puspa* equals "poospa").

Where necessary for the grammatical coherence of the writing, the plural forms of nouns are indicated by the addition of an *s,* as in English. This is only for the sake of convenience and does not reflect practices of pluralization used in the Indonesian or Balinese languages.

The italicized words *gong* and *gongs* are used in this book with specific reference to the instruments known as *gong ageng* (great gongs). Two forms of this instrument are normally employed in beleganjur music: the "female" *gong wadon* and the higher-pitched "male" *gong lanang.* The unitalicized terms "gong" and "gongs" are used as generic references for the various gong-type instruments discussed, or for sets of gong-type instruments (which may or may not include one or two gong ageng).

STSI (Sekolah Tinggi Seni Indonesia), the government college of the arts, and SMKI (Sekolah Menengah Kesenian Indonesia), the government high school of the arts, are sometimes referred to in the text by their former names, ASTI (Akademi Seni Tari Indonesia) and KOKAR (Konservatori Karawitan Indonesia), respectively. ASTI became STSI in 1988; KOKAR became SMKI in 1976. Depending on the historical period being discussed, I use whichever name was current at the time.

Some of the more technical discussions of musical structures and forms found in chapters 1 and 3 may prove difficult for readers without formal training in music. Such readers may prefer to skim-read or skip over these sections.

This book was completed shortly before the political upheavals in Indonesia that led to the resignation of President Suharto, among other significant changes.

Part One

Awit-Awit

Introduction

Bali: Summer 1995

The wave caught me in its curl, smashing me head-first into a sandbank and snapping my legs over my back as though I were a contortionist acrobat in a Chinese circus. I heard two terrifying cracks, one from my neck, the other from my back. Time went into slow motion as water crashed down around me with deafening force. Then, all seemed completely still. I found myself washed up on the shore of an isolated beach, alone and scared and not daring to move for fear that I would be unable to. Eventually I mustered the courage to attempt to stand up. Fortunately, I could. I was lucky; I was not paralyzed, but I was badly hurt, and the injuries would never fully heal.

A few days before the accident, I had arrived in Bali with the intention of completing field research for a book on *gamelan beleganjur,* the Balinese "gamelan of walking warriors," [1] a processional orchestra of gongs, drums, and cymbals that has been an integral part of the ritual and ceremonial musical life of this island culture for centuries and has taken on new significance since the mid-1980s as the basis of an extremely popular type of music competition. This was my fourth beleganjur research expedition to Bali in six years. It was to be a follow-up project, providing refinements and finishing touches. From the time of the accident, however, a series of bizarre occurrences powerfully challenged my efforts to carry out the work I had planned.

It was the dog bite that changed things most profoundly. I was on my way to work one day about a month into my stay when I stopped to pet Doggie, who was tied to the post by the gate of the guest house in Denpasar where I was residing. He wagged his tail excitedly, seemingly enjoying the attention. Then, without warning and for no apparent reason, he attacked me savagely. I jumped back, but not soon enough. Blood was streaming from my right hand. I was terrified. One of the boys from the house rushed me to the back and wrapped the wound. I began to feel faint and had to lie down. After attending to the hand, the boy rolled up my right pant leg and gasped. I managed to sit up and looked downward. There was blood everywhere; the wound was extremely deep. While my hand ended up healing quickly, my leg did not. It became badly infected and I took months to recover. The pain and sickness from infection made working almost unbearable, but I was compulsively persistent. Eventually I managed to meet my research "objectives," but the Bali I had constructed through my earlier experiences there, and the self I had conceived in relation to that Bali, largely disappeared along the way.

Departing

While earlier departures had always led to feelings of sadness and pre-nostalgic sentiment, on this occasion I felt only relief. I had been through enough. The cumulative impact of the body-surfing accident, the dog bite, a severe illness brought on by food poisoning, implication in a bitter feud between my two principal teachers, and daily reminders of a great romance that had bloomed in Bali in 1989 and was now dying in a failed marriage back home had drained my energy and left me unsure of just where I stood relative to this fascinating place that had been such an important part of my life these last six-plus years. Moreover, exposure to real-life problems of Balinese friends of mine—alcoholism, family dysfunction, poverty, disease, and consequences of political corruption, problems that had previously been either hidden from my view or somehow obscured by the haze of romantic illusion—forced me to embrace a new perception of what Bali was, one in which the romance, passion, and wonder that opportunity had allowed me during earlier visits were brought into check by darker, more troubling realities.

I settled into my seat on the airplane and took a deep breath. I had survived and was on my way home. I had to laugh at the thought of "surviving" Bali. It was hardly as though I had climbed Mount Everest or was escaping the ravages of a war-torn nation. This was, after all, Bali I was leaving: "the morning of the world," "the last paradise," the ultimate fantasy escape destination of the twentieth century; and this was a place where I had fallen in love, where so many cherished memories resided, where new musical worlds had opened up to me, and where great musicians such as I Ketut Sukarata and I Ketut Gedé Asnawa[2] had invited me into their lives and inspired me with their genius. Now, though, while the beauty and inspiration and cheerfulness and ease of Bali had not disappeared altogether, their susceptibility to forces of ugliness and violence and depression and hardship had been laid bare to an unprecedented degree. On the long plane ride home, I tried to retrace my steps, as it were, in an effort to reconcile my Balinese present with my Balinese past.

I first went to Bali in 1989 to escape certain troubles of my own, to "find myself" somewhere on the other side of the world, and to perhaps discover a good dissertation topic in the process. As it turned out, new music, new love, the discovery of new ways of looking at things and living through them, and the luck of circumstance made me feel reborn there. Like countless others before me, I was consumed by Bali's magic and beauty, captivated by this enchanted place that made so much sense and wonder.

But over time, and then rather dramatically in 1995, "my Bali" got complicated. More and more, obstacles seemed to stand in the way of my ability to do what I wanted and needed to do; more and more, I became enmeshed in the troubles and hardships of my Balinese friends and all too often found myself not knowing how to respond to them, or, even worse, not wanting to respond at all. My work—my "book"— became an obsessive concern, and somehow, the more confusing things became, the more convinced I became that the book was the place where I could make it all right again.

The course of my earlier fieldwork in Bali had been predicated largely on commitment to an ideal of exploring experiential possibilities, especially musical ones. I sought out opportunities to play the music I was studying in as many contexts as possible and put a high priority on establishing a place of belonging for myself within the communities of Balinese musicians with whom I worked. My experiences as a musician in Bali shaped the questions I asked and the issues I addressed as a scholar, provided the core data upon which much of my analysis and interpretation ultimately came to rely, and centrally defined the terms of both my personal and professional relationships with Balinese people I came to know.

By 1995, though, the situation was dramatically different. I had become like a walking cipher, moving ghost-like through the very kinds of musical experiences and situations that had formerly constituted the lifeblood of my study. Accomplishing specific "objectives" became the driving force behind my work; documenting, transcribing, recording, and videotaping under quite formal conditions took precedence over all else. I turned down invitations to perform in events so that I could videotape them instead, became less committed to really connecting musically with my Balinese teachers and peers than to accumulating new repertoire and amassing large amounts of information.

In short, I became more concerned with what I was getting done than with what I was doing, and in the process I became the kind of ethnomusicologist I had always thought I should be but had never wanted to be. In retrospect, it was almost as though I had to go through a process of divorcing myself from the experiences I was living through in order to prepare for the imminent transition to a state where, thousands of miles away, I would endeavor to bring those now-dead experiences back to life in words.

Reflections and Offerings

Balinese Hindus conceive of their cultural history in three main periods: a precivilized age of chaos and barbarism predating the arrival of Hinduism; a golden age of civilization initiated by the introduction of Hindu-Javanese religion and culture several centuries ago; and a long period of gradual spiritual and moral decline since the culmination of the golden age, throughout which the diligent and profuse practice of religious ritual has served as the primary force militating against a return to chaos (Asnawa, pers. comm., 1992;[3] see also Hobart, Ramseyer, and Leemann 1996, 33–45; Hood 1990, 14–15).

Reflecting back upon the experiences and activities that have resulted in the creation of this book, I think that the "history" of a fieldwork-based research project such as this one may also be seen to comprise a progression through periods of chaos, golden age, and ritualized resistance to the return of a chaotic state. As scholars, we typically begin in chaos, possessing little or no knowledge of the things we hope eventually to understand. We learn what we can before traveling to our chosen "field site" and may think we know quite a lot by the time we get there. Almost inevitably, though, our preconceptions and expectations, however well founded they might be, dissolve in the face of the realities we encounter, and we find ourselves confronting something close to chaos once again.

If we are lucky and diligent and approach new situations with flexibility and open-mindedness, perhaps we recover, figure out what we are doing anew, and move ahead. Armed with the excitement of new discoveries and new understandings, a sense of enlightenment premised on an increasing capacity to solve puzzles and mysteries that formerly per-plexed us, and a feeling of belonging in a place that previously felt alien, we enter a kind of golden age ourselves. As the purpose of the work becomes crystallized and the theories upon which it is based vali-dated, we come to believe both in the value of what we are doing and in our ability to do it successfully.

But there is usually a point where things turn back upon themselves. And it is here that fear of the possibility of a regression back to a state of chaos may come to the fore. New discoveries now begin to under-mine our achieved understandings rather than enhance them; the people with whom we work frequently appear more in conflict with systems of cultural rules and structures than operating smoothly within them; even the perceived "cultural order" itself often seems more inclined to crum-ble in the face of what is actually happening than to productively define people's actions, or is perhaps revealed as, at best, a hollow, more or less articulated, dogmatic ideology that serves to suppress rather than guide people in the way they live their lives.

Our perceptions of ourselves may change too. As we become increas-ingly drawn into the complexities of other people's worlds—emotion-ally, economically, politically, and ideologically—the complexities of our own situation may cause us to question whether we are the benevo-lent seekers of knowledge we endeavor to be, to wonder whether we have the right to do what we are doing and to ponder whether its pur-pose is worthwhile even assuming that we do.

Then, when we finally "finish" the research and arrive at the point where we must "write up our findings," we face the demoralizing real-ization that whatever small and hard-won claim we may have gained to truth or knowledge in "the area" of our research, the possibility that we will be able to effectively communicate what we have learned in a way that truly does justice to the music and people we have "studied" is slim indeed.

It is ritual that saves us from the perils of a descent into unbridled cynicism, from a regression into chaos. Like Balinese Hindus, we too must make our offerings to the forces that threaten our civility, which often take the form of our own doubts and insecurities about what we are up to. Perhaps more than any other activity, writing is the one through which we ritualize experience and turn the lives we live and share with others into offerings, into symbols of faith that we send out into the world like containers of ashes thrown out to sea at the conclu-sion of a Balinese *memukur* ceremony.

Memukur represents the "second cremation" in the Hindu-Balinese cycle of mortuary rituals. It is preceded by the cremation ceremony proper, *ngaben,* which culminates with the burning of the actual body of the deceased, making of an effigy containing the cremated ashes, and tossing of this effigy out to sea.[4] Whereas ngaben is devoted to liberating the human soul *(atma)* from its corporeal bonds, memukur focuses ritual attention specifically on the final purification and release of the soul itself. A new effigy of the deceased is constructed and "cremated," its ashes in turn becoming the inner contents of yet another effigy made from the shell of a young coconut surrounded by flowers, leaves, and ornamental filigree. At the end of the final procession of memukur, this effigy is thrown into the sea with joy and abandon, a celebration of the final liberation of the soul of the departed.[5]

For scholars, one might say that the first cremation—the *ngaben*—occurs as soon as the fieldwork process proper ends, at the moment when we get on the airplane or boat or whatever it is that will transport us to another world with the realization that we have "finished" our work in the one we are leaving and that our task now is to transform our experiences into words that describe them. We take what has happened to us and burn it down to our best approximation of its essence, then, through a long series of elaborate rituals of writing, endeavor to re-create that essence as representation, creating and cremating one effigy after another: draft, manuscript, revised manuscript, edited manuscript, galley proofs, and finally book, each emerging from a core of the ashes of the last. We encase the final effigy in the most attractive possible outer shell, the book cover, and with that mixed sense of loss and promise that accompanies all moments when death in one world signifies a beginning of life in another, toss it forth into an unknown future.

The Gamelan Beleganjur: Music of Death and New Creation

This book is my offering to the musical world of the gamelan beleganjur[6] and to people who inhabit that world. Beleganjur is one of more than twenty distinct gamelan ensemble types found in modern-day Bali (Tenzer 1985, 1991), each of which has specific associations with particular religious rituals, dance-dramas, competitive events, or other performance contexts.[7]

Gamelan is the generic term for a large and diverse class of mainly percussion-dominated Indonesian music ensembles found on Java and Bali, and on other Indonesian islands including Madura and Lombok.

The Balinese usually employ an alternate spelling, "gambelan," reflecting their unique pronunciation of the word. Related types of ensembles, generically known as gong-chime orchestras, are found in other parts of Southeast Asia as well.

The different Balinese gamelan ensembles are classified into two main categories: *gamelan krawang,* that is, ensembles in which bronze forms the resonant material for the main body of instruments (i.e., the different-sized gongs, gong-chimes, and metallophones); and ensembles where other materials—iron, bamboo, and wood,[8] either separately or in combination—produce instrumental sound (McPhee 1966, 23).

Each gamelan is conceived as an inseparable set of instruments with its own distinctive tuning, timbre, size, design, and other characteristics. In contrast to the instruments of a Western orchestra or band, gamelan instruments are not interchangeable between different ensembles, and individual instruments are normally not owned by the musicians who play them.

The instrumental set that makes up a gamelan is owned most often by a *banjar,* a neighborhood organization (often described as a village ward or hamlet) typically consisting of between fifty and five hundred families, which is responsible for planning and producing most of the core communal, religious, and social activities of its membership (Eiseman 1990, 72–73). Alternatively, a gamelan may belong to a *desa,* or village, a different (usually larger) unit of social organization that may comprise an aggregation of several associated banjars linked together by temple affiliations, participation in collaborative rituals and ceremonies, and other criteria. A banjar may be a subdivision of a desa, although this is not always the case; in fact, some banjars include residents from more than one desa.[9]

The personnel of a Balinese gamelan performance organization is normally drawn from the ranks of members of a single banjar. Less often, a desa may serve as the pool from which an ensemble's membership derives. In even rarer instances, a group made up of employees of a particular corporation or business (such as a hotel) or a selected "all-star" group representing an entire Balinese regency *(kabupaten)*—or even the entire province *(propinsi)* of Bali—is formed.

A gamelan performance organization is known as a *sekehe gong.* The term *sekehe (seka, sekaa, sekaha)* means, literally, "to be as one" (Geertz and Geertz 1975, 30) but is usually translated as "club" or "voluntary organization." The performing members in sekehe gongs are almost exclusively male, although women's clubs *(sekehe gong wanita)* have formed with increasing frequency in recent years (see chapter 6).

It should be noted that there are sekehes, or clubs, not only for music, but for activities as varied as dancing, kite-flying, badminton, making of religious offerings, sacred singing, or most anything else for which a social organization might be imagined. Membership in a sekehe generally requires payment of dues and committed dedication to the goals and activities of the club. All members, including the *klian,* or head administrator (who, in a music club, may or may not actually perform with the group), have equal say and an equal vote in all group decisions, at least in theory.[10]

The number of active sekehe gongs in Bali runs into the thousands. Banjars with active gamelan programs may sponsor several "sub-sekehes," each devoted to a particular type of gamelan performance; for example, a separate *sekehe beleganjur* and *sekehe angklung* may function quasi-independently under the umbrella of a banjar's sekehe gong. Overlap in personnel between such sub-sekehes is common. Only about half of the members of a sekehe gong function as performing musicians. The nonplaying members take on a variety of responsibilities, such as carrying and maintaining instruments, preparing food and drink for rehearsals and performance events, designing costumes, making offerings, and attending to various aspects of group administration.

Provision of beleganjur music during processional occasions is one of the primary responsibilities of any banjar's sekehe gong. Beleganjur music has been an indispensable part of Balinese death ritual processions such as ngaben and memukur for centuries and is employed in a great many other religious contexts as well, including grand temple festival *(odalan)* processions. In precolonial times, beleganjur was also used to accompany Balinese soldiers as they descended upon their enemies in battle.

The gamelan beleganjur's function as an ensemble of war has been rendered obsolete in modern, peacetime Bali, but the martial power and foreboding sonic impact of its music live on in other domains, especially in the modern *lomba beleganjur,* or beleganjur contest. The emergence of the lomba beleganjur has provided a new life for the traditional, "functional" music of the gamelan beleganjur. The first such contest was held in Bali's capital city, Denpasar, in 1986. By the end of the 1980s, contests of the same type were being held all over the island, from major urban centers to remote mountain villages, attracting audiences often numbering in the thousands.

Along with the new performance context has come a new musical style, *kreasi beleganjur,* which is more formally complex, virtuosic, and display-oriented than its antecedent forms. *Kreasi* means "creation," and in the context of kreasi beleganjur is short for *kreasi baru,* or "new creation," a term used in connection with other neo-traditional repertoires as well, especially those connected with the most well known type of modern Balinese gamelan, the *gamelan gong kebyar.* Kreasi style has sparked a revolution in beleganjur; its impact on a traditional music of death has been largely responsible for the emergence of a modern music of new creation. Kreasi beleganjur and the competition-driven musical world in which it lives—especially within the lifeworlds of two Denpasar-based master musicians, my principal teachers and colleagues I Ketut Sukarata and I Ketut Gedé Asnawa—will be the primary foci of this book.

Beleganjur music, whether heard in traditional ritualistic contexts or modern contest settings, is grounded in a standard Balinese musical form known as *gilak.* Gilak is one of a number of foundational cyclic structures heard in Balinese gamelan music. Each is known as a *tabuh* and is characterized by a specific recurring sequence of gong tones. The musicological term "colotomic structure" is often used in connection with such forms. Gilak is outlined by a short (eight-beat), cyclically recurring sequence of strokes on different-sized gongs. Each "gong cycle" is known as a *gongan.* The booming resonance of a distinctive gilak "gong melody" ostinato created by the three lowest-pitched gongs (the two *gong ageng* and the *kempur*) anchors a timbrally diverse collage of loud and intense percussive sound.

With the possible exception of the gamelan gong kebyar, the gamelan beleganjur is the most ubiquitous type of music ensemble in contemporary Bali. Beyond its newfound popularity as a vehicle for competitive musical display, it is, according to ethnomusicologist and composer I Ketut Gedé Asnawa (pers. comm., 1992), the one gamelan that is "absolutely essential" for meeting the most fundamental musical requirements in the ritual life of every Hindu-Balinese banjar. While in theory every banjar should possess a minimum of three gamelans in order to fulfill its annual cycle of ritual obligations—these being a gamelan gong (today usually a gong kebyar), a gamelan angklung, and a gamelan beleganjur (McPhee 1966, 6)—many modern banjars, especially in Denpasar, manage to make do with only a gamelan beleganjur, adapting ceremonial pieces from other gamelan repertoires to its relatively limited tonal and instrumental resources as necessary (see chapters 1 and 2).

Today, the gamelan beleganjur continues to function centrally in the traditional life of Hindu-Balinese ritual and custom while thriving in a modern kreasi musical world, operating in the latter case under a broad hegemonic imperative to fuse traditional Balinese culture with modern Indonesian cultural nationalism. It is a vehicle for some of the most exciting and creative musical invention of modern Balinese music-makers; a locus for real and symbolic manifestation of alliances, tensions, and conflicts in the aesthetic, ideological, and spiritual domains of Balinese life; and a musical embodiment of many of the core values, priorities, and realities that define present-day Balinese culture and society.

Through its multiple identities and meanings, beleganjur reflects and affects Balinese worldviews, mediating and problematizing dialectical interactions of tradition and modernity, culture and ideology, individual and communal identity, hegemony and marginality, and masculinity and femininity. In its examination of beleganjur music and its world, this book addresses all of these interactions. It is, in the first instance, a study of a particular musical tradition, a music ethnography that relies on a variety of interpenetrating descriptive, analytical, and interpretive modes of presentation. Additionally, however, it is a study of musical interculturality, an epistemological exploration of ways in which people experience and understand music not only in culture, but between and around cultures as well.

Ethnomusicology: Differing Conceptions

There is a basic tension throughout this book, especially in its last chapters, between a conception of ethnomusicology rooted in the "music and culture"–type definitions that have oriented the discipline over the last four decades, and an alternative conception premised on a reconfiguration of conventional epistemological priorities. The latter may appear to violate one of ethnomusicology's basic tenets: the notion that relevant musical experience is the exclusive province of the culture-bearer, and that consequently the musical experiences of the ethnomusicologist in the field—like those of any other "cultural outsider"—are ethnomusicologically significant only to the extent that they provide insights into the thoughts, concepts, practices, and beliefs of the musical/cultural "Other." That this notion has gained wide acceptance in a discipline whose central premise is that music must be studied first and foremost as a phenomenon of culture is neither surprising nor illogical. Still, it has had the effect of limiting the range of ethnomusicological thought in significant ways, and in this study I have felt compelled to move outside these limits—in particular, to propose an alternative ethnomusicology in which culture's authority over music is decentered in ways that allow for the subject positions of all experiencers and potential experiencers of any music to be treated as ethnomusicologically relevant.

This book is in part a detailed study of a music, beleganjur, that holds deep meaning for most Balinese people, and that is created and performed by them and used in a vast array of contexts for a variety of purposes. In this sense it is conventionally ethnomusicological. But it is also a study of my own relationship with beleganjur music, and with its makers and its world, for while ethnomusicology is what we do as ethnomusicologists, it is also who we are before the doing, and what happens to us and what we make of it all through a long process of exploring and trying to understand things that our love of music inspired us to care about and communicate about in the first place. As Merleau-Ponty suggests, "Our situation is for us the source of our curiosity, our investigations, and our interest." It is "what links us to the whole of human experience, no less than what separates us from it" ([1960] 1964, 110). In this book I will explicitly address my "situation," conceiving of it as an integral—at times even central—aspect of a musical world in which I have no rightful claim to membership according to ethnomusicological convention. My reasons for placing myself in this peculiar and unorthodox position are explored in the following discussion.

How Music Lives: Toward an Alternative Epistemology

The "science" of ethnomusicology inevitably begins and ends in understandings and perceptions that stem from the researcher's personal experiences, especially during the fieldwork process. Thus, the ethnomusicologist who chooses to write unreflexively about a particular music "in culture" (Merriam 1960) or "as culture" (Merriam 1977; Herndon and McLeod 1980) faces an unenviable, or at least complicated, predicament: without self-reference, she must describe events and phenomena that she has come to understand largely through participatory experience; and in adopting this mode of cultural representation, she is implicitly denied the opportunity to openly and honestly address the many ways in which her own participation has altered the normal flow of human action and interaction among members of the culture she studies.

The willful imposition of such limiting constraints would seem to be

counterproductive; yet historically it has been common, even normative. Fieldwork is regarded as the foundation of ethnomusicological
method, but ethnomusicologists' actual experiences in the field have
paradoxically been seen to distort, or at least dilute, the purity and authenticity of the very musical/cultural phenomena they write about.
Fieldwork experience, then, as understood in the most literal sense of
the term, is doomed to marginalization. It may be acknowledged as
an inevitable but essentially undesirable consequence of the scholar's
"situatedness," or may be sidestepped altogether beyond some rather
cursory and perfunctory account buried in the "Methodology" section
of a book's introduction.

It is my belief that this peculiar form of disenfranchisement relating
to fieldwork, "the most critical stage of ethnomusicology research"
(Myers 1992, 21), is a vestige of an outmoded but pervasive legacy of
idealizing "objectivity" in the human sciences. This view is supported
by Helen Myers's astute observation that historically in fieldwork,
"[w]hile invoking the name of objectivity, emphasis in fact was placed
on insight, intuition, personal charm, happenstance and luck. Because
the topic is individual and personal, scholars were reluctant to write
candidly about their own experiences in the field" (ibid., 22).

The reflexive and dialogical turns of ethnomusicology in recent
years, many inspired by phenomenological, hermeneutical, or postmod-
ernist epistemologies and methods of inquiry, have loosened the grip
of the former objectivity-centered paradigm considerably and moved
ethnomusicologists toward modes of ethnographic discourse, narrative,
analysis, interpretation, and critique that more candidly account for the
lived experiences of both the people whose cultures they study and
themselves.[11]

Still, despite a widespread and ever increasing belief in the inherent
value of reflexive research methods and writing strategies, certain
spheres of potentially revealing reflexive inquiry have remained largely
unexplored, almost as though they were taboo. For all of the various
advances and developments that have occurred, the experiences ethnomusicologists have while sharing their lives with people in places and
cultural worlds foreign to their own continue to be regarded as essentially unworthy of explicit scholarly attention unless they can be shown
to have direct relevance in terms of our understandings of the cultural
Other. Indeed, this premise is so firmly entrenched in ethnomusicological epistemology that it appears to represent a "commonsense"
notion.

The continuing influence on contemporary ethnomusicology of certain ideas proposed by Alan Merriam thirty-five years ago provides evidence in support of this assertion. In *The Anthropology of Music,* Merriam claimed that ethnomusicology should be a discipline centered in "sciencing about music" (1964, 25). While contemporary scholars frequently argue against the continued applicability of this characterization for present-day ethnomusicology, it is notable that certain of the basic tenets underlying Merriam's "sciencing about music" concept have gone largely unchallenged. In particular, most ethnomusicologists would still support Merriam's claim that the ethnomusicologist "does not seek the aesthetic experience for himself as a primary goal (though this may be a personal by-product of his studies), but rather he seeks to perceive the meaning of the aesthetic experience of others" (ibid., 25). What is most telling here is not the substance of the statement itself, but Merriam's use of the implicitly pejorative term "by-product" in connection with the ethnomusicologist's aesthetic experience, which I suspect was neither incidental nor the result of a careless choice of words. The "insider/outsider or emic/etic dichotomy that has loomed so large in ethnomusicological theory" (Rice 1994, 64) since Merriam and before has effectively pitted "insider" and "outsider" experiential perspectives against one another in the discipline's epistemology, and the dictates of cultural relativism have ensured that the latter would be privileged over the former (at least ostensibly) in most ethnographic representations. This tension is reflected in Merriam's "by-product" allusion and in the character of his writings generally. As Jeff Titon has written, for Merriam and most ethnomusicologists of his generation, "the personal experiences of the ethnomusicologist, including all the relations with others in the field that not merely affected but constituted the meaningfulness of data, were absent" (1993, 2).

Titon's comment is from his essay "Knowing People Making Music: Toward a New Epistemology for Ethnomusicology," [12] in which he develops a compelling and innovative model for approaching ethnomusicological studies from a phenomenological perspective. He presents a convincing argument that the lived experiences of the ethnomusicologist, as music-maker and fieldworker, are central to scholarly understanding, and should thus be explicitly addressed through phenomenology-derived reflexive methods.

In proposing the application of such methods, however, Titon executes a partial retreat from the bold epistemological stance initially implied, which might otherwise have posed a real challenge to the unquestioned assumption that the experience of the cultural Other ought rightly to be the subject of ethnomusicological inquiry. Citing Clifford Geertz's assertion (1988) that ethnographers are primarily authors, not reporters, Titon warns that as authors, ethnomusicologists must contend with the risk of "displacing the reader's interest from the people making music whom we are writing about, to ourselves" (1993, 6). He notes that the frequent accusations of self-indulgence and unprofessionalism that have been leveled against writers of "autobiographical narrative ethnography" are indicative of this risk, but insists that such problems can be avoided by ethnomusicologists: "[N]arrative ethnography need not displace the attention from people making music to authors' consciousness. Instead, an author may skillfully work up a scene and cast herself in the role of a bit player, someone whose participation isn't very important during the event, but whose reflections upon it afterwards serve as a kind of interpretation" (ibid.).

Titon cites Geertz's "Deep Play: Notes on the Balinese Cockfight" (1973a) and his own preface and first chapter from *Powerhouse for God* (Titon 1988) as effective examples of the proposed "bit player" approach. Certainly this approach represents a valid ethnographic option for documenting the experiences of the researcher during the fieldwork process, but if understanding does indeed derive from "experiences of music and fieldwork, from knowing people making music," as Titon suggests (ibid., 5), then why must the ethnomusicologist feel obliged to relegate himself to the role of a subordinate experiencer? Apparently, even in an approach as challenging and progressive as Titon's, the assumption that the ethnomusicologist's own fieldwork experiences and interactions lack scholarly relevance in and of themselves prevails; there are perhaps more vestiges of the Merriamesque influence here than initial appearances would suggest.

Throughout most of this book my primary concern, in common with that of a great many ethnomusicologists, is to accurately depict, represent, and evoke the perspectives, experiences, and situations of people belonging to a musical and cultural world foreign to my own: this is a study of beleganjur music in Bali, people who make such music, and the historical, social, spiritual, cultural, ideological, and political frameworks in which it exists and to which it contributes. More specifically, as was mentioned earlier, the book's central focus is the modern world of competitive beleganjur in Denpasar, which is portrayed not in its entirety but rather within the limits of what I was able to learn about it on the basis of my studies with two of its most prominent musicians, Asnawa and Sukarata.

Where I depart from the foundational epistemological tenets of ethnomusicology is in those sections of the book in which I portray myself as a central character of the story (especially chapters 8 and 9). In these sections I am often less concerned with the Balinese beleganjur world per se than with examining more broadly how musicians experience one another musically, learn from each other, negotiate relationships, and personally interact under circumstances of intercultural encounter. I am, for example, interested as an ethnomusicologist in the "music culture" created by myself and one of my Balinese teachers, Sukarata, during the course of my efforts to become a beleganjur drummer, not so much because of what that process revealed about Balinese music or culture, but rather because of what it revealed about intercultural musical experience.

In pursuing this alternative epistemological agenda, attempts at casting myself in the role of a "bit player" have proved unsatisfactory; so too have efforts to limit my discussions of personal fieldwork experiences (particularly musical ones) to those instances that have had direct, demonstrable relevance to my ethnomusicological understanding of the music and culture of Bali, or of the experiential worlds of Balinese musicians themselves (see Herbst 1997; also Rice 1994, on Bulgarian music). In short, working within the parameters I perceive to exist in current ethnomusicology has been frustratingly limiting, and I have therefore been motivated to seek other options.

In accounting for my own experiences as explicitly as I have in certain passages, and in pursuing modes of analysis and interpretation whose relevance in terms of the study of beleganjur music in Bali may be questioned, I have created a book that may seem to defy fundamental priorities of ethnomusicology. This is especially true for those priorities that pertain to the notion that representation of the experiences and perspectives of the cultural Others of our investigations should unquestionably constitute the ethnographic core of an ethnomusicological study. I must emphasize my realization that such priorities have been, and indeed continue to be, of great significance to the growth and development of a discipline that has long struggled with its legacy of ethnocentrism. My intention has not been to disregard their importance; it has only been to expand the range of possibilities in ethnomusicological thinking and discourse.

Of much value in this regard is a definition of ethnomusicology that has helped me to at least partially resolve the inherent tension between the conflicting epistemological orientations presented above. By defining ethnomusicology as *the study of how music lives in the lives of people who make and experience it, and of how people live in the music they make,* I shift the primary focus away from "culture" and toward people.[13] This allows for the experiences and creative agency of all who participate in a musical world—insiders and outsiders, culture-bearers and ethnomusicologists, music-makers and music-listeners, professionals and novices—to be included within the parameters of significant ethnomusicological investigation. Such a definition diminishes the power of problematic dichotomies such as "insider versus outsider," "emic versus etic," and "musician versus scholar" to constrain thought, while still allowing the "culture concept," which has been of such great value to ethnomusicology, to be employed productively.

Music lives within people and articulates what matters to us. It is an expression that reflects, embodies, and informs feelings and thoughts through which we define ourselves as human. Thus, musicologists have a responsibility to attempt to understand how music humanizes people and how and why people humanize sounds into music. In addressing this responsibility, we must consider the possibility that any music may be culturally grounded but that no music is culturally bounded.

Book Form and Musical Form

The opening demonstration section of a kreasi beleganjur contest piece normally features four main parts, or movements, which are played without pause: the introductory *awit-awit,* consisting of a virtuosic, cadenza-like display of unaccompanied two-part drumming; the *kawitan,* or first movement proper, which represents the core of the work[14] and presents its main thematic materials in a series of fast-tempoed "mini-compositions" or "variations" *(pukulan)* played by the full ensemble; the more melodically conceived *pengawak,* or slow movement, in which the "heroic"-themed *(kepahlawanan)* character of the kawitan is reinterpreted in ways that create both reinforcement of and contrast with the preceding material; and the concluding *pengecet,* where the fast tempo of the kawitan returns but the music's character typically becomes more playful and lighthearted than in the preceding sections. Colin McPhee, in his monumental study *Music in Bali,* described the pengecet as being "essentially a movement of freedom and release" (1966, 92). While he was referring specifically to music of the gamelan gong repertoire, the depiction transfers well to the beleganjur context.[15]

In a general and impressionistic way, the formal design of this book is similar to that of the beleganjur contest demonstration described, and

I have therefore taken the liberty of entitling the book's four main parts Awit-Awit, Kawitan, Pengawak, and Pengecet. Like an awit-awit drum prelude, the introduction is cadenza-like, shifting quickly and unpredictably between different segments of text that contrast with one another, but that collectively are intended to set up, contextualize, and foreshadow what is to come. The core music ethnography of beleganjur is presented in the four chapters of the Kawitan, the last of which functions as a kind of transition. The discussions and interpretations of chapters 5 and 6, which alternately reinforce and problematize the portrait of beleganjur contained in the first set of chapters, constitute the Pengawak. The book's "movement of freedom and release," the Pengecet, includes the final three chapters (7–9), in which beleganjur becomes the basis of an experimental, self-reflexive study of intercultural musical experience and learning.

Chapter 1 discusses the gamelan beleganjur in terms of its instrumentation, historical development, and classification within the broader spectrum of Balinese music ensembles. It provides a detailed examination of "traditional" beleganjur musical style and describes the conventional use of such music in ritualistic contexts. Chapter 2 is concerned with the modern context of competitive beleganjur—the lomba beleganjur, or beleganjur contest. It describes the origin and historical development of the contest phenomenon and examines how contests have been designed to serve political ends as symbols of mediation between localized Balinese cultural interests and Indonesian national ideology. Chapter 3 is devoted to analytical discussion of the contest musical style, kreasi beleganjur. The first section outlines the formal, structural, and aesthetic features that distinguish the kreasi style and also investigates the impact of ideological priorities on musical design. The second section explores similar issues with specific reference to the works and ideas of three leading kreasi beleganjur composers—Asnawa, Sukarata, and I Ketut Suandita—and concludes with a section on contest beleganjur choreography (gerak). Chapter 4 contains biographical portraits of Sukarata and Asnawa. Special attention is paid to the beleganjur-related dimensions of their multifaceted musical careers. The related yet vastly contrasting life stories of these two eminent musicians, and additionally their respective concerns, fears, and aspirations and the different challenges and obstacles they have faced, provide important insights relative to the larger social and political issues addressed in other chapters.

Chapter 5 is an interpretive study of the high competitive stakes that exist in the beleganjur world. It features detailed analyses of two "dys-functional" 1992 beleganjur contests, both of which were compromised by the impact of covert, politically motivated acts of corruption. In the course of the discussion, numerous issues are addressed: individual resistance to institutional authority, hegemonic and coercive political strategies, the ideological uses of "culture," the slippery and contestable nature of ethical propriety. Chapter 6 broaches many of these same issues in a discussion of what has arguably been the most controversial development in modern beleganjur: the advent of women's beleganjur performance ensembles. Here gender moves to the center of a conflict that has brought traditional Balinese notions of cultural integrity and modern Indonesian ideological agendas into a direct and awkward confrontation. Beleganjur is a quintessentially "male" music, and the politically inspired phenomenon of women's beleganjur has been as problematic as it has been compelling.

In the final three chapters, the book's focus shifts to issues of music-learning and musical experience, with specific attention devoted to the complex art of beleganjur drumming. Chapter 7 examines the normative Balinese music pedagogy process, *maguru panggul,* through an analysis of beleganjur drum lessons of Balinese students taught by Sukarata. Chapter 8 is a highly self-reflexive examination of my own very different process of learning to drum beleganjur with Sukarata, and explores the complex and idiosyncratic musical world the two of us created and shared. It is prefaced by a discussion in which I challenge conventional ethnomusicological notions of what constitutes "musical understanding" and propose an alternative perspective based on my own experiences as a performer of beleganjur music in Bali. Chapter 9 completes the story of my odyssey as a student of beleganjur drumming, culminating with an account of my final 1992 drum lesson with Sukarata. The experiences of this lesson resulted in a profound transformation of my conceptions of beleganjur drumming in particular and of musical experience of and musical understanding more broadly. This transformation and the ideas and perspectives it generated are the main subjects of the final portion of the chapter, with which the book concludes.

Bali: Summer 1989

Marilyn and I sat close together in the back seat of the minivan *bemo.* Finally, we were getting away from the tourist crowds and insanity of

Kuta Beach, heading north to the mountains. Just minutes outside of claustrophobic Kuta, we entered a different world: picturesque terraced rice paddies, doe-eyed cows of almost deer-like beauty sauntering along the roadside, a massive water buffalo trudging purposefully through a field under the gentle guidance of an aged yet ageless plow master. Postcard-perfect Bali: my first glimpse of it, really. Maybe things were going to work out here for me after all.

Had it not been for Marilyn, I might well have already been on my way back to the States by that time. My first impressions of Bali had all but shattered my fantasies of the world's most famous paradise. I arrived late at night in the middle of a steamy tropical downpour and followed Raoul, the manic Peruvian surfer seated next to me on the plane, to a beachside hotel in Kuta. I ventured out, got hopelessly lost, and ended up in a seedy area of town declining the wares of drug dealers and prostitutes on every corner. Eventually I found my way back to the hotel. It was 3:00 A.M. I collapsed onto the sweaty, board-hard bed and fell asleep instantly, only to be startled awake a couple of hours later by the sound of smashing glass. Raoul's room next door was being ransacked by some loud, drunken hooligans. They shouted and swore in Spanish as they made off with his camera and surfboards. I cowered in the bed, at least a little terrified.

My first full day in paradise was spent on the beach at Kuta. I had hoped to relax and unwind in solitude, but instead spent my time trying to convince several dozen peddlers—each more persistent than the last—that I was not interested in buying anything. The range of goods and services offered was astounding, with everything from carved wooden elephants and woven friendship bracelets to full-body massages being offered at "very special for you, mister" prices; but I was in no mood to be tempted.

Things went from bad to worse that evening. Somehow I ended up attending a big party at a beachfront restaurant. I had a horrible time. The low point was an encounter with a bleached-blonde, sunbaked woman clad in a skin-tight purple mini-dress. She backed into me while fake-laughing excessively, causing some of the drink I was holding to spill onto her dress. The collision was entirely her fault, but I apologized for the mishap nevertheless. She turned and scowled at me, then called me a "scumbag" and walked away. I left the party wondering why on earth I had chosen to divest myself of all my savings to travel halfway around the world to such a miserable place as Bali.

Stumbling through the darkness on my way back from the party, I got lost again trying to find the hotel. A silhouette emerged out of the black, walking briskly in my direction along a dirt path. As the figure came closer, the dim night light revealed a strikingly attractive young woman. My pulse quickened a few beats; I was smitten. I managed to get her attention and asked if she could point me toward the Blue Ocean Hotel. She looked at me as though I were an idiot, pointed directly behind me, and said "It's right there," her annoyed condescension accentuated by a haughty, vaguely English-sounding accent.

I turned around and, sure enough, there was the hotel; then I turned back, hoping to strike up a conversation with the enchanting young woman. Alas, she was gone, but we would meet again, and eventually we would marry.

Discovering Beleganjur

Half an hour north of Kuta, the road curved sharply to the left. As the *bemo* driver gamely negotiated the curve, I heard a faint but unmistakable sound of large, deep gongs. A gamelan, I thought excitedly, the first I had heard since my arrival. Other sounds came into focus soon after the gongs: first drums, then small, high-pitched gongs. The road curved back to the right, and suddenly the ensemble came into view. Just at that moment, a chorus of cymbals came crashing in over the drums and gongs. I leaped forward to the front of the *bemo* and frantically asked the driver to pull over and stop. He did, and Marilyn and I jumped out.

The music was intoxicating. It was unlike anything I had encountered before, bearing little evident resemblance to any of the gamelan recordings or performances I had heard back home. Loud, brash, and forcefully energetic, it pumped along with a contagious groove and a motoric rhythmic drive, propelled forward by a pair of drummers and a gang of eight cymbal players, sustained by a repetitive eight-beat "gong melody" and a simple two-toned melodic ostinato, and ornamented by the short, rapid-fire figurations of a set of four small hand-held kettle gongs played by four of the musicians in an intricate interlocking style. The drummers too played fast interlocking patterns, which were executed with a variety of right-hand mallet and left-hand palm strokes. The cymbal section switched between performing short bursts of unison rhythm and an intriguing set of interlocking patterns that created a continuous stream of delicious, cacophonous sound.

The musicians—young, middle-aged, and older men wearing traditional Balinese ceremonial attire—sat cross-legged near the roadside on a small ridge near an open-air temple. As they played, they seemed to take no notice of Marilyn and me, who had positioned ourselves about fifteen meters away on the far side of the ridge so as not to be obtrusive. They seemed to take little notice of each other either. They sat almost completely motionless, playing with a marked blankness of facial expression and staring straight ahead at nothing in particular, or at least nothing I could see. Further back from the road, a ceremony of some type was being held. All kinds of interesting things were taking place, but I took little notice of any of them. I was transfixed by the music. It mesmerized me, enveloping me in the richness and purity of its percussive strength.

What kind of music was this? I asked the driver upon returning to the *bemo*. "Gamelan," he replied. This much I already knew, but between my lack of proficiency in Indonesian and his in English, that was as far as we were able to get. My ignorance piqued my curiosity and also my anxiety. Maybe this music was extremely rare, I thought; maybe I would never hear it again.

But my fears proved unwarranted. After a few days in the mountains, Marilyn and I moved on to Ubud, the "cultural tourism" center of Bali. We found a nice two-floor bungalow to rent in neighboring Campuan. As I sat on the verandah looking out over the terraced rice paddies my first evening there, I reveled in the beautiful scenery and serene night sounds of frogs, crickets, and gentle running streams, all pure and peaceful but for the tortured howlings of a thousand Balinese dogs.

About an hour after sunset, I was surprised by a distant sound of gongs. A few minutes later, there were more—closer, and entering the night soundscape from a different direction. Now I could faintly hear drums and cymbals as well, and then a third group started up. In the next forty-five minutes, four additional groups joined the fray, creating a cacophonous and disjointed fugue of distant percussive sound. All were too far away for me to hear distinctly, but it soon became evident that the music they were playing resembled that which I had heard during the roadside ceremony the other day. Again there were the energetic drum and cymbal parts, the short gong cycles, and the melodic ostinatos and rapid elaborative figurations.

I was fascinated, excited, and a little confused. I had listened to my share of Balinese music before coming to Bali without encountering anything like this. And now that I was here, it seemed as though almost no other kind of music was even played. I jumped prematurely to the romantic conclusion that this must be the genuine, authentic Balinese music, the kind played by and for Balinese people in Bali alone. It was a notion that was as compelling as it was naive, one born of particularities of circumstance, timing, and chance. A variety of factors—my ignorance, the fascinating newness of my situation, a heightened sense of romanticism inspired by my blossoming love for Marilyn—contributed to my romanticized perception of this unfamiliar and "exotic" music. But beyond all of this, the music possessed for me a real and deep affective power. Long before I ever heard it, long before I ever came to Bali, my musical tastes and sensibilities ensured that it would draw me in. As the alluring sound of drums, cymbals, and gongs surrounded me on all sides that first night in Campuan, it was as though I were experiencing a calling; I was convinced that this music would become an important part of my life. My reasons for perceiving this sense of "destiny" may have been misguided, but the feelings behind them were real and strong. As much as anything else, those feelings belong to the store of ethnographic data from which this study has evolved.

Playing in the Beleganjur World

The next morning, Marilyn and I walked into town. After wandering about in the hot sun for several hours, we ended up on Padang Tegal Road, where we came across a large, open, brick-paved temple courtyard. Four teenage boys were sitting in the courtyard, relaxing, chatting, and smoking. Resting in a haphazard arrangement near the boys were four small kettle gongs and a bundle of mallets. It appeared that a rehearsal of some kind was about to begin.

Thoroughly fatigued from the afternoon heat and hours of walking, we sat down on a step underneath a tree to rest and to see what might unfold. Several more teenagers and young men arrived. Two of them entered a small room in an open-sided pavilion on the far side of the courtyard, emerging with large wicker mats and laying them out in the center of the area. Next, more instruments, some gong stands, and various mallets were brought out from the room and laid out on the mats. There were bossed (knobbed) gongs in a range of sizes, a pair of drums (each wrapped in a black, white, and red checker-patterned cloth), and several pairs of the large crash cymbals that I had first seen played by the group on the road outside of Kuta. Clearly this was the same type of ensemble, although the musicians here were much younger. I guessed this to be one of the groups I had heard from the verandah the night before.

As the ensemble grew larger, some of the musicians began picking up instruments and playing, while others continued socializing casually. There were some who managed to converse, smoke, and warm up on their instruments all at the same time, which I found impressive. What playing there was seemed random and haphazard. Initially, none of the musicians appeared to pay any attention to what the others were doing. At some point, two cymbal players paired up and worked out an interlocking pattern. One fellow got up and walked over to a drum, picked up a mallet, banged out a couple of rhythms with style and flair for about ten seconds, then put down the mallet and returned to the group he had been sitting with to rejoin their conversation.

A group of three young boys, aged seven or eight at most, wandered over from the street and ran around the courtyard playing a game of tag. Occasionally one of them would strike a gong, or pick up a stray pair of cymbals and knock out a short rhythmic flourish, usually in imitation of a pattern being played by one of the older boys. In the midst of all of this, the four teenagers who had been sitting and chatting when we first arrived each picked up one of the small kettle gongs, which looked like—and as I would later discover actually were—single "pots" abstracted from a *reyong,* an instrument of the gamelan gong kebyar consisting of a set of twelve small tuned gongs of this type. They began working out a rapid four-part interlocking pattern on the reyong kettles that sounded rather difficult. Apparently it was, especially for the boy with the second-highest-pitched pot, who kept dropping out of the texture, shaking his head, and trying to jump back in.

The chaos of sound continued for a very long time, perhaps twenty minutes. Never had I witnessed such a long warm-up to a rehearsal. Eventually, all of the instruments were taken up by players and some sense of musical pattern and interaction began to emerge in spots; yet there was still nothing to suggest that any kind of structured ensemble music-making would take place anytime soon. After a half hour or so, I began to wonder whether there would even *be* a real rehearsal. Maybe this was just some kind of a noise-making social hour. I was prepared to wait longer and see what developed, but I could tell Marilyn was getting tired and impatient and would want to leave shortly if things didn't pick up. We still had a long uphill walk to the bungalow ahead of us.

Then, quite suddenly, the entire group began to play as an ensemble.

With uncanny smoothness and ease, everything came together in a most organic way. The seamless transition from the warm-up session to the actual rehearsal was striking and surprising to me.

Once the group began to play as a unit, I immediately recognized the eight-beat ostinato cycle of the low gongs; it was the same one I had heard from the verandah the night before and at the roadside ceremony outside Kuta. The instrumentation—two drums, eight pairs of cymbals, and various hand-held and hanging gongs—confirmed that this was the same type of gamelan. The music was different in significant ways, however. There were greater contrasts in tempo and dynamics than I had heard in the music at the ceremony, and the sound was slicker and more "arranged." This was most obvious in the cymbal parts, which featured some brilliantly complex unison passages, as well as the distinctive continuous rhythmic texture generated by interlocking patterns, with which I was by now becoming familiar.

As I listened, my attention was drawn mainly to the cymbal players. I was able to figure out the rhythms of most of their interlocking patterns with careful observation. I also began to mentally transcribe the unison passages. As for the drumming, it seemed impossibly complex. Despite my many years of training and professional performance experience as a percussionist, I realized immediately that even an elementary understanding of this drumming style would require intensive formal study.

The group played continuously for over forty-five minutes. I listened intently throughout. A few minutes before they stopped, a somewhat older man arrived. He was very handsome, with perfectly coifed hair and a neatly trimmed mustache, and looked to be in his late twenties or early thirties. He acknowledged Marilyn and me with a polite smile (the rest of the group had ignored us to that point) and then focused his attention on the music. When the group stopped playing, he addressed them. It appeared that he was commenting on their performance, and I guessed that he must be either the leader of the group or its teacher.

After speaking for a minute or two, the handsome newcomer sat down, laid a drum across his lap, and began to play. He was brilliant. The drummers who had been playing prior to his arrival had sounded good to me, but this man was clearly on a different level. His playing was so rhythmically crisp and precise, his sound so strong and centered.

After about fifteen seconds of virtuosic solo drumming, the full group joined in all at once. For the next twenty-five minutes, the performance continued. Through an elegant "dance" of drumming cues, hand signals, and pantomimed demonstrations of various instrumental parts, the new lead drummer directed the ensemble through a complex and varied musical arrangement. The difference in precision and cohesiveness before and after his arrival was remarkable. At the conclusion of the piece, the players put down their instruments and he made some comments. An elderly man brought out a tray of black coffee and cigarettes. Apparently the rehearsal was over.

By now it was getting dark, the mosquitoes were out, and Marilyn and I were hungry. It was time to go. We stood up and smiled at the musicians, bidding them farewell. They smiled back, and then one of the young cymbal players gestured for us to come join them. Marilyn chose to stay where she was, but encouraged me to go ahead. As I approached the group, the cymbal player smiled and held out his cymbals. "You want try?" he asked.

I took the cymbals and sat down with the other musicians, exchanging smiles and head nods with them while strategically locating myself next to the player who, from what I had observed, had functioned as a kind of cymbal section leader. I had noticed that whenever any of the other players experienced moments of confusion or fell out of sync with the group, they would look to him to bring them back into line. He was about eighteen and had an early Beatles mop-top haircut, large white teeth, and a radiant smile. His muscular arms appeared disproportionately large for his otherwise slight build. He played with animated flair and a clear style that was easy to follow, his rhythmic sense was very strong, and he seemed to have a better command of the arrangement than the other players. After I had settled into my space on the wicker mat, he tapped me on the knee to get my attention, then smiled and nodded his head in greeting, introducing himself as Madé. He pointed first at me and then at himself, indicating that I should watch and follow him. I nodded.

The drumming started. I had no idea how to pick up the entrance cue, so I kept my eyes glued on Madé's hands. He sprung into action, and I followed. CENG - CENG - CENG - CENG - CENG - CENG - CENG, then immediately the two drums in a rapid interlocking pattern: pa-ka-pa-pa-ka-pa-ka-ka-pa-ka-pa-pa-ka-pa-ka; and again, CENG-CENG-CENG-CENG-CENG-CENG-CENG, pa-ka-pa-pa-ka-pa-ka-ka-pa-ka-pa-pa-ka-pa-ka, then CENG - - CENG - - CENG - - CENG - CENG - CENG-CENG-CENG, leading straight into a constant stream of interlocking cymbal rhythm. I doubled Madé's pattern. CENG - ceCENG -

ceCENG - CENG - ceCENG - ceCENG - CENG - ceCENG -ceCENG - CENG - ceCENG - ceCENG - CENG - ceCENG - ceCENG - CENG - ceCENG - ceCENG - CENG - ceCENG - ceCENG . . . The whole cymbal section suddenly came together to pound out a powerful cadence on the last two strokes: CENG! - CENG!

We were off and running, and so far, thanks largely to Madé's clear lead, my playing had been on target. As I waited for our next entrance, he smiled at me, laughed, and gave a thumbs-up sign. He seemed pleased to discover that I could keep up.

I was having a great time. Here I was, halfway around the world, playing a type of music I had only just discovered, with a group of musicians that I did not know and with whom I did not even share a common language. Yet we were playing together, the music was working, and everybody seemed to be enjoying the experience.

Madé gave me a signal. I caught it too late and missed the first note of the phrase, but managed to jump in by the second. CENG - - - CENG - - - CENG - - CENG - CENG-CENG-CENG, and then back to the interlocking patterns, which continued for a very long duration this time around. I loved the feeling generated by playing these patterns: like gears of a machine meshing together in perfect synchronization, each dependent on the other to keep the motor running.

With every successive entry, I became a little more self-assured. I even started experimenting with different patterns in the interlocking sections, which seemed to amuse the other players. After about ten minutes I began to develop a sense of the music's overall structure; I came to realize that a specific sequence of variation-like musical passages was being repeated over and over again. Soon I was able to predict quite accurately where the next cymbal entry was going to occur, and which sequence of rhythmic patterns it would comprise. On some entries, I would not even look to Madé for guidance, except perhaps out of the corner of my eye. Then I got a little too confident. I "felt" an entry coming and went for it. CENG!! A strong, powerful crash; unfortunately, one gong cycle too early. My face turned red and I managed an embarrassed chuckle amid the gales of mocking laughter around me. From that point on, I kept my eyes on Madé.

After about thirty minutes of playing, the tempo accelerated dramatically, and an energetic, cadential flourish of sound brought the piece to a close. I was given thumbs-up signs and nods of approval all around. Madé offered me a cigarette. Although I was not a smoker, I accepted, not wishing to offend him. I took a drag and began coughing uncontrollably. This brought even more hysterical laughter than my faux pas cymbal "solo" had, not to mention hilarious impersonations of my smoking "technique" by various members of the group.

Once things had settled down after my smoking mishap, the teacher made an announcement. This was followed by about five minutes of animated group discussion, during which there seemed never to be fewer than three people talking at any given moment. The discussion concluded, and all eyes suddenly turned in my direction. Then one of the group members, who spoke a little English, addressed me.

"You come back tomorrow, seven o'clock," he said. It was not so much a question or a request as an order.

"Yes," I responded, "I'll come back."

He looked at the teacher and nodded; the teacher looked at me and smiled.

I asked the English-speaking musician (who later introduced himself as Wayan) what kind of music we had been playing.

"Gamelan music," Wayan answered.

"Gamelan what?" I asked. "What kind of gamelan?"

"Gamelan beleganjur," he replied. I pulled out a pen and a pad of paper from my fanny pack and jotted down the unfamiliar name.

The Contest

After the rehearsal, Marilyn and I walked back to the bungalow. En route, we came across another beleganjur group rehearsing. They were sharp, probably a little more polished-sounding than "my" group. We listened for five minutes and then moved on, stopping at a restaurant for some much-needed dinner. Our meal was accompanied by the sounds of at least seven different beleganjur groups, coming at us from all directions. By now, we were very tired and badly dehydrated. My hands had been chafed by the cymbal straps, and my forearm muscles and biceps were getting sorer by the minute. But I could hardly wait until the next rehearsal, when I would get the chance to play this exciting and captivating beleganjur music again.

The next evening, I headed into town by myself to practice with the group. Marilyn opted to go shopping rather than accompany me. (This was to become something of a pattern.) The rehearsal went very well. My knowledge of the arrangement increased considerably, and I became less dependent on Madé for cues. The climax of the evening was a beleganjur procession through the village led by the two drummers. The large, heavy *gong ageng,* or "great gongs," which were hung from poles and carried on the shoulders of nonplaying members of the group, shored up the rear. I took my place next to Madé in the cymbal section directly behind the drummers. We played energetically as we marched down Padang Tegal Road and back, holding up traffic all the while. The villagers who lined the street seemed surprised, amused, and at times a little confused by my involvement in the parade.

Following the procession, there was another short group meeting, after which Wayan instructed me that I was to come to rehearsals every evening from now on, but that I would not be allowed to play "in contest" because only residents of the village were allowed to compete. I had no idea what he was talking about.

"What contest? When contest?" I asked.

"Big contest; many groups. Two weeks, contest. But you no can play," he answered.

So that was why there were beleganjur groups rehearsing all over Ubud every night; they were all preparing for some kind of a competition.

If I was not going to play in the contest, I feared that my participation in rehearsals might prove a hindrance to the group's preparations. I asked Wayan if it would be best for me to stop practicing with them, since I did not want to interfere with their progress.

"You play, good you play, no problem. You extra one," he said reassuringly.

A pair of cymbals was provided for me—so that there were nine players in the section instead of the usual eight—and I participated in all of the sessions other than the final one the night before the contest.

* * *

On contest day, the unpaved parking lot outside the Peliatan dance theater near Ubud was ablaze with color. Beleganjur ensembles from around the region arrived on foot or in the backs of large, open-topped trucks, their shiny silk shirts glistening in the hot noon sun. One group wore yellow, another turquoise, a third pink. As I looked down from a hilltop on the opposite side of the road, they appeared to me as a human rose garden, each group a patch of brilliant color against the background of the drab and dusty parking lot. The group with which I had been working, from Banjar Padang Tegal Kaja, was scheduled to play third. They looked sharp and dignified in their white silk shirts, dark blue wraparound skirts, and black-and-white checker-cloth waist sashes. The painted gold-leaf design of their red wrap-headdresses flashed in a play of light. Their instruments and mallets were also colorfully ornamented, with red yarn pom-pons. While some of the other groups wore black tai chi slippers or rubber thongs, the Padang Tegal musicians had chosen to go barefoot. Since the contest procession would involve walking a course of over a mile on blistering-hot pavement, I was relieved that contest rules had prevented me from competing.

Joining the musicians were a number of other elaborately costumed individuals: girls in traditional ceremonial clothes and dance regalia; boys and young men dressed as clowns, warriors, ministers, and spirit beings from Balinese myth and legend. These non-musicians carried an assortment of ceremonial objects, including silver trays of offerings, brightly colored and decorated umbrellas and fans, banners, spears, lances, daggers, and Indonesian flags.

The parking lot became increasingly crowded as contest time approached; musicians and other contest participants, as well as hundreds of spectators from the community and a smattering of tourists curious to see what all the commotion was about, jammed the area. Most Balinese audience members crowded into the juncture of the main road and a narrow dirt path leading up to the parking area; this was where the groups would play their opening demonstration performances. The jockeying for position there became intensely aggressive as the crowd grew and the excitement mounted. A few of the more passive spectators decided to escape the throng and join me atop the hill, where I had positioned myself early in the day to ensure a good view for taking photographs.

Nestled in a protected and shaded spot on the edge of the demonstration area was a small portable table, behind which sat a young man in sunglasses wearing a yellow GOLKAR T-shirt and a baseball cap with KORPRI inscribed above the brim, both insignias indicating his status as a government employee. A pad of paper, a scoring sheet, and a pen lay on the table behind a sign on which was hand-painted the single word "Juri."

The day's proceedings got under way with a long speech by a government official dressed in an odd green outfit that appeared to be a cross between a military uniform and a 1970s-style double-knit polyester leisure suit. The sound of his voice distorted by an inferior yet remarkably loud public address system, the official droned on through his oratory with passion and conviction, undaunted by the intermittent ear-piercing shrieks of feedback that shot through the loudspeakers or by the fact that, as far as I could tell, no one seemed to be listening to him.

Finally the speech came to a close, and there was a bustle of activity as policemen, soldiers, and contest officials attempted to push back the audience and clear a path for the first beleganjur group to enter the performance area, at the same time trying to assure a clear line of vision for the gentleman seated at the "Juri" table. But frustrated spectators in the back layers of the crowd started pushing aggressively forward, attempting to get as close to the front as possible. From my comfortable perch in the crook of a tree above the fray, the real victims appeared to be the folks in the middle of the crowd, who were being crushed and flattened into one another from both front and back. There seemed to be no concern for the safety of the young children, women, and elderly people among them. They were shoved and jostled just as mercilessly as the teenage boys and young men who made up the majority of the crowd, and some of the children and old women and men were actually highly aggressive themselves, pushing their way determinedly to the front. Surprisingly (to me), everyone looked to be having a grand time with all this. The faces in the crowd exuded pleasure and excitement, not the pain, annoyance, and frustration I was sure I would have been feeling had I been caught in the middle of the melee.

Eventually, the area was cleared for the first group's performance. Leading the procession was a girl dressed in elaborate traditional costume and hoisting a long pole topped by a placard, on which was inscribed the name of the represented banjar and the number 1. Flanking her on either side were two other girls, identically costumed, each carrying a silver bowl filled with offerings of flowers, rice, and incense. Loud hoots, whistles, and catcalls from men and teenage boys in the audience accompanied the girls' entrance, but they remained composed, elegant, and dignified. Directly behind the three girls came a pair of young men dressed as royal ministers *(patih);* ornate ceremonial daggers *(kris)* were wedged against their backs by their waist scarves, and each carried a red-and-white Indonesian flag. Next came two traditional "warriors" carrying impressive-looking spears at least eight feet in length. Finally came the musicians in their turquoise silk shirts, bright red wraparound skirts, and gold cloth waist sashes. The two drummers entered the arena first, followed by two lines of cymbal players, a row of reyong players, several musicians playing the larger hand-held kettle gongs, and finally the players of the large hanging gongs and the gong carriers.

Once assembled before the judge's table, the musicians stood motionless, with stone-faced expressions. The human ring around them closed in tightly, but the contest officials managed to force back the suffocating swarm, maintaining at least a small space between the performers and the audience. A second man dressed in a government "uniform" of T-shirt and baseball cap blew sharply on a whistle, then raised and dropped a green flag.

Immediately, the two drummers hammered out a short, rapid flourish of interlocking rhythm, which was followed by a single gong stroke and a synchronized bow by the entire group. The audience cheered loudly; again there was frantic pushing from the back. The drummers started up again, this time playing a longer cadenza-like duet with virtuosic flair. The crowd became quiet and still, listening with rapt attention. The tempo slowed momentarily, then rushed ahead. With a resounding crash, the entire ensemble entered, joining the drummers with a brilliant flash of rhythmic energy. A flurry of motion ensued as the musicians propelled themselves into new configurations: drummers facing each other in the center, reyong players forming a line behind them and dropping to one knee, cymbal players fanning out in a semicircle behind the reyong section. A young man marking out the basic pulse on a smallish hand-held gong charged forward and began to dance freely, clowning and interacting with other members of the group. The crowd burst into wild applause as the drummers executed an intricate choreographic twist and the cymbal players performed a series of unison steps and turns without missing a beat.

Following the scintillating opening came a more relaxed section at a slower tempo. Here the music became more melodic, especially in the reyong part. But after a while the frenetic energy and fast tempo of the opening were reestablished in a short third "movement," which rounded out the form and culminated in a climactic cadence. Finally, at the end of the demonstration, the group returned to its original processional formation, slowed the tempo down briefly once again, bowed to the judge, and, still playing, headed calmly away from the demonstration area along the parade route after a path was cleared for them by contest officials.

Group 2 was a bit of a disappointment after the impressive performance of Group 1. They were neither as exciting nor as virtuosic as the first team, and sounded a bit under-rehearsed. At one point, a cymbal player lost his concentration and made a mistake, playing an inadvertent "solo" note much as I had during my first rehearsal in Padang Tegal. The crowd hooted and jeered mercilessly.

Padang Tegal was third on the docket. Their opening demonstration was very exciting and technically precise. At its conclusion, I ran down to the road and followed along with the group as they proceeded along the parade route. The street was lined about three deep with people on either side. Most were middle-aged and older Balinese or else small children. There were quite a few tourists as well. Unlike the aggressive crowd at the opening demonstration area, these viewers were generally passive and relaxed, preferring to take in all the sounds and pageantry with the comfort of a bit of shade and breathing room rather than be crushed and knocked about at one of the main judging posts. Behind them, banners and Indonesian flags hung listlessly from restaurant and shop entrances in the sweltering midday air, waiting in vain for a gust of wind to set them in motion.

After marching for some thirty minutes, Padang Tegal reached the final demonstration area at Ubud Palace, where a swarm of eager viewers was pushed aside to make way for their entrance by about a dozen policemen, soldiers, and screaming, megaphone-happy contest officials. I took advantage of the shifting position of the mob to break through to a reasonable vantage point from which to photograph and record the group. Being taller (and larger generally) than virtually anyone else in the crowd, I presumed that with a bit of effort I would be able to get in quite close. I managed to squeeze through a few human layers before the trouble started.

CENG - CENG - CENG - CENG - CENG - CENG - CENG. Padang Tegal broke into their closing demonstration with an energetic round of cymbal crashes. At that moment, I felt a tremendous push from behind and fell forward, my chin crashing into the back of the head of a woman in front of me, who did not even flinch as she strained her neck to try to catch a glimpse of the group. CENG - CENG - CENG - CENG - CENG - CENG - CENG. Suddenly there was a sharp pain in my left lower ribs as a small boy pushed his way beneath my arm, jabbing me with his elbow and knocking the tape recorder out of my hand. I grabbed desperately for the recorder as it dangled precariously from the end of the microphone cable. The lunging motion caused my camera to swing dangerously through the air. CENG - - CENG - - CENG - - CENG - CENG - CENG-CENG-CENG. Now I was off balance. Taking advantage of my vulnerable position, a teenage boy shot forward into a tiny space left vacant by my near fall, his knee ramming me in the backside, causing me to lose my balance and fall sideways into the shoulder of a young woman, who was then knocked back in my direction from the other side. I was losing ground, and despite my height, I still could not see a thing. CENG - ceCENG - ceCENG - CENG - ceCENG - ceCENG - CENG - ceCENG - ceCENG - CENG - ceCENG - ceCENG -

CENG - ceCENG - ceCENG - CENG - ceCENG - ceCENG - CENG - ceCENG - ceCENG - CENG - CENG. There was a roar from the crowd as the exciting opening was brought to a brilliant conclusion. An ecstatic, high-pitched holler from a young man on my right fired straight into my ear from about two inches away, causing me several seconds of partial deafness.

As the tempo decreased during an unaccompanied reyong transition to the slow movement, there was a shifting in the audience, apparently in response to some new choreographic configuration by the ensemble. A slim channel opened up in front of me and I popped through it, advancing about ten feet. Although still far back in the crowd, I could now see the musicians clearly. I could also see behind them some kind of a large, covered, unwalled pavilion structure facing out onto the street. A panel of three judges sat in padded chairs behind a long table at the front of this temporary structure, viewing the performance and occasionally jotting down notes on their score sheets. They had pitchers of water, plates of fruit, and white cardboard lunch boxes. Behind them were several more rows of chairs, mainly occupied by official-looking types, some wearing green polyester leisure suits, others attired in blue-and-white Javanese batik shirts that identified them as government bureaucrats. They too had lunch boxes, and some snacked as they listened. Battered, bruised, thirsty, and sunburned as I was, I could not help but feel envious.

Padang Tegal put on an excellent show. They were followed by nine other groups, some of whom were outstanding, others quite good, and a few mediocre at best. After the final group's performance, the crowd dispersed immediately. There were no final ceremonies. No one lingered to find out the results. No sentiment whatsoever seemed to be displayed; it was as though nothing had happened at all. Even before the resonance of the final gong stroke had fully decayed, everyone was on their way, seemingly in a great hurry, like a high school class leaving the room at the final bell. An announcement came over the public address system, but no one paid any attention to it. It all seemed rather peculiar.

After the contest, I caught up with Wayan and some of the other Padang Tegal musicians, who were walking back to the banjar with their instruments in tow. I asked him how he felt about the group's performance.

"Good," he said matter-of-factly.

"Who won the contest?" I wanted to know.

Wayan shrugged. "Don't know. No matter," he replied.

"When will we start practicing again?" I queried, presuming my continued membership in the group.

He looked at me quizzically. "Habis," he stated, saying one of the few Indonesian words I knew at that time—"finished."

The group never rehearsed again that summer, and when I returned to Bali about a year later, they had disbanded. But the compelling music they played, this beleganjur music that had so captivated me, lived on, in the musical life of Bali and in my life as well.

Part Two

Kawitan

One

The Gamelan Beleganjur
in Traditional Balinese Musical Life

> In the years I lived on the island the air was constantly stirred by musical sounds. At night hills and valleys faintly echoed with the vibrant tones of great bronze gongs. By day drums thundered along the roads to the clash of cymbals as chanting processions of men and women carried offerings to the far-off sea or followed tall cremation towers to the village cremation grounds.
>
> Colin McPhee, *Music in Bali*

Colin McPhee's evocative description of drums thundering to the clash of cymbals in elaborate Balinese processions gloriously brings to life the traditional *(kuno)* world of the gamelan beleganjur. For centuries, the powerful sound and rhythmic intensity of beleganjur music have been used to inspire warriors in battle, intimidate enemy soldiers, drive away evil spirits, and bring physical and spiritual strength and energy to Balinese engaged in the performance of ritual duties.

This chapter provides an introduction to the gamelan beleganjur and its place in the traditional life of Balinese culture. The first part of the chapter focuses on classifications of the ensemble, its historical development, its various configurations and musical "relatives," and aspects of instrumentation and ensemble organization. The second part is devoted to the description of fundamental formal, structural, and design features of what I define as "traditional" beleganjur musical style. The third part examines traditional beleganjur performance contexts, focusing on a number of religious rituals in which the music figures prominently. The fourth part explores the problematic infiltration of the modern contest style, kreasi beleganjur, into ritualistic contexts.

Classifications of the Gamelan Beleganjur

Within the broad range of different types of gamelans found in Bali (see Tenzer 1985, 1991; McPhee 1966), the gamelan beleganjur cuts across several systems of classification.[1] In its instrumentation, it belongs to the *pegongan* family of gamelans. Pegongan gamelans are the only Balinese ensembles that feature the *gong ageng,* or "great gongs," which represent the musical and symbolic heart of all gamelan music. These instruments may exceed ninety centimeters in diameter. A stroke on the gong ageng, which generally marks simultaneously the ending of one and the beginning of another formal cycle of a composition, symbolizes in sound the point in the universe from which all emanates and to which all shall ultimately return.[2] Likewise, the *gong* itself can be interpreted symbolically as the source from which the entire gamelan was born and to which it will ultimately return. The gong ageng is thus to the gamelan what the sacred volcano, Mount Agung (lit., "the Great Mountain"), is to Bali, and what the trinity of supreme Hindu deities—Brahma, Wisnu, and Siwa, collectively the *trimurti* (three shapes) of God—is to the universe itself: the ultimate creator, protector, and destroyer of all that is.[3] Morphologically, with its protruding central boss or "knob" *(moncol* or *pencu),* bent-down rim (*bibih,* lit., "lip"), and tiered surface (*awak,* lit., "body"), the gong ageng, which originated in neighboring Java, is the prototype for a host of other gong-type gamelan instruments and is distinct from flat- or convex-surfaced gongs such as those found in China and India (McPhee 1966, 28).[4]

Other than the gamelan beleganjur, the pegongan gamelans all belong to the family of the *gamelan gong,* described by McPhee (1966, 63) as the "[f]oremost of Balinese gamelans . . . , whose stately ceremonial music may be heard at all formal and festive occasions." There are three basic types of gamelan gong: the grand, ancient *gamelan gong gedé,* or "gamelan of the great gongs," which in precolonial times furnished the core ceremonial *lelambatan* repertoire for temple festivals and other events; the more streamlined ensemble known simply as *gamelan gong,* which enjoyed a brief period of popularity around the turn of the twentieth century; and the modern *gamelan gong kebyar,* which emerged in northern Bali around 1914–15 and quickly surpassed all other types of gamelan in popularity to become the dominant ensemble of twentieth-century Balinese musical life. Today, the gong kebyar is used for adapted renditions of traditional gamelan gong compositions and for the seemingly endless stream of newly created, ever more virtuosic kebyar compositions that have revolutionized Balinese music over the past eight or nine decades. The gamelan beleganjur may comprise a discrete set of instruments or it may be abstracted from the instrumentation of one of the gamelan gong ensembles, such as a gong kebyar (provided that there are several pairs of *cengceng* cymbals in addition to the standard gong kebyar instruments).

In terms of material construction, the gamelan beleganjur is classified as a *krawang* ensemble, that is, an ensemble featuring bronze instruments. Krawang gamelans are distinguished from a variety of other types in which the principal sounding material is something other than bronze: for example, iron *(gamelan selonding),* wood *(gamelan gambang),* or bamboo *(gamelan joged).* Within the krawang group, which also includes the various forms of gamelan gong, the classical court *gamelan Semar pegulingan* (see Rai 1996; Hood 1990), and the small, four-toned *gamelan angklung,* beleganjur is distinctive on account of a conspicuous absence of bronze-keyed metallophones (e.g., *gangsa, gendèr*).

Both the origins and the age of the gamelan beleganjur are, at present, largely matters for conjecture. Within the historical classification system usually applied by Balinese scholars, gamelan beleganjur is placed within the *golongan madya,* or middle period, of gamelan development, on the basis of the leadership function of the drums. Drums are either entirely absent or function in a very limited capacity in ensembles of the *golongan tua (golongan kuno),* or old period, such as the gamelan selonding, *gamelan luang,* and gamelan gambang. Whether beleganjur predated or was derived from its closest relative, the gamelan gong gedé, is not known.

Finally, the gamelan beleganjur can be classified in terms of function. In precolonial Bali, the powerful sound and rhythmic intensity of processional beleganjur music were integral affective presences in most domains of religious ritual and state ceremony, and also in the contested spaces of inter-kingdom warfare.[5] As was noted earlier, gamelan beleganjur literally means "gamelan of walking warriors," and in former times a primary task of beleganjur ensembles was to accompany armies into battle, inspiring soldiers to bravery and striking terror in the hearts of their enemies (S. Willner [1992] 1996, 11). With a faint hum of gongs advancing like the sound of a distant storm before an explosion of lightning cymbals and thunderous drums, beleganjur heralded the impending battle with foreboding power and force.

Today, the role of beleganjur in Hindu-Balinese religious life remains vital. In the all-important mortuary rituals *ngaben* (cremation) and *memukur* (post-cremation purification), processional beleganjur music is indispensable; from grand temple festivals *(odalan)* to exorcistic rites *(mecaru)* and majestic ceremonies in honor of the gods and deified ancestors *(melis)*, the functional presence of beleganjur sound is of crucial importance.[6] The latter portion of this chapter provides a detailed examination of the gamelan beleganjur's role and character in such contexts, while the next chapter will discuss the most prominent vestige of beleganjur's martial past: the modern beleganjur contest.

Ensemble Types and Instrumentation
Historical Predecessors of the Modern Gamelan Beleganjur

Throughout this study, the terms *beleganjur* and *gamelan beleganjur* will be employed to refer to the standard modern form of the ensemble, the *gamelan beleganjur bebonangan*. There are, however, two other types of gamelan beleganjur: the *gamelan beleganjur bebatelan* and the *gamelan beleganjur peponggangan*. Neither is commonly used today, and both are significant mainly as historical predecessors of the modern ensemble type.[7]

The smallest, and likely the oldest, form of beleganjur is the bebatelan. Its instrumentation forms the nucleus of the other, larger beleganjur ensembles, comprising one gong ageng, one *bendé* (sunken-bossed hanging gong), one *kempli* (hand-held bossed kettle gong), four pairs of crash cymbals *(cengceng kopyak),* and two drums *(kendang).* As in modern beleganjur style, the ensemble is led by the drummers (in particular by the player of the *kendang lanang,* or "male" drum), the drumming and cymbal parts feature interlocking patterns, and the gongs outline the underlying cyclic colotomic structure. Rather than *gilak,* the colotomic form *(tabuh)* characteristically employed here is *batel,* the structure of which is simpler.[8] Its form is illustrated in fig. 1 and on the first track of this book's accompanying compact disc (CD #1).

k	k	k	k	k
		B		
G				G

Figure 1.   Colotomic structure of batel. *k*, kempli; *G,* gong ageng; *B,* bendé.

The intermediary phase in the gamelan beleganjur's historical development is likely represented by the beleganjur peponggangan, or "beleganjur with ponggang." To the instrumentation of the bebatelan ensemble is added a *ponggang,* a pair of medium-sized hand-held kettle gongs—tuned approximately a semitone apart—that provides the sole melodic *(lagu)* component of peponggangan-style music. The expanded instrumentation further comprises three colotomic punctuating instruments not found in bebatelan: a second gong ageng; a *kempur* (medium-sized, bossed hanging gong); and either a *kajar* (sunken-bossed hand-held kettle gong) or a *kempluk* (raised-bossed hand held kettle gong). The standard peponggangan colotomic underlay is gilak, the formal structure of which will be discussed shortly.

Gamelan Gong Bheri and Other Related Ensembles

Another ensemble type relevant to an examination of the historical antecedents of the standard modern gamelan beleganjur is the *gamelan gong bheri,* a sacred, ancient ensemble that is possibly of Chinese origin (see Tenzer 1991, 97). The only extant example is found in the village of Renon, not far from the tourist enclaves of Sanur Beach on Bali's southeastern coast. In bheri music, which accompanies a rarely performed sacred dance called Baris Cina (Chinese Baris), the basic gilak gong cycle and the interlocking drum rhythms and cymbal patterns suggest close historical ties to beleganjur. These similarities have prompted the noted Balinese ethnomusicologist I Madé Bandem to speculate that bheri might represent "the oldest form of beleganjur," predating all other beleganjur ensembles as a processional ensemble of war (Bandem, pers. comm., 1992; see also Bandem 1983, 3).[9] Bheri is distinguished from beleganjur (and indeed from all other forms of Balinese gamelan) by the flat surfaces of its gongs[10] and by the employment of a *bedug*—a large, two-headed barrel drum played with two mallets by a single player—rather than a pair of kendang for the drumming part.

Other "relatives" of the gamelan beleganjur include the non-processional *gamelan gong bebonangan* and the modern *gamelan Adi Merdangga* (CD #2), a massive ensemble that may include sixty or more drummers and over two hundred musicians and dancers.[11] The core instrumentation of both is derived from the gamelan beleganjur bebonangan, to which we will now turn our attention.

The Modern Gamelan Beleganjur: Beleganjur Bebonangan

Beleganjur bebonangan, meaning "beleganjur with bonang," is the standard modern form of the gamelan beleganjur, whether the music is heard in ritual, competition, or other contexts.[12] This ensemble, which serves as the focus of the present study, is commonly referred to in Bali simply as *beleganjur.*

The beleganjur bebonangan is an enlarged version of the beleganjur peponggangan, adding four extra pairs of cengceng (for a total of eight) and the bonang, an unmounted set of four small, tuned kettle gongs, each of which is played by a separate player. (The archaic gamelan gong gedé includes a trough-mounted version of this instrument.) Traditionally, the bonang employed a special type of kettle gong, slightly larger and different in shape than its reyong counterpart in the gamelan gong kebyar (McPhee 1966, 29) and more closely resembling its Javanese namesake. Today, though, the bonang part in beleganjur is typically played on four standard reyong kettles (often temporarily detached from the reyong gong-chime of a gong kebyar), and the term *reyong* is most commonly used to identify the instrument.

The full instrumentation of the beleganjur bebonangan ensemble, listed in standard processional performance order, is found in fig. 2. Plates 1, 4, 5, 6, and 13 show beleganjur instruments being played.

First line of performers:
   1 kendang lanang: male drum
   1 kendang wadon: female drum, heavier and lower pitched than lanang

Second and third lines:
   8 cengceng (i.e., cengceng kopyak): eight pairs of crash cymbals; eight players

Fourth line:
   1 reyong (bonang): gong-chime comprising four small hand-held, bossed kettle gongs;
       four players

Fifth line:
   1 ponggang: gong-chime comprising two medium-sized hand-held, bossed kettle gongs;
       two players
   1 kajar (or kempluk): medium-sized hand-held gong, sunken-bossed (kajar) or bossed
       (kempluk)
   1 kempli: like the kempluk, but larger and lower in pitch

Sixth line:
   1 bendé (bebendé): large sunken-bossed hanging gong
   1 kempur: large bossed hanging gong
   1 gong lanang: very large bossed hanging gong, male*
   1 gong wadon: largest and lowest-pitched hanging gong, female*

---

*Both *gongs* are normally played by one performer.

Figure 2.   Standard instrumentation of the gamelan beleganjur (bebonangan)

Altogether, twenty-one musicians are employed in performance. Each is known as a *juru* or a *tukang* (*juru kendang, tukang cengceng,* etc.). *Juru* is the more formal of the two designations, both of which basically translate as "skilled worker." A pair of gong carriers is required for each of the large hanging gongs of the sixth line: bendé, kempur, gong lanang, and gong wadon. Each of these instruments is suspended from a thick, decorated wooden pole that is balanced on the shoulders of two gong carriers: one in front of the instrument and the other behind it (the latter sometimes being the performer himself).

Beaters or mallets *(panggul)* are used on all beleganjur instruments, except for the cengceng crash cymbals.[13] All the mallet handles are carved into shapes that fit nicely in the hand and are visually appealing. The players of the various gongs hold a beater in one hand (typically the right) and use the other hand, if at all, to hold (and/or to dampen or to stabilize the position of) their instrument. The beaters used vary in length, weight, shape, design, and hardness, each being suited to the size, shape, and function of a specific instrument: large, padded beaters are used for the *gongs* and the kempur; long-shafted, cord-wrapped, straight mallets for the kempli, kempluk, ponggang, and reyong; and hard wooden beaters in the shape of an elongated "S" on the bendé and kajar. The kendang are slung over the shoulder by a thick strap, enabling the drummers to play with both hands as they march, using mallet strokes on the right-hand drum head and palm strokes on the left (i.e., playing in *cedugan* style; see McPhee 1966, 99). Their mallets are elegantly carved and consist of a shaped handle, a tapered shaft, and a carved round head made of either wood or water buffalo *(kerbau)* horn.

As with most gamelans, the instruments of the beleganjur bebonangan (henceforth referred to simply as *beleganjur*) can be classified into two functional types: *irama* and *lagu.* The irama instruments are responsible for establishing and maintaining temporal elements of the music, while the lagu instruments are involved with its pitch-centered aspects.[14] An oversimplified but useful distinction is to think of irama instruments as "rhythmic" and lagu instruments as "melodic" in function. The irama instruments in beleganjur may be further subdivided into two categories: *pemurba irama,* or "supervisors of the rhythm," in this case the drums, reinforced by the cymbals; and *pemangku irama,* or "supporters of the rhythm," the pulse- and phrase-marking instruments.

The standard processional order of instruments in beleganjur performance, as shown in fig. 2, is actually reflective of the functional hierarchy and structural organization of beleganjur music. The two kendang drums lead the ensemble, defining rhythmic design and linear form while directing changes in tempo, dynamics, and texture; they are followed directly by their closely related but subordinate associates, the cengcengs, which essentially enhance and highlight the foundational rhythms of the drumming part and can therefore also be classified within the pemurba irama section. Next come the lagu instruments: first the reyong, providing elaborative melodic figuration; then the pong-gang, providing the core melody ostinato upon which the reyong figuration is based. Finally, there are the pemangku irama instruments: the kajar (or kempluk), the kempli, the kempur, and the *gongs*. These instruments collectively serve to outline the main structural points of the music's colotomic underpinning, which is normally in the gilak form. The one functionally ambiguous instrument of the ensemble is the bendé, which normally contributes a brash-sounding, syncopated ostinato pattern to the gong colotomy but may occasionally deviate from its basic pattern with improvised rhythms that correspond to and supplement rhythms heard in the cymbal parts. The functional categories of the different instruments are summarized in fig. 3.

1. **Pemurba irama:** kendang (leadership of ensemble); cengceng (subordinate associates)

2. **Lagu:** reyong (elaboration of core melody); ponggang (core melody)

3. **Pemangku irama:** kajar (or kempluk), kempli, kempur, gong lanang, and gong wadon (colotomic punctuation); bendé (ambiguous; usually colotomic but sometimes shifts functions to join with cengcengs)

Figure 3.   Functional categories of beleganjur instruments

Traditional Beleganjur: The Music Itself

Having discussed the standard instrumentation of the modern beleganjur ensemble and the basic functional categories of its instruments, we may now look more closely at how beleganjur music itself is structured, organized, and performed in what I will term "traditional" contexts. In this discussion, we will move through the instruments of the ensemble in reverse performance order: colotomic punctuating gongs first, then melodic instruments, and finally drums and cymbals. First, however, I must provide some qualifying remarks about how I am defining "traditional" and about the basis of my knowledge and understanding concerning what I am calling traditional beleganjur.

Research Problems in the Study of Traditional Beleganjur

It is important that I acknowledge from the outset that my understanding of "traditional" beleganjur music is based primarily on information provided by my teachers (especially Asnawa) rather than on observation of or participation in performances featuring such music. Because of the pervasive impact of the modern contest style on all types of beleganjur performance since 1986 (at least in the areas where my work was conducted), opportunities for me to hear the music played as I will describe it below were almost nonexistent. (The third selection on the accompanying CD, recorded during a 1995 ngaben procession in Denpasar, is an excerpt from the most "traditional" beleganjur performance I heard during my research.)

Prior to the advent of kreasi beleganjur in 1986, the musical form, mood, and character of a beleganjur performance were dictated almost exclusively by contextual demands (Asnawa, pers. comm., 1992). A flexible, open-ended approach to rendering linear musical form over the constantly recurring underpinning of gilak colotomy and ponggang core melody facilitated spontaneous invention of "arrangements" that could be easily molded to the functional requirements of particular ritual events, such as cremation and temple ceremony processions. Linear musical form in a processional beleganjur performance was determined mainly by a simple alternation of passages that included drums and cymbals *(rangkep* or *rangkap)* with those that did not *(pengisep).*[15] Each full-ensemble section was introduced by a short unison lead-in figure in the drum and cymbal part (often reinforced by the reyong section) and concluded with either a regular *(bawak)* or long *(lantang)* cadential closing figure, or *angsel.* Framing the entire performance were an unaccompanied drumming prelude *(awit-awit)* leading directly into an extended unison drum/cymbal passage at the beginning (the *kawitan*), and a coda-like section—possibly also featuring extended unison drum/cymbal passages—at the end (the *pekaad*).

The lead drummer of the ensemble, the *juru kendang lanang,* was charged with translating musical needs into beleganjur sound. If the energy or pace of the procession lagged, he directed the ensemble to play at a faster tempo and with increased intensity; if the overall mood of the event seemed anxious and unsettled, he pulled the tempo back and the dynamic level down; if the tower carriers in a cremation procession appeared to be tiring under their heavy burden, he cued a *malpal* passage, in which the motoric drive of drum and cymbal parts prompted a rush of adrenaline (CD #4). The quality of a musical performance was judged almost entirely in terms of its meeting specific, context-determined needs, whether of human or spirit origin. Other criteria, such as virtuosity, originality, and compositional development, had little relevance beyond perhaps contributing in some manner to the music's functional efficacy (Asnawa, pers. comm., 1992).

According to Asnawa and others, this flexible, function-driven approach to beleganjur "composition" and performance has become "all but extinct today," at least in Denpasar and its vicinity. Beleganjur is rarely played in the traditional way anymore. Even in sacred ritual contexts, it is extremely unusual to hear the music performed in a manner that does not bear the distinctive mark of kreasi style, where virtuosity and originality are prized and highlighted in largely fixed, relatively inflexible musical arrangements (CD #5).

While this situation has considerable ramifications for Hindu-Balinese religious life that will be discussed briefly at the end of this chapter, my main reason for drawing attention to it now is that it is integral to the methodology of this study. My attempts to reconstruct a "traditional" or "root" beleganjur style have of necessity been based on secondary sources of information rather than direct observation, since I have never truly had the opportunity to experience such music in context (though I have learned about it, been taught to play it, and even performed it in rehearsal situations).

Furthermore, I have had to work in the absence of any significant body of preexisting documentation. In a continuum of Balinese music from the functional to the artistic, beleganjur has historically been located at or near the extreme of function. In contrast to the repertoires of other gamelan types, such as *gambuh,* Semar pegulingan, and kebyar, the development of beleganjur musical style prior to the 1980s was not defined in terms of artistic or aesthetic motivations. Balinese musicians (including my teachers) do not talk about "classic" beleganjur compositions of the pre-kreasi period, or of a beleganjur "repertoire" per se. As Asnawa once explained to me, beleganjur was always "just beleganjur" prior to the mid-1980s.[16] Because neither Indonesian nor Western musicians or scholars have devoted serious scholarly attention to beleganjur until recently, historical information is extremely rare. Other than isolated references (e.g., McPhee 1966, 380) and a single commercial recording (*Gong Beleganjur,* Aneka 212; see the discography), there is little in the way of tangible materials with which to work.

This analytical portrait is thus necessarily limited and partially speculative, but it is nonetheless of critical importance to an understanding of all types of beleganjur music heard in Bali today, including the modern kreasi style that has transformed and in many cases supplanted the traditional.

Beleganjur Building Blocks: Colotomic Structure and Rhythmic Stratification

The foundation of beleganjur music is gilak colotomic structure. Almost all beleganjur performance events—ritualistic, ceremonial, and competitive—are built upon a base of *tabuh gilak,* or gilak form; usually the distinctive gilak ostinato is heard continuously from the beginning to the end of a beleganjur performance.[17]

Gilak is defined by a standardized, cyclically recurring pattern of gong strokes encompassing eight beats on the pulse-marking kajar (or kempluk). The basic pattern is illustrated in fig. 4 (CD #6).

K	K	K	K	K	K	K	K	K
k		k		k		k		k
	(P)		(P)		P		P	
				L				
W								W

Figure 4.   Basic colotomic structure of gilak beleganjur. *K,* kajar; *k,* kempli; *L,* gong lanang; *W,* gong wadon; *P,* kempur; *(P),* "omitted kempur."

A modified Western notation version of fig. 4 is provided in example 1.

$\mathbf{\downarrow}$ = 48-196

Gong wadon   Gong lanang   Kempur   Bendé   Kempli   Kajar (or Kempluk)

Example 1.   Gilak colotomy in Western notation

Each gilak "gong cycle," or *gongan,* culminates with a stroke on one of the two great *gongs,* usually the lower-pitched, female gong wadon.[18] The male gong lanang bisects the cycle at its midpoint, while the kempur and kempli subdivide the cycle through alternating strokes at a higher rate of rhythmic density. The "omission" of kempur strokes between the main stroke of the gong wadon and that of the gong lanang ensures the undisturbed resonance of the gong wadon. It also creates a compelling rhythmic asymmetry that results in what might be described (if only from a Western perspective) as a characteristic gilak "gong melody." This "gong melody," in turn, is rhythmically highlighted by the syncopated ostinato pattern of the clangy-toned bendé, which weaves in and out between the main low gong strokes and the steady punctuation of the kempli (except in sections where it deviates by improvising in cengceng-like style), as can be seen in fig. 5 (CD #8).

—	—	B	B	—	—	B	B	—	—	B	B	—	B	—	B	—
k	—	—	—	k	—	—	—	k	—	—	—	k	—	—	—	k
—	—	—	—	—	—	—	—	—	—	P	—	—	—	P	—	—
—	—	—	—	—	—	—	—	L	—	—	—	—	—	—	—	—
W	—	—	—	—	—	—	—	—	—	—	—	—	—	—	—	W

Figure 5. Bendé part as "colotomic counterpoint." *B,* bendé; *k,* kempli; *L,* gong lanang; *W,* gong wadon; *P,* kempur.

The kajar (or the kempluk) provides a steady, eight-beat pulse that essentially coalesces the rhythms of the slower-moving punctuating gongs into a single composite part while serving as a point of reference for the fastest-played, or density referent, instruments (see Hood 1982, 114–16; see also Vetter 1981): kendang, reyong, and cengceng. These density referent–level instruments normally share a rate of rhythmic density four times as fast as the kajar's. They sit at the top of what may be described as an inverted pyramid of rhythmic activity, in which each level of the pyramid represents a doubling or quadrupling of the rhythmic density of the one below it.[19] The full gilak beleganjur pyramid can be seen in fig. 6 (CD #9). The isolation of selected instrument parts in fig. 7 makes the pyramidic structure more readily observable.

kendang	XXXX	XXXX	XXXX	XXXX	XXXX	XXXX	XXXX	XXXX	XXXX
cengceng	XXXX	XXXX	XXXX	XXXX	XXXX	XXXX	XXXX	XXXX	XXXX
reyong	XXXX	XXXX	XXXX	XXXX	XXXX	XXXX	XXXX	XXXX	XXXX
bendé		X X		X X		X X	X	X	
ponggang	X		X	X	X	X		X	X
kempluk	X	X	X	X	X	X	X	X	X
kempli	X		X		X		X		X
kempur						X		X	
gong lanang					X				
gong wadon	X								X

Figure 6. Full inverted pyramid of rhythmic activity (gilak beleganjur).

reyong	XXXX	XXXX	XXXX	XXXX	XXXX	XXXX	XXXX	XXXX	XXXX
kajar	X	X	X	X	X	X	X	X	X
kempli	X		X		X		X		X
gong lanang					X				
gong wadon	X								X

Figure 7.   Inverted pyramid, partial

Located on the same plane of the pyramid as the kajar is the ponggang, which provides the music's core melody, or *pokok,* a two-toned ostinato that repeats every gong cycle. Rapid, four-toned interlocking figurations in the reyong part serve as elaborations of the pokok, as is shown in example 2 (which also illustrates the relation of the melodic parts to the underlying colotomy, now including the bendé part in the second space from the top of the staff).

Example 2.   Reyong and ponggang

The ponggang and reyong together constitute the entire lagu (melodic) dimension of the music; they will be discussed in more detail shortly.

Joining the reyong on the uppermost planes of the pyramid are the two kendang and the eight cengceng. In contrast to the punctuating gongs and the ponggang, the kendang, cengceng, and reyong may enter and exit the musical texture at different points. These instruments alternate between playing either interlocking patterns that fill in the entire rhythmic texture or syncopated unison rhythms, collectively engaging in what Michael Tenzer (1991, 97) describes as "a three-way musical dialogue of commanding power."[20] Let us now look in somewhat more detail at how the reyong, kendang, and cengceng parts typically work in traditional modes of performance, after first examining a basic feature of musical structure that is common to all three: interlocking textures.

A Note on Interlocking Textures

Thus far, we have seen that gilak colotomy and rhythmic density stratification (as represented in the inverted pyramid) are fundamental building blocks of beleganjur musical design. Interdependent, interlocking instrumental parts constitute a third such building block. At every level of the pyramid—from the *gongs* at the bottom to the kendang, reyong, and cengceng at the top—the instruments of the gamelan beleganjur are engaged with one another in interlocking pairs or sets, which may even be identified as male-female unions (e.g., the two gong ageng and the two drums). The alternation of male and female *gong* strokes, the interaction of these strokes with the kempur, the kempur's own dialogue with the kempli, and the collective conversation of all these instruments with the bendé can be interpreted as examples of the interlocking principle. The higher- and lower-pitched kettle gongs of the ponggang— each typically played by a separate player—also form an interlocking set, one that is devoted to the outlining of core melody (pokok) rather than to colotomic punctuation per se.

It is at the uppermost level of rhythmic density that the most complex interlocking structures are created, between the four reyong players, the eight cengceng players, and the two kendang players. Each interlocking set or pair generates a musical composite, the individual parts of which always lack the capacity for self-sufficient musical coherence. It is characteristic for the musical composite of each instrumental section to "fill in" the entire texture; thus, if we label the density referent an eighth note, we find that it is characteristic for the reyong, kendang, and cengceng sections to each produce an uninterrupted flow of eighth-note rhythm during all interlocking passages, even though no one player actually performs a continuous eighth-note pattern.

Different terms are used to describe the interlocking of different instruments. *Kotekan* is a useful general term for interlocking (although it is perhaps most specifically associated in modern times with the *pemadé* and *kantilan* metallophones of the gamelan gong kebyar); *reyongan* is often used for reyong interlocks, *kilitan* or *candetan* for interlocking cymbal patterns. The correct term for the interlocking patterns of the male and female drum parts is simply *lanang-wadon.*

Melodic Figuration in Traditional Beleganjur Music: The Reyong Part

As we have seen, the different forms of gamelan beleganjur are primarily distinguished from one another by the presence or absence of lagu, or melodic, instruments. In the beleganjur bebatelan, there are no such instruments; the peponggangan ensemble employs only the limited tonal resources of the two-toned ponggang; finally, the modern beleganjur bebonangan expands the melodic element by including both core melody in the ponggang part and elaborative figuration of that core melody in the reyong (bonang) part. Even in its bebonangan form, however, the gamelan beleganjur is, at least relative to other forms of Balinese gamelan, extremely limited in its melodic and tonal range, especially in traditional modes of performance, where there is seldom deviation from the standard ponggang ostinato core melody and a stock repertoire of idiomatic figurations in the reyong part.

In its bebonangan form, the gamelan beleganjur features a unique four-pitch tonal system abstracted from *saih selisir,* the *pelog*-type scale system whose full five-tone version is heard in the gamelan gong kebyar. The selisir tones *dong, deng, dung,* and *dang* are employed. Intervalically (though not necessarily in absolute pitch) these can be translated into the Western concert pitches D–E–G#–A, respectively (see McPhee 1966, 49). *Ding* (C#), the other pitch of saih selisir, is omitted in the beleganjur scale.

The four reyong kettles (one per player) are each tuned to one of these four pitches; the ponggang kettles are tuned to the *dung* and *dang* (G# and A) notes an octave below the top two reyong pots. Most often, the reyong players perform fast interlocking patterns that serve to embellish the oscillating core melody of the ponggang at a rate of four notes to one (e.g., eighth notes to half notes; see example 2), while at the same time providing a reinforcing melodic dimension to the constant eighth-note rhythmic motion of drums and cymbals.

Two main performance techniques are involved in reyong playing: striking the kettles *(gegedig)* and damping them *(tetekep)*. The latter is as crucial to an effective performance as is the former. In the absence of proper damping technique, all sense of rhythmic articulation and melodic line is lost in a blurred ringing of multiple reyong tones. To dampen, a stopped stroke on the central boss of the kettle must be used to deaden the tone immediately following each main stroke; thus, a single mallet is used for both striking *and* damping. The main, open stroke is called "byong"; the closed, damping stroke is "cek" (pronounced "chek").

The striking and damping patterns executed on the four kettles in a typical interlocking reyong texture are illustrated in the breakdown of example 3. Both medium (or slow) and fast tempo versions are included.

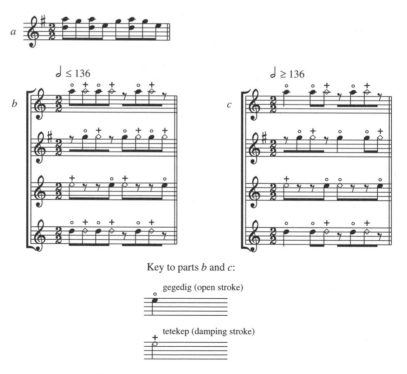

Example 3.   Reyong striking and damping. *a,* Sounded composite reyong part. *b,* Striking and damping pattern at medium (or slow) tempo. *c,* Striking and damping pattern at fast tempo.

At points where the drum and cymbal parts shift to unison rhythmic textures (see discussion below), the reyong players may join them, playing percussively on the edges of their kettles with the wooden tips of their mallets rather than in the usual melodic manner (CD #10, third section). The technique is known as *lambé,* which literally means "edge." In lambé, the open and closed strokes are known as "ceng" and "cet" (pronounced "chéng" and "chet"), respectively, reflecting the identical onomatopoeic terms used for the open and closed cymbal strokes they reinforce in such passages.

The reyong's elaborative melodic figurations, alternately referred to as *reyongan* or *pepayasan,* relate either directly or indirectly to the shape of the core melody in the ponggang part. Reyongan in beleganjur music fall into two main categories: the *noltol* type and the *ngubit* type (Asnawa, pers. comm., 1995). The noltol version (example 4; CD #10, first section) consists of a single four-note melodic cell that is repeated each kajar beat (each half note). This cell begins with a stroke on the highest reyong pot, which is followed by an ascending "sweep" through the other three pitches and back to the top. The pattern repeats eight times per gong cycle.

♩ = 84-196

Example 4.   Reyongan noltol

The "hocketing" effect created by the four reyong players in noltol figuration requires extremely precise execution; while structurally simple, noltol is very difficult to perform, especially at fast tempos.

More structurally complex than reyongan noltol is reyongan ngubit. This style of figuration highlights three-note rhythmic groupings that create syncopated cross-rhythmic relationships with the ponggang part. (Rhythmically, the effect might be likened to the three-against-four syncopations heard in ragtime piano music.) The structure of ngubit patterns in beleganjur is closely related to that of *kotekan empat* patterns in gong kebyar. (See Vitale 1990 for detailed discussion of the latter.) The two outer reyong kettles, which form a kind of consonant tonal sonority known as *empat,* are always struck together in ngubit, resulting in an implicit accentuation pattern that emphasizes the music's syncopated character. Ngubit figurations come in two lengths: the short patterns (example 5; CD #10, last section) repeat four times per gong cycle (i.e., every measure).

Example 5.   Reyongan ngubit, short pattern

The long patterns (example 6; CD #10, second section) extend through an entire gong cycle before repeating.

Example 6.   Reyongan ngubit, long pattern

Kendang: Leaders of the Ensemble

Not only are the drummers the leaders of a beleganjur ensemble, but the composite male and female drum part, a combination of all kendang lanang and kendang wadon patterns, represents the heart of the music's linear design and rhythmic complexity. Drumming is the engine that drives beleganjur as surely as gilak colotomy is the anchor that grounds it.

The kendang beleganjur are rather large versions of a form of instrument found in most types of Balinese gamelan: horizontally held two-headed conical drums that taper slightly so that the drum head played by the left hand is somewhat smaller than the right-hand head and produces a higher pitch. Balinese kendang are carved from a solid log in such a manner that the external shape is conical but the internal shape is that of an hourglass. As Mantle Hood has suggested, it is the hourglass shape of the interior of such drums that primarily accounts for their distinctive acoustical qualities and the broad range of timbres they can produce (1982, 127–28). The drum heads are made from water buffalo (kerbau) hide, as is the strapping that connects the heads across the length of the drum in a zigzagging series of V-shaped patterns.[21] Both drums arc about the same size as their male and female counterparts in the gong kebyar, but they are lighter. This is a concession to the physical demands of processional performance, although the instruments are quite heavy nonetheless.

During processions, each drum is hung horizontally from opposite ends of a thick, padded rope that the drummers drape around their necks and shoulders. The rope is hooked onto two small rings screwed into the body of the drum, one near the right-hand head, the other near the left.[22] Carrying and playing a kendang in a long procession, especially the heavier wadon, is taxing; neck and shoulder pain (which may become chronic) is an occupational hazard with which many beleganjur drummers must eventually contend. The conventional association between beleganjur music and male youth in Bali is more than a symbolic correlate of musical style and gendered conceptions of energy and spirit; it is also simply a matter of physical strength and endurance. Most middle-aged and older musicians, especially drummers, prefer not to subject themselves to the physical rigors of playing beleganjur and avoid doing so when they can. And until quite recently, the very idea of women playing beleganjur instruments—most especially the drums—was unconscionable to many Balinese (see chapter 6).

As was mentioned earlier, the technique of beleganjur drumming involves playing the right-hand head with a mallet and the left-hand head with palm strokes. There are three main types of drum strokes; all have onomatopoeic names, and these names differ depending on whether the strokes are played on the lanang or the wadon drum. Most important is the open mallet stroke on the right-hand head, known as "dug" on the lanang and "dag" on the wadon. Second in importance is a "slap" stroke on the left-hand head, known as "pak" on lanang and "ka" on wadon. A "closed" right-hand mallet stroke ("tit" on lanang, "tat" on wadon), in which the sound is deadened by pressing the mallet into the drum head as the left hand presses into the center of the opposite head, is the third type of stroke.

In addition to these main strokes, there are a number of auxiliary strokes for both hands that "fill in" the rhythmic texture. Most of these do not have specific names, but are known collectively as *maye* (Asnawa, pers. comm., 1995). (I have also heard the term *anak pukulan,* "children of the strokes," used in reference to these incidental or filler strokes.) The most important of the various *maye* is a soft right-hand mallet stroke preceding by an eighth note a main "dug" or "dag" stroke. The anticipatory and main stroke together produce a kind of double stroke ("di-DUG" or "de-DAG") that is highly idiomatic of beleganjur and other Balinese drumming styles. One additional type of stroke, used only rarely in beleganjur, is "pung" (lanang) or "peng" (wadon), which involves pressing in with the thumb of the right hand while simultaneously striking with the outer fingers; this produces a kind of high "harmonic" effect.

In the musical examples referred to in the following discussion, the different drum strokes are notated as indicated in fig. 8. Also note that the double-bar sign is used to mark the start/endpoint of each gong cycle.

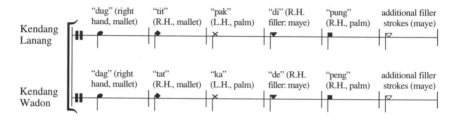

Figure 8.   Drumming notation index

The player of the male kendang lanang serves as the performing conductor of the beleganjur group. He commences the performance with the unaccompanied drum introduction, awit-awit, which is played either solo or in interlocked collaboration with the wadon. A traditional-style awit-awit, such as the one illustrated in example 7, typically begins with a series of six "pak-dug" patterns on the lanang. Their spatial arrangement creates an impression of acceleration and increased intensity. The opening is followed by a brief pause, then a virtuosic solo drum improvisation stressing the "pak" stroke accents of the left hand. The improvised passage closes with an abridged restatement of the opening flourish of "pak-dug" patterns, which closes this time with a single loud "pak" accent. Following another pause, there is an interlocking six-note lead-in figure performed by both drummers. This lead-in is the cue for the full ensemble to enter (commencing the first rangkep, which constitutes the ensemble introduction, or kawitan, section of the performance).

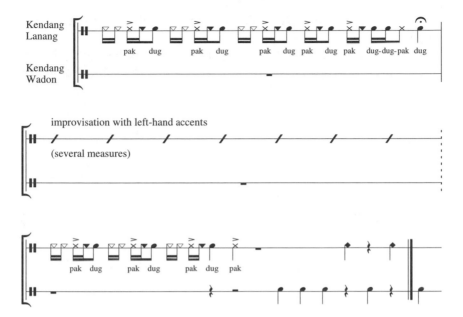

Example 7.   Traditional-style awit-awit

The lanang drummer takes on multiple leadership functions once the ensemble enters, directing all changes in tempo and dynamics, cueing the entrances and exits of the different instrumental sections, mediating between the musical performance of his ensemble and the particular demands inherent in the event for which the music is being furnished, and eventually bringing the performance to a close. In all of these tasks he is aided and supported by the kendang wadon player, who functions as a kind of co-conductor.[23] The two drum parts are completely interdependent and together constitute an indivisible composite whole. While the lanang may be described as the leader of the ensemble, the wadon is in a certain sense the foundation of the music's rhythmic design. In passages where the cymbals play together in unison (sometimes joined by the reyong and, very rarely, by the bendé as well), outlining and reinforcing the rhythm of the drum part, it is the wadon rather than the lanang whose part they double in the great majority of instances. Meanwhile, the lanang anticipates each of the wadon/cymbal unison notes. This characteristic texture of unison wadon drum and cymbals (and in this case reyong as well), with anticipatory lanang strokes, is evident in the third, fourth, and eighth measures of example 8. (A similar texture is heard in the third section of CD #10.)

The anticipation-and-follow interplay that occurs between the two drums reveals one of the great fascinations of beleganjur drumming

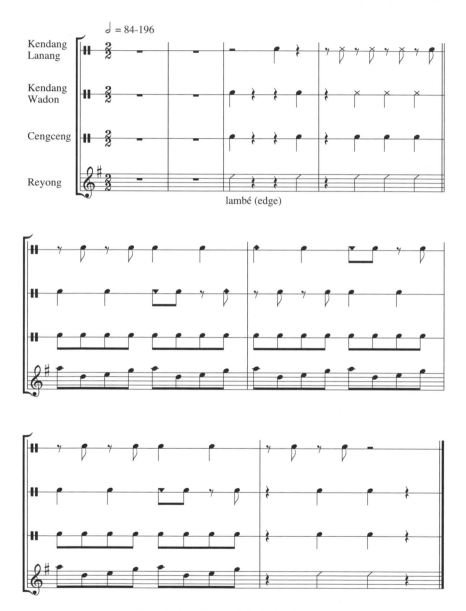

Example 8. Characteristic "unison" texture

(and Balinese two-part drumming styles generally): that the individual parts played by the two drummers are, with rare exception, virtually identical but for the fact that they are rhythmically displaced from one another, usually by a single density referent–level rhythmic unit. The result is what might be described as a hocketing rhythmic canon at the dazzlingly short distance of an "eighth note." The rhythm, unfolding in a blur of perpetual motion, moves along at such a quick pace that the "canonic" structure is very difficult to hear (at least for most Western listeners). Characteristically, it is the lanang that "anticipates" and the wadon that "follows," but the order may be reversed, sometimes even in the middle of a passage.

Clear examples of the anticipate-and-follow kendang interplay are to be found in the drum rhythms of standard cadential patterns, or *angsels:* the "regular"-length *angsel bawak* and the extended *angsel lantang.* Let us first examine a typical angsel bawak drum part, which is notated in example 9 (CD #11).

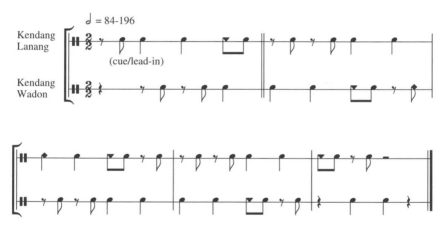

Example 9.   Angsel bawak kendang interlock

Following the one-measure interlocking lead-in figure, the two drum parts essentially become mirror images of each other through their criss-crossing syncopated patterns in the two successive measures; one measure of the lanang pattern is identical to the following measure of the wadon pattern, and vice versa. The two parts collectively fill in a continuous stream of eighth notes until the arrival of the angsel proper, which is marked by the two final notes of the wadon part in the last measure, both of which are anticipated by single lanang strokes (and would be reinforced by unison cymbal strokes—and perhaps unison reyong punctuations as well—in performance).

Angsel lantang, a typical version of which appears in example 10 (a variant version is heard on CD #12), exhibits a similar structural design but in an extended format.

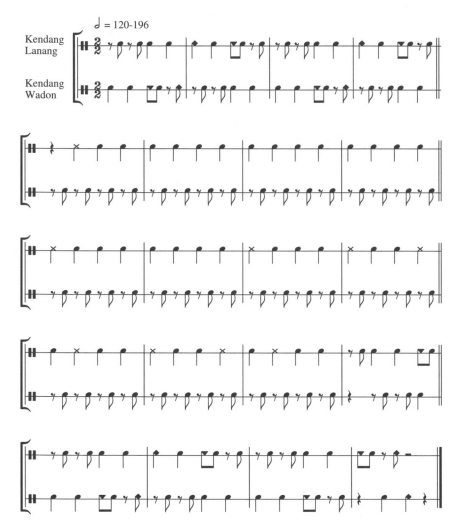

Example 10.   Angsel lantang kendang interlock

In the lantang version, the arrival of the regular angsel drum pattern (measure 16) that signals the end of the whole passage is preceded by two or more gong cycles (three cycles in the transcribed example) of straight alternating strokes between the two drums, which create a sense of added tension and excitement leading up to the closing angsel figure. Here, rather than simply anticipating each "off-beat" "dug" wadon stroke with an "on-beat" "dag" stroke of its own, the male drum mixes things up by substituting left-hand "pak" strokes at certain key points and with increasing frequency as the passage unfolds. Timbral variety is thereby employed to enrich the drumming texture and increase the rhythmic energy in a drive to the cadence.

A notable exception to the usual interlocking style of drumming heard in angsels and other sections of beleganjur performances occurs during passages known as *batu-batu* (CD #13). Batu-batu are distinctive by virtue of their emphasis on improvised drumming, which is otherwise relatively rare in two-drum Balinese styles. Usually (though not always) it is the kendang wadon player who improvises, playing in a way that highlights rapid patterns of mallet strokes on the lowest-pitched drum head. The wadon's syncopated rhythmic figures tend to create a kind of "rolling" effect, like rocks rolling down a hill, and since *batu-batu* means "stones," it is perhaps reasonable to posit a connection between the name and its associated musical style. The kendang lanang accompanies the wadon with a constant eighth-note figure in which the second and fourth quarter notes of each measure are accented, thus creating a kind of "back-beat" effect. Occasionally, the lanang player may break away from the standard pattern and react spontaneously to the wadon's improvisations with syncopated patterns of his own.

Example 11 is a transcription of the drum parts for what may be described as a typical batu-batu. This transcription is from a recording of one of my drum lessons in 1992. My teacher, I Ketut Sukarata, performed the improvised wadon drum part. Note how he manipulated the basic rhythmic motive introduced in the first two measures, altering the rhythm slightly in measures 3–4, repeating the standard pattern at the beginning of the next gong cycle (mm. 5–6), then altering the pattern in a new way in the two successive measures (mm. 7–8) before introducing transitional material to set up the arrival of the angsel.

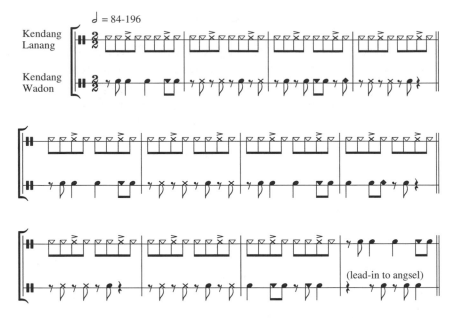

Example 11.   Batu-batu kendang improvisation

The Cengceng Part: A Rhythmic Blueprint

As has been mentioned at various points in this chapter, the cymbal section in a traditional beleganjur performance functions mainly to reinforce the drum part, rhythmically and timbrally. If compressed into a single "composite" of the rhythms of all eight cymbal players, the collective cengceng part can be helpful for analysis purposes as a kind of blueprint of the linear (vertical) rhythmic outline of the drumming part.[24] Alternatively, examining how the various individual cymbal parts work together in interlocking passages provides excellent illustrations of how the interlocking principle so characteristic of gamelan music is achieved through horizontal rhythmic layering. The following analyses will incorporate both of these perspectives.

The eight-member cengceng section creates two distinct textures during the course of a performance: unison and interlocking. In passages where the two drummers together generate a continuous flow of interlocking eighth notes, the cymbal section does likewise, creating its constant rhythm through the layering of three or more interdependent patterns; in sections where the wadon drummer outlines a more distinct rhythm of accented mallet strokes—each typically anticipated by a mallet stroke on the kendang lanang—all eight cymbal players join in unison to outline the fundamental rhythm of the wadon part (often together with the reyong section playing in lambé style as well). In traditional beleganjur style, the "unison" texture is normally limited to the short lead-ins preceding and the cadential angsels concluding full-ensemble rangkep sections, with the continuous interlocking texture filling in all of the "space" in between.

The lead-in figures and angsels alike tend to be highly formulaic, exhibiting only limited variation. The different patterns included in example 12 collectively represent the main "types" of patterns, while perhaps providing a sense of the usual range of variation as well (although not of the full range of possibilities).

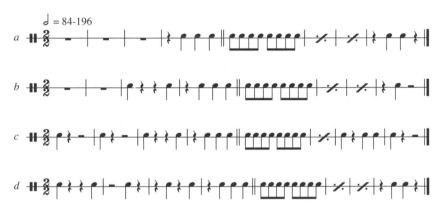

Example 12.   Traditional lead-in and angsel figures: cengceng rhythms

In example 12a, the interlocking cymbal pattern passage (here, as elsewhere, compressed into a single line of eighth notes for purposes of illustration) is preceded by a series of three unison strokes, and the angsel concludes after the interlocking section with two more such strokes. This might be described as the basic form, which corresponds to the standard angsel bawak drumming pattern notated in example 9. In example 12b, the unison lead-in is extended by one measure and the angsel concludes with one unison stroke rather than two. Example 12c extends the lead-in even further, so that it comes to encompass one complete gong cycle, and furthermore varies the closing angsel figure. Finally, example 12d represents a more syncopated and rhythmically

active lead-in of one gong cycle's duration, although it closes with
the more standard two-stroke cadential figure. As we will see in chapter 3, the range of variation in kreasi-style unison patterns is far more
extensive.

Having looked briefly at the kinds of unison rhythmic figures that
frame sections of continuous interlocking cymbal rhythm in the traditional style, let us now examine the internal rhythmic organization of
these interlocking sections themselves. Interlocking cymbal patterns are
known as *kilitan cengceng* (CD #14). The core of the interlocked texture is always a set of three interdependent patterns known as the *kilitan
cengceng telu,* or "cymbal patterns of three" (typically shortened to just
kilitan telu). The designation *telu,* or "three," refers to the number of
main cymbal strokes heard in each pattern before it is repeated.

The three rhythms of the kilitan telu are known as *megbeg, nyandet,*
and *ngilit.* These are notated in score form in example 13.

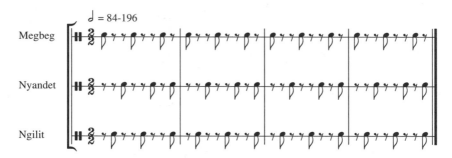

Example 13.   Kilitan telu interlocking cengceng patterns

Megbeg is the *polos,* or basic rhythm, from which nyandet and ngilit
are derived. As is illustrated in example 14, all three of the patterns are
in fact just rhythmically displaced variants of a single rhythmic figure.

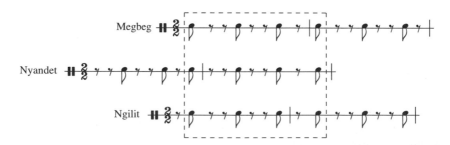

Example 14.   Identical fundamental rhythmic structure of kilitan telu patterns

In accordance with the same basic structural principle underlying interlocking drum parts, then, the imitative rhythmic counterpoint of the cymbal section is generated by different players executing the "same" rhythm at different points in the cycle: nyandet anticipates megbeg by a single eighth note; ngilit follows megbeg in like fashion. Together the three parts create the continuous, multilayered rhythmic flow that is so characteristic of the beleganjur cymbal section's texture.

In performance, the kilitan telu may be performed in either of two different ways. In the first, *gebug polos,* only the three principal notes of each pattern are struck, resulting in a "thin" overall texture in which only one cymbal stroke is heard on each eighth-note beat (with the exception of the last stroke of each measure, where nyandet and ngilit sound together). This is the style represented in example 13. In the other style, *ngejer,* the texture is significantly thickened by a "filling in" of each of the three basic, skeletal rhythmic patterns with double-stroke executions. The resultant texture is illustrated in example 15 (CD #14).

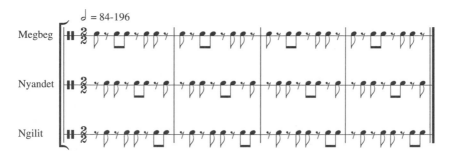

Example 15.   Ngejer version of kilitan telu

One may observe from the transcription that, in ngejer style, each eighth note of the cycle is sounded in two of the three parts (except for the first note, which is marked by megbeg alone); the sound is thus richer and more powerful. According to Asnawa, the ngejer style is used far more frequently in beleganjur performance than the gebug polos style. (My research supports this claim.)

In both traditional and modern beleganjur performance contexts, the standard kilitan telu patterns may constitute the entire range of ceng-ceng "polyphony" or may represent but a subset of a more variegated polyphonic cymbal texture; the continuous stream of interlocked cymbal sound may be divided among the eight players into between three and eight distinct parts. If only the three basic patterns are employed, each one is either doubled or tripled. If there are additional patterns, less doubling occurs. Supplementary patterns are added in interlocking pairs or sets of three. Increasing the number of different parts enriches the texture of beleganjur music, as multiple kilitan tumble over each other in a metallic waterfall of sound. We will return to a more detailed discussion of complex forms of polyphonic cengceng layering in chapter 3, since such textures are most characteristic of kreasi beleganjur styles.

The kilitan telu rhythmic patterns are fundamental not only to bele-ganjur but to most other forms of Balinese music as well. Beyond the obvious connections with cymbal interplay in the gamelan gong gedé (see McPhee 1966, 79–82) and beleganjur-derived gamelan types such as Adi Merdangga, one finds the same set of rhythms woven through everything from Balinese women's rice-pounding music *(oncongan* or *gebyog)* to the "vocal percussion" of *sanghyang dedari* and *kecak*[25] and the sophisticated melodic kotekan patterns of modern gong kebyar (see Vitale 1990; also Ornstein 1971, 1:238–52).

In Its Cultural Context: The Gamelan Beleganjur in Traditional Hindu-Balinese Ritual Life

Processions are central to religious life in Bali. There are thousands of processions every year, a great many of which involve gamelan perfor-mance of one or more types. While other gamelans, such as the gamelan angklung, are frequently played processionally, none is utilized more widely or in a greater array of contexts than the gamelan beleganjur. Beleganjur musical style may have been significantly transformed by kreasi beleganjur's broad-based influence, but the gamelan beleganjur's great functional importance as an integral part of religious ritual life remains intact. Processional events produced in connection with reli-gious occasions provide the primary contexts through which beleganjur maintains its inseparable connection to traditional Balinese lifeways, practices, and values, even in situations where the music is played dif-ferently than in the past.

Five categories of ritual offerings are central to the Hindu-Balinese religion. These are known collectively as the *panca yadnya,* meaning the "five sacrifices" or the "five offerings":

1. *Dewa yadnya:* ritual offerings to gods and deities
2. *Manusa yadnya:* ritual offerings for human beings (life-cycle ceremonies, rites of transi-tion)

3. *Resi yadnya:* ritual offerings for the consecration of priests and priestesses

4. *Pitra yadnya:* ritual offerings to the souls of the dead and to the ancestor spirits (mortuary rites and rituals involved in the purification of souls)

5. *Bhuta yadnya:* ritual offerings to evil spirits

It is through the making of yadnya that humans contribute to their own spiritual evolution and to preserving the natural order, which depends upon achieving a state of balance between earthly microcosm *(buana alit)* and universal macrocosm *(buana agung)* (Phalgunadi 1991, 105). The practice of yadnya ranges from personal daily disciplines of meditation to large communal temple festivals and, at the grandest level, to colossal ceremonials such as the Bali-wide purification ritual Eka Dasa Rudra, which is held only once every one hundred years (i.e., in the Balinese calendrical system where each year is 210 days long). In most communal yadnya ceremonials, specific forms of gamelan music are required. The music's presence is aesthetically and functionally important to the people involved, but music is also presented as a form of offering to supernatural powers, in and of itself.

Providing accompaniment for yadnya processions is the principal task of the gamelan beleganjur in Balinese ritual life. In certain of the pitra yadnya and bhuta yadnya rituals, the role of beleganjur music is especially crucial. In two of the pitra yadnya, the mortuary rituals *ngaben* (cremation) and *memukur* (purification of the soul), beleganjur music serves at several levels to assist deceased human souls in their afterlife journeys. The exorcistic bhuta yadnya rituals *mecaru* and *ngerupuk* employ the forceful sound and volume of beleganjur to frighten and ward off evil spirits *(bhutas)*. In the dewa yadnya realm, beleganjur music accompanies the procession to the sea and ritual bathing of invited deities during *melis (mekiis)* rituals for the holiday Nyepi; beleganjur music is also featured prominently in processions for *odalan* (temple festivals), another form of dewa yadnya at which the gods are honored and entertained.

Through the next portion of our discussion, we will explore the roles and functions of the gamelan beleganjur in these various ritual contexts. Looked at collectively, beleganjur's uses in the different yadnyas support DeVale's claim that "enlivening and protective aspects always underlie the ritual functions" of the gamelan beleganjur (1990, 62). The enlivening aspects are manifest in the music's power to generate energy and strength for people involved in physically demanding ritual tasks, in its more general capacity to help set and adjust the mood and energy flow during processional events, and in its contribution to the overall sense of *ramé*, or crowdedness, so crucial to the success of Balinese ritual occasions. From religious rites to warfare to modern music competitions, beleganjur music is for the Balinese a symbol of strength, power, and energy, and its presence is highly valued in situations where people require stamina and endurance. As for its protective function, beleganjur music acts in behalf of people against the evil spirits who might harm them. It frightens away the *bhutas, kalas,* and *leyaks* through sheer volume and intensity, and it inspires a sense of internal strength in its human beneficiaries, who are made to feel less vulnerable to these evil forces on account of the music's protective power.

Ngaben: Beleganjur in the Balinese Cremation Ceremony

As DeVale has observed, "No matter how rudimentary and humble a cremation is, or how high or low the caste of the deceased is, *gamelan baleganjur,* or *gamelan bebonangan,* is one ensemble that is always used" (1990, 60). The cremation ceremony, ngaben, commences the night before the day of cremation with the striking of a *kul-kul* (large wooden slit-drum), which is used to inform all residents of the banjar that they are to assemble at the deceased's home compound *(natah)*. There, the body of the deceased is ritually prepared for cremation by a high priest *(pedanda),* who summons the gods and deified ancestors and asks them to provide instructions on how to carry out the ceremony.[26] Gamelan music is performed, ideally by the gamelan angklung, whose melancholy character is thought by Balinese to be best suited to the mood of the occasion. Many banjars, however, do not own a gamelan angklung, and beleganjur music is often played as a substitute.

On the morning of the cremation, all members of the host banjar, together with invited relatives and guests, assemble at the deceased's home compound.[27] Amidst socializing and final preparations for the procession, gamelan music is performed in the houseyard in order to set a proper mood of *ramé,* which translates literally as "crowded" and refers to the "aesthetically desired state of heightened excitement" essential to the success of any Balinese social occasion (DeVale 1990, 61). Ideally, the musical sense of ramé is created collectively by multiple gamelans all playing at once but not in coordination with each other. Ancient ceremonial music played on the gamelan gong (usually a gong kebyar nowadays) (CD #15) is complemented by the plaintive tones of a gamelan angklung across the courtyard and preferably also by a rare, sacred ensemble with specific associations to cremation rituals, the gamelan gambang (see Schaareman 1980) (CD #16).[28]

Just before the procession to the *kuburan,* the grounds where the actual cremation will take place, the beleganjur musicians assemble and prepare for their long, tiring march with a special high-protein lunch, often consisting of hard-boiled eggs, *saté* (skewered meats), *lawar* (a ground-meat and vegetable delicacy), sweet rice cakes, and sweet black coffee. They then carry their instruments to the roadside and begin playing when instructed to do so by a member of the host family. The music energizes the crowd and serves as a signal to all congregants to move to the street. The performance will continue uninterrupted until the ensemble's arrival at the cremation grounds.

When the members of the banjar and the other guests are all assembled on the street outside the houseyard, the body of the deceased,[29] wrapped in a very long white cloth *(lancingan),* is carried out and placed in the cremation tower *(wadah* or *badé)* amidst much ritual activity. In its construction and design, the multi-tiered tower symbolizes the lower, middle, and upper worlds of the Balinese universe, with the uppermost tiers representing the world of the gods and deified ancestors to which the soul of the deceased will hopefully ascend (see Eiseman 1989, 119; and DeVale 1990). At the front of the procession, women gracefully balancing colorful trays of fruit on their heads are followed by men carrying sacred daggers *(kris)* and other heirlooms. Next comes the gamelan angklung (if there is one), the tower, the beleganjur group (CD #3, #5), and the remainder of the crowd; in grand cremations, a pair of *gendèr wayang* (bronze-keyed metallophones that are mainly identified with Balinese shadow-puppetry performances) may be played from opposite sides of the base of the tower as it is carried along.

Once the body of the deceased is securely in place, the tower is lifted off the ground by a group of men (usually composed mainly of young men and teenagers). Depending on the status and wealth of the deceased, the tower may be quite small, requiring as few as nine or ten carriers, or it may be massive, needing twenty or more handlers and sometimes as many as a hundred. If the deceased is from a high-caste family *(brahmana, kesatria,* or *wesia),* a male relative sits atop the tower as it is carried from the houseyard to the cremation ground. If he or she is a low-caste *sudra* or *jaba* (as are about 90 percent of the Balinese population), a high-caste *brahmana* or *kesatria* rides on the tower. In either case, the official task of this individual is to help protect the deceased's soul from harm; in a less official capacity, he often also entertains the crowd with humorous antics from his lofty perch.

Just before the tower is first lifted up, officially commencing the procession, the beleganjur group breaks into a musical style of great energy and intensity, the power of the music symbolizing and inspiring strength in the tower bearers for their difficult task. Shouting by the crowd in response to the rocking and tilting of the tower as the young men hoist it up onto their shoulders fortifies the sonic energy of the beleganjur. The music may simply get louder and faster overall at this point, or new rhythms specifically suited to the mood of intensity may be introduced, especially in the cengceng part. The procession proper now gets under way, and the tower is carried boisterously toward the cremation ground, which may be over a mile away.

The beleganjur group maintains its position immediately to the rear of the tower throughout the march. This enables the lead drummer to carefully monitor the overall tempo of the procession and especially the mood and energy level of the tower carriers. Musical tempo and intensity are adjusted in accordance with the situational needs he observes. The ngaben procession should move along at a relatively quick pace, so the lead drummer is especially attentive and responsive to signs of fatigue or lethargy among the ceremony's participants. Any perceived lag prompts more-energetic playing from the ensemble. Conversely, if the pace of the procession becomes too fast, or if signs of overexcitement become evident among participants, then contrastingly slower, less intense music is used to calm things down. Regardless of whether the tempo is fast or slow, the continuous gilak underpinning is maintained.

The importance of the beleganjur group becomes especially great when the procession reaches a crossroads. At every such intersection, the wadah must be rapidly spun around in a circle three times. The purpose of these circumambulations is twofold. First, the spinning of the body disorients the soul of the deceased and prevents it from attempting to "escape" and return home, where it might haunt and harass surviving family members. Second, crossroads are prime gathering places for evil spirits (bhutas and leyaks), who may try to interfere with the deceased's safe passage to the upper world. Since bhutas and leyaks can only travel in straight lines, the spinning of the tower deters their potentially damaging meddling.

The turning of the cumbersome wadah is a difficult task, and one that must be undertaken with much gusto if the desired spiritual ends are to be achieved. For stimulation of energy and strength, the tower carriers feed off of the beleganjur ensemble. Thus, the tempo and the dynamic intensity of the music played at crossroads along the procession route reach peak levels, and the rhythms heard at such moments are especially driving and forceful. The most common of these is the *malpal* (CD #4), which means "to fight or come into conflict" (Barber 1979, 1:376). Here, the kendang wadon and half of the cengcengs play a strong and constant rhythmic pulse that doubles the rhythm of the kajar, while the "off-beat" of each main beat is filled in by the kendang lanang and the other half of the cengceng section, combining to create a relentlessly driving flow of continuous "quarter notes." Historically, during times of war, malpal was reportedly the standard style of beleganjur music played during battles (Asnawa, pers. comm., 1992). In ngaben, it animates the crossroads battles between deceased souls and evil spirits in two ways: empowering the tower carriers with spiritual energy and, more directly, creating a sound frightening enough to drive away bhutas and leyaks.

When the procession reaches the kuburan cremation grounds, the beleganjur group concludes its performance with a climactic passage *(pekaad)*, which is played just after the tower is lowered to the ground. The kuburan is typically a large, open field at the "seaward-most" *(kelod)* extreme of the banjar district, near the Pura Dalem, the Temple of the Dead, dedicated to Siwa. Balinese concepts of directionality are centered on the notion of *kaja-kelod,* or the "mountainward-seaward" axis. Kaja (mountainward) is associated with that which is pure, holy, and good; kelod with that which is impure, profane, and evil (see Bandem and deBoer 1995, vii–viii; Eiseman 1989, 2–10). The kuburan is also a temporary burial ground, and therefore a dangerous place populated by angry, frustrated souls of deceased individuals awaiting ngaben, souls who until their liberation through cremation will take every opportunity to wreak havoc upon those who have survived them. This explains its location at the kelod edge of the banjar.

After finishing their processional performance, the beleganjur musicians are escorted to a shaded area across the field from where the burning of the body, the *meancung,* will occur. There they relax, sitting on wicker mats and enjoying snacks, coffee, and tea provided by the host family. Meanwhile, the body (or the exhumed bones) is removed from the wadah and the white lancingan cloth is cut away, exposing whatever is left of the deceased for a last glimpse by family members and others in attendance. The body is placed in a sarcophagus, often in the form of a black or white bull (for men) or a cow (for women),[30] together with magically powerful sacred objects that will assist the soul on its journey. Everything is covered in a "magic cloth," the *rurub kajeng,* and then doused with several types of holy water *(tirta)* in a series of offerings directed by the priest. The body is then set ablaze, either atop a wood fire or by a huge kerosene blowtorch.

As soon as the burning commences, the beleganjur group begins to play again, now from a seated position. The music helps to set the proper mood for the occasion and, most importantly, accompanies the departing soul on its journey. Compared to the processional performance, it is slow and soft, creating a calmer and more relaxed mood. Sometimes a style called *ocok-ocokan* is heard, in which the lead drummer's part includes more improvisation and the melodic figurations of the reyong are highlighted. Alternatively, a beleganjur arrangement of a tabuh telu–form piece from the gamelan gong repertoire may be performed, in which case the role of the ponggang is transformed from its usual ostinato nuclear melody function in gilak beleganjur to that of a lower melodic extension of the reyong part. Other gamelans may also be heard performing elsewhere on the kuburan grounds; again, a gamelan gambang performance is particularly desirable. The sacred ritual dance Baris Gedé may be presented as well. As in the pre-procession ritual activities, an atmosphere of ramé is strived for, musically and otherwise.

The beleganjur performance that accompanies the burning ceremony concludes the group's official obligations. They may opt to play two or three additional pieces if requested to do so by the host family, however. For example, they may perform during a special ritual held after the cremation, during which an effigy of the deceased is created by placing the person's ashes *(abu)* in the shell of a young coconut. Through invocations *(mantra),* the priest encourages the effigy to come to life. Since beleganjur music is thought to possess power to inspire the deceased soul's desire for rebirth, it is customary for the host family to request this performance. Standard gilak beleganjur pieces or beleganjur arrangements of tabuh telu compositions or others (e.g., "Bapang Selisir") may be played, the ensemble leader choosing selections from the group's repertoire in accordance with his sense of what will best enhance the event.

Late in the afternoon or early in the evening, the ngaben concludes with a procession to the sea, where the effigy created earlier is thrown into the water.[31] Again, beleganjur musical accompaniment is desirable but optional, and whether it is included in the procession depends on arrangements made between the beleganjur club and the host family. If beleganjur is played, the music is again slower and more restrained than that which was performed in the pre-cremation procession. Tossing the effigy out to sea symbolizes the release of the soul from earth. As Eiseman (1989, 124–25) explains, "Now the five elements of the body have been returned to the macrocosm whence they came, and the spirit has been released to the sea where its impurities will fall as sediment, and from which its purer essences will be summoned for the next and final major series of ceremonies"—the memukur.

At whatever point in the ceremony the host family decides that the beleganjur group has completed its required services, a family representative presents a large plate of fruit to the musicians. An envelope containing a small honorarium (usually about twenty-five thousand rupiah, or $12.50 U.S.) is placed on top of the fruit. The ensemble plays a closing piece *(penyuwud)* before the lead musician discreetly removes this envelope. Then the musicians eat, and afterward they may throw fruit seeds at each other and engage in other food-fight games. If the relationship between the host family and the members of the beleganjur ensemble is close, the leader of the ensemble will pick up the envelope as though planning to keep it, only to quietly hand it back to a member of the host family. This indicates that the offer of remuneration is appreciated but unnecessary, that only symbolic capital need be exchanged.

Memukur: Beleganjur in Final Purification Rites

Through the pitra yadnya of memukur—also known as *ngasti* or *nyekah*[32]—the *atma* (soul) of a deceased Balinese person receives its final rites of purification. It is the ritual that "grants the soul the purity it requires for reincarnation" and for entry into the domain of the ancestor spirits (see Hobart, Ramseyer, and Leemann 1996, 125–26). Memukur ceremonials may last for a full week, culminating with a marathon twenty-four-hour ceremony that concludes with a procession to the sea.[33] There an effigy *(sekar),* containing the ashes of another effigy *(sekah)* burned earlier in the ceremony and representing the now fully purified soul, is tossed into ocean waters as a final signification of liberation from earthly bonds. The procession to the sea is accompanied by beleganjur music, as are several other processions that occur during the weeklong period of observance.

Memukurs are often multiple affairs during which several—sometimes dozens—of cremated individuals receive their last rites of purification. In a large-scale memukur, a wealthy, high-caste host family honoring a departed family member often acts as a sponsor for several less well-to-do families. A wait of up to two years between ngaben and memukur is not uncommon among poor commoner-caste families who need a sponsor. Ideally, a deceased commoner undergoes memukur together with his or her *surya* (lit., "sun"), the brahmana priest to whose temple congregation she or he belonged, or else with a member of the surya's family. Thus, it is characteristic for the memukur of a deceased brahmana to also encompass the memukurs of perhaps fifty other people.

The final, climactic ceremony of a memukur is a long one indeed, commencing the morning of the second-to-last day of the ritual and continuing through to the morning of the final day. Ideally, several different gamelans perform during this span, the most important being the rare and sacred *gamelan luang,* or *gamelan saron* (see Toth 1975), an ensemble that has exclusive associations with memukur (CD #17). The luang musicians' job is demanding, since they cannot leave the ceremony area during the entire twenty-four-hour period of ritual activity leading up to the final procession to the sea. The ensemble does not play continuously, but must remain "on call" at all times. Large quantities of sweet coffee, special energy drinks, clove cigarettes, sweet rice cakes, and a couple of high-protein meals help keep the musicians awake and alert throughout the night.

In addition to the gamelan luang, a gamelan gong (today usually a gong kebyar) and gamelan *gendèr wayang* are typically involved in memukur activities. At certain points, the role of these ensembles is simply to provide musical sound that contributes to the overall mood of ramé. Their main function, however, is to accompany special dance and shadow puppetry *(wayang)* performances. The most important of the dances is the sacred Baris Punia, during which the solo dancer also acts as assistant to a high priest in a ritual collecting of offerings. In smaller, more modest memukurs (perhaps the more appropriate term here is nyekah), procuring a gamelan gong, let alone a luang, may prove impossible. In such cases, a gamelan beleganjur may have to suffice as a substitute ensemble.

The focal point of memukur is the *sekah,* an ornate effigy with a bamboo frame, which represents the soul of a cremated individual. Toward the end of the memukur, usually at around 4:00 A.M., the sekah is

burned in a symbolic "second cremation," purifying the soul in preparation for its ascent to the upper world. The ashes from the sekah are
then placed in the shell of a young coconut and adorned with flowers,
Chinese coins, and other decorative items; thus, another effigy, the sekar
or *puspa* ("blossom" or "flower"), is created (Eiseman 1989, 125).
This effigy is carried to various family shrines to receive prayers and
offerings before being placed in a special tower *(bukur)*. Except for its
colors—white and yellow, symbolizing the state of purity now achieved
(the clothing of the ritual participants is likewise predominantly white
and yellow)—the tower (see plate 2) closely resembles in appearance
the one that was employed in the original cremation procession.

By dawn, all the sekar have been placed in their towers. When it is
time for the procession to the sea to begin, the beleganjur musicians
assemble on the road and start to play, signaling the rest of the congregation to gather and prepare for departure. A gamelan angklung typically leads the procession, while the beleganjur ensemble falls in near
the rear.[34] At the beginning the beleganjur musicians play with considerable volume and intensity to generate energy for the long trek, which
may last for up to four hours; but once the procession is under way, the
playing becomes slower and more subdued (CD #18), in notable contrast to the robust beleganjur style heard during ngaben processions.

Upon arrival at their seaside destination, the beleganjur group's official duties are complete, although both they and the angklung ensemble
often continue to play through to the end of the final memukur rite,
nganyut. In nganyut, the sekar are removed from their towers and
thrown or carried out to sea by family members following a lengthy
ceremony of prayers and offerings (see plate 3). The mood is excited
and playful; nganyut is a joyous occasion, since now "[t]he soul has
finally been sent on its way to God" (Eiseman 1989, 126) and the departed individual can be invited to rejoin his or her family as a deified
ancestor.

Mecaru: Beleganjur in Rituals for the Appeasement and Exorcism of Evil Spirits

Mecaru are ceremonies of the bhuta yadnya type, in which offerings are
made to appease bhutas and kalas, evil spirit beings of the lower world.
The ceremonies are held when there is a perceived need for protection
against evil spirits—for example, when a family moves into a new
home, immediately before a sacred ritual, or during a village epidemic.

Mecaru typically conclude with a purification of the ceremonial grounds, or *ngilehin caru,* during which the bhutas and kalas are encouraged to depart after a ritual "feeding." At the culmination of a ngilehin caru, all the ceremony participants circle the grounds three times, making as much noise as possible. Some strike coconut-leaf stems against the ground; others play loudly and forcefully on hand-held wooden slit-drums *(kul-kul).* A chaotic and terrifying cacophony is generated in an effort to ensure that any evil spirits who remain unappeased after their ritual feast are driven away. Often of significant value in this endeavor is a beleganjur group playing as loudly and frantically as possible.

Mecaru may occur at any time of the year, but the most auspicious time for them is immediately prior to Hari Nyepi, the Day of Silence marking the Balinese New Year. Nyepi is when "everything begins anew and nature becomes neutral" (Asnawa, pers. comm., 1992). On this day, Balinese must observe three basic rules, collectively known as the Amati: Amati Lelungan, which forbids leaving the home; Amati Geni, which forbids making or using fire (including for cooking); [35] and Amati Karya, which forbids working.

To assure a "clean slate" of ritual purity at the beginning of the new year, evil spirits of all kinds must be appeased on the day before Nyepi. This is achieved by means of two different ceremonies: in the morning, Tawur Agung, a large-scale mecaru dedicated to eradication of bhutas and kalas; and in the evening, *ngerupuk,* devoted to the expulsion of earth-dwelling evil spirits known as leyaks, who terrorize their human victims with "black magic" (see Jensen and Suryani 1992, 22). In both ceremonies, the gamelan beleganjur may play a significant role.

Tawur Agung

All over Bali on the morning before Nyepi, the entire congregations of village temple associations *(desa adat)* gather in fields near the main temple for the Tawur Agung ("great payment" or "great offering"). Offerings of many kinds, including animal sacrifices, are made to placate the bhutas and kalas. A piglet may be decapitated while held by the hind legs so that blood will flow freely for the delight of the demon spirits; a cockfight may also be held, the bloodshed of the cocks similarly satiating the desires of the demons (Hooykaas 1973, 15).

The Tawur Agung concludes with a grand mecaru, held at the village's main crossroads. There the *sengguhu,* a priest specializing in exorcistic rites, drones a litany aimed at chasing away the evil spirits as he rings a small handbell *(genta)* in uninterrupted rhythm. His efforts are strengthened by the playing of a small hand drum and a tambourine-like instrument at maximum volume by two assistants, and by explosions created by the lighting of small fires under stalks of unripe bamboo. Burning torches may also be used to drive away the demons, the torches "flung back and forth by groups of young men in a kind of fire battle" (Bandem and deBoer 1995, 58). Filling out the soundscape is beleganjur music, which is used to enhance the priest's exorcistic power. As Hooykaas (1973, 15) explains, "the averting of . . . disaster can be effectuated by adding the maximum of noise to be caused by a complete *gong* [by implication, a gamelan beleganjur] to the din already made by the *sengguhu* and his helper."

The largest Tawur Agung ceremony by far is the one held annually at the Puputan Badung Memorial Park (Taman Puputan Badung) in downtown Denpasar. Balinese come to this event from all over the island; the governor of Bali and other important dignitaries normally attend as well.

Ngerupuk

Ngerupuk rituals commence at dusk on the evening before Nyepi ("New Year's Eve"). On this night, every Balinese family must rid its home compound of leyaks in anticipation of the new year; this is achieved through participation in a ngerupuk procession. The procession traces completely around the perimeter of the houseyard, beginning and ending at the family temple. It is led by an individual carrying a special bamboo gas torch known as an *obor*. All participants function as noisemakers, yelling and banging on boxes, metal cans, slit-drums, and other objects to drive away the leyaks. Things become especially raucous at each of the four corners of the houseyard, where the leyaks are thought to congregate.

The individual family ngerupuks are often followed by a communal one in which all the villagers can participate. Here, the village beleganjur group is often called upon to contribute to the anti-leyak din. In some instances, two or more neighboring or otherwise associated banjars (often belonging to the same desa) join forces to produce an even larger ngerupuk; several beleganjur ensembles may be featured.

And then there is the grand ngerupuk held each year in Denpasar. Since 1983, the government of Bali has sponsored the production of a huge ceremony at Puputan Badung Memorial Park, making an important religious event into a major tourist attraction. Entourages from over a hundred village associations congregate at the park; there are thousands of participants. Each entourage features one or more *ogoh-ogohan,* huge life-like statues (fifteen to twenty feet tall) of grotesque but benevolent protective creatures who possess special powers for frightening leyaks. Every imaginable sound-producing object and form of vocalization is used to create an overwhelming wall of sound, but the greatest volume comes from the collective efforts of approximately one hundred beleganjur groups playing as forcefully as possible in what As-nawa describes as "the loudest of all Balinese ceremonies" (pers. comm., 1992).

Melis (Mekiis): Honoring the Deities

Yet another major ceremonial featuring beleganjur music is *melis* (or *mekiis*), which also normally occurs on the day before Nyepi. In contrast to the different forms of mecaru, melis is a dewa yadnya, a ritual presented in offering to the gods, rather than to evil spirits. It involves a complex network of long, elaborate, ever-expanding processions in which effigies representing various deities are carried to the sea and symbolically bathed. The effigies are in the image of humans and are known as *arca* or *pratima.* They are carried high above people's heads on thronelike chairs made especially for the occasion. Statues of tigers, serpents, birds, and other animals are also included in the procession. These represent the *auban,* the spirit beings responsible for transporting deities to earth for this special event; each god is associated with a particular auban. Also included in the procession are spiritually empowered objects *(pelawatan)* such as masks *(topéng),* daggers *(kris),* Barongs of various kinds,[36] and other sacred heirlooms, all of which possess magical powers that help protect the villagers from evil spirits.

Each of several processions grows as one banjar after another joins in along several prescribed routes that begin at various inland points and proceed toward the ocean. With each new banjar entourage, a new beleganjur group is added, its sounds mixing chaotically with all the others and with the singing of sacred verses in honor of the gods. According to Bandem and deBoer, "On this day, it seems that everyone in Bali is on the march with umbrellas and banners and *gamelan,* going in procession down the highways and byways to the sea or to a river that leads to the sea" (1995, 126). The desired "crowded" sense of ramé increases with the addition of each new group, reaching its apex when all of the different processions finally congregate at some designated seaside point (often either Kuta or Sanur Beach) to form a visual and sonic mass of "hundreds of thousands of people" and as many as "a thousand Barong" (Bandem and deBoer 1995, 126), all united in a common act of spiritual devotion. At the ocean's shore, the ceremony concludes with a ritual bathing of the effigies of the gods and their bird and animal spirit transporters, although none of the spiritually empowered objects are actually placed in the water or made wet.

Odalan: Beleganjur in Temple Festivals

A final important dewa yadnya context for the performance of beleganjur music is the large temple festival, or *odalan*, held in honor of the anniversary of a temple's dedication. The main ceremonial events of an odalan are usually preceded by a large procession, in which an entourage from each banjar of the village temple association brings offerings to the temple. Each of the banjars includes its beleganjur ensemble as part of the entourage. Beleganjur music, which is typically played in an energetic style and at a relatively fast tempo on such occasions, contributes to the festive mood of the event and also serves as a form of offering itself; the chaotic collage of sound created by the multiple beleganjur groups and other processional gamelans (especially angklung) contributes significantly to the achievement of a desired spirit of ramé.

Upon arrival at the temple, each beleganjur group in turn concludes its performance with a short demonstration. There is often a sense of rivalry as the groups attempt to outdo one another, each trying to show its banjar to be the best and proudest of all. In such informal "competitions" one finds something of the spirit, and perhaps even the roots, of the modern formal beleganjur contest, or lomba beleganjur, which will be the focus of the next chapter.

A Clash of Old and New: Ritual Beleganjur Music in Crisis

As was discussed earlier, new musical realities have transformed the formal shape and stylistic character of beleganjur music heard in ritual contexts since the mid-1980s. In endeavoring to meet their religious obligations, Balinese today must contend not only with spirit-world antagonists, but also with the compromising forces of musical modernity. The modern, kreasi-inspired style of beleganjur music most often heard today during cremation processions and in other religious contexts (CD #5) is frequently painfully at odds with its contextual setting. A portion of a procession calling for calmness and tranquility may be disrupted by loud and frantically fast kreasi pyrotechnics, while a sudden need for music of energetic intensity may be thwarted by the arrival of a slow, lyrical passage of a fixed, kreasi-style arrangement. Even where the degree of inappropriateness is less marked, the fundamental incongruity between largely fixed beleganjur forms designed for contest performance and traditional religious forms requiring a subtly complex and ever-changing interplay between music and its surrounding ritual activities undermines the proper fulfillment of religious obligations.

For many older Balinese, including the revered composer I Wayan Beratha, now in his mid-seventies, the potential consequences of this situation are alarming. During his long and illustrious career, Pak Beratha[37] has contributed profoundly to revolutionizing Balinese music through his innovations in gong kebyar and many other genres. On account of his central involvement in the establishment and development of the Balinese arts conservatories and other major cultural institutions, such as the Bali Arts Festival—and his more recent activities as a senior advisor in the development of an array of neo-traditional genres, including kreasi beleganjur and kreasi lelambatan—Beratha has also been a significant force in the shaping and defining of Bali's "modern traditional" culture (see chapter 2) more broadly. For decades he has thus promoted and actively contributed to the kinds of musical and cultural change that have given rise to forms such as kreasi beleganjur, but he sees great danger in the use of new modes of expression for old purposes.

"Each type of ceremony has its own unique character, and the music of the beleganjur should reflect that character," Beratha explained to me in 1992. "The mood for the cremation procession is one thing; for the temple festival, it is something else. Very holy processions like melis are different again. The style of the music needs to be different for each of these, but nowadays, because [beleganjur groups] learn kreasi style, they always use it, even though it is usually not right. We are afraid of this! Young people like the strong and energetic character of the new style. They get carried away and forget where they are. For example, in the melis [ceremony], at the same time as the beleganjur is playing we also have singing of *kidung* sacred verses. The beleganjur should be soft and calm to go along with the kidung, but very often now, it is not. They play loud and fast and that is not right. It is dangerous."

So why have protective measures not been taken against the potential consequences of the inappropriate employment of kreasi style? "It is a difficult question to answer," states Beratha. "The young people are very excited by the new beleganjur music. They like to play it very much, and this is good, because it means that they stay interested in the Balinese culture instead of just going to the discos and things like that. If we try to tell them not to play their style, maybe they will not want to play anymore for the ceremonies. We cannot take that chance. Even if we are not so happy with how they play the beleganjur all the time, and even if we are afraid that the wrong way of playing may be bad for the ceremony, it is still better than if they decide not to play. That would be worse. If they are staying involved with the traditions, we do not want to discourage them. That is the most important thing."

Beratha's sentiments are shared by younger musical luminaries. The very individuals who pioneered kreasi beleganjur and helped to establish its prominence in the modern Balinese musicscape are often among the harshest critics of the new style's indiscriminate use in ritual settings. Composer and kreasi beleganjur innovator I Komang Astita, some thirty years Beratha's junior, is a case in point.

"If a beleganjur group has worked up a piece in kreasi style," states Astita, "they will play in that style no matter what. The young people do not seem to care if this sets the wrong mood for the ceremony. The new style is exciting for them, so they want to play it all the time."

Inappropriate use of kreasi beleganjur style in religious contexts by the young musicians who dominate the beleganjur performance world is a source of major concern—even fear—for middle-aged and older Balinese Hindus. Critics such as Beratha and Astita warn that employment of modern-style music in ritual situations lessens the likelihood that the rituals will achieve their desired spiritual ends. As a result, the delicate and vulnerable balance between human and spiritual forces essential to human survival may be threatened.

Nonetheless, at least in Denpasar, the rampant use of kreasi style in ritualistic settings is generally tolerated in the interest of promoting an embracing of traditional culture and lifeways by Balinese youth. Paradoxically, this compromising concession to modernity is seen as a necessary sacrifice for the continuance of Hindu-Balinese religious practices and values. Where the sustenance of traditional life is concerned, members of the Balinese establishment appear to be more comfortable relying on the benevolence of supernatural powers than wagering against the capricious fancies of youth in a rapidly changing society. Beleganjur contests and the flashy musical style of kreasi beleganjur have galvanized the interest of youth in "tradition" *(tradisi),* and this apparently outweighs all other considerations in the eyes of many Balinese—especially in urban areas such as Denpasar and tourist centers such as Kuta, Sanur, and Ubud, where alternatives to conventional Balinese lifeways are most readily available to young people.

A clear indication of kreasi beleganjur's perceived social value as a catalyst for revitalization of youth interest in *tradisi* is evident in the following anecdote related to me by I Wayan Rai. Rai, who holds a Ph.D. in ethnomusicology from the University of Maryland, Baltimore County, is a highly respected composer and conservatory music professor. He has been a major figure in the "cultural renaissance" of his native Ubud. In 1989, he produced Ubud's first beleganjur contest and organized a group from his own banjar to compete in the event.[38] One of his nephews was a key member of that ensemble.

"When he was younger, he was quite a bad boy," Rai told me in 1992. "He would always get in trouble. All he wanted to do was ride his motorcycle and go to [the] disco. When I began to organize the first beleganjur contest for Ubud in 1989, I thought maybe I could get him involved, so I put him in our banjar's group. It was amazing. Right away, he really loved the beleganjur. He even got some friends to come. 'Put away the motorcycles and let's play,' he would tell them. Every day, he would go to the *balé banjar* [community center] to practice with the group. He would even come to the village's religious ceremonies so that he could play beleganjur. Playing in the contest was very exciting for him, and then, because the group had success, he got to play on television. We are so pleased. Instead of being 'motorcycle boy,' now he is 'beleganjur boy.' This is why beleganjur and the contests are so important. To make the young people interested in the traditional culture you have to make a program for them. You have to make particular events for them to practice for where they get to do things that they really like, things that make them excited. Beleganjur is very good that way."

Two

Lomba Beleganjur:
The Modern Competitive Context

Since 1986, the gamelan beleganjur's status and role in Balinese musical culture and the style and aesthetics of its music have greatly changed with the advent and development of the *lomba beleganjur,* or formal beleganjur contest. The widespread popularity and official endorsement of contests have resulted in the development of a new, important cultural institution from the synthesis of an old, function-driven music with modern artistic and sociopolitical sensibilities. The modern lomba beleganjur has placed beleganjur music and imagery in the ideological service of Indonesian cultural nationalism, making it a symbol of mediation among traditional Balinese cultural values, modern Indonesian political ideals, and the realities of contemporary Balinese-Indonesian life. In addition, it has furnished a hospitable and stimulating environment for creative musical endeavor, as is manifest in the innovations of the kreasi beleganjur style.

From the contest to the cremation procession, beleganjur music today is profoundly different than it was in the past. Its forms and structures are more fixed and complex; the performance aesthetic is more exhibitionistic and the technical demands greater; there is an unprecedented emphasis on musical innovation and virtuosity; and the beleganjur performance domain, while traditionally male-dominated, has become largely the province of teenage boys and young, unmarried men specifically.[1] All of these changes have been inspired by the new expectations and possibilities of the competitive lomba environment, a forum for musical display that is deeply implicated in certain ideological agendas of "culture" in New Order Indonesia.

This chapter presents an ethnographic portrait of the modern beleganjur contest phenomenon. I begin by locating the lomba beleganjur within two broader contexts: first, the lomba institution of Indonesian cultural nationalism; and second, a particularized musical history of the Denpasar region. This is followed by a section on the original and foremost beleganjur contest, the Lomba Beleganjur Puputan Badung, which includes a detailed examination of the performance evaluation criteria used in that event. The next sections are a survey of the Bali-wide growth and spread of the beleganjur contest phenomenon from the late 1980s through the mid-1990s, and a description of how beleganjur groups prepare for competition performances. I conclude by discussing the role of the lomba beleganjur as a sanctioned cultural medium for the release and expression of certain kinds of intense energies and emotions, both for contest performers and their audiences.

The Indonesian Lomba

The lomba beleganjur originated in the musical culture of Badung regency, in southern Bali, and most specifically in the city of Denpasar. *Lomba* simply means "contest," but the term is usually used in connection with a broad category of formal, institutionalized competitive events held throughout Indonesia and produced with government sponsorship by provincial *(propinsi)*, regency *(kabupaten)*, or district *(kecamatan, kelurahan)* administrative branches, most often under the auspices of the Ministry of Education and Culture.

Government-sponsored gong kebyar contests in Bali date back to at least 1968, when a major lomba featuring groups from different Balinese regencies was produced (Asnawa, pers. comm., 1992). This event essentially formalized a legacy of kebyar competitions stemming from the early part of the century (see Lendra 1983, 65), which was in turn grounded in a long history of competitions between royal court gamelans in the precolonial era. Today, the annual gong kebyar competition of the Bali Arts Festival, established in 1978 and enhanced by the addition of a women's division in 1985 (see chapter 6), stands as the defining institution of the modern music lomba tradition.

The first lomba beleganjur, entitled Beleganjur Contest in Honor of the 80th Anniversary of the Puputan Badung (Lomba Beleganjur Dalam Rangka ke 80 Puputan Badung), was produced in Denpasar in September 1986. Its success led to the establishment of the Lomba Beleganjur Puputan Badung (LBPB) as an annual event, and the contest subsequently became the basic model for a plethora of others held all over Bali. We will return to the LBPB in more detail shortly.

A tremendous diversity of activities are encompassed within the Indonesian institution of lomba. In Bali, it seems that just about any activity warranting the organization of sekehes (clubs) also warrants the production of formal contests between such groups. Thus, one finds lombas not only for music, but for dance, military-style marching, oratory, even garbage collection efficiency.[2] Beyond their local significance as community or regional events, lombas typically serve larger interests; most importantly, they are central to the government's efforts to promote Indonesian cultural nationalism. The evaluative criteria applied to lomba performances characteristically center on the "development, expansion, and preservation of traditional arts" (membina, mengembangkan, dan melestarikan kesenian tradisional), on the "upgrading" of localized cultural traditions. There is a "recurring theme in policy statements . . . that the arts as they currently exist are imperfect, in need of improvement, and can serve at best as the foundation for something new" (Sutton 1991, 189). The desired "something new" comprises a merging of the "local" and the "national," the "traditional" and the "modern." Lomba participants, as R. Anderson Sutton explains (in specific reference to Central Java), "are all urged, in accordance with government policy, both to maintain the best of regional arts and to contribute to 'national culture'—as Indonesians and not just as Yogyanese, or Javanese" (ibid., 191).

This notion of regional and national interest being mutually reinforcing lies at the heart of Indonesia's national motto, Unity in Diversity (Bhinnéka Tunggal Ika), the semantic cornerstone of an officially prescribed national philosophy or "civil religion" (Geertz 1990) known as the Pancasila (Five Principles). As one government publication explains, the Pancasila represents a crystallization of "the national ideology: the principle, the aims and the views that make peoples from different [Indonesian] subcultures or ethnic groups commit themselves to national goals, get motivated by the national spirit, develop national sentiment vis-a-vis the world at large, in other words, acquire his [sic] national identity" (Dahlan and Walean 1995, 16).

Lombas, like other government-endorsed "cultural events," create highlighted public spaces for the reification of what I have elsewhere described as "culturally-elevated authenticity" (Bakan 1998b, 455–58). The products and performances displayed and comparatively assessed in lombas reference the specific, localized cultural worlds of their origin, while symbolically transforming those worlds into something more globally "Indonesian." Those entered in the competition who best succeed in molding their "native" cultural expression to the prescribed dictates of the "national culture" garner the rewards of official approval and legitimization: prizes, trophies, certificates, appearances at official state functions, financial remuneration. Through the vehicles of their invented traditions (Hobsbawm and Ranger 1983), lomba champions are granted the privilege of representing themselves not just as Balinese, Javanese, Sumbawans, or what have you, but as model Indonesians in a more encompassing sense. They are the select Diversities ordained to symbolize Unity: the diverse Others who manifest the unity of the Indonesian collective Self. The stages upon which they perform may be local, national, or even international, but however modest or grand the scale, a status is accrued that sets the selected individual, group, village, region, or even entire province (e.g., Bali) on a pedestal above its peers.

"Balinese culture," as represented in the culturally elevated artistic forms featured in contests, festivals, official public demonstrations, radio and television broadcasts, recordings, and tourist and international performances, holds a place of great prominence within the Indonesian "national culture" that has been constructed by government and corporate interests (often one and the same thing) to promote Indonesia, both to the rest of the world and to itself. The nation's present and future political and economic good fortune—both internally and internationally—relies to a great extent on its public images of "culture," and the predominant images employed are mainly linked to the arts of Central Java and Bali, with music and dance forms serving in especially significant roles.

Kreasi beleganjur, as defined through the institution of the lomba beleganjur, has become an important modern addition to Bali's officially sanctioned cultural image. Contest beleganjur style and the contest event to which it is integrally related enframe a historic, noble Balinese past within a progressively nationalistic Indonesian present; the proper balance of "development, expansion, and preservation" is achieved.

Denpasar/Badung: Historical Antecedents of the Modern Beleganjur Contest

Denpasar/Badung's status as the birthplace of the modern beleganjur contest is consistent with the region's reputation as a place where the gamelan beleganjur has played an unusually prominent role in musical life historically, especially since Indonesia became an independent nation in 1945.[3] According to Asnawa and his principal musical mentors, I Wayan Beratha of Denpasar and I Nyoman Rembang of Sesetan (both natives of the Badung region who are now in their seventies), unique patterns of urban development in Badung fostered a musical environment where the gamelan beleganjur came to function in a more diverse array of contexts than elsewhere in Bali. Denpasar-area musicians were thus especially well suited to the creative challenges of developing a new style of beleganjur appropriate to contest performance, as the following discussion will help to illustrate.

Beleganjur's prominence in Denpasar/Badung prior to the kreasi period apparently grew out of practical necessity more than anything else, mainly in connection with the musical needs of a large number of newly incorporated banjars formed in the wake of large-scale and rapid urbanization during a politically and economically volatile period. Denpasar's dual status as the capital of Bali and the new hub of a burgeoning international tourism industry brought job-seeking Balinese to the area by the thousands—especially beginning in the late 1960s, when an international airport built in nearby Kuta[4] helped generate a tourism boom following a traumatic period of brutal, politically inspired violence, devastating natural disasters, and deteriorating economic conditions that left much of rural Bali in a state of socioeconomic disarray (see Robinson 1995; Vickers 1989).

Despite rapid urban growth, new and old residents alike placed a high priority on maintaining the status of the banjar as the basic unit of social and political organization. Consequently, Denpasar developed less as a city proper than as a densely populated tapestry consisting of hundreds of contiguous but largely autonomous "urban villages." Some of its new banjars were founded by residents from rural areas intent on maintaining their former banjar-centered social networks, others by splinter factions of existing banjars who chose to break away for social, economic, or political reasons. In the latter scenario, the pressures of rapid and overwhelming population growth and its attendant tensions were most often at the root of the splits. These two processes of urban banjar formation were often closely interrelated (Asnawa, pers. comm., 1992).

While a banjar-centered system of social and political organization was maintained, continuation of traditional banjar-based ritual and ceremonial practices presented formidable challenges. Separated or alienated from their native communities and limited by financial constraints, residents of the new banjars frequently found themselves lacking the basic material needs of cultural life. The procurement of gamelans was especially problematic. Due to considerable cost and space requirements, many new banjars were unable to purchase or store a gamelan gong (e.g., a gong kebyar), let alone a gamelan angklung or more specialized orchestra, such as a Semar pegulingan.

The low cost and minimal space demands of a gamelan beleganjur made it attainable where other gamelans were not, and, inspired by the need to furnish appropriate music for rites and ceremonies, musicians in the new banjars fashioned ways to convert the gamelan beleganjur into an all-purpose ensemble, using it both in conventional contexts and in arrangements of compositions from other gamelan repertories, especially core pieces of the gamelan gong repertoire. Working with very limited melodic and instrumental resources, beleganjur arrangers had to be clever and flexible to adapt works originally intended for ensembles employing five-toned scale systems, multi-octave ranges, and multiple layers of melodic stratification to the constraints of a four-toned gamelan with a melodic range of just over an octave and only six possible melody notes. Through the use of pitch substitutions (e.g., using *dung* [G#] in places where the missing *ding* [C#] would normally occur),[5] unconventional melodic organization (e.g., treating the ponggang as a lower melodic extension of the reyong), and colotomic structures other than gilak (e.g., *tabuh pisan, tabuh dua, tabuh telu*), the gamelan beleganjur could be made to function passably in renditions of ceremonial *lelambatan* compositions, *topéng* masked dance accompaniments, and other standard pieces such as "Bapang Selisir."

Initially, such beleganjur arrangements were surely received as poor substitutes. According to Rembang (pers. comm., 1992), however, greater familiarity over time ultimately led to their increased acceptance, to the degree that a gamelan beleganjur sometimes came to be used in place of a gong kebyar or other large gamelan simply for the sake of convenience, even when there was access to the larger ensemble. This trend continues to the present day, and for Rembang it represents a general decline in both musical standards and the quality and integrity of cultural life in Denpasar/Badung.

The seemingly disproportionate prominence of gamelan beleganjur in post-independence Denpasar/Badung may be perceived by critics as an undesirable consequence of a complex urbanization process that has had an ultimately detrimental impact on the region's musical culture. It can, however, also be viewed as a key contributing factor explaining the dominant position of Denpasar and its environs in the modern world of competitive beleganjur. With relatively limited access to other types of gamelan, Badung music-makers, especially those in the newly established banjars, had to rely on their beleganjur ingenuity and inventiveness to meet community musical needs and were likely more compelled than others to seek opportunities for creative musical expression within the medium of beleganjur music. Thus, it may be inferred that out of the particularities of sociopolitical circumstance emerged a predisposition for creative endeavor in the beleganjur sphere, and that this predisposition found its ideal host environment with the introduction of a major beleganjur contest as part of the commemorative ceremonies for the eightieth anniversary of a decisive moment in Badung's history: the Puputan Badung.

The Puputan Badung

On 20 September 1906, the Balinese kingdom of Badung fell to Dutch colonial forces. Rather than surrender, the king of Badung, his family, and thousands of his subjects took their own lives or marched directly into the line of enemy fire. This incident, depicted by Hobart, Ramseyer, and Leemann (1996, 202) as a "heroic and distressing mass ritual suicide," is today commemorated as the Puputan Badung. *Puputan* means "fight to the death" or "die before surrender" (Asnawa, pers. comm., 1992).[6] The Puputan Badung was among the earliest and largest of a series of puputans that occurred between 1906 and 1908 during the Dutch takeover of Bali.[7] It heralded the beginning of the end of more than five centuries of Balinese monarchies, of the long-waning golden age of Hindu-Majapahit Bali.[8] Historian Willard Hanna offers a vivid re-creation of the Puputan Badung:

> The Dutch troops, marching in orderly ranks along a long roadway, walled on either side, which led to the royal palace, were not surprised to find the town apparently deserted and flames and smoke rising over the *puri,* the most disquieting factor being the sound of the wild beating of drums within their palace walls. As they drew closer, they observed a strange, silent procession emerging from the main gate of the *puri.* It was led by the Radja [king] himself, seated in his state palanquin carried by four bearers, dressed in white cremation garments but splendidly bejeweled and armed with a magnificent *kris* [sacred dagger]. The Radja was followed by the officials of his court, the armed guards, the priests, his wives, his children, and his retainers, likewise dressed in white, flowers in their hair, many of them almost as richly ornamented and as splendidly armed as the Radja himself.
>
> One hundred paces from the startled Dutch, the Radja halted his bearers, stepped from his palanquin, gave the signal, and the ghastly ceremony began. A priest plunged his dagger into the Radja's breast, and others of the company began turning their

daggers upon themselves or upon one another. The Dutch troops, startled into action by a stray gunshot and reacting to attack by lance and spear, directed rifle and even artillery fire into the surging crowd. Some of the women mockingly threw jewels and gold to the soldiers, and as more and more persons kept emerging from the palace gate, the mounds of corpses rose higher and higher. Soon to the scene of carnage was added the spectacle of looting as the soldiers stripped the valuables from the corpses and then set themselves to sacking the palace ruins. It was a slaughter and self-slaughter of the innocents and a plundering of the dead made all the more appalling by reason of its recurrence that same afternoon in nearby Pematjutan, a minor appendage of Badung. (1976, 73)

Today, the site of the Puputan Badung sits at the center of bustling downtown Denpasar. On 20 September and during the weeks leading up to it each year, people come from all over Bali to Puputan Badung Memorial Park, located directly across from the former site of the royal palace, to pay tribute to the Badung martyrs, honor their noble history, and celebrate the present glory of Bali in an independent Indonesia. A multitude of parades, ceremonies, and contests are presented, all of them highlighting in their symbols, rhetoric, and strong government presence a prescribed perception of sameness between the royal heroism of precolonial Balinese kingdoms and the greatness of the modern Indonesian republic.

The First Beleganjur Contest:
Lomba Beleganjur Puputan Badung, 1986
The Kreteria Lomba

For the eightieth anniversary of the Puputan Badung, a proposal for a special music contest featuring beleganjur groups from all over the regency was brought before the Badung Senate by I Wayan Sudhama, president of the now-defunct Badung Young Artists' Association, HSR (Himpunan Seniman Remaja). Sudhama, the oldest son of I Wayan Beratha and a leader in the Denpasar music community prior to his untimely death from cancer in 1990, presented his case convincingly, and the contest proposal was approved. Given the gamelan beleganjur's traditional associations with heroic warfare, noble death, and the pageantry of royal processions, the appropriateness of a lomba beleganjur on such an occasion could hardly be challenged. HSR was put in charge of the contest, receiving government sponsorship and a set of general formal guidelines outlining the ideological priorities of such events.

HSR's first order of business was to draft a contest evaluation criteria document, the *Kreteria Lomba*. Principal authorship of the *Kreteria* was assigned to the talented young composer Asnawa, vice-president of HSR. His main collaborators on the project were his brother, I Komang Astita, and his teachers, Beratha and Rembang.

The contest grading scheme outlined five main evaluative categories, listed here in descending order of percentage weight with summary explanations of what each comprised:

1. Technique/appearance *(teknik/keterampilan):* comprises rhythmic precision, note accuracy, dynamic range and control, striking and damping techniques, uniformity and quality of physical appearance in the act of playing, accordance with proper standards of performance, and *komposisi,* the technical quality of the musical arrangement itself.

2. Expressiveness and "harmony" *(ekspresi dan keharmonisan):* relates to the integratedness of group "feeling" during performance, to how well the desired musical character is expressed by the musicians as an ensemble.

3. Compositional quality/originality *(kreasi/kreativitas):* assessment of the innovativeness, novelty, and "character" of the musical work; these criteria are related to but distinct from the more technical procedures of *komposisi,* noted above. The focus here is on the evaluation of *pepayasan,* a term often translated as "ornamentation" that refers to innovative variations in the drum, cymbal, and reyong parts.

4. Proper instrumentation/sound quality of instruments *(instrumentasi/suara gambelan):* grade penalties in this category result from any failure to conform exactly to the standardized beleganjur bebonangan instrumentation (see fig. 2), and also from assessments of deficiency in the tone quality, maintenance, appearance, or tuning of instruments.

5. Presentation *(penampilan):* refers to all "extramusical" aspects of performance, including choreography, costumes, and the attitude and deportment *(sikap)* of both the musicians and the nonplaying members of the sekehe who take part in the contest procession. The latter include gong carriers and a number of individuals (both male and female) attired in traditional ceremonial regalia and bearing a variety of lances, banners, trays of offerings, sacred daggers, flags, and other items. Costumed characters representing clowns, legendary heroes and villains, or mythological beings may also take part in the procession.

Three prescribed elements outlined in the *Kreteria*—the first relating to musical design, the second to musical style, and the third to performance presentation—were of particular significance in essentially predefining the new contest music, kreasi beleganjur, as a new genre rooted in, but distinct from, its antecedent traditional beleganjur forms: the use in judged demonstration sections *(demonstrasi)* of three-part (fast-slow-fast) formal schemes derived from the "classical" Balinese kawitan (pengawit)–pengawak–pengecet musical model; an emphasis on musical and technical innovations, variety, and virtuosity far more akin to a kebyar aesthetic than to a conventional beleganjur one; and a call for elaborate choreographed sequences, identified as *gerak* (lit., "movement"), which were to be executed by the musicians as they played.

All of these elements, which will be discussed in greater detail in the next chapter, underscored a fundamental issue involved in the gamelan beleganjur's institution as a public forum for competitive musical display: the official recognition of beleganjur performance as a legitimate focus of aesthetic interest warranting serious attention. The prescribed three-movement form—comprising a level of formal complexity not found in conventional beleganjur music and a distinctive slow middle section, the pengawak, in which significant melodic development was to occur in the reyong part—helped justify an "elevated" artistic status for kreasi beleganjur through an implied (albeit superficial) association with the musical repertories of lelambatan, Semar pegulingan, *legong* (a dance-drama featuring three young female dancers), and other forms embodying Balinese conceptions of classical musical artistry. The kebyar-inspired aesthetic allocated to the new kreasi style fostered an expansion of the beleganjur ensemble's range, molding beleganjur sound to musical priorities that have become virtually paradigmatic of Balinese musical modernity in the wake of kebyar's dominant impact. The incorporation of an elaborate choreographic element served to emphasize beleganjur's new status as the centerpiece of a public music performance medium.

Also of fundamental importance in the *Kreteria* was a detailed description of the contest's designated "theme" *(tema).* Prospective competing groups were instructed to conceive all aspects of their contest presentations in relation to an overarching theme of *kepahlawanan,* which means "heroism" but refers more specifically to a form of idealized martial heroism through which symbolic links are formed—both in official ideology and in the public imagination—between heroic warriors and martyrs of historical Bali and military heroes of the modern Indonesian nation. Musically, choreographically, and visually, performances were to represent an embodiment of kepahlawanan ideals, and the competitive success or failure of each group would hinge largely on its ability to achieve the proper "heroic" character. In the *Kreteria,* the kepahlawanan theme served as the basis for numerous details of performance protocol, right down to the mandatory inclusion of an Indonesian flag as part of each group's processional regalia.

As Beratha explained to me in an interview at his Denpasar home in 1992, "On the flag, red stands for bravery, strength, and courage; white symbolizes holiness and virtue. Thus, as Indonesians, we must always be brave and courageous in service of the righteous cause. This is to be kepahlawanan. As Balinese, the same is true, and that is why the Puputan Badung is so important to us. The flag and the Puputan mean the same thing, and so does beleganjur. The music, the choreography, the feeling, the presentation—everything should be kepahlawanan. This is most important."

Through its defining impact on musical form and style, categories of evaluation, choreography and presentation, and thematic content in the original lomba beleganjur, and through its acknowledged status today as the basic model for all subsequent documents of its kind, the LBPB *Kreteria Lomba* drafted by Asnawa and his colleagues in 1986 largely shaped the course of beleganjur's development as a competition-rooted, contemporary musical genre. As we shall see later in the chapter, Asnawa also led by example, creating for the contest a musical work that would eventually become the standard model for kreasi beleganjur composition.

The Contest Event

The contest was scheduled for the afternoon of 13 September 1986, a week prior to the actual anniversary of the Puputan Badung. It was to be a processional affair, each group commencing its performance with a flashy, three-minute opening demonstration before a panel of distinguished adjudicators at Puputan Badung Memorial Park, then proceeding along a two-kilometer route through the streets of downtown Denpasar, playing continuously throughout. Besides the opening graded demonstration, three additional ones were scheduled at designated judging stations: a five-minute presentation at the Panggung Kehormatan, or VIP Stage, where the distinguished musical elders Beratha and Rembang were to be among the judges and where prominent politicians and other dignitaries would be present; a four-minute performance at Jury Post III, located somewhat further along the parade route; and a three-minute concluding demonstration at Jury Post IV, the contest route's terminus. The performances of the various competing groups were to be staggered, each beginning approximately five minutes after the one before. A crew of contest officials would be employed to ensure a proper pace for the proceedings, and to enforce the demonstration performance time limits.

Registration packages containing a copy of the *Kreteria Lomba*, a formal letter of invitation, and informational materials were assembled by HSR and sent to the hundreds of banjars in the Denpasar/Badung area. The packages were directed to the *sekehe teruna* of each banjar, male youth clubs composed of unmarried young men and teenage boys. No age or gender limitations were specified, but it was generally understood that the competing groups would be made up of males in their teens and early twenties (Asnawa, pers. comm., 1992). In order to register, a sekehe was required to submit a card listing its name and the title of the composition it would perform; both were to reflect the contest's "heroic" theme.

News of the contest was greeted with great enthusiasm. Official endorsements were offered by the Ministry of Education and Culture, the Government Council on the Arts, and the Badung Honorary Council of Musicians (Pembina Tabuh), among others. "When I first heard about the contest," recalls Beratha, a senior member of the Honorary Council, "I felt joy deep in my heart. For the young generation, stimulating interest in the traditional arts is crucial. I saw this contest as an excellent opportunity for generating this kind of interest."

Throughout the region, beleganjur groups could be heard rehearsing late into the night during the weeks leading up to the contest. The services of top gamelan teachers and composers were eagerly sought by sekehes endeavoring to gain the greatest possible competitive advantage.

On 13 September, colorfully attired beleganjur groups and their entourages began arriving at Puputan Badung park in the early morning hours, instruments and processional regalia in tow. Also arriving early was the first wave of spectators, who would eventually blend into an audience of thousands lining the streets of the contest route and congregating with greatest density at the four judging stations.

The contest finally got under way following an opening address by the Regent (Bupati) of Badung at 2:00 and several additional speeches by assorted political dignitaries. For some three hours, downtown Denpasar was vibrant with the fresh and exciting sounds of a new beleganjur music, as over two dozen ensembles paraded one after another along the procession route, dazzling the assembled masses with their virtuosic music, choreographic feats, colorful costumes, and noble pageantry. The pyrotechnics and innovative musical variations of the fast-tempoed sections, and the surprising melodicism of the slow, curiously novel "pengawak" passages, delighted the judges and audience members. The first-ever lomba beleganjur was an unqualified success.

Immediately following the contest, the fifteen-member adjudication committee convened to determine the results, which were not made public until a special Puputan Day ceremony a week later. The top three groups selected were honored as First, Second, and Third Champions (Juara), receiving trophies and sizable monetary prizes; the fourth-through sixth-place finishers (Harapan) were recognized with honorable mention certificates and small cash awards.

First prize went to the group representing Banjar Belaluan Sadmerta, second prize to the rival sekehe from Banjar Kaliungu Kaja. Separated by just two city blocks in downtown Denpasar, these two banjars are home to some of Bali's greatest musicians. Belaluan Sadmerta's ensemble was led by the extraordinary drummer I Ketut Sukarata, youngest son of the legendary I Wayan Beratha. Sukarata's energetic virtuosity, charismatic leadership, and innovative rhythmic exploits in the new kreasi beleganjur style helped carry his hometown group to the championship. Kaliungu Kaja finished a close second with its performance of the brilliant "Beleganjur Angga Yowana," arguably the most influential of all kreasi beleganjur compositions, which was created especially for the occasion by Asnawa. Although Asnawa (together with his brother, Astita) prepared his native banjar's group for the performance, he did not participate in it, serving instead on the adjudication committee.

With their successes in the 1986 Lomba Beleganjur Puputan Badung, Sukarata and Asnawa were established as leaders in the emergent kreasi beleganjur world. As we will see throughout the course of this study, the subsequent impact and influence of both men on the genre's development have been far-reaching and profound.

Lomba Beleganjur Puputan Badung, 1987–1994

From 1987 through 1992, the LBPB took place annually in Denpasar, with each year's contest modeled closely on the format of the original 1986 event. Some notable changes did occur over time, however: the administration and sponsorship of the competition were taken over from HSR in 1987 by the government's Ministry of Education and Culture, innovative developments in musical style were introduced, the *Kreteria Lomba* was modified from year to year, the scope of the contest eventually expanded to comprise both a gamelan angklung competition (starting in 1989) and a student-division lomba beleganjur (beginning in 1990), and the growing interest of local commercial recording companies in contest-style beleganjur music became an important factor.

The government's decision to take administrative control of the

LBPB likely stemmed from recognition of the contest's value as an ideological tool. Linking demonstrated mass appeal and the capacity to inculcate fervent patriotic sentiment with the symbolic power of an idealized synthesis of local and national values, the event clearly could be a highly effective vehicle of cultural nationalism. A nine-member contest organizing committee under the direction of I Madé Ebuh, head of cultural affairs for Badung regency, was appointed.[9] Government investment in the event became substantial, with approximately seven thousand dollars U.S. (a large sum by Indonesian standards) being committed annually; some 10 percent of that total was given out in prizes. Government sponsorship of hundreds of other beleganjur contests produced throughout Bali over the years, the majority held in connection with occasions of local and/or national patriotic significance, further evidenced a deep commitment to the lomba beleganjur project.

Musical and other creative developments in kreasi beleganjur style (which will be described in more detail in the next chapter) followed several directions. Some were initiated by the innovations of individual musicians and groups seeking to both expand the range of creative expression and gain competitive advantages through their innovations. Others emerged from modifications of evaluative criteria instituted by the contest's adjudication committee with the intent of improving the aesthetic and ideological quality of the event as a whole. Still others represented the musical results of an ongoing creative dialogue between participating musicians and contest administrators. Among the developments that came to have a genre-wide impact were a tendency toward greater length and formal complexity in the pengawak sections, or slow movements, of compositions; an increasing preference for more complex and unpredictable formal designs and orchestration techniques generally; a more liberal attitude toward the incorporation of non-Balinese musical elements, both from other parts of Indonesia and from the West; and greater emphasis on both choreographic presentation and proper evocation through performance of the contest's "heroic" (kepahlawanan) theme.

An unofficial but important association between the LBPB and Bali's two major recording companies, Bali Record and Maharani Records, was established following the original 1986 LBPB, when the second-place group from Kaliungu Kaja received a contract to record their prize-winning piece, "Beleganjur Angga Yowana" (along with a few supplementary selections), for Bali Record. In subsequent years, every LBPB champion but one was featured on a commercial recording for

Bali Record or Maharani, including the championship groups from Ubung Kaja (1987), Pandé Sumerta Kaja (1989), Kehen (1990), Sedang (1991), Meranggi (1992), and Bindu Mambal (1994). (The LBPB was not held in 1993; see below). Recordings by several other groups who, like Kaliungu Kaja, finished high in the LBPB standings but did not win the contest, were also produced.

The production of a commercial recording has become an important status symbol for sekehes vying for a place among the beleganjur elite. Recordings are equated with prestige, influence, and at least some financial gain, and the opportunity to be represented on one is a virtual given for champions of the LBPB, Bali's most prestigious lomba beleganjur. Thus, the absence of a recording by either the 1986 or 1988 LBPB champions—Belaluan Sadmerta and Tatasan Kaja, respectively—appears oddly conspicuous; so too does the absence in kreasi beleganjur's discography of a representative example of the work of I Ketut Sukarata, the composer, musical director, and lead drummer for both of these groups and undoubtedly one of the most important innovators in the area of kreasi beleganjur composition. As I will argue in chapter 4, Sukarata's omission from the ranks of recorded kreasi beleganjur composers is likely the result of certain political agendas.

In 1993, the LBPB was canceled, probably on account of a political restructuring of the Badung area that resulted in incorporation of the city of Denpasar (Kodya Denpasar) as a separate administrative district with regency-like political autonomy. When the event was reestablished in 1994, it was held at Kuta Beach rather than in Denpasar. A number of changes, including the new location, the replacement of certain long-standing members of the contest jury by new adjudicators, and the absence of a number of beleganjur groups (most from banjars within the Kodya Denpasar district) from the list of invited contest participants, suggest that tensions and rivalries inflamed during the 1993 political restructuring effort may have been reflected in the structure and priorities of the post-1993 LBPB.

Beyond Denpasar/Badung: The Spread of Kreasi Beleganjur

By the end of the 1980s, formal beleganjur contests were a basic institution of musical life not only in Denpasar/Badung but in virtually every region of Bali. The scope and size of such events varied greatly, from small, modest lombas in rural areas featuring just a handful of groups to grand competitions in urban regions including upwards of two dozen ensembles. The first island-wide beleganjur contest, with champion sekehes from all eight Balinese regencies in head-to-head competition, was held in Denpasar during the 1990 Bali Arts Festival. (It was won by the 1989 LBPB champions from Banjar Pandé Sumerta Kaja.) Other island-wide contests have included a school-groups competition sponsored in 1991 by STSI (Sekolah Tinggi Seni Indonesia, the government college of the arts) and an election-campaign lomba produced in conjunction with the Indonesian national election of 1992 (see chapter 5), both of which were held in Denpasar as well.

The original LBPB has served, directly or indirectly, as the model for all subsequent contests, and in keeping with its spirit, lomba beleganjur of every type and size have come to be linked by a common thread of "patriotic" themes and associations. Anniversary commemorations of puputans, important battles, and other major events in a region's history; national holidays such as Indonesian Independence Day and Kartini Day;[10] and important political occasions all provide opportunities for the production of contests. Sporting events such as soccer matches, badminton tournaments, kite-flying contests, and regional sports and arts festivals known as PORSENI[11] also offer good environments for beleganjur contests, as they too tend to be closely tied to patriotic themes and occasions. Additionally, the period leading up to Nyepi (the Balinese New Year) witnesses a profusion of lomba beleganjur all over the island each year.

Different beleganjur contests are also linked by their common reliance on Indonesian government agencies for support and legitimization. Government involvement and sponsorship are a virtual given, although levels of support vary considerably from contest to contest. In exchange for providing funding and official valuation for contest events, government representatives gain the power to mold such events to the dictates of their cultural nationalism agenda. Thus, whether presented in honor of a national holiday or the founding of a small village, beleganjur contests tend to reflect nationalist ideology as surely as they do localized interest.

While government sponsorship extends across a broad range of areas, including a variety of contest production–related costs and the provision of trophies and prizes, it does not extend to financial support of individual competing beleganjur groups, who must generate their own funds or seek outside sources of sponsorship (as will be discussed later in this chapter).

Center and Periphery:
Denpasar and the Kreasi Beleganjur Tradition

Throughout Bali, Denpasar has come to symbolize the modern, competitive beleganjur tradition with near-iconic power. Wherever beleganjur contest music is heard, it seems that there is a preference for groups said to possess the "Denpasar style." Leading teachers from the Denpasar/Badung area are frequently hired by beleganjur groups in other parts of the island to prepare them for contests, often at considerable expense; LBPB adjudicators are a fixture on judging committees for contests in outlying regions, their recognized authority lending distinction to these events; LBPB prize-winning compositions featured on commercial recordings are heard in imitation versions at contests island-wide.

As the birthplace of the lomba beleganjur and of kreasi beleganjur music, the centerpoint of the genre's creative evolution, the home of most of its leading innovators, and the central location of the government agencies that administer beleganjur contests generally, Denpasar's centrality is indisputable. But Denpasar's relationship to other "beleganjur communities" in Bali has been characterized more by dialectical interaction than by top-down dominance. In characteristic Balinese fashion, regional diversity and cross-pollination have become hallmarks of lomba beleganjur culture. Innovations in musical and performance style, and even in the structure of contest events themselves, have issued with increasing frequency from areas outside the Denpasar/Badung hub, especially from neighboring Gianyar, whose top groups have fared well in interregional competitions and produced influential commercial recordings.

By about 1992, Badung musicians were probably as likely to be influenced by beleganjur developments in other areas as they were to influence such developments themselves. Moreover, at least on the basis of my own research findings, it may be inferred that musicians and contest administrators in areas far from the Denpasar/Badung hub and other prominent musical centers such as Ubud, Peliatan, and Singapadu (all in Gianyar regency) take the greatest creative liberties, departing from established norms and conventions in interesting, progressive, even radical ways, sometimes with widely influential results. Indonesian government officials have tended to have less direct involvement with—and therefore less direct control over—small contests in remote areas than with high-profile contests in the larger population centers. Thus, somewhat paradoxically, local contest organizers and participants in small contests have often operated with greater autonomy and creative latitude than their more prominent peers in the major cultural centers.

For example, the use of dancers in beleganjur contest demonstrations (separate from the choreographic sequences executed by the musicians) and the addition of a *tektekan* (bamboo slit-drum) section to the standard beleganjur orchestra were both innovations first introduced in small regional beleganjur contests of the early 1990s. At the time I concluded field research in 1995, however, proposals for the allowance of dancers and tektekan players in the LBPB, both of which were formerly forbidden under the contest's rules, were being seriously considered. It was the reported success of these novel elements in smaller contests that prompted LBPB officials to contemplate incorporating them.

Liberal attitudes held by organizers of an August 1990 pre–Independence Day lomba beleganjur in the north-central Balinese mountain village of Kintamani were responsible for my own contest debut as a beleganjur musician (plate 17). The month before the contest, a chance encounter I had with one of the participating ensembles (representing Batur Tengah) resulted in an opportunity for me to sit in with the group as a cengceng player during a rehearsal. This, in turn, led to my being invited to join as an honorary member. The situation was virtually identical to the one in which I had found myself a year earlier in Ubud. Again, I would have the opportunity to rehearse with the ensemble throughout the contest-preparation period, taking part fully in all rehearsals and other group activities, but again, I would not be allowed to actually play in the contest. A rule common to all beleganjur contests, with which I had by this point in my research become very familiar, specified that each member of a competing sekehe must be a native and/or a permanent resident of the banjar (or other administrative unit, e.g., desa) he represented.[12] Clearly, an outsider like myself was ineligible.

It thus came as a tremendous surprise to me when, about a week after my first encounter with the group, the lead drummer, I Nengah Jejel, asked me whether I would like to play cengceng in the contest. I told him that I would of course love to play, and also that I was flattered by the invitation; but how, I asked, could I be granted such an opportunity, given the restrictive rules regarding contest participants? Jejel smiled wryly, almost as though he were going to wink. "It will be taken care of," he assured me.

I played in the contest, and Batur Tengah won (although I did not find this out until two years later). According to Jejel, our victory was the result of two main factors: first, thanks to him, we had the "Denpasar style," which he claimed was lacking in the performances of all the other sekehes; and second, thanks to me, we had an unbeatable edge in terms of novelty, a valued commodity in beleganjur contests and Balinese cultural production generally.

In 1990, I considered myself fortunate to have had the opportunity to play in a beleganjur contest, but I did not realize at the time, as I would come to understand later, that my participation in the lomba had constituted a radical defiance of established convention. In subsequent years, I performed with numerous contest beleganjur groups around Bali, several of whom petitioned for special permission to have me included as an eligible participant in upcoming contest performances. In all cases, though, I was barred from competing.[13] Outsiders, I was informed over and over again—in Denpasar, Baturiti, and several other locations— simply could not be allowed to play. In ceremonial, ritual, and pure demonstration performance contexts, my involvement as a performer apparently posed no problems, but in competitions it was *dilarang:* forbidden.

So why *had* I been granted permission to perform with Batur Tengah in the 1990 contest? In 1992, I returned to Kintamani in search of an answer to this question, and was eventually directed to Luh Tirta Wardani. She, I was informed, had been the individual responsible for authorizing my participation in the lomba. Previously, I had known Wardani only as the wife of Pak Gunawan, who owned the small hotel *(losmen)* in Kintamani where I had stayed. Gunawan had also been the principal financial sponsor of the Batur Tengah beleganjur group. As for Wardani, in 1990 I had had no idea that she was the village headperson *(kepala desa),* nor that she held the distinction of being the first Balinese woman ever appointed to such a position, nor that she was the chair of the organizing committee for the beleganjur contest in which I had performed.

Over tea and rice cakes, Wardani explained to me (in excellent English) why I had been permitted to play in the contest. The key factor, she stated, was that the event, though endorsed by the Indonesian government, had been produced without any direct involvement of government officials or adjudicators. Consequently, it had been a truly local production, so that she and her collaborators had been left to their own progressive-minded devices.

"It was our contest and I made [the] decision," she told me. "If the jury had been from Denpasar, or the government had given us money, maybe you would not have been able to play. But it was not like that. I thought that it would be *good* to have [a] tourist play. Then Balinese people would see you and think, 'If [a] tourist can play, why not me?' This make them more interested in the beleganjur music, and this is a good thing. Also," Wardani added with a mischievous smile, "because you play good and make the group different, I think that if you play, maybe we win because the jury likes it."

Preparing for a Beleganjur Contest:
Priorities, Challenges, Methods, and Strategies

Ensembles who compete in beleganjur contests on behalf of banjars, desas, regencies, or other organizations bring pride and prestige to the people and institutions they represent; the lomba beleganjur has become a popular and respected social institution, endorsed and supported across all sectors of Balinese society. This being the case, it may seem surprising that only a small percentage of eligible beleganjur groups actually compete in contests. For example, between 1986 and 1992, well under 10 percent of the eligible banjars in the Denpasar/Badung region were represented in the LBPB during any given year. The reasons that sekehes choose not to compete are many and varied, and are typically interrelated: lack of sufficient funds, failure to procure the services of a first-rate teacher, and fears of competitive failure and unfavorable public response (see chapter 5) are among the primary ones.

Sekehes who do choose to take part in lombas must commit to a long and challenging preparation process. In the major contests, at least, only the most accomplished, dedicated, and rigorously trained groups stand any chance of being ranked among the champions. Furthermore, contest audiences and judges alike are notoriously merciless in their reactions to and evaluations of subpar performances, so much so that competing groups must exhibit a very high level of competence just to avoid public humiliation.

When a sekehe receives an invitation to compete in a beleganjur contest, the first order of business is for all club members to vote on whether or not the group should register. In general, if it is determined that there are enough available musicians to ensure a full complement of players, the vote will be positive, even in cases where financial or other obstacles are known by everyone involved to be insurmountable. The support of actions and decisions that symbolize community pride and solidarity is essential to Balinese communal spirit, and a decision to compete in a beleganjur contest falls within this category. This helps to explain why many more sekehes typically register for beleganjur contests than end up actually competing in them.

Once a sekehe has decided to compete in a contest and determined who will perform in it, the next major challenges are to raise funds and to secure the services of a good teacher. Taking part in a contest is expensive, costing a sekehe the equivalent of between $150 and $500 U.S., sums that are prohibitively large within the Balinese context. Costumes, transportation, food, coffee, and cigarettes must be provided for all sekehe members; instruments must be repaired and decorated, sometimes even purchased; expensive ritual offerings must be prepared; and the teacher must be paid. In short, a major investment is required.

Sources of funding vary. Profits from performances for tourists are used by some of the groups based in resort areas, but the vast majority of sekehes in Bali generate little if any revenue through their musical activities and must look elsewhere for support. They may turn to their banjar's excess revenue pool, a kind of community slush fund built on profits from agricultural sales and other business ventures. More often, though, primary funding comes in the form of sponsorship from a wealthy individual or local business. In rare cases, a large corporation, possibly even a multinational one such as the Coca-Cola Company, will choose to underwrite a sekehe's contest-related expenses in exchange for promotional opportunities.[14]

Next to obtaining funding, procuring a quality teacher is perhaps the greatest challenge faced by an aspiring contest beleganjur group. The teacher's role is crucial and multifaceted. It usually involves composing and choreographing the musical work to be performed, as well as preparing the ensemble to play in the competition; it may also include actually performing as one of the group's drummers.[15]

The cost of hiring a well-known teacher on a freelance basis is normally high, ranging from $12.50 to $17.50 per rehearsal, plus meals, a transportation allowance, and possibly other expenses. Some teachers insist that an assistant instructor be hired as well, which increases the overall fee considerably. It is relatively rare, however, for teachers to be remunerated on a straight work-for-pay basis, since this is considered rather crass. Some arrangement involving a symbolic, rather than real, exchange of capital is greatly preferred. Ideally, a teacher's services to a beleganjur group become part of a complex credit system, one based on culturally defined norms and expectations of reciprocity and gratitude. Perhaps at some later date, members of the ensemble will help him build a new house, or will assist him in producing a family ceremony. Terms are rarely specified; a mutual, unspoken understanding of future obligation is simply assumed.

Leading beleganjur teachers typically find themselves in great demand during contest periods, and often must choose between several groups vying for their services. In making decisions, they are guided by certain priorities that tend to be hierarchical. Of utmost importance is allegiance to the native banjar. Banjars who count among their membership a distinguished music teacher are virtually assured of his commitment to the local beleganjur group, regardless of other factors. Next in terms of priority come ensembles representing banjars that include members of the teacher's extended family. Such sekehes receive first consideration in instances where the native banjar is not competing. Third in importance are groups associated with the teacher's close friends and professional colleagues. Social and professional ties in Bali may be almost as close as familial ones (that is, in cases where they are not one and the same thing) and carry with them similar expectations of mutual obligation. Next come groups who have had success in prior contests. Barring specific allegiances such as those outlined above, teachers tend to align themselves with sekehes whose competitive prospects are good, thus maximizing their own chances of garnering the prestige and rewards that come with a lomba championship. Finally, all other things being equal, money may become the determining factor in a teacher's decision to work with one group rather than another.

Because the demand for quality teachers tends to exceed the supply, especially where large contests such as the LBPB are concerned, many sekehes that wish to compete ultimately fail to attract an appropriate instructor. This is perhaps the most common reason why groups withdraw from contests for which they have registered; the risk of public embarrassment resulting from a performance deemed inadequate by far outweighs the potential benefits that participation for its own sake might engender. Sekehes competing in small, rural contests may be sufficiently daring to prepare for a lomba without the aid of a bona fide teacher, perhaps using a commercial cassette recording as their model; but in the major, high-profile contests, such an approach is rare.

One program that has been especially helpful to sekehes who wish to compete in beleganjur contests but lack access to qualified teachers is Kuliah Kerja Nyata (KKN), the government's "Putting Learning into Practical Work" educational initiative. Under KKN, conservatory students in the final semester of their graduating year at STSI are required to reside full-time in a selected banjar for a period of three months, contributing significantly to the artistic and cultural development of the community during their residency. Preparing a group for a lomba beleganjur or some other type of gamelan contest is a common undertaking of KKN candidates in the music area (Bandem, pers. comm., 1992).

The Rehearsal Process

The methods and strategies used by different beleganjur groups to prepare for contests vary widely. Some approach the process with great seriousness of purpose, investing large amounts of time, money, and energy, and rehearsing an average of four hours per night over a period of two to four months. Others are surprisingly casual—for example, a group with whom I worked briefly in 1992 that went from never having played contest-style beleganjur to performing in a competition within one week! They did not win.

On the basis of my research, it seems that an average contest-preparation process involves seven to nine weeks of rehearsal: three to four sessions per week for the first six or seven weeks, followed by one or two weeks of daily practice. Practices are held at the *balé banjar,* an open-sided pavilion that serves as a combined meeting hall, performance venue, rehearsal space, community center, and social gathering place. They normally take place in the evening, beginning around seven o'clock and running until ten or eleven. Refreshments are provided during a fifteen-minute intermission and again at the end of the rehearsal, at which time the sekehe's administrative director, or *klian,* presides over a short meeting. During the meeting, announcements are made and there is open discussion of the sekehe's activities and operations. Certain matters are voted upon, with all sekehe members—from the klian to the gong carriers—receiving an equal vote.

Everyone belonging to the sekehe is expected to attend every rehearsal. Unexcused absences or tardiness can result in fines. The teacher, however, need not necessarily be present at all practices, unless he is himself a sekehe member. Sometimes the task of running a rehearsal is left to one of his assistants, other times to the group's lead drummer. It is the mutual responsibility of the klian and the teacher to work out a satisfactory arrangement concerning the teacher's level of involvement in the overall preparation process.

Each teacher approaches the job of preparing a sekehe for competition in a unique manner. As an example, we might look to the different strategies for dealing with choreography *(gerak)* employed by Asnawa and Sukarata. Asnawa treats choreography as an integral part of musical performance. From the earliest stages of the rehearsal process, groups under his tutelage learn to perform music while "dancing." Sukarata takes a very different approach. His groups focus exclusively on the music for the majority of the pre-contest preparation period. Not until the last week of rehearsals is the choreographic element added, during a short period of intensive practice. As we shall see in the following chapters, profound differences between these two beleganjur masters are further reflected in their contrasting compositional approaches and philosophical worldviews.

Contest Day Preparations

The final phase of a sekehe's preparations for a lomba beleganjur is reserved for the day of the contest itself. Early in the morning, all club members assemble at the balé banjar to dress. Painstaking attention is devoted to every sartorial detail; everything must appear perfectly matched and symmetrical. The musicians and gong carriers all wear the same outfit, usually consisting of flower-adorned peaked headbands *(udeng)* with gold-leaf or batik decorative patterns; solid-color silk shirts; special cloth belts; and wraparound "skirts" *(kain)* with batik or other design patterns, around which are tied an additional cloth with an embroidered bottom hem *(saput)*. Footwear is optional. Black tai chi slippers, white athletic shoes, or sandals may be worn, although the latter are disallowed in certain contests on account of their being too casual.

The musical instruments are also "dressed" with great attention and care. The drums are covered in matching cloth wrappings, since they, like human beings, are believed to possess living souls and must therefore be properly attired for the event. Brightly colored yarn or shredded waxed-paper pom-pons are affixed to the ends of all the mallet handles. Meanwhile, similar yarn or waxed-paper pom-pons already attached to the cengceng grips are combed through and fluffed.

In one corner of the balé banjar, a village priest *(pemangku)* intones a series of prayers in honor of the instruments, which are sprinkled with holy water *(tirta)* and presented with large trays of flowers, rice, and incense. The most lavish attention is devoted to the *gongs*. By the end of the priest's service, the *gong* stands are almost totally obscured by a plethora of offerings. The kendang are also ritually prepared. Male (lanang) and female (wadon) are joined together in "wedlock" when the priest touches the two drums in rapid succession with an egg, symbolizing their fertile union.

Leaving the balé banjar, the sekehe members walk to the village temple, where they take part in a long group prayer ceremony *(sembahyang)* directed by a high priest *(pedanda)*. Prayers are offered to the deities, who are invited to enter the musicians' bodies and called upon to provide them with strength, energy, and inspiration *(taksu)*, ensuring a good performance and a favorable outcome to the contest. Communal prayer, private meditation, the sprinkling of holy water, and the making of various forms of offerings all occur simultaneously during the sembahyang ceremony, whose devotional character evidences the fact that in Bali, even ostensibly secular events such as beleganjur contests are imbued with deep spirituality.

Following the prayer ceremony, there is usually a short dress rehearsal. Then a high-protein lunch of meat and rice is consumed, along with special energy-enhancing beverages and herbal supplements *(jamu);* one "Hemaviton" tablet washed down with a cup of condensed milk, sugar, and raw egg is an especially popular formula.

Finally, it is time to depart for the contest. The beleganjur warriors are now ready for battle.

Energy, Solidarity, and Release:
Beleganjur Performers and Their Audiences

The young musicians who perform in beleganjur contests claim that the social aspects of the experience take priority over all else. Musicians with whom I spoke unanimously stressed the primary importance of group membership, of belonging to the sekehe and making a significant contribution to the collective whole. As one young reyong player, I Wayan Sumendra, explained to me in 1992, "The competition is important, but more important is the group, everyone cooperating and working together, being all together and keeping the traditional culture alive." While the actual relative priorities of participation and competition are debatable, as will be explored in chapter 5, there can be no doubt that issues of social solidarity are indeed of fundamental significance.

The character of beleganjur music itself facilitates the forging of strong social bonds. It is in the communal stylistic expression and emotional release of a certain kind of masculine energy, *gaya laki-laki,* that contest beleganjur music finds its core identity. "The character of beleganjur is very appealing to [male] youth," states I Wayan Beratha. "Playing the music is a good way for them to express their feelings and use their *gaya* [their distinctive energy and style]. It is very appropriate for them. This is why the kreasi [beleganjur] style became popular so quickly from the beginning."

Proper expression of gaya laki-laki spirit is imperative in contest beleganjur performance. It is a quality that must be shared and cultivated by everyone in the group, and its achievement is by no means a given. The level and intensity of youthful masculine energy required in beleganjur performance arguably exceeds even that demanded in kebyar performance. I have encountered excellent kebyar musicians who opt not to play beleganjur because they consider it too taxing. Some even claim to lack the capacity to produce the kind of energy that is needed, whether because of age or other factors. To this category belongs I Wayan "Gara" (a pseudonym), a gifted young kebyar and *musik kontémporér* composer and performer, and a self-described *playboy* as well.

"I am weak because of too many girls," Gara told me in 1995. "They steal my energy, so I don't have the strength for beleganjur. But 'Nyoman,'" he continued, making reference to a highly talented and successful young kreasi beleganjur composer from Badung, "he is so strong, because he has never been with a girl, so all his strength is still in his music, in his playing. That's what makes him so great for beleganjur. Not me, though," he concluded, waving his hand limply in the air and laughing, "my mind, my hand—not so strong like that."

In Bali, where true privacy is rare, and where a modest, reserved, and graceful bearing is demanded of individuals in the majority of social situations (see Wikan 1990; M. Hobart 1986; and Geertz 1973c), culturally sanctioned opportunities for the release of pent-up energies serve very important social and psychological functions. For teenage boys and young bachelors like Gara's friend Nyoman—the primary inhabitants of the competitive beleganjur world—provision of such opportunities is deemed especially crucial. As is likely the case in every society, finding ways to productively channel the passions and exuberance of male youth presents serious challenges to the Balinese establishment. The banjar-based male youth club, or *sekehe teruna,* is the primary social institution to which such challenges are assigned, and music and sports organizations operating under the umbrella of the sekehe teruna, such as beleganjur clubs, are of key importance.

Contest-style beleganjur has proven highly effective in its assigned "sociological" task on behalf of Balinese male youth culture. Its strong, forceful, and exciting musical character makes it an ideal manifestation of gaya laki-laki spirit. Beleganjur is tougher and rawer than other kinds of gamelan music, one might even say more macho. Within the context of Balinese musical expression (at least relative to other gamelan forms), it occupies a position somewhat akin to that of heavy-metal rock music in the West: both convey an essentialized youthful ideal of powerful masculine energy, and both furnish a medium for the productive release of such energy.

There is a further level where this comparison may be relevant. Kreasi beleganjur, by virtue of its inherent intensity and excitement, its immanent gaya, has actually been promoted in Bali as a viable alternative to Western popular music forms such as rock, hip-hop, and reggae. The alluring images of Western wealth, power, and freedom contained in such musics, as embodied primarily in their sonic force and energy, have captivated a great many Balinese young people, inspiring a movement away from Bali and toward the West in the musical preferences-cum-cultural allegiances of youth culture. There is hope among middle-aged and older Balinese that the heightened energetic quality of a music like kreasi beleganjur, in its seeming capacity to push some of the same emotional and sensate buttons as, say, rock or hip-hop, can help to convince the young that they need not categorically reject their heritage in their efforts to accommodate the modern sensibilities of an increasingly cosmopolitan world. At this level, kreasi beleganjur has been presented as a bridge to youthful proclivities, as a specific symbol invested with more broad-based cultural implications concerning the nature and possibilities of contemporary Balinese identity. Pak Rai's story of his nephew, the "motorcycle boy" who became "beleganjur boy," suggests that the bridge is at least sometimes willingly crossed.

While kreasi beleganjur's role as a medium for the productive release of gaya laki-laki may be most important relative to meeting the social and psychological needs of its practitioners, this role also extends outward to the people who attend contests. Beyond providing a forum for competitive musical display, the lomba beleganjur may be said to offer a prescribed opportunity for controlled public mayhem. The music's energy and the intensity of the performers both feed into and feed off of an atmosphere in which uncharacteristically rough and aggressive, even unseemly, public behaviors are allowed. Audience members scream out lewd comments and insults, whistle rudely at the elegantly attired teenage girls heading up the processional entourages, engage in rambunctious horseplay, throw food, and shove each other mercilessly in order to gain prime viewing positions.

They can also be ruthless in their responses to the performers themselves. Music contest audiences in Bali, as Elaine Barkin has aptly put it, "are irrepressibly enthusiastic and merciless" (1990, 2). To a far greater degree than their Western counterparts, Balinese spectators are acutely aware of the minute details that define performance competence and distinction. To quote Margaret Mead, "Every [Balinese] audience is composed of individuals interested in how it is done" ([1942] 1970b, 343); and such individuals are rarely shy in demonstrating either their appreciation of excellence or their disdain of ineptitude.

The combination of keen critical perception and volatility that characterizes Balinese audiences puts great pressure on the boys and young men who play in beleganjur contests. Expectations are high, and any slip-up on the part of a performer can have disastrous consequences (see also Geertz 1973c, 402). Gaya laki-laki is a powerful expressive force, but it is inescapably subject to the foibles of human vulnerability; composure is as essential as it is fragile. I have seen a teenage cengceng player crumble in the face of a hostile, jeering crowd when his waist skirt *(kain)* came undone in the middle of a contest performance, leaving him standing before an audience of over a thousand in his underwear, so terrified and ashamed that his hands and legs shook uncontrollably as he tried unsuccessfully to retie his costume for some two minutes before exiting in disgrace along with the rest of his group, accompanied by a chorus of boos and demeaning taunts from the audience; I have witnessed a group being completely drowned out and then driven away from the performance area by an angry audience chanting "Enough!" ("Cukup!") when their time limit was exceeded (by a considerable amount) during a *demonstrasi;* and I have seen a contest (for which I served on the adjudication committee) in which one group was barely able to complete its performance because of a deluge of nasty barbs and insults, prompted by nothing more than the audience's displeasure with the somewhat old and outmoded costumes worn by the musicians.

The rambunctious behavior of beleganjur contest audiences, whether within the crowd itself or directed toward the performers, is most often led by groups of teenage (or younger) boys, but they are by no means the sole protagonists. People of all ages, male and female, from all walks of life—elderly women, esteemed community leaders, young mothers with babies in tow—"act out" at beleganjur contests, taking advantage of an opportunity to express sides of themselves that must normally remain concealed from public view. As Unni Wikan has written, "Big ceremonies and crowds, where ego occupies spectator status and the attention is focused on others, are safest. . . . A failure to 'manage one's heart' [that is, to control one's outer expression by shaping feelings into appropriate molds (1990, 95–97)] in such settings is of much less consequence than in any other kind of interpersonal gathering" (1990, 83).

To an even greater extent than for the musicians, who are constrained by the pressure of performance expectations, the beleganjur contest represents for the spectators an enframed moment of cathartic release, of temporary liberation from the normally tight reins of social propriety. The dimensions of the frame, it should be noted, are surprisingly exact; the mayhem ends as suddenly as it begins. Audiences normally appear relaxed and subdued throughout all the pre-contest speeches and other preliminary activities; but from the moment the first beleganjur group enters the demonstration area, the crowd springs into action, swarming around the musicians like a giant parasitic organism in order to get a better view, crushing forward against the resistance of the security officers, tightening the circle around the performers to a sometimes suffocating degree, and then, with the sounding of the first *gong* stroke, bursting forth with a great collective howl of excitement. With this, the proper tone is set, and although the energy level and intensity will rise and fall over the course of the competition, the fever pitch of the opening should ideally endure quite consistently through to the final note of the last performance. In large measure, both the audience and the jury will gauge the quality and rank of each group according to its ability to generate, maintain, rekindle, or, best of all, exceed the frenetic level of energy initially established, to sustain the euphoric state.

As soon as the final *gong* sounds, though, everyone abruptly reverts to normal behavior. The moment of revelry is over. There is a return to courtesy and polite manners, and a strange, almost anxious quiet descends over the contest site as the crowd quickly disperses. People appear almost embarrassed, as though they might be trying to suddenly dissociate themselves from the madness of the moment just past. I will never forget the occasion of a 1992 lomba beleganjur in Denpasar, during which a boy of perhaps fourteen shoved and hacked at me incessantly for the better part of three hours, vainly attempting to push ahead of me in the crowd. During the assault, I suffered numerous bruises and came dangerously close to having my video camera smashed to the ground at least four times. When the contest finally ended, I turned around and glared at the boy. I was expecting an equally unfriendly glare in return (although I was hoping for an apology), but instead I was confronted by the most innocent-looking face imaginable, by a smile that could only be described as angelic. The boy attempted to start up a conversation with me, in quite proficient English yet; he was nothing if not shy, gentle, and humble. The rude and obnoxious teenager of just seconds before had completely disappeared; it was a total transformation. I was dumbfounded and confused, and as I walked home I found myself thinking about Gregory Bateson's and Margaret Mead's observations on the "cultural schizophrenia" of Balinese people (Bateson and Mead 1942), concisely summarized by Adrian Vickers (1989, 122) in the following passage: "On the one hand, people would be calm, harmonious, and almost too restrained. On the other, they would be prone to culturally-controlled outbursts which allowed them to express the otherwise hidden aspects of their personalities."

Three

Kreasi Beleganjur: The Contest Musical Style

Having examined the root forms of modern contest-style beleganjur in chapter 1 and the music's primary performance context, the lomba beleganjur, in chapter 2, we now turn our attention to a detailed study of kreasi beleganjur music itself. In this chapter, John Blacking's notion of the importance of drawing distinctions "between innovations within a musical system and changes of the system" ([1977] 1990, 277), or in other words between "radical change from variation" on the one hand and "innovation within a flexible system" on the other (259), provides a framework for a study of selected structures, forms, and stylistic features that define kreasi beleganjur music. Through analysis that combines Balinese concepts and categories with Western-derived methods, kreasi beleganjur is examined as a product of innovations that have emerged from within the broader beleganjur "musical system" to which it belongs, and also as the result of changes of that system.

The first part of the discussion focuses on general musical features that define the kreasi beleganjur genre, distinguish it from its antecedent forms, and symbolically link it to certain other forms and styles of Balinese gamelan music. The second part examines the creative attitudes, choices, and innovations of selected individual musicians through analysis of kreasi beleganjur music by three leading composers: Asnawa, Sukarata, and I Ketut Suandita. (Since there are no written scores for any of this music, the points of reference for the analyses are my own transcriptions and recorded examples included on the compact disc accompanying this book.) A section on contest beleganjur choreography, or *gerak,* the medium through which kreasi beleganjur's essential spirit and character are brought to life in physical motion, concludes the chapter.

Comparisons of the modern contest style and its antecedent forms are employed here to explore not only the "whats" of musical innovation and change, but the "whys" as well. Why have some traditional beleganjur musical features been maintained, others modified, and still others fundamentally altered? Why, and how, have certain musical sources outside the beleganjur sphere been selected, drawn upon, and adapted to foster the modern style's transformation and development?

In the engagement of such questions, continuity, innovation, and change are treated as interacting forces in a complex musical dialectic of traditionalism and modernity. Officialized cultural ideologies, creative individual agency, and aesthetic priorities rooted in desires for competitive success appear to alternately align and collide within this matrix. Beyond the musical analysis itself, therefore, a broader interest here is to consider how certain extramusical, contextual factors and forces implicated in the beleganjur world are reflected musically, that is, to interpret how music as structured sound reflects, embodies, and informs cultural and ideological priorities as well as the particular priorities of individual music-makers.

Musical Design in Kreasi Beleganjur

The foundations of kreasi beleganjur music lie in traditional beleganjur. Standard beleganjur bebonangan instrumentation, unaccompanied awit-awit drumming introductions, gilak colotomy, stock interlocking patterns (played on drums, cymbals, and reyong), and musical forms built on an alternation of full ensemble sections *(rangkep)* and passages without cymbals or drums *(pengisep)* are basic features of virtually all beleganjur music, even that heard in the most progressive contest pieces.

Beyond its adherence to such fundamental formal and structural features, however, musical design in kreasi beleganjur departs dramatically from that of earlier beleganjur forms. Aesthetically, conventional beleganjur provided relatively little from which to develop a legitimate contest performance style, for the older music had only to be appropriate to the functional demands of ritual and ceremonial occasions in order to be effective. The needs of a competition-centered style were different. The music had to stand alone, to impress, to provide criteria for the comparative assessment of different pieces and performances; the inherent capacity to foreground displays of musical sophistication, innovation, novelty, and virtuosity was required.

In their efforts to transform beleganjur into a viable contest music, kreasi beleganjur's pioneers grafted certain formal, structural, and stylistic features derived from other Balinese musics onto a traditional beleganjur base, consciously endeavoring to elevate beleganjur's artistic credibility and popular appeal by incorporating elements associated

with modern gong kebyar and classical gamelan genres (e.g., lelambatan), in particular. The flexible, malleable character of traditional beleganjur form, which had always been central to the music's effectiveness
in accommodating sudden and unpredictable changes in the musical
needs of ritual processions and the like, took on a new kind of importance as beleganjur was molded into a competition style. Composers
exploited the music's immanent potential for adaptability, liberally expanding and varying the standard drum, cymbal, and reyong patterns
and cadences; experimenting with novel textures and combinations
of instruments within the ensemble; developing the conventional alternation of passages with and without drums and cymbals into a
more complex theme-and-variations-type design; and integrating musical materials from a wide range of sources into the gamelan beleganjur's vocabulary.

Kebyarization

The principal stylistic model and inspiration for this creative expansion
was found in the fiery and explosive character of kebyar music.[1] Kebyar
has been the predominant aesthetic force in Balinese music of the twentieth century. As Tenzer asserts, "There are many who bemoan kebyar's
near-hegemony, but such certainly is the reality" (1991, 77). Despite its
primary identification with the gamelan gong kebyar, itself an invention
of the early part of this century, "kebyar style" has permeated most
other types of Balinese gamelan music as well.

   Through a process of "kebyarization" (my term), beleganjur became
modern as kreasi beleganjur. Kebyar's direct impact on the new contest
style was evident on multiple levels: extremely fast tempos, unprecedented rhythmic intricacy, exhibitionistic virtuosity, and the privileging
of musical innovation, novelty, formal complexity, and variety over
conventional "functional" priorities. There was a sociological dimension to the kebyar connection as well. It was mainly through the infu-
sion of kebyar spirit, long associated with the energy of youth, that a
strong youth appeal came to be identified with beleganjur in its new
manifestation as kreasi beleganjur (Asnawa, pers. comm., 1992).

Classicization

The numerous innovations introduced into beleganjur via the stylistic
impact of kebyar were associated with a more fundamental change of
the beleganjur "musical system," one deriving from the influence of

classical Balinese musical models: the introduction and standardization of multipart musical designs for the demonstration sections, or *demonstrasi,* of contest performance pieces. The musical results of this development and their symbolic significance, although noted briefly in chapter 2, require more detailed consideration at this point in our discussion.

The modern contest-style demonstrasi typically comprises three connected main sections: an opening kawitan, a middle pengawak, and a concluding pengecet. Transitional passages *(pengalihan)* link the sections together over an uninterrupted flow of gilak colotomic punctuation. A contest performance normally includes two to four demonstrasi, one for each of the jury posts along the contest procession route.

The kawitan and the pengecet feature fast tempos. Both are made up of a series of discrete subsections, or *pukulan,* each highlighting some combination of drum, cymbal, and/or reyong variations *(pepayasan).* The subsections, in turn, are separated from one another by passages where the drums and cymbals rest (and sometimes the reyong as well). Thus, the conventional alternation of full- and partial-ensemble textures heard in traditional beleganjur remains, but with an important difference: whereas all of the full-ensemble passages, or rangkep, in a traditional-style beleganjur performance tend to feature essentially the same (or at least very similar) musical material (rhythmic patterns, cadences, etc.), each such passage in a kreasi piece is musically unique, mainly because of distinctive variations in the drum and cymbal parts.

As Asnawa explains (pers. comm., 1995), a *pukulan,* in kreasi beleganjur terms, is "a segment within a larger formal section of the piece based on a particular musical idea or style";[2] it is, in essence, a self-contained "mini-composition" framed by an introductory lead-in and a cadential angsel, a single segment within a succession of variations that unfolds over the cyclically recurring "ground bass" of gilak colotomy. A diversity of musical sources may be drawn upon to provide the "particular musical idea or style" for a given pukulan, and a variety of techniques may be employed in its development. Primary among these techniques are the following six:

1. Extension in the length of a traditional beleganjur rhythmic phrase. For example, the ceng-ceng part for a traditional two-measure-long angsel lead-in, measures 3–4 of example 16a, is expanded into the eight-measure-long kreasi variant, measures 1–8 of example 16b (from a kreasi beleganjur piece by Sukarata), which encompasses a full two gong cycles. Example 16c is an even longer and more rhythmically complex extension of the same lead-in, this from a composition by Asnawa.

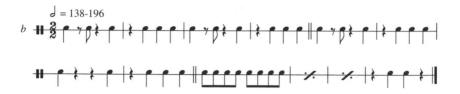

Example 16.   Kreasi-style extensions of a traditional angsel lead-in, cengceng. *a,* Traditional version. *b,* Extension 1. *c,* Extension 2. A dot over a note indicates a stopped, or damped, stroke.

2. Rhythmic variation of a traditional beleganjur phrase, an example of which can be seen by comparing the traditional-style angsel lead-in of example 17a to the modified kreasi version (again from a work by Sukarata) of example 17b.

Example 17.   Kreasi-style rhythmic variation on a traditional angsel lead-in, cengceng. *a,* Traditional version. *b,* Kreasi version. A dot over a note indicates a stopped, or damped, stroke.

3. Arrangement of musical materials adapted directly from other gamelan repertoires (especially gamelan gong repertoires, including lelambatan and kebyar).

4. Invention of musical material that is essentially newly composed but that derives stylistically and/or formally from another musical genre, usually Balinese (e.g., kebyar) but occasionally non-Balinese (e.g., Sundanese *jaipongan,* African-American funk).

5. Creation of new musical material that does not derive from any identifiable preexisting source.

6. Merging together of two or more distinct pukulan segments (usually with the aid of a transition) within a single, continuous musical passage.

Any or all of these six techniques may be employed in a given musical work.

The middle section of the demonstrasi, the pengawak, is slower in tempo than the outer two. It is also distinct in musical mood and character, emphasizing melodic development and variation, especially in the reyong part.[3] Melodicism such as that heard in kreasi-style pengawaks had no real precedent in traditional, gilak-based beleganjur music. Prior to the advent of kreasi beleganjur, only the beleganjur-ized versions, or arrangements, of compositions that were originally composed for other types of ensembles featured anything similar in terms of exploitation of the gamelan beleganjur's relatively limited melodic resources (Asnawa, pers. comm., 1992).

Perhaps even more significantly, it was the interpolation of a pengawak between the two fast outer sections that, more than any other single factor, was responsible for redefining beleganjur formal structure in the kreasi context. The presence of interrelated but contrasting musical sections—movements, in essence—represented a decisive break from the past. Older styles of beleganjur provided no model for formal complexity of this order.

It is at this level, the transformation of formal musical design, that kreasi beleganjur might be said to have brought a basic change to the beleganjur musical system, as opposed to innovation within that system. On the one hand, the incorporation of the pengawak definitively distinguished kreasi beleganjur from its antecedent forms; on the other, it brought the new style into alignment with other repertoires of Balinese music, specifically those identified in the cultural nationalism rhetoric as *klasik* (classic): lelambatan, legong, gambuh, etc. If "kebyarization" rendered the new beleganjur modern, then "classicization"—mainly as symbolized in the three-movement, kawitan-pengawak-pengecet forms of the new demonstrasi—rendered it artistically respectable in an essentialized historiographic sense. Beleganjur's "elevation" and "improvement," in accordance with the basic tenets of cultural nationalism ideology, were premised to a large extent on the genre's appropriation of formal musical symbols of classic musical design.

It is important to note that symbol, rather than substance, was the key issue. While the kawitan-pengawak-pengecet forms of kreasi beleganjur reflected the overall fast-slow-fast tempo design structure of klasik compositions, they did not adopt the *internal* features of formal design that define and characterize kawitans, pengawaks, and pengecets in such compositions (see McPhee 1966 and Astita 1993 for discussion of the latter). Beyond a rather loose formal correspondence to their counterpart forms in the klasik genres, the different movements of demonstrasi in contest-style beleganjur were (and are) kawitans, pengawaks, or pengecets in name only. Thus, it was at least as much from the adoption of names as from the specific musical forms referenced by such names that kreasi beleganjur drew its power to claim legitimacy as a musical object of autonomous aesthetic interest and value.

Through its synthesis of traditional beleganjur roots, a kebyar-based stylistic orientation, and the liberal adaptation of three-part formal designs from classical Balinese models, kreasi beleganjur came to represent a unique distillation of musical influences and priorities, one in which matters of continuity, innovation, and change were guided by both aesthetic and ideological factors from the outset. The principal issue to be addressed in the later sections of this chapter is how individual composers have creatively navigated kreasi beleganjur's multifaceted, "neo-traditional" musical terrain, but first it will be helpful to outline, with the aid of specific examples, the main musical components of beleganjur contest-style demonstrasi.

The Formal Components of Kreasi Beleganjur Demonstrasi
Awit-Awit: The Drumming "Prelude"

Like traditional beleganjur performances, kreasi beleganjur pieces normally commence with an awit-awit: an unaccompanied, essentially nonmetric[4] drum introduction. According to McPhee (1966, 94 n. 10), the root word, *ngawit,* means "to alert, prepare beforehand," a translation that accurately captures both the spirit and function of the awit-awit relative to the musical performance itself and the performance event overall, whether in a cremation procession or a beleganjur contest.

In terms of basic function, kreasi-style awit-awits are similar to traditional ones, but they differ greatly in musical style. As we saw in chapter 1, the traditional awit-awit form typically comprised a brief, improvised solo played on the kendang lanang followed by a short lead-in cue involving straightforward interlocking patterns between the two drums. In contrast, the kreasi form of the awit-awit features a series of highly complex, pre-composed two-drum interlocking passages. The virtuosic, cadenza-like display serves not only to "alert" and "prepare," but also to impress and draw attention. At the risk of overstating an analogy, one might say that the kreasi-style awit-awit is to its traditional counterpart what the virtuosic ensemble kebyar introductions of

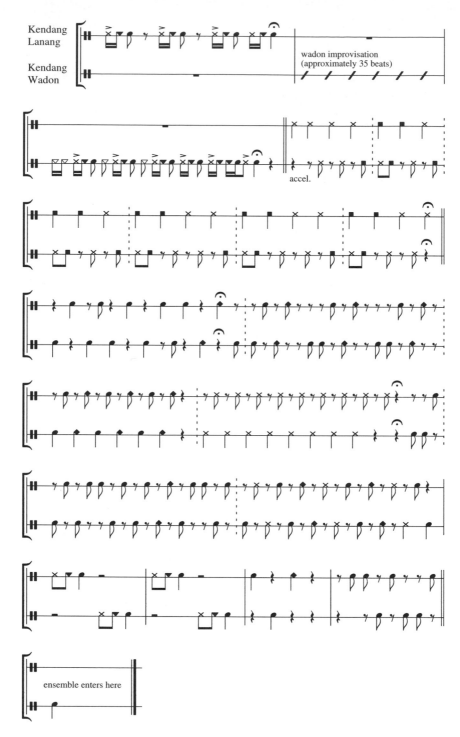

Example 18.   Kreasi-style awit-awit drum introduction (Sukarata)

gong kebyar pieces are to the semi-improvised solo *trompong* introductions of traditional ceremonial gamelan gong pieces. (See McPhee 1966, 67, for discussion of the latter).

Example 18 (CD #19), a transcription of a kreasi awit-awit composed by Sukarata, provides a good example of the modern, virtuosic style.

The solo opening here is similar to that of the traditional awit-awit discussed in chapter 1 (compare to example 7), as is the free-improvisation section featuring left-hand accents that follows directly. The remaining portion of the kreasi version departs dramatically from its traditional antecedent, however. In place of the conventional six-beat lead-in figure between the two drums, one now finds an elaborate sequence of fast-tempoed flourishes of interlocking drum rhythm. These might be likened to the quick-tempoed, virtuosic fragments of interconnected melody heard in the introductions of gong kebyar compositions.[5]

Kawitan

In the opening demonstration, the awit-awit leads directly into the kawitan, the first and main movement. *Kawitan,* according to McPhee (1966, 94 n. 10), means "begin," and it is at the inception of the kawitan, marked by the first *gong* stroke and the entry of the full beleganjur orchestra, that the piece proper does indeed commence.[6] The first full-ensemble section, or opening rangkep, which features powerful rhythms performed in unison by the drum, cymbal, and reyong sections (the latter sometimes playing on the edges of the reyong kettles), establishes the overall character of the kawitan and of the composition as a whole.

The opening rangkeps heard in kreasi pieces, with their kebyar-inspired syncopations and other novel features, represent a stylistic departure from earlier beleganjur music. In terms of formal design, however, the link between new and old is direct. The basic model for most contest-style opening rangkeps derives from a particular form of extended ensemble introduction that, according to Asnawa (pers. comm., 1992), had already been developed well before the advent of kreasi beleganjur. In the extended traditional format, the opening rangkep comprised three distinct subsections spanning several gong cycles (at least three) and involving continuous playing by the drummers. Following the opening "statement" and concluding angsel performed by the full ensemble (usually of one gong cycle's duration) came a cymbal-less "interlude" section featuring drumming with just the gongs accompanying. This interlude led directly into a second angsel, of either the "regular" bawak or the "long" lantang type, with the cymbals again joining in to close out the introduction.

Analysis of two kreasi beleganjur opening rangkeps, one composed by Asnawa ("Beleganjur Angga Yowana"), the other by Sukarata ("Beleganjur Padma Mudra"), illustrates how this traditional three-part "model" is transformed in creative ways within the modern beleganjur contest-style milieu. I will begin with discussion of the Asnawa work, which relates to example 19 (CD #20).

Asnawa begins the piece unconventionally (there is no awit-awit drum prelude) with a brief melodic introduction played on the reyong (mm. 1–4).[7] A two-measure drum lead-in (mm. 3–4) sets up the opening rangkep, which begins at "A" (m. 5) with the entry of the gongs and driving unison rhythms executed by the cymbals, drums, and reyong. Following the first angsel (m. 12) comes a drum interlude at "B" (m. 13), during which the cymbal and reyong sections rest. Beginning at "C" (m. 21), the arrival of the final angsel is delayed by an extended preparatory buildup; in this segment, accented unison strokes on the cymbals, reinforced by glissando-like melodic "sweeps" in the reyong part (mm. 22–27), build tension and excitement underneath a repeating two-measure drum figure (mm. 21–22, 23–24, 25–26). Finally, at "D" (m. 29), the drums, cymbals, and reyong all simultaneously break into their characteristic gilak interlocking patterns for the first time, driving to the climactic section-closing angsel at measure 32.

Throughout this opening section, Asnawa cleverly manipulates the listener's expectations, evading the establishment of a sense of structural stability by delaying the arrival of the standard, complete pattern of gilak colotomic punctuation that normally grounds a beleganjur performance from the outset. The two *gongs* are played at an unusual "half-speed" rate from "A" to "B," and the kempur, bendé, and ponggang are, surprisingly, not even heard at all until after the conclusion of the introduction section, at "E," at which point the familiar gilak underpinning finally begins to settle into place.[8] At "E" also, the drums rest for the first time (the cymbals also lay out), taking pause for several gong cycles before leading the way through the sequence of pukulans that will constitute the rest of the kawitan portion of the demonstrasi. (Detailed analyses of selected pukulans will be provided later in the chapter.) This pause is customary in kreasi beleganjur arrangements.

Sukarata's approach to the opening rangkep represents both more and less of a departure from the traditional three-part "model" than Asnawa's. This should be evident from the following analysis, which

Example 19.   Kreasi ensemble introduction: opening rangkep (Asnawa)

Example 19. (*Continued*)

Example 19. (*Continued*)

corresponds to example 20 (CD #21). (Note: The transcription of example 20 begins with the first *gong* stroke of the piece, which arrives where the full ensemble enters at "A" after the awit-awit drum prelude, about thirty-five seconds into the recorded version on the CD. Since the colotomic instruments simply mark out a conventional gilak cycle throughout the example [unlike in example 19], I have elected not to include these instruments in the notation.)

The entry of the ensemble is announced by a rousing opening at "A," which highlights a sparse, syncopated motive (played in unison by the wadon drum, the cymbals, and the reyong) repeated three times in succession (mm. 1–2, 3–4, 5–6). The spaces between the three statements of this motive are filled in by continuous streams of interlocking "pak" strokes between the two drums; added excitement and intensity are generated by the propulsive, steady quarter-note rhythm of the ponggang melody, which contrasts with the usual slower-moving pokok core melody played on that instrument. The section at "B" (mm. 9–12) leads to the first angsel, an angsel bawak that cadences at "C" (m. 13). With the arrival of "C," the cymbals and reyong drop out and the drum interlude commences; at the same time, the ponggang switches to playing its conventional core melody ostinato. It is at the point of the drum interlude that the distinctively kreasi character of the piece first becomes clearly evident; this interlude covers a surprisingly vast terrain of syncopated rhythm in the short space of just two gong cycles. The cymbals and reyong re-enter at "D," where the energy builds for three gong cycles (mm. 21–32) through an angsel lantang, or long-type angsel passage. This appears to be leading to a cadential close to the entire introductory section at "E," but Sukarata defies expectations by appending a lengthy, coda-like extension to the angsel. This extension continues through six full gong cycles (mm. 33–56), highlighting an exciting array of drum-cymbal-reyong unison rhythmic figures before drawing to an end. After this, as in the Asnawa piece, the drummers rest for the first time in the performance before proceeding to the various remaining pukulans of the kawitan movement.

Pengawak

The pengawak follows the kawitan without pause. It may commence with a sudden and dramatic slowing of tempo, or its arrival may be anticipated by a decelerating transitional passage *(pengalihan,* or *pengiba).* In either case, the movement proper will typically be preceded

Example 20.   Kreasi ensemble introduction: opening rangkep (Sukarata)

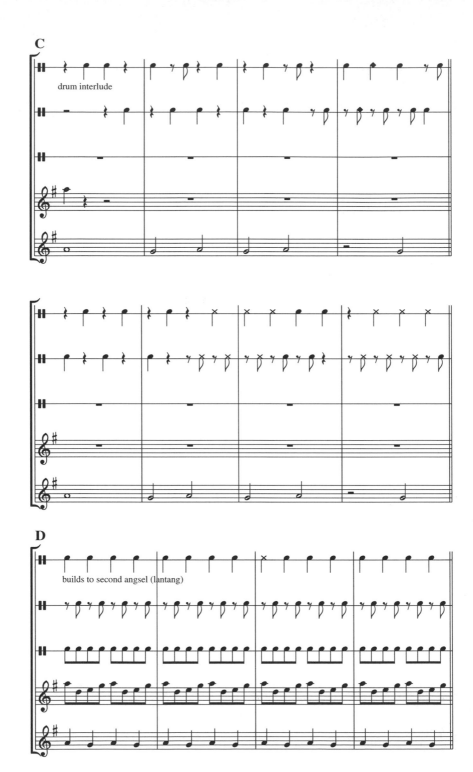

Example 20. (*Continued*)

Example 20. (*Continued*)

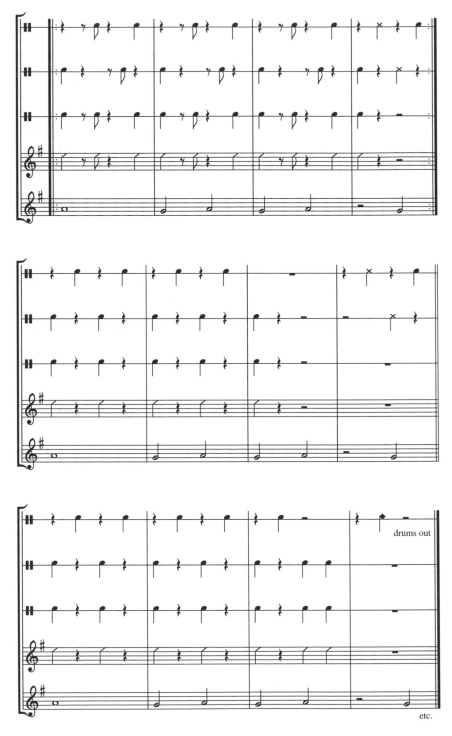

drums out

etc.

Example 20. (*Continued*)

by a short (usually one-phrase) melodic introduction played by the reyong, such as the one in example 21, from Asnawa's "Beleganjur
Angga Yowana."

Example 21.   Pengawak lead-in, reyong

This lead-in serves to set the slower tempo and to create a more relaxed and subdued mood.

After the introductory phrase comes a relatively long reyong melody,
comprising several phrases. This melody, the *lagu pengawak,* repeats at
least three times as it spins out over the standard ponggang core melody
ostinato and gilak colotomy, which now move along at about half their
former tempo. The reyong melody includes an "A" and a "B" section;
the latter is known as the *penyelah,* and is typically more intense and
energetic than its "A" counterpart. Contrast between the "A" and "B"
sections may emerge from the use of different melodic materials, from
gradual or sudden changes in tempo and dynamics, or from special
rhythmic devices such as the use of "double-time" drum or cymbal
patterns during the penyelah. Specific examples and analysis will be
provided later in the chapter.

The penyelah section serves not only to generate musical contrast
within the design of the pengawak itself, but also to link the pengawak
to the two fast outer movements that frame it. The rhythmic and dynamic intensity of the penyelah echo the energetic spirit of the opening
kawitan movement and foreshadow the eventual return of a similar
spirit in the fast-tempoed pengecet closing movement—the latter connection apparently accounting for the name *penyelah,* which in the Indonesian language means "prophesier" or "forecaster" (Echols and
Shadily 1989, 561).[9]

Pengecet (Pengecet Gegilakan)

The final statement of the penyelah, performed with a dramatic acceleration in tempo, normally serves as the transition to the pengecet.
With the arrival of the pengecet, the original tempo of the kawitan is
reestablished. The mood of the pengecet also recalls the opening movement, but with a twist. According to Asnawa, the pengecet should be

the section of a demonstrasi in which a "happier, lighter, wittier" side of kreasi beleganjur's heroic (kepahlawanan) character is expressed (pers. comm., 1992). It should be of a musical character that contrasts with both the earnestness of the kawitan and the introspectiveness of the pengawak.

Like the term *pengawak, pengecet* is something of a misnomer in the kreasi beleganjur context. In classical Balinese repertoires such as lelambatan, the form of a pengecet involves "several melodic sections, each based on a metrical contraction of the preceding meter, with a corresponding contraction in gong punctuation" (McPhee 1966, 83). Not so with the beleganjur version of the pengecet, which, formally speaking, is in actuality just another series of varied pukulans performed over gilak colotomy at a fast tempo, much like the kawitan; [10] as Asnawa told me in 1992, it is really a "pengecet gegilakan" rather than a pengecet proper.

Again, stylistic impression rather than formal design connects the beleganjur-type pengecet to its non-beleganjur namesake. In most beleganjur pengecets, there is an escalation in intensity and virtuosic flair with each successive pukulan, culminating with a climactic drive to the final cadence. The sense of "increasing animation and rising rhythmic tension" that McPhee (1966, 83) attributes to the metric and colotomic "contractions" of conventional pengecet forms finds impressionistic parallels in the freer formal structures of their beleganjur correlates.

Depending on the particular demonstrasi in which it is heard, the pengecet may range in length from a full-scale movement consisting of several pukulans to a brief passage that serves to do little more than round out the three-part, fast-slow-fast form of the demonstrasi overall. Normally, the pengecets of the opening and mid-route demonstrasi of contest performances are relatively short; the more extended and compositionally developed pengecet form is reserved for the final demonstrasi, where it is used to build to the climactic close of the piece, usually terminating with a coda-like section known as the *pekaad*.

Jejalanan: Processional Music between the Main Demonstrasi

In all but the final demonstrasi of a contest performance, the pengecet movements transition directly into slow processional, or *jejalanan,* music, which usually begins just as an ensemble bows before the adjudicators and prepares to march to the next judging post along the contest route. This music typically contrasts with the flashy graded demonstration sections of the piece. Its relative simplicity and repetitiveness link it stylistically and symbolically to more traditional beleganjur styles.

Mid-Procession and Final Demonstrasi of Contest Performances

While the basic three-part, fast-slow-fast, kawitan-pengawak-pengecet formal design of the opening demonstrasi is replicated in the subsequent judged demonstrations of a contest performance, the duration, musical content, internal formal structure, and integration of musical materials vary considerably from one demonstration to the next. In all but the opening demonstrasi, the kawitan movement emerges directly and without interruption out of slow processional jejalanan music. Because of the direct transition, no awit-awit drumming introduction is used after the first demonstrasi; furthermore, the opening ensemble sections (opening rangkeps) of mid-procession and closing-demonstration kawitan movements may be significantly shorter than that of the first. Just as the closing pengecet of a kreasi beleganjur performance may be more expansive than those that precede it, the opening kawitan may be more developed than those that follow it. Only the pengawak movements tend to be consistent in length and design from one demonstrasi to the next.

In the kawitan and pengecet movements of successive demonstrasi, the same or different musical materials may be developed in the various pukulans, and the number of pukulans may also change or remain uniform. The varied time limits imposed on competing groups at the different judging stations along the contest route significantly influence creative decisions on what materials to include in a demonstrasi and how to arrange and integrate them within a particular musical segment of the performance.

Batu-Batu and "Jagul"

In virtually every contest beleganjur composition, two specific types of pukulan are included in the kawitan and/or pengecet sections: batu-batu and "Jagul." Batu-batu in the kreasi context features the same improvisation-based style of drumming that was discussed in connection with traditional beleganjur in chapter 1 (see example 11). "Jagul" is built around the drumming part *(kendangan)* of a section from an ancient ceremonial lelambatan composition for gamelan gong, "Tabuh Pat Jagul," and thus might be seen to reinforce the "klasik" associations of the "elevated" beleganjur style.[11] A section of "Tabuh Pat

Jagul" featuring this distinctive drumming form is included on the accompanying compact disc (CD #22). The standard kreasi beleganjur rendition of the Jagul drumming is notated in example 22 (CD #23; the transcribed drumming part begins at about nine seconds in).

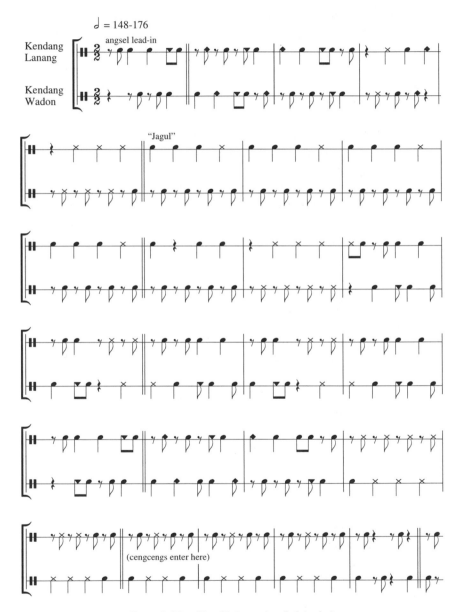

Example 22.   "Jagul" drum parts (beleganjur)

Both the batu-batu and "Jagul" passages of kreasi beleganjur arrangements highlight the skills of the drummers. They therefore are essentially treated as drumming test pieces, providing a standard basis for comparison from which contest judges (and audiences) assess the talents of the lead musicians of the different competing groups. Batu-batu tests improvisational abilities (it is normally the only portion of a kreasi beleganjur arrangement that allows for improvisation); "Jagul" tests rhythmic precision in a fast-tempoed, technically demanding interlocking drumming texture. In many contest beleganjur pieces, batu-batu and "Jagul" are linked together within an arrangement, so that a more or less standardized "drum feature" section is incorporated into each demonstrasi.

Creative Strategies and Priorities
in Kreasi Beleganjur Composition

How have prominent composers worked creatively within the kreasi beleganjur "formal model" outlined above? And through their creative endeavors, how have these composers defined and articulated distinctive musical identities and achieved status and prestige within the competitive beleganjur scene? The purpose of the following analysis of musical examples from kreasi beleganjur compositions by Asnawa, Sukarata, and Suandita is to shed light on these matters.

According to Asnawa, Balinese composers who create kreasi compositions, whether of the beleganjur type or any other, treat the full spectrum of past and present Balinese music as a common pool of musical resources: an inexhaustible reservoir for the creative adaptation, development, and revitalization of existing musical materials found in older Balinese musical traditions. In the Balinese music world, imitation is still regarded as the sincerest form of flattery. "The test of a piece of music, a style, or any kind of art," I Wayan Beratha told me in 1992, "is found in its ability to touch people's souls. The power to do this can be measured by how widely and quickly it spreads, by how much it is copied." It is not difficult to comprehend why Western-derived concepts, laws, and policies relating to copyright and the like have met with resistance in the Balinese gamelan world (despite their significance in the realm of Western-inspired Balinese commercial popular music forms).[12] Innovation and originality are prized in kreasi beleganjur, as they are in the kreasi genres generally, but Balinese attitudes concerning what constitutes the "original" are profoundly different from those in the West. Composition, in the words of Asnawa, is "a process of putting things in order to make what is old new." The goal is not to break with tradition but to build upon, renew, and revitalize that which has come before (see also Herbst 1997, 111–33).[13] This idea should be kept in mind during the following discussion of creative strategies in the work of kreasi beleganjur composers.

Compositional Approaches and Priorities:
The Pengawak Beleganjur

In the kawitan and pengecet sections of kreasi beleganjur contest pieces, rhythmic invention and variation, mainly centered in or generated from the drumming part, determine the music's creative dimensions and parameters. Virtuosity, technical brilliance, and novelty in beleganjur performance are highlighted primarily through the medium of rhythm in these movements. In the pengawak, however, the melodic aspect becomes the principal focus, both as a gauge of the musical sensitivity and expressiveness of the performers and, most significantly for our present purposes, as a forum for display of the musical artistry and craftsmanship of the composer.

Most of the beleganjur composers with whom I spoke during my research stated that the creation of pengawaks offered the most interesting creative opportunities and challenges in the beleganjur composition process. Moreover, in commenting on the musical quality of their own beleganjur creations or those of their peers and rivals, these composers were far more likely to focus on pengawaks than on anything else.

The inherent challenges of pengawak composition reside in the small number of melodic instruments, narrow melodic range, and limited four-toned scale system of the gamelan beleganjur. Working with the resources of an ensemble that was essentially designed to play music in which melodic development plays a minor role renders the task of creating attractive, compelling melodies a difficult one. To accommodate the gamelan beleganjur's limited melodic scope, kreasi beleganjur composers, building to some extent on previously discussed techniques that convert non-beleganjur pieces into beleganjur arrangements, have developed a linear melodic style for the reyong part, wherein the reyong's functional relationship to the rest of the ensemble is essentially inverted. Rather than furnishing ornamental figuration derived from the ponggang's two-toned core melody, as in the fast movements (and in traditional beleganjur style as well), the reyong takes on an entirely new role as the main melody instrument in the pengawak; in addition, it becomes the central focus of the musical design overall instead of a subordinate element to the drum and cymbal parts.

"When I compose a pengawak," explains Asnawa, "all of the parts tend to be built around the reyong melody, unlike [in] the fast sections, where the ideas come from the rhythms of the kendang. In the pengawak, even the kendang and cengceng rhythms are like ornamentations of the reyong, and the pokok [core melody of the ponggang] becomes more like an accompaniment to the reyong than the actual main melody. It's a very different process" (pers. comm., 1992).

A good illustration of the linear melodic style characteristic of beleganjur pengawaks is provided in example 23, a transcription of a reyong part composed by Sukarata.

Example 23.   Lagu pengawak, reyong (Sukarata)

Throughout almost the entire "A" section, the reyong is heard playing what amounts to a lyrical, single-line melody,[14] not even hinting at the more conventionally beleganjur-like continuous eighth-note figuration style until the last two measures of the passage. Beginning at "B," the penyelah section, single-line melodic treatment and the more standard eighth-note reyong figuration texture begin to merge, becoming increasingly blurred; finally, the figuration style takes over completely during the last four measures. This, together with the faster tempo, is a musical device that links the penyelah section to the enframing kawitan and pengecet movements.

In contrast to Sukarata, Asnawa maintains constant eighth-note motion in the reyong part throughout the Pengawak of his "Beleganjur Angga Yowana." A further distinction is that the lagu pengawak heard in the reyong consists of just a single melodic theme that repeats throughout the entire movement (a total of nine times), rather than of contrasting "A" and "B" (penyelah) melodic themes stated in alternation. This melody, or lagu, is transcribed in example 24 (CD #24).

Example 24.   Lagu pengawak, reyong (Asnawa)

At first glance, the lagu may appear to represent little more than a "slow-motion" version of conventional beleganjur-style reyong figuration. The appearance is deceptive, however, since Asnawa cleverly weaves a lyrical melodic line into the seemingly conventional figuration texture. As is illustrated in example 25, the basic theme is composed of four distinct melodic motives encompassing two slow-tempoed gilak gong cycles (eight measures).

Example 25.   Melodic motives of the lagu pengawak of "Beleganjur Angga Yowana," reyong (Asnawa)

In accordance with Asnawa's earlier-quoted comments concerning his process of composing pengawak beleganjur melodies, one notes in example 26 that the standard "core melody" of the ponggang part is actually altered to accommodate the reyong's melodic development. In addition, the order of *gong* tones is reversed, seemingly to accommodate the melodic shape of the reyong part as well.[15]

Example 26.   Altered ponggang and gong ageng

Through these various melodic techniques and manipulations, Asnawa subtly infuses a lyrical sense of melodic line into a musical framework that on the surface appears to conform to a more traditional-style beleganjur structure. This represents an exemplary synthesis of "tradition" (conventional beleganjur melodic figuration) and "progress" (innovative melodic development) in the kreasi beleganjur context.

Beyond its highly effective treatment of melody, the Pengawak of "Beleganjur Angga Yowana" can be studied as a model example of internal formal balance on the one hand, and integrated connection with the fast outer movements that frame it on the other. The root of the word *pengawak* is *awak,* literally meaning "body." As was alluded to earlier, in klasik repertoires such as lelambatan, the pengawak movement constitutes the body of a composition; it is the centerpiece around which all other sections of a piece of music are built. However, according to the original contest criteria *(Kreteria Lomba)* of the 1986 LBPB, the beleganjur version of a pengawak should be different; it should be supportive of and subordinate to—rather than supported by and more prominent than—the kawitan that precedes it. The kawitan is the rightful locus of the core heroic spirit of a kreasi beleganjur piece, the designated focal point of the music's character and expression. The pengawak must always complement and never overwhelm the kawitan if a proper sense of musical balance is to be achieved.

The formal design of the "Angga Yowana" Pengawak brilliantly facilitates achievement of such balance. As was mentioned earlier, the lagu pengawak is repeated nine times. Although the melody never changes, a distinctive "A"-"B" structure for the movement *overall* emerges through the course of these nine repetitions. In the absence of a penyelah melody section, Asnawa uses other devices to generate contrast: changes in tempo and dynamics, new rhythmic patterns in the drum part, and "double-time" (i.e., sixteenth-note) cymbal interlocking patterns in particular. These result in an asymmetrical "A"-"B" design, in which the music played during the final seven repetitions of the lagu pengawak essentially comes to function as a macro-level penyelah. Approximately 75 percent of the movement is thus contained within the "B" part of the form, which not incidentally is the part that relates most closely in character to the "main" movement of the piece, the Kawitan. An analysis of example 27 (CD #25), a complete transcription of the Pengawak, minus the ponggang and colotomy, will help to illustrate this formal structure and also to show how the movement is integrated with the fast-tempoed outer ones.

The first statement of the lagu pengawak at "A" (beginning at measure 5 following the transitional opening) is performed at a slow tempo, about one-third that of the preceding Kawitan. The music's design draws attention to the melody itself; the drums are barely audible and the cymbals are tacit. The second lagu statement occurs during a repetition of the "A" material, but now there is some acceleration in the tempo and louder drumming, foreshadowing change. A sudden increase in tempo and more active drumming patterns heard at the outset of the third statement of the lagu at "B" signal the arrival of the contrasting penyelah section, from which point the listener's attention is increasingly diverted away from primary focus on the reyong melody. The basic contrast between this and the preceding sections becomes most

Example 27. Pengawak, "Beleganjur Angga Yowana" (Asnawa)

"double time" cymbals (interlocking)

Example 27. (*Continued*)

B2

Example 27.   (*Continued*)

Example 27. (*Continued*)

Example 27.   (*Continued*)

clearly evident with the entry of the cymbal section five measures later. The double-time rhythmic rate of the cymbals (whose interlocking parts are compressed into a single line of sixteenth-notes in the transcription) results in a rhythmic effect that is essentially identical to that heard earlier in the Kawitan movement, but for the fact that the underlying gilak colotomy is now being marked out at about half the original tempo (compare CD #26 to CD #27). Through this clever use of double-time cymbal patterns, a juxtaposition between the Pengawak and the movement it is designed to support and complement, the Kawitan, is achieved. Concomitantly, the musical autonomy of the Pengawak is subverted by its "kawitan-like" features of rhythm and instrumentation.

Through the successive repetitions of the lagu pengawak that follow "B," the linear development and forward motion of the music are achieved mainly through changes in the respective roles of the drums and cymbals, and through shifting relationships between these instruments. At "B2" the drums drop out of the texture temporarily, allowing the cymbals (playing double-time patterns that are now extended in length) to be foregrounded in the texture to an even greater extent than previously. Thirteen measures later (at the second ending of "B2," which arrives halfway through the seventh statement of the lagu), the drums re-enter to join with the cymbals in punctuating a series of unison rhythmic figures that serve to further reinforce the double-time feel formerly emphasized in the cymbal part alone. With the ninth and final statement of the lagu at "B3," the cymbals exit and the drums come fully to the fore with a dazzling passage of interlocking rhythm that accelerates dramatically (ultimately arriving back at the original fast tempo of the Kawitan) and cadences into the opening of the concluding Pengecet movement.

A fascinating feature of the entire penyelah section is that although it is the drum and cymbal rhythm rather than the reyong melody that changes throughout the passage, the specific *ways* in which the rhythm changes occur may lead the listener to perceive that the melody is changing even though it is not. Because of the shifting contexts of rhythm and texture that enframe it, the lagu sounds (at least to me) as though it is being developed and transformed during successive repetitions. A further point of musical interest is that virtually every rhythm introduced in the drum and cymbal parts throughout the penyelah is derived directly from the Kawitan (although in many cases these inter-movement connections have become evident to me—at least at a conscious level—only through the analysis of my transcriptions).

The Pengawak of "Beleganjur Angga Yowana" is a masterpiece of formal balance and compositional integration. In terms of both musical structure and character, it remains distinct from, yet related to, the Kawitan and Pengecet movements that surround it. At a broader level, it represents a consummately skillful integration of the various strands of "traditional," "classical," and "progressive" aesthetic priorities that have contributed to kreasi beleganjur's distinctive character as a musical genre. Asnawa allows for these varied streams of influence to alternately converge and compete but never to consume or overwhelm each other. Thus, even beyond the fact that it was featured on the first commercial kreasi beleganjur recording, it is not surprising that this pengawak became the model for the genre as a whole. Nothing in the kreasi beleganjur repertoire has been more influential or more widely imitated.

The exemplary formal balance achieved by Asnawa in his "Angga Yowana" Pengawak was no mere product of chance; it was, rather, the result of diligent and disciplined effort. For Asnawa and other Balinese composers, the pursuit of compositional balance is not just an aesthetic priority, but in a sense an ethical concern as well. Together with his mentors Beratha and Rembang, Asnawa has been perturbed in recent years by the increasing tendency of many composers, especially younger ones, to create pengawaks that are disproportionately long and complex, so much so that they overwhelm the compositions to which they belong, distorting the essential heroic character of the music in the process. The results of this tendency, in Asnawa's view, are not only musically unappealing but disrespectful and inappropriate as well; they undermine the dignity and integrity of the music's moral character.

"If the pengawak is too long or too broad," states Asnawa, "this devalues the music's heroic quality. This is why I think it is better for the melody to be short rather than long and why the moments of soft-ness and calmness should be short and concise. I think many composers now must disagree with me, because they make the pengawak so long and fancy. Maybe they think this represents a more sophisticated rep-resentation of kepahlawanan, but for me, it is no good, because then the music sounds more like dance accompaniment than beleganjur. I think it is true that in the pengawak, for a composer, this is where you can do [the] most interesting things, especially with the melody. The challenge is to make the music creative and interesting without making the pen-gawak so long and complicated that it does not fit the character of the piece anymore" (pers. comm., 1992).

Despite the concerns and criticisms of Asnawa and others of like mind, younger beleganjur composers have continued to push the enve-lope of beleganjur "propriety" by inventing ever longer and more com-plex pengawaks—some built on newly composed melodies, others based on melodies adapted from other repertoires where the pengawak is *supposed* to be the centerpiece of the work, still others developed through the combining and fusing of two or more formerly distinct melodies. Such tendencies emerge both from the adventurous creative spirit of the music-makers themselves and from their efforts to satisfy a seemingly insatiable public appetite for musical novelty and virtuosic display. Critics fear that the tendency toward "overindulgence" that has become rampant in pengawak beleganjur composition is moving the new style so far from its roots in traditional beleganjur that the music risks losing the core essence of its identity.

These same critics, however, recognize exceptions. One young com-poser whose works are often cited as evidence of the fact that the longer, more complex pengawak forms favored by younger musicians and au-diences need not diminish the integrity of kreasi beleganjur's essential character and balance is I Ketut Suandita. By age twenty-three, Suan-dita, a protégé of Asnawa who now teaches at SMKI (Sekolah Menen-gah Kesenian Indonesia, the government high school of the arts), had achieved the unprecedented distinction of serving as composer and mu-sical director for three consecutive LBPB championship groups (Kehen in 1990,[16] Sedang in 1991, and Meranggi in 1992). But according to Suandita, such success did not come easily. For some two years prior to his first major contest victory in 1990, his kreasi beleganjur works re-ceived mediocre grades in contest performances.

Suandita believes that the central distinction between his unheralded early works and the championship-caliber later ones was in the differing quality of their respective pengawak movements. Motivated by his initial lack of competitive success as a beleganjur composer *(penata)* in the late 1980s, Suandita sought guidance from his teachers, I Wayan Sinti and I Gusti Ngurah Padang, who both stressed that better integration of his pengawaks with the outer movements of his contest demonstrasi, both formally and in terms of consistent evocation of the properly kepahlawanan theme, would be the key to increasing the effectiveness of his works. Suandita experimented with a variety of compositional methods aimed at facilitating such integration. These included doubling the rate of melodic motion in the reyong part during the penyelah sections in order to form musical links to the fast movements, employing sudden and dramatic contrasts in tempo and dynamics at key structural points, and paying very close attention to the relationship between reyong melody, drum rhythm, and underlying colotomic punctuation in even the most adventurously unconventional passages. His disciplined yet creative approach ultimately enabled Suandita to successfully fuse novelty and formal complexity in his pengawaks, and to create the impression of a near-seamless connectedness with the surrounding movements. Such qualities are well exemplified in the opening demonstrasi of his 1992 LBPB championship-winning composition, "Wira Ghorava Cakti," an excerpt of which (from a 1995 performance) is included on the accompanying compact disc (CD #28).

Innovative Cymbals

Another innovative musical feature that helped Suandita achieve distinction as the most successful contest beleganjur composer of the early 1990s was his novel approach to interlocking cymbal textures. Through kreasi beleganjur's early years of development in the mid- to late 1980s, composers had typically retained the traditional-style beleganjur cymbal interplay of three standard interlocking patterns: the *kilitan telu*— megbeg, nyandet, and ngilit—discussed in chapter 1 (see example 13), which were distributed among the eight cymbal players (Asnawa, pers. comm., 1992). Although additional patterns were added in some pieces, subtly enriching the degree of polyrhythmic stratification, the doubled (or tripled) kilitan telu patterns predominated.

In his efforts to develop a uniquely compelling beleganjur style, Suandita devised a new multipart format for interlocking cymbal passages, one in which each of the eight players performed a different rhythmic pattern. He found the model for this more complex rhythmic texture in the music of the kecak dance-drama. In kecak performances, which employ a "vocal gamelan" *(gamelan suara)* that may include hundreds of members, voice interplay similar to the cymbal interplay in beleganjur is a central feature of musical design. The kilitan telu rhythms of beleganjur are fundamental in kecak as well, where they are executed vocally in a percussive style, usually on the syllable "cak" ("chak"). (In the kecak context, the kilitan telu are usually referred to as the *cak telu.*) Over the course of kecak's historical development, the nuclear three-part set of interlocking rhythms was eventually expanded to include additional sets, resulting in polyphonic textures of upwards of nine parts being divided among the massive choral forces employed. Beyond the basic telu patterns, two other sets of patterns ultimately became standardized: the *nem-lima* (five- and six-note patterns) and the *besik* (one-note patterns). Each interlocking set was composed of three separate parts.

Suandita's innovation was to compress the nine rhythmic patterns of the telu, nem-lima, and besik sets of kecak into an eight-part beleganjur cymbal-section arrangement in which no doubling of parts occurred. In order to accommodate the nine-part polyphony with only eight players, the nyandet pattern of the telu set was omitted. One gilak gong cycle of the resulting cymbal-interplay texture is represented in example 28 (CD #29). It should be noted, however, that the interrelationships of the different rhythmic patterns actually continue to shift through three full gong cycles before repeating. This is due to the fact that the besik pattern set, notated on the top staff of the transcription, is generated from a continuous three-way alternation of single cymbal strokes. This structure produces shifting cross-rhythmic relationships against the other cymbal patterns and against the duple-metered gilak underpinning, delaying repetition until the beginning of the fourth gilak cycle (illustrated in several sections of CD #28).

Example 28.   Kecak-inspired beleganjur cymbal interplay (Suandita)

Suandita's innovative treatment of the cengceng section, a result of clever borrowing from within the Balinese musical sphere, brought new levels of complexity and sophistication to cymbal interplay in the kreasi beleganjur style. The absence of doubled rhythms and the vastly expanded degree of rhythmic stratification yielded a streamlined texture of intriguing rhythmic and timbral variety. "The difference is profound," Asnawa told me in 1992. "The cengceng part becomes much richer, much more interesting." The "Suandita cengceng style" has been widely imitated. The difficulties it presents for performers, however, have prevented its adoption by all but the most competent—and confident—beleganjur groups.

The Jejagulan of Sukarata

In kreasi beleganjur, where drumming resides at the heart of musical design and expression, the drum feature pukulan known as "Jagul" is generally regarded as a quintessential test of drumming ability, as has been discussed. But this is not where the significance of "Jagul" ends, since it also serves as the basic theme for an abundance of musical variations. Beleganjur composers are almost invariably drummers, and many take delight in the invention of new drum feature sections rooted in the basic "Jagul" formal shape and structure. These variations are generically known as *jejagulans*. They provide excellent examples of the process through which old music becomes new in the context of kreasi beleganjur.

Sukarata is a self-described "jejagulan specialist." In 1992, he told me that he was the creator of "hundreds of jejagulans. I am always coming up with new ones, all the time." His best friend and drumming partner, I Wayan Jaya, added that Sukarata "has composed more jejagulans than anyone else in Bali. Of that I am certain."

Example 29 (CD #30, which begins with a short ensemble passage and a drum lead-in that are not included in the notated example) is a transcription of Sukarata's best-known jejagulan. It has been featured in several of his award-winning contest beleganjur works.

It is interesting to compare this jejagulan to the original beleganjur "Jagul." The brief comparative analysis that follows relates to example 30, in which the opening eight measures (two gong cycles) of the lanang drum part of Sukarata's jejagulan is juxtaposed with its standard "Jagul" form counterpart.

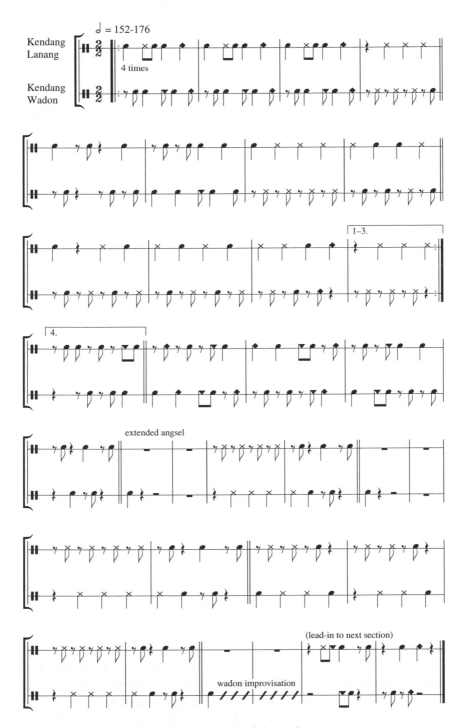

Example 29.   Jejagulan by Sukarata, drum parts

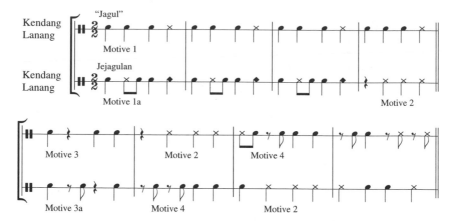

Example 30.   Comparison of standard "Jagul" and Sukarata jejagulan openings, lanang drum parts

Four short rhythmic motives that occur in both versions are identified in example 30. Motive 1 is first stated in the opening measure of the standard "Jagul." This corresponds to motive 1a of the Sukarata jejagulan, which is simply a variant of the same pattern. In both pieces the opening motive is heard three times in succession at the outset. At measure 4, it is repeated once again in the standard version, but at this point Sukarata diverges by introducing motive 2, consisting of a quick succession of left-hand "pak" strokes; motive 2 is not heard in the standard form until the sixth measure. Measure 5 sees the two versions coming back into alignment with the simultaneous introduction of a third motive, which is presented in a syncopated variant form by Sukarata. At measure 6, there is a parting of paths again. While motive 2 is being introduced in the standard version, Sukarata is introducing yet another new motive, motive 4, which does not arrive in the original "Jagul" until one bar later, in measure 7. Meanwhile, at measure 7 Sukarata restates motive 2.

On the basis of even a cursory examination such as this, one can begin to understand the ways in which beleganjur composers recast existing musical works into new ones. As I have attempted to illustrate, Sukarata was able to create a distinctive opening to his jejagulan merely by reordering and varying the rhythmic motives found in the opening passage of the standard "Jagul." How a particular composer transforms an existing piece of music into a unique musical expression is one interesting issue to examine in the study of beleganjur creative process. What materials that composer chooses to adapt and employ in the first place is another, and as we shall now explore, in the case of Sukarata, the range of materials is broad and eclectic indeed.

Foreign Musical Influences in Kreasi Beleganjur: Examples from the Work of Sukarata

The free use and adaptation of musical materials drawn from within the Balinese musical sphere constitutes an accepted and expected practice in kreasi beleganjur composition. The incorporation of musical source material of non-Balinese origin, however, is controversial. Kreasi beleganjur is conceived of primarily as a musical expression of contemporary Balinese identity and values, and most composers with whom I have spoken (and whose compositions I have studied) maintain that the music's range should not extend beyond Bali itself. Asnawa and Suandita, for example, each told me during separate 1992 interviews that Balinese musical repertoires represented the only proper and appropriate foundations from which to develop kreasi beleganjur works, adding that looking elsewhere for ideas or inspiration was unnecessary in any case, since Bali's musical heritage was so abundantly rich and varied.

But kreasi beleganjur is not just "Balinese." It is also a symbolic manifestation of "Indonesian-ness" in the cultural nationalism–defined sense of the term, and is therefore implicated in Indonesian agendas of nationalization, internationalization, and modernization. For some composers whose musical interests extend beyond the Balinese domain, a broader conception of what kreasi beleganjur might be seen to represent with respect to "Balinese identity" has served as inspiration and justification for the innovative use of non-indigenous musical source materials in the kreasi beleganjur context. Three years after our 1992 conversation, even Asnawa acknowledged that he had become increasingly drawn to the idea of employing non-Balinese elements in his beleganjur creations, provided that "the practice does not become over-indulgent." "It's about creativity," he told me in 1995, "and if fresh musical ideas from the outside can make the music more vital, maybe it's okay."

How particular composers approach the issue of whether or not it is appropriate to employ "foreign" musical elements in their beleganjur works—and if so, to what degree—reveals much about the range of individual attitudes that shapes the scope of creative production in an identity-defining medium of culture. What does it mean to be Balinese in contemporary Indonesia? The varied source materials that different composers choose to include or not include in their beleganjur compositions, and their comments concerning their choices, provide partial answers to this question while engendering an awareness of its unending complexity. Every composer must define his or her personal creative parameters within a complex matrix of negotiable musical and ideological priorities. In a genre whose legitimacy rests on a partially prescribed synthesis of traditional roots, appropriated historicity, and adopted modernity, the creative parameters and musical choices of music-makers ultimately issue from personal decisions. Such decisions are largely concerned with what balance of "traditional," "classic," and "modern" will best facilitate the forging of a distinctive and novel musical expression conducive to competitive success, and with what kinds of musical materials will best serve that expression. Where the "modern" component of the equation is concerned, "foreign" musical material is one important element.

One composer who has embraced the employment of non-Balinese musical sources in kreasi beleganjur with great enthusiasm and seemingly little ambivalence is Sukarata. From the inception of the genre in 1986, his competition showpieces have normally included compositional "vignettes" inspired by one form or another of non-Balinese music, from Sundanese *jaipongan* of West Java to American marching band, funk, and hip-hop. He has been criticized by some and praised by others for his musical cosmopolitanism. In his own view, it is simply an expression of who he is: as a person, a musician, and a Balinese Indonesian.

Sukarata has had a deeper personal involvement with Western popular music forms than have the great majority of his peers in the Denpasar musical elite. His musical tastes are eclectic, as is evidenced by his listing of Pat Boone (whom he inadvertently refers to as "Fat Boone") and The Police among his favorite musical artists. Until recently, he frequented the discotheques of Kuta and Sanur, developing a passion for the rhythmic grooves and textures of various Western and Indonesian popular dance music styles.

Sukarata's compositional innovations in the kreasi beleganjur medium have drawn significantly on his broad-based musical tastes and experiences, as is exemplified in the concluding segments of his composition "Beleganjur Padma Mudra," the 1988 LBPB championship-winning piece created for the beleganjur club of Banjar Tatasan Kaja, Denpasar.

The last three pukulans of the Pengecet of "Padma Mudra" are transcribed in example 31 (CD #31).

Example 31.   Foreign influences: Pengecet, "Beleganjur Padma Mudra" (Sukarata). A dot over a note indicates a stopped, or damped, stroke. An asterisk represents a "cupped" stroke produced by pressing the edge of one cymbal into the center "bell" of the other.

Example 31. (*Continued*)

Example 31.   (*Continued*)

Example 31. (*Continued*)

Example 31. (*Continued*)

Example 31. (*Continued*)

Example 31.   (*Continued*)

The first pukulan of the transcription, which begins at "A," is entitled "Brek Dan," Sukarata's creolized pronunciation of "break dance." According to the composer, the rhythmic design of "Brek Dan" was directly inspired by American funk and rap music he heard in the discos during the mid- to late 1980s, when break-dance styles originating in African American hip-hop culture of several years prior spawned a new dance craze in the nightclubs of Bali's tourist enclaves. Sukarata's beleganjur gloss on funk and rap rhythms is not linked to any particular Western piece of music; it is, rather, an impressionistic vignette that cleverly adapts a generic, slow-tempoed (half-time) funk drumset (or perhaps drum machine) groove to the context of beleganjur drum and cymbal rhythms.

At the commencement of "Brek Dan" ("A"), a constant quarter-note rhythm produced by the cymbals, the reyong, and the lanang drum together (the latter playing left-hand "pak" strokes) outlines a standard hi-hat cymbal-type pattern. (This rhythm would normally be notated in one-measure units of sixteenth notes rather than in four-measure units of quarter notes in a conventional drumset transcription.) The open and closed strokes on the reyong kettles (played with the wooden ends of the mallets), together with the divided rhythmic pattern of the cymbal part (four players performing the "stems down" notes, the other four the "stems up" notes), approximate the differing timbres of open and closed hi-hat strokes. Meanwhile, the subdividing wadon drum part effects a doubling of the basic rhythmic rate, evoking the feel of slow funk tunes in which the hi-hat "doubles up the rhythm" and at the same time maintaining the beleganjur convention of having unison rhythms preceded by anticipatory drum strokes. The syncopated funk "bass drum" rhythm is located in the low-pitched open "dag" strokes of the wadon drum part, while the back-beats and syncopated accents of a "snare drum" part are converted to open "dug" strokes on the lanang drum. The same beleganjur-to-drumset instrument correspondences are maintained through the section commencing at "B," where the rhythmic "doubling" effect subtly implied at "A" intensifies due to a more active drum accent pattern. Contrast between the two sections also occurs as a result of the altered musical role of the reyong at "B," whose quarter-note motion suddenly takes on a melodic rather than purely rhythmic function. Each of the three statements of "B" climaxes with a "break," notated in the eighth measure of the passage. Finally, this break leads to a conventionally beleganjur-like extended buildup to the "Brek Dan's" final angsel, which arrives at "D."

Example 32 represents a drumset "translation" of the "A" and "B" portions of the kendang and cengceng parts of "Brek Dan," employing the beleganjur-to-drumset instrumental correspondences outlined in the foregoing analysis.

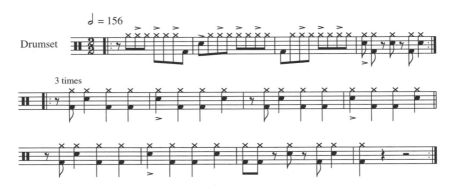

Example 32.   Drumset "translation" of Sukarata's "Brek Dan"

In including this translation, my intention is to evoke a sense of the sound Sukarata may have heard in his head as he transformed his impressions of Western drum beats into beleganjur rhythms and timbres. The bass drum part is notated in the bottom space of the staff, the snare drum in the middle, and the hi-hat on the top (in "x"-headed notes). (I have taken the liberty of adding accent patterns idiomatic of funk-style drumming.)

Returning now to example 31, "Brek Dan" is followed by a pukulan of a very different character. The brief, decelerating transitional passage heard at "D" presents a melodic motive in the reyong part that proves deceptive. It creates the illusion that Sukarata is for some reason setting up a second pengawak to be interpolated into the middle of the Pengecet. The melodic treatment of the reyong at "E," along with the relaxed tempo, initially reinforces this illusion, but it soon becomes evident that something other than a pengawak is being developed. Again, the listener is transported to a "foreign" musical world through the familiar medium of beleganjur sound, this time through a vignette based on the popular dance music style of West Java (Sunda) known as *jaipongan*.[17]

As with "Brek Dan," the relationship of Sukarata's "Jaipongan" pukulan and genuine jaipongan music is more impressionistic than literal; "Jaipongan" represents a stylistic gloss rather than an arrangement of a specific Sundanese piece. The original's sound quality and character are appropriated to the gamelan beleganjur through the clever use of specific kinds of rhythms, melodies, and instrumental techniques (as well as choreography) that are evocative: a staccato, syncopated interlocking ostinato figure in the cymbal section that emphasizes "backbeat" accents; a repeating eight-measure melodic progression in the reyong part whose angular contour unfolds over a lightly syncopated, recurring rhythmic pattern; and a rhythmic motif featuring alternating open and closed strokes between the two drums (see, for example, mm. 2–3 of "E"), by means of which a distinctive pitch-bending effect characteristic of jaipongan drumming is approximated.[18] The playfully exaggerated choreography executed by the musicians gently caricatures the subtle eroticism inherent in actual jaipongan dance style, which achieved great popularity in Balinese discotheques in the late 1980s.

Sukarata's "Jaipongan" is a crowd-pleaser, enjoyed and appreciated for its novelty and clever wit. Contest adjudicators, however, have sometimes been skeptical, claiming that it is too lighthearted and undermines the essential heroic spirit of kreasi beleganjur. Sukarata scoffs at such criticisms. "It's a good pukulan," he says. "It's fun and it's different, and I think it has helped groups win more often than it has caused them to lose."

After its adventurous forays into American and Sundanese musical territories, "Beleganjur Padma Mudra" finally comes home to Bali in Sukarata's "Tektekan" (beginning at "G" of the transcription), a pukulan loosely based on the musical style of a type of Balinese gamelan in which bamboo slit-drums *(tektekan)* perform interlocking rhythms similar to those heard in beleganjur cymbal interplay. "Tektekan" segues directly to the Pekaad, or Coda, which arrives at "H" and builds to a rousing finale.

Musical cosmopolitanism such as that found in the concluding sections of "Beleganjur Padma Mudra" is a trademark of the Sukarata kreasi beleganjur style. It is a reflection of his personal musical tastes and preferences, and perhaps also of his notion of what "Balinese identity" and "Balinese culture" comprise within the nationalized and internationalized spheres of contemporary Balinese life.

Musical works embody the perspectives and ideals of their creators: personal and communal; aesthetic, cultural, and ideological. Analyzing the ways in which composers such as Sukarata, Asnawa, and Suandita choose and develop musical materials provides insights into the techniques and creative processes involved in kreasi beleganjur composition. But as I have tried to illustrate, it also moves us toward understandings of who the people who make the music are, and of what matters to them both as individuals and as representatives of a highly complex contemporary Balinese culture.

Gerak: Music in Motion

Kreasi beleganjur composers do not just create musical works; they are also responsible for teaching their music to the groups that perform it in competitions (see chapter 7) and for inventing the choreographic sequences executed by the musicians. Choreography, or *gerak,* is an integral aspect of beleganjur composition. As Michael Tenzer (1991, 12–13) has observed, Balinese dance and music are "two art forms wedded in spirit, nuance, structure and even terminology. Balinese choreography, in its purest interpretation, is a detailed and subtle, physical embodiment of the music that accompanies it. Music and dance together are a mutually reflective duet—two realizations of the same abstract beauty, each clothed in the attributes of its form."

In most Balinese genres, this "mutually reflective duet" involves the performance of both dancers and musicians, but in kreasi beleganjur the musicians *are* the dancers to a unique degree.[19] The "physical embodiment of the music" through choreography occurs within the musical performance itself, where movement is used to highlight, enhance, contextualize, integrate, and even comment upon aspects of the music's spirit, character, and formal structure. "The music comes first," composer I Wayan Rai explained to me in 1992, "but [the choreography] is very important. It is really the physical indication of how well the musicians feel the music. It should have a feeling of naturalness, of having come out of the music."

The prescribed purposes of gerak are, first, to animate the heroic spirit of the music; and, second, to enhance the spectacle and excitement of the musical performance. Most of the choreographic sequences are devoted to rather serious-minded symbolic depictions of military action; they evoke the essentialized martial heroism identified with the kepahlawanan ideal. Such sequences bear a close resemblance to (and may in some instances be derived from) the stylized army-like formations of certain ancient ritual dances, especially Baris Gedé, in which martial movements and war cries figure prominently in a ritualized representation of royal Balinese armies of bygone eras (see Bandem and deBoer 1995, 18–21).

Most active in gerak are the cengceng players. Swinging and twirling their cymbals through the air, moving quickly from one formation to another, forming a ring and circling around the two drummers at its center, and clashing cymbals with their neighbors, the eight *juru cengceng* engage in carefully coordinated sequences of energetic movements, poses, and stances intended to replicate the battle-like postures and actions of noble warriors, from swashbuckling to martial arts maneuvers. In pengawak sections, their movements become more subtle and graceful, but should nonetheless remain strong in their evocation of the appropriately kepahlawanan spirit.

The drummers, especially the lanang player, are the other central figures in beleganjur choreographic presentations. Their cues and signals to the rest of the ensemble become dramatically exaggerated and stylized in contest performances, adding visual flair and energy to the demonstrasi. During "drum feature" passages, such as awit-awits, "Jagul," and jejagulans, the kendang players engage in choreographed interactions with each other, sometimes involving the other musicians as well. One especially popular sequence features the two drummers approaching each other from opposite sides of the performance area until they meet face-to-face at its center. The wadon player kneels down on one knee, while the lanang player remains standing but leans forward until the two drums are in perfect vertical alignment. This "locking together" of the male and female kendangs is an expression of their essential unity and cooperation, a visual correlate of the ideal of total interdependence symbolized in the interlocking rhythms of the drumming part (Asnawa, pers. comm., 1995).

The roles of the reyong section in kreasi beleganjur choreography are typically limited and understated, those of the ponggang and gong players even more so. According to Asnawa, the entire hierarchical structure is army-like: "The kendang are the generals and the cengceng are the soldiers. The reyong are [like military personnel] who work behind the scenes. They are important, but not so flashy. And the gongs are there to provide the foundation" (pers. comm., 1992).

The one key instrument missing from Asnawa's analogy is the kajar (kempluk). Clowning is an important component of most Balinese theatrical forms and other performance genres, and a clowning role often finds its way into contest beleganjur choreography through the antics of the kajar player. Comical movements, gestures, and facial expressions, mocking impersonations of other musicians or audience members, and any number of slapstick-like routines may be worked into the kajar player's performance, so long as these do not interfere with his principal responsibility of marking out the music's basic pulse with rock-steady assurance. The humor and wit of a good kajar player can add much to a performance, increasing a group's audience appeal and thus its prospects for competitive success.

The kajar player may be the designated clown of the beleganjur army, but he is seldom the only member who contributes a sense of humor to the choreographic presentation of a contest beleganjur performance. The earnest martial heroism idealized in the majority of group gerak sequences is occasionally counterbalanced, at least briefly, by comical, sometimes satirical, routines. Playful choreographic caricatures of legendary nobles and warriors may be used to poke fun at the lofty conventions and ideals of the more standard kepahlawanan characterizations. Even sexually suggestive antics, subtle and not so subtle, may be included: pelvic thrusts, gyrations, protruding backsides turned toward the audience.

All of this is generally deemed acceptable by contest audiences and judges alike. The humor speaks to an irrepressible youthful spirit that characterizes the teenage boys and young men with whom kreasi beleganjur is identified. It is, in effect, part and parcel of the young warrior's *berani,* or "brave," persona; as Wikan has written, "Berani has connotations of being challenging, unruly, even obstinate. It is fitting in men, on occasion and within limits" (1990, 295 n. 17). It is also consistent with the long-established theatrical clowning conventions referred to earlier, in which satire and sexual innuendo often figure prominently.[20] Employed judiciously, the right touch of irreverence in a choreographic presentation can improve a group's chances of winning a beleganjur contest. But the line between good and bad taste, between clever wit and desecration of the kepahlawanan ideal, is a fine one, and its cross-ing, whether perceived as intentional or inadvertent, can lead to a group's demotion in the contest standings or to an outright disqualifi-cation (see Bakan 1998b). In their roles as choreographers and teachers, beleganjur composers must therefore take great care in designing gerak sequences for competition performances and in training the young mu-sicians with whom they work to perform with appropriately tempered exuberance. As with the incorporation of foreign musical elements or the composition of long and complex pengawaks, advantageous novelty value and credibility-destroying overindulgence can prove to be just a hair's-breadth away from one another where the assessment of gerak is concerned, and being able to predict where the line will fall is no easy matter.

The intersection at which culture, ideology, and creative musical and choreographic expression meet in kreasi beleganjur is a congested one, a space where the normative appearance of order is occasionally disrupted by collisions, some predictable and others not. As we move in the forthcoming chapters more deeply into lives and institutions be-hind the music, we will encounter some of the myriad personal, social, and political complexities that underlie the kinds of musical choices, preferences, possibilities, and restrictions addressed in the preceding discussion.

Four

Two Musicians: I Ketut Sukarata, I Ketut Gedé Asnawa

Of the many fine beleganjur groups that competed in the original Lomba Beleganjur Puputan Badung of 1986, those of two Denpasar banjars, Belaluan Sadmerta and Kaliungu Kaja, were judged to be above the rest. These ensembles were directed by Sukarata and Asnawa, respectively. Today these two musicians are among the most sought-after beleganjur composer/teachers in Bali; in addition, both have served on adjudication committees for prestigious beleganjur contests. Asnawa, in particular, has been a perennial presence on major contest juries and has worked in various capacities on government projects connected with beleganjur contest administration and development island-wide. Though Sukarata's involvement in administrative activities has been minimal, he has been more active than Asnawa in recent years as a teacher and coach. Several of the groups prepared under his direction have won major contest championships, and the others have consistently been ranked highly in competition standings.

Beyond being major contributors to kreasi beleganjur, Sukarata and Asnawa have much else in common. They were both born into musical families in Denpasar in the mid-1950s and grew up in homes less than three blocks apart. As youths, they enjoyed a close friendship and musical relationship, especially during a period when they lived together while Asnawa was studying with Pak Beratha, his mentor and Sukarata's father. Asnawa, too, looked to Beratha as a father figure, and is actually related to both him and Sukarata through marriage. The culmination of Sukarata's and Asnawa's youthful partnership occurred in 1978, when the pair led Badung regency's entry in the first annual Bali Arts Festival gong kebyar competition to the contest championship, serving as the group's drummers.

Here, though, the similarities end. Sukarata and Asnawa share a past and continue to live in closely connected musical, familial, and social worlds, but they are otherwise a study in contrasts. Asnawa has risen to prominence through the official channels of the modern conservatory system to become an established and highly respected composer, educator, and scholar. He is employed as a government-appointed music faculty member by the SMKI and STSI conservatories and is one of the few Balinese musicians to hold a Master of Arts degree from a U.S. university. Performances of his compositions in foreign countries and teaching engagements at several North American universities have led to his international reputation as a representative of Balinese musical culture. Asnawa is a leading composer in the areas of kebyar, musik kontémporér, and kreasi lelambatan, as well as kreasi beleganjur, and he has conducted important scholarly research on the Balinese gamelan gambuh as well (see Asnawa 1991). By virtue of his many achievements, he has gained acceptance into the elite ranks of Denpasar musical society, where government affiliations and sponsorship calibrate measures of success.

Sukarata's position in the Denpasar musical hierarchy is an odd and ambiguous one. In a culture where family lineage has traditionally been a principal factor in social determinations of musical talent and prestige, he is heir to a regal musical legacy, being a son of the revered Beratha and a grandson of the venerable I Gedé Regog. Moreover, in a society saturated with exceptional musicians, his status as one of the truly great kebyar and beleganjur drummers of his generation is commonly acknowledged.

But in the competitive modern musical world of Denpasar, where advanced degrees and conservatory or other government appointments have become the primary criteria by which the ranks of professional musicians are defined, Sukarata is a fish out of water. He is, by his own description, a *seniman alam,* or "natural artist," a "self-taught" musician born into a generation that prizes formal musical education and degrees. He never finished elementary school and does not hold a steady job. His freelance musical career is marked by chronic instability, since the Balinese cultural economy is not set up to support musicians operating outside the purview of either government affiliation or full-time employment in the tourist industry. Sukarata's consummate musical skills and esteemed pedigree are recognized and respected by representatives of the upper echelon of Denpasar's musical society, but Sukarata himself is both of their world and excluded from it; it may be his birthright to belong, but he has lived outside the standards and expectations of his peers and has suffered the consequences.

In profoundly different ways, Asnawa and Sukarata have used kreasi beleganjur to define who they are: as musicians; as members of families, banjars, musical communities, and social networks; and as representatives of both Balinese culture and the Indonesian nation. As they have mapped and navigated the terrain of an important new musical genre, they have also been shaped by it. Their experiences, achievements, and perspectives fundamentally inform an understanding of kreasi beleganjur and its world, and at a more general level provide insights into how a music lives in the lives of its makers.

I Ketut Sukarata
Life History

I Ketut Sukarata was born on 12 April 1954 in Banjar Belaluan Sadmerta, Denpasar, to I Wayan Beratha and Ni Madé Sukri. He and his wife, Ni Mas Putra Mahandayani, have been married for over twenty years and have three daughters: Ni Putu Duniari, born in 1975; Ni Madé Ira Handayani, born in 1976; and Ni Nyoman Dewi Ernawati, born in 1981. They are also grandparents. "I've got three kids and one grandchild—all girls, no boys," Sukarata jokingly complained to me in 1995 just after hearing that his second daughter, Madé, was pregnant. "And now there's one more from Madé on the way, but so far none with an *ékor*" (lit., "tail," slang for "penis").

When he was a small child, Sukarata and several of his siblings were moved from his father's home to his paternal grandfather's after Beratha left Sukri to marry another woman. Grandfather Regog sold gamelans, and gamelan music was a constant presence in his household. There was always an abundance of instruments on hand, and the children, especially the boys, treated them as their personal toys. Figuring out the melodies and interlocking patterns they heard at the local gamelan rehearsals became a favorite pastime for Sukarata and his big brother Sudhama, and by age nine young Sukarata had already developed prodigious musical skills. It was around this time that he acquired the nickname "Tutnang," short for "Ketut Kelenang." As the story goes, Pak Regog gave the boy a *kelenang,* a very small gong, as a gift. He liked his new toy so much that he took to running around the neighborhood and banging on it at all hours of the day. Sukarata is still called "Tutnang" by his friends.

When Tutnang was eleven, his grandfather gave him another present, a miniature kendang, explaining that it was "a special drum, just for him and not for anybody else." Tutnang took to the drum with great enthusiasm, and when his grandfather would play with the gamelan at the balé banjar, he would always watch and listen to the old man carefully and try to play along. Everything was informal. Drumming was just a part of everyday life, and it is perhaps for this reason that Sukarata conceives of himself as musically "untrained" and his musicianship as *alam,* "natural." He denies ever having "learned" or "studied" music; music just "entered him," he claims, adding that it could not have been otherwise given his inherited attributes and the environment in which he was raised. "Studying" music was the province of others, of individuals such as Asnawa, I Komang Astita, and I Wayan Suweca, who grew up with Sukarata in a burgeoning community of young Denpasar musicians but moved in a very different direction after becoming involved as teenagers with the musical culture of the conservatories. Sukarata sees irony in the fact that his own father, as a leading founder and teacher at first the KOKAR (now SMKI) performing arts high school and later the ASTI (now STSI) college of the arts, came to be a patriarchal mentor to all of these other musicians, to the eventual leaders of a musical establishment that would ultimately relegate Sukarata himself to its margins.

One of Sukarata's older brothers, I Nyoman Yuda, became part of this establishment, studying music at STSI and securing a position with the Ministry of Education and Culture. (Yuda's son, I Gedé Yudartha, is now on the music faculty of STSI.) In recounting the story of his life, however, Sukarata never mentioned Pak Yuda to me. The only brother about whom he ever spoke was Sudhama, a seniman alam like himself. More than anyone else, it was Sudhama who he claims was responsible for nurturing and inspiring his musical development. To the extent that he is willing to acknowledge having been taught music at all, Sukarata credits Sudhama as his teacher, and Sudhama was much more to him as well.

"I was very, very close to Wayan [Sudhama]," Sukarata told me during a 1995 conversation at his home, the tone of his voice revealing the great sadness he still feels over the tragic loss of his brother and best friend. "We slept in the same bed; we were never apart. He was my drum partner, my favorite partner. And he taught me gamelan." Sudhama's death from cancer in 1990 at age forty-two devastated Sukarata, and deprived the Denpasar musical community of one of its most gifted and charismatic leaders.

Sukarata's academic career was short-lived. By his own recollection, he left school at age twelve before completing the fifth grade; others claim that he was even younger. His passions for playing gamelan, hunting and fishing, nighttime socializing, and attending cockfights were not conducive to academic success. "At that time, I never had time to go to

school because what I really wanted to do was play gamelan," he recalls. "Also, I liked to go out at night with my friends and go fishing
and hunting. We would hunt squirrels. We'd cook them up as *saté* or in
a soup. Delicious. Better than goat! School wasn't for me. I just didn't
like it."

Interestingly, it was fishing that most inspired Sukarata's musical
creativity when he was a young teenager. He remembers coming up
with one inventive rhythmic idea after another while idling away the
hours at the local stream. The results of such rhythmic play and experimentation, he claims, reside at the heart of the distinctive kendang improvisations and kreasi beleganjur compositions for which he is now
known.

At age fourteen, in 1968, Sukarata was invited to join his banjar's
gamelan club. During this period, the sekehe of Belaluan Sadmerta,
under the guidance of Regog and the leadership of Beratha, was one of
the leading gamelan organizations in Bali (see Tenzer 1991, 80). By the
time Sukarata joined, Sudhama and Yuda were already members; the
group thus comprised the talents of three generations of one of modern
Bali's great musical families. Initially Sukarata played *kantilan* (a small
metallophone) and then *pemadé* (a larger metallophone), but within a
year he had been promoted to playing kendang along with Sudhama.
Since then he has served Belaluan Sadmerta exclusively as a drummer,
and both inside and outside the banjar he has rarely performed on any
other instrument since 1974. He admits to occasionally desiring the opportunity to play something else, if only for the sake of variety, but what
is expected of him precludes that possibility. "I always must play kendang," he states matter-of-factly, "because my friends demand that of
me." Between 1968 and 1990, Sukarata's principal drumming partner
was always Sudhama, although he was also paired with other drummers
on occasion, performing with the likes of Suweca, Asnawa, and his
close friend I Wayan Jaya at various festivals, competitions, and other
special performances outside the banjar context.

In 1971, Sukarata performed outside of Bali for the first time, playing with a gong kebyar group that toured Java as representatives of the
Denpasar Council of the Arts. A year later he again visited Java, this
time as a "ringer" kantilan player in a group otherwise composed of
KOKAR students that was organized by Pak Beratha for a performance
at the international Festival Ramayana in Surabaya. The year 1974 saw
Sukarata's first performance as a drummer at a major Balinese arts festival, the Badung Topéng Festival. Pak Suweca was his drumming partner on that occasion.

A source of great personal pride for Sukarata is the musical relationship he had with I Gedé Manik, the individual primarily responsible for
revolutionizing Balinese gamelan music in the early twentieth century
through his pioneering innovations as a kebyar composer. Pak Beratha
had introduced his son to the great north Balinese kebyar master. Manik
was considerably older than Beratha, but the two were longtime drumming partners and lifelong friends. When Manik needed a teacher in
1975 to direct a kebyar group in his native Jagaraga, he asked Beratha
for a reference, and Beratha recommended Sukarata. Manik invited the
young drumming virtuoso to Jagaraga for a six-week period and was so
impressed by his abilities that he ended up enlisting him as his drumming partner for numerous performances. Sukarata deeply cherishes
the memory of one such occasion, when Manik told him that with the
possible exception of Beratha himself, he had never worked with a finer
kendang player (Sukarata, pers. comm., 1995).

Sukarata toured Europe for the first time in 1975 as Manik's drumming partner in an all-star group organized by Beratha. The ensemble's
personnel was unusual for that time, being composed exclusively of
seniman alam during a period when touring Balinese musical troupes
were almost invariably dominated by conservatory faculty members
and students. The nine-nation tour also featured performances by ensembles from Central Java and Sumatra. "We went to Greece, Holland,
Austria, England, and five other countries," Sukarata recalls, "but I
don't remember what the other five were."

In 1978, as was noted earlier, Sukarata joined Asnawa in leading
Badung regency to the championship of the first annual Bali Arts Festival gong kebyar competition. "I liked playing with Tutdé [Asnawa]
very much, very much indeed," Sukarata once told me. But the two
have not been drumming partners since. The divergent paths of their
lives over the past two decades have both limited their opportunities for
collaboration and led to interpersonal tensions and rivalries that have
greatly strained their formerly close friendship. This has effectively prevented them from pursuing opportunities to work together even where
the potential might have existed.

Through the 1980s, Sukarata maintained an active performing and
teaching career. He returned to Europe in 1986, leading a gamelan tektekan group on a monthlong tour of Germany. This, of course, was also
the year in which he led Belaluan Sadmerta to victory in the original
LBPB. While he took great pride in the championship, events in the
aftermath gave Sukarata cause for bitterness. He was hurt and humili-
ated when Bali Record chose to feature the second-place group from

Kaliungu Kaja on the first commercial kreasi beleganjur recording. As we have seen, that recording, which featured Asnawa's "Beleganjur Angga Yowana," proved highly influential, setting the course for the new genre's development for years to come. Beyond Denpasar, it was not Belaluan Sadmerta but Kaliungu Kaja that became the central icon of the new musical style, and even within Denpasar, the popular recording likely caused many to forget that Kaliungu Kaja had not been the contest's champions.

Despite the injurious snub, Sukarata's services as a composer and teacher were in great demand among prospective LBPB competing groups of the late 1980s, and the ensembles he chose to work with were invariably successful. Tegal finished second in 1987, Tatasan Kaja won the 1988 championship, and Belong Sanur earned a third-place ranking in 1989. (Outside of the original 1986 contest, the 1988 LBPB was the only one in which Sukarata actually performed.)

In 1990 and 1991, Sukarata did not work with beleganjur groups, devoting his energies instead to preparing men's and women's kebyar ensembles for performances in the Bali Arts Festival gamelan competitions of those years. He also toured Korea for two weeks in 1991, performing there with a government-organized ensemble that also included Asnawa and Beratha. Two years later he would journey to eastern Asia again to teach gamelan at Japan's Sangkokan University.

Nineteen ninety-two witnessed a triumphant return to the beleganjur contest world for Sukarata, when he and fellow drummer I Wayan Jaya led Tatasan Kaja, the 1988 LBPB champions, to a prestigious victory in another major contest. The event was held in Denpasar but featured leading groups from all over Bali. Sukarata also prepared a rather interesting group for the LBPB that year—an ensemble representing not a banjar or a desa, but a major Kuta Beach tourist hotel, the Kartika Plaza.[1] All of the musicians were hotel employees.

In both 1992 and 1993, Sukarata was honored by being selected to play kendang wadon for Badung in the Bali Arts Festival kebyar competition. Badung won the 1992 championship and finished third the following year. Sukarata received a long-overdue token of recognition for his years of distinguished achievement in kreasi beleganjur in 1994: an appointment to the adjudication committee of the LBPB, to which Jaya was also appointed. He and Jaya additionally served as coaches and advisors for the 1994 and 1995 Badung ensembles featured in the Bali Arts Festival kebyar contest. Both groups finished second. The 1995 loss, to Kodya Denpasar, was an especially bitter one for Sukarata, and

it fueled the fires of his long-escalating rivalry with his old friend Asnawa, one of the principal coaches for Kodya. Recently, in 1997, Sukarata toured North America for the first time as a member of a large
Badung government music-and-dance troupe that performed in Vancouver, Montreal, Boston, and Los Angeles.

Sukarata's lengthy list of accomplishments, distinctions, and honors
would suggest that he occupies a secure and well-entrenched position
within the Denpasar/Badung musical elite. But as the following discussion aims to illustrate, his is a largely disenfranchised voice that exists
at or beyond the margins of the inner circle.

"Where Is My Cassette?" Commercial Recordings and the Marginalization of Sukarata

I Ketut Sukarata is a gracious and charming man, warm and generous
by nature. But there is a contrastingly bitter and defensive side of his
personality that surfaces occasionally. He believes that he has been
unfairly treated and under-appreciated by the powers that be within
Bali's Denpasar-centered musical establishment, and when he is compelled to reflect upon events he regards as emblematic of the injustices
he has suffered, or to respond to new situations that salt the wounds of
his self-perceived marginalization, his normally bright demeanor dark-
ens dramatically.

The subject of commercial beleganjur recordings is one that invariably invokes Sukarata's ire. The facts are simple enough. The championship sekehe of every LBPB has recorded a commercial cassette for
either Bali Record or Maharani Records, with two exceptions: the 1986
champions from Belaluan Sadmerta and the 1988 winners from Tatasan
Kaja—in other words, the two sekehes guided to victory by Sukarata,
the individual who in turn holds the dubious distinction of being the
only LBPB championship-winning composer not represented on a recording. This is particularly conspicuous because, in addition to the
various championship groups, several non-champion LBPB contenders
have made recordings over the years as well; and in Sukarata's view, the
irony of the situation is rendered all the more poignant by the fact that
several composers whose beleganjur works *have* been recorded studied
the craft of beleganjur composition with him.

"Suandita, Murna—all the young composers who win the cham-
pionships, who make the cassettes—they all come to me for beleganjur," Sukarata told me during a 1995 conversation at his home.[2] "They

all come to study with me, to learn my style, my pukulan. But Bali Record, Maharani . . . aaah, they take them [for the recordings]. Me? Where is my cassette?" he says with an ironic chuckle, waving his hand in disgust. "Well, forget that. I can't worry about that."

But he does worry about it, and his disenchantment with the situation does indeed seem justified. The absence of Sukarata's compositions from the shelves of Balinese cassette shops is not likely the consequence of some accidental oversight by the recording companies. Sukarata is indisputably one of the leading composers in the kreasi beleganjur arena (a good example of his innovative style may be heard on selection #32 of the accompanying CD), and the groups that have won championships performing his music are among Bali's finest. The granting of a recording contract to the annual LBPB champion has been a virtual given, and the fact that not one but two championship groups associated with Sukarata have failed to gain an opportunity to record would certainly appear to support his conviction that his omission from the kreasi beleganjur discography is not arbitrary.

It seems reasonable to surmise that Sukarata has been marginalized by the government-centered culture elite that dominates Denpasar/ Badung musical society and defines the hegemonic center of Balinese musical culture at large. His exclusion from the ranks of recorded beleganjur composers is but one example of this, albeit a rather glaring one. But why has Sukarata been marginalized? A closer look at certain priorities and complexities of the Denpasar musical "community" itself may provide partial answers to this question.

Kreasi beleganjur has been conceived and promoted from its beginning as a banjar-centered musical phenomenon. Beleganjur contests present an opportunity for the playing out of inter-banjar rivalries, for healthy competition between representatives of the different neighborhood associations within an area or region. The scale of contest events varies, and the banjar-based model has in some cases been adapted to alternate contexts such as school-group or interregional lombas; still, the format of banjar groups squaring off against one another, established with the original 1986 LBPB, remains the defining standard.

Beleganjur contests, then, at least ostensibly, are events by and for the communities that produce them. Kreasi beleganjur is not taught in the government conservatories; moreover, conservatory-affiliated musicians, whether faculty members or students, are barred from performing in the contests. They are, however, permitted to compose for, teach, and administratively direct competing groups, and it is largely on account of this situation that kreasi beleganjur's identity as a community-centered music has become problematized, especially in its "native" musical community, Denpasar.

As we saw in chapter 2, Denpasar has a dual status in the kreasi beleganjur world. At a localized level, it is the center of an expansive musical "community" comprising hundreds of banjars in the urban area and surrounding regions of Badung, a community that in a sense is reified by the institution of the LBPB itself; at a broader level, it is the central icon for a Bali-wide kreasi beleganjur phenomenon. Denpasar is the source: the birthplace of the genre, the primary locus for the music's creative growth, and the center from which the contest tradition has spread. While Denpasar musicians have been increasingly influenced by musical developments in other areas of Bali over the last few years, it is still to Denpasar that Bali as a whole looks for innovations, progress, and standards of excellence in kreasi beleganjur. And it is the commercial recordings of the top Denpasar groups, especially LBPB champions, that largely define the celebrated and influential "Denpasar style."

Theoretically, all banjars within the Denpasar/Badung community have equal opportunities to achieve success and receive honors in the competitive domain of kreasi beleganjur. Yet in reality, LBPB champions and the few other groups who have "represented" Denpasar beleganjur through the medium of commercial recordings have mainly hailed from banjars that include highly prominent musicians among their membership—musicians such as Asnawa, Suandita, I Madé Murna, and I Wayan Sinti who are affiliated with the government conservatories and the Ministry of Education and Culture especially. Furthermore, the sekehes from outside the Denpasar/Badung hub who have had the highest levels of success, in some cases defeating the best Denpasar groups in major interregional competitions, have most often come from the native banjars of conservatory-affiliated musicians as well (I Wayan Rai, I Nyoman Windha, and Pandé Gedé Mustika, to list a few examples).

Esteemed and highly visible musicians such as those noted above have been actively involved when sekehes representing their native banjars perform in beleganjur contests. Their participation is essentially expected as a service to the banjar community. They may function as composers, teachers, coaches, administrators, or in some combination of these roles. Neither their specific contributions nor those of any other individuals, however, tend to be explicitly acknowledged relative to the group's contest performances or successes; and even on commercial beleganjur cassettes, composers *(penata tabuh)* and other behind-the-scenes personnel are unacknowledged but for perhaps a credit line in the tiniest of print. It is the sekehe as a whole, and to an even greater extent the entire banjar represented by that sekehe, whose accomplishments are celebrated in a contest victory. Individuals do not and should not stand out in the public images that accompany competitive success, for it is the group, and by extension the community, whose achievements are to be emphasized. Thus, while there is clearly a correspondence between sekehes that win beleganjur contests and banjars that include within their constituencies members of Denpasar's government-affiliated musical elite, the connection is rarely noted, at least publicly. To the extent that it does receive attention, it is treated as a matter of course: obviously, a master musician's commitment to an aspiring beleganjur group will bode well for that sekehe's competitive prospects, and in Denpasar the inner circle of the musical elite is populated mainly by individuals who hold government appointments.

Such logic is not lost on Sukarata, but he is not willing to accept that it fully explains the overwhelming dominance of sekehes whose banjars are home to representatives of the officially sanctioned musical elite. In his view, this dominance is not merely the product of a meritocracy premised on objective comparative assessments of different community musical organizations; it is, rather, at least partially attributable to politically motivated agendas centered around the statuses and reputations of particular individuals. When Sukarata speaks to this issue, he implies that it is likely due to these same agendas that neither his beleganjur music nor the championship groups with whom he has been associated over the years are represented on recordings. It is such agendas, too, he believes, that prevented him from being appointed to the jury of the LBPB until 1994, that account for his not holding a position on Badung's Pembina Tabuh (the honorary council consisting of the region's most distinguished musicians), and that have caused him to be denied numerous other deserved opportunities and recognitions over the course of his musical career.

Sukarata does not explicitly identify or delineate the specific agendas that have in his opinion worked against him, and it sometimes appears that his tendency to blame "the system" for his own frustrations is a form of rationalization. But kreasi beleganjur's involvement in the politicized arena of Indonesian cultural nationalism, combined with Denpasar's central yet complexly multiple identity in the competitive beleganjur world, suggests that his suspicions may well be warranted. Beleganjur contests may be localized community events, but they are typically produced under the watchful and purposeful eye of government officials whose interests are motivated by political goals and incentives.

Sukarata is on the one hand an ideal representative of the Denpasar "school," kreasi beleganjur's central, standard-defining musical community. As a seniman alam who comes from a most distinguished Denpasar musical family, his status as a symbol of that community is particularly "pure." Unlike his government-affiliated peers, including other Denpasar-area natives such as Asnawa, Sukarata has a quintessentially "local" Denpasar musical identity. Musicians associated with the conservatories and other government arts agencies are identified not only with the particular musical traditions of their native communities, but also with an essentially pan-Balinese modern musical culture that extends outward from its Denpasar bureaucratic core to encompass the entire island, defining what Balinese music is in the eyes of the Indonesian nation and the world. Sukarata has in actuality participated extensively in this more broadly Balinese musical world centered in Denpasar, as we have already seen, but he is nonetheless perceived in Bali as a musician who belongs less to that world than to the other Denpasar, the one where people live their daily lives, working and playing and constituting a large yet geographically specific community.

Sukarata the local Denpasar community musical leader is well qualified for his designated role. His numerous contest victories and honors testify to this. He is the real thing from the real place, an important symbol and champion of kreasi beleganjur music in its most "authentic" form: the Denpasar style. In these respects he is valued both by the public and by controlling government interests, whose commitment to maintaining kreasi beleganjur's community-based image forms a paradoxical but critically important link to cultural nationalism ideology.

Sukarata, however, does not fill the bill nearly so well where kreasi beleganjur's position in the broader, pan-Balinese musical spectrum is concerned. *Because* he is not employed by the government, and because of his limited educational background, lack of a steady livelihood, and close personal and professional associations with "controversial" individuals such as I Wayan Jaya—whose maverick business ventures and bold irreverence have generated hostility among at least some factions of the empowered elite—he does not convey the officially desired image of the broadly *Balinese* musical champion. It is perhaps at least partially for this reason that his compositions have not been made available on recordings, which function importantly in Bali to objectify that which is legitimately culture and to differentiate it from that which is not (or is at least less so).

The conspicuously large percentage of recordings by beleganjur groups originating from the native banjars of highly placed, government-employed musicians may be primarily related to the exemplary musicianship of those groups, but it may also be related to the establishment's tendency to place its trust in those musicians who are most closely in tune with its values and priorities. Although the contributions of particular individuals may be de-emphasized in competitive beleganjur's public culture, their significance and impact are in actuality profound. Professional musicians employed by the official, government-sanctioned institutions bring competitive advantages to their village groups that extend beyond the purely musical domain. They are the chosen few who have been selected by the establishment to shape, propagate, and represent "Balinese culture" writ large, and it is therefore not unreasonable to infer that even the localized, community-based musical organizations that they serve, despite having no official ties to the conservatories or to other government cultural institutions, would have a distinct edge in areas where "proper" cultural representation is a leading priority.

The Balinese recording industry is one such area. Recording companies are not government agencies per se, but in Indonesia, where the line between private enterprise and political prerogative is fine and often blurry, they are deeply entrenched in the business of filling the government's cultural prescriptions. Recordings produced by companies such as Bali Record and Maharani—especially in the traditional/classical (as opposed to popular) catalogs—reify, index, and sanction Bali's musical culture in tandem with the priorities of the government arts agencies.[3] Beleganjur contests and the champions they produce may represent particular communities, but beleganjur recordings make the winners of community-based championships into icons of Balinese music in the broader sense, and it appears that the hegemonic powers have not seen fit to entrust Sukarata with such a status, or have at least found others—such as Asnawa, Suandita, Murna, and Sinti, via the successful LBPB sekehes with whom they have been associated—to be better suited to the role.

As I was told by one conservatory faculty member, Sukarata is thought by the establishment to be "too district-minded, too Denpasarminded. All he wants is Denpasar. He's always thinking only he's good, that only Denpasar is good. Whatever else is going on—in Gianyar, Karangasem, wherever—he does not recognize it. He is not objective, maybe because—you know—[he's] not so educated. Because it is like this, the government wants others to represent the beleganjur. Maybe the group of [another composer] gets a score of seven and Tutnang's group a score of eight. If [it is] like that, the government still wants to promote [the other composer's group] with a recording."

Sukarata apparently faces additional, though not unrelated, obstacles as well. Beyond actually living outside the loop of government-sanctioned musical professionalism, he is resented for doing so, or so he claims. Whether speaking about his exclusion from the ranks of recorded beleganjur composers or about other situations where apparently earned statuses, opportunities, or recognitions have been denied him, he sees his treatment as a form of punishment. Because of his lineage, he explains, and because of his exceptional musical talents, he inherited a responsibility to follow in his father's footsteps as a leader of not only the Denpasar musical community but Balinese musical culture at large. But in the transformed modern context of a musical world defined by government appointments and educational degrees, he has been unable to assume the leadership role for which he believes he was destined. Sukarata, in his own estimation, has failed to live up to the expectations of others, and for that reason he believes he has been penalized, again and again.

Flip-Flopping: Marginality, Ambivalence, and Self-Presentation

In reflecting and commenting upon his self-proclaimed marginality, Sukarata vacillates between attitudes of self-righteous indignation, feigned indifference, resigned acceptance, and self-deprecation. At times he casts himself as the heroic rebel, a superior musician of noble blood unfettered by the petty constraints and bureaucratic agendas of a misguided musical regime; at other times, though, he savagely denigrates his own musicianship, achievements, and lifestyle, especially in those instances where the accomplishments and skills of certain of his highly educated and stationed musical peers are treated as foils for his own self-perceived inadequacies, limitations, or failures.

Sometimes the superior and inferior modes of self-presentation alternate with stunning rapidity, and it is often difficult to discern whether Sukarata is expressing the way he actually feels at a given moment or is using one attitudinal stance as a rhetorical strategy for setting up another. I recall, for example, an occasion when he was visited at his home during one of my drum lessons by a man I had never met before. The man stayed for only a few minutes. After he left, Sukarata explained to me that he was a teacher at one of the conservatories, an exceptionally clever musician who not only could compose and perform in many different styles but was skilled in the use of musical notation as well.

"Me, though, I am rather stupid," Sukarata continued with a self-deprecating turn. "I only compose beleganjur, and I don't know notation at all. Those guys at [the conservatories], like him, they are so clever. They know so much more than I do." He seemed genuinely humbled and in awe, but then, unexpectedly, he changed his tune completely. "You know, Michael," he said, "I'm a better musician than he is. They just don't appreciate me, because I'm a seniman alam, because I don't have the fancy degree and all that. But I have the feeling for the music, like my father. That guy, all those guys, they all learned with Pak Beratha, but I know more of his pukulan. No one else knows as many. When Badung wants a drummer they come to me, not him. Why do you think so? But him, he's the big teacher at [the conservatory], ya?"

My initial exposure to Sukarata's "flip-flopping" self-presentational style occurred on the day I first met him, by chance, at a 1992 wedding ceremony in Seminyak, just north of the busy tourist beach communities of Legian and Kuta on Bali's southwestern coast. Just a few days into my third visit to Bali, I was riding through town on the back of a motorcycle with Marilyn when I happened to hear beleganjur music coming from behind the gates of the village temple. Curious, I asked her to let me off. I put on a temple belt (which happened to be in my shoulder bag) and wandered in tentatively.

A wedding ceremony was in progress. The beleganjur group was seated just to the right of the entrance gate in a small *balé* (open-sided, roofed pavilion structure) of the temple's outer courtyard. Their playing seemed rather lethargic. A couple of the musicians smiled at me, so I approached the balé, seating myself on the steps next to the cymbal section. The musicians continued to play for about ten minutes, then stopped to take a break.

One of the reyong players gestured for me to come over and sit with him. He introduced himself as Nyoman, handed me a glass of coffee, and asked me who I was and where I was from. I answered, then told him about my interest in beleganjur, explaining that I was writing my thesis on the subject and had had some experience playing the music during my two previous trips to Bali.

Nyoman smiled, complimented me on my Indonesian, and offered me a cigarette. I politely declined.

"Has this group performed in beleganjur contests?" I asked. My query prompted unexpected laughter from Nyoman and several of the other players, who were now following the conversation.

"No, no. This group is not commercial, just social. We are too lazy to play in the contests," Nyoman replied, inspiring further laughter.

"Do you know of any upcoming contests in this area?" I continued. He did not, but had a suggestion.

"Our *guru* [mentor], he is from Denpasar. You must speak with him."

Nyoman paused and looked out toward the courtyard. He then gestured in the direction of the older of a pair of men walking toward the balé. "Here he comes now," he announced.

The guru was a large man. He was not especially tall, but his broad shoulders, solid build, dark complexion, and charismatic bearing made it appear as though he were. As he approached, he joked with his younger companion, and each time he laughed his face lit up with a most beautifully radiant smile. Immediately upon entering the balé, he sat down on the floor, placed the kendang lanang across his lap, and began to play. From the opening note, I sensed that I was in the presence of a master musician. The quality was there in his sound, in his style; he possessed that intangible something that immediately jumps out and grabs your attention, demanding respect and admiration. Within moments, I was convinced that this man was one of the greatest drummers I had ever heard. His playing was magical, completely captivating, and when the rest of the group joined in after his stunning awit-awit introduction, it was as though they had been transformed into a completely different—and vastly better—ensemble.

At the conclusion of the performance, the guru looked over at me and smiled warmly. His acknowledgment caught me by surprise, since up to that point I had suspected he was not even aware of my presence. Nyoman introduced me as "Pak Michael," explaining that I claimed to know how to play beleganjur and to be writing some kind of a book on the topic. The guru nodded and smiled and told me that his name was Pak Ketut. He gestured for me to come and sit next to him, then picked up the kendang wadon and laid it across my lap. I had taken a few drum lessons at STSI with Pak Suweca and knew some of the basic patterns, but beyond this I was completely inexperienced in beleganjur drumming. I explained this to Pak Ketut and asked whether it might be all right if I played cengceng instead; to my surprise, he shook his head, indicating that it would not be. "It doesn't matter," he said, pushing the drum rather forcefully into my stomach. "Go ahead and try."

During my very brief course of study with Suweca, I had concentrated on transcribing some of the standard beleganjur drumming patterns and forms. My "repertoire" comprised nothing beyond a rudimentary, traditional-style awit-awit; a few regular and long angsel forms; and the opening section of one of the "Jagul" drum parts (see example 22 in chapter 3). And I had not yet fully memorized even this small corpus of musical material.

I felt desperately underprepared for the situation at hand, and reasoned that my only hope of avoiding abject humiliation rested in relying on my transcriptions to get me through. As luck would have it, they happened to be in my bag. I reached in and pulled out a shabby pad of manuscript paper. Ketut stared at the pad, apparently perplexed. The notations were scrawled haphazardly on the front and back sides of three dog-eared sheets. I tore them out and laid them down side by side in front of me. Ketut and the rest of the group stared curiously at the pages and waited patiently. Then, just when I was about ready to begin, a gust of wind caught the corner of the third sheet and sent it flying; fortunately, I was quick enough to catch it in midair. Ketut responded by impersonating my paper-grabbing performance, inspiring fits of hysterical laughter from the other musicians. This broke the tension and put me somewhat at ease.

I reassembled the pages and nodded at Ketut, indicating that I was ready to start. He smiled and gestured for me to begin. I proceeded to play a straightforward gilak pattern, and Ketut came in immediately with the interlocking part. This threw me off and caused me to stop. Embarrassed, I apologized, then started up again. Things worked out better this time. With eyes glued firmly to the page, I kept the pattern going as first Ketut and then the rest of the group joined in. With each successive cycle, I gained more self-assurance. Finally, I chanced looking up and away from the notation for a moment. Ketut caught my eye. He smiled widely and nodded enthusiastically. Apparently I was doing all right.

I loosened up, and my playing started to flow more. I was amazed at how easy it was to play with Ketut. No matter what I did—even when I faltered—he was there with me, keeping everything together and making me sound good, even when I probably did not. It seemed that if I just trusted in Ketut, it was impossible to go too far wrong. At certain moments, I even found myself losing awareness of which drum part was which altogether. Ketut seemed so in tune with my rhythmic sense that I began to feel as though I were playing both drum parts myself, or that I was not playing either of them. It was a strange and magical feeling.

Just as I felt myself really settling into the groove, I was snapped back to my formerly anxious state by a jarring and unanticipated escalation in the volume and intensity of Ketut's drumming. He was cueing the arrival of an angsel. I scanned my notations, looking desperately for the appropriate pattern, but for some reason I could not locate it. I froze up and stopped. Once again I felt embarrassed, but when I looked up to apologize, Pak Ketut was beaming excitedly.

"Bagus! Bagus!" he exclaimed, assuring me that my playing had been good, that there was nothing to worry about. He gave me a hearty thumbs-up sign, and we started up again. This time the groove felt solid right from the outset, and I managed to execute the angsel successfully as well. The basic sequence of gilak pattern to angsel was then repeated over and over and over again; we played without pause for nearly an hour. Finally Ketut cued a concluding angsel, and the performance was brought to a close.

My hands and arms were tired and sore, but I was buzzing with excitement. Playing kendang with Ketut and a real, live beleganjur ensemble was an incredible rush. I did not want the experience to end, so I asked whether we could now work "Jagul" into the little impromptu arrangement. In retrospect, this was a rather bold request, if not an odd one, given that I had only completed about half of the "Jagul" transcription.

Ketut and the group seemed glad to oblige me, and after a couple of false starts I managed to play successfully with them through to the point where my transcription ended. And there, for lack of any other apparent option, I stopped. Now it was Ketut who seemed to have been caught off guard. His eyebrows went up in a startled expression as he continued to play and signaled for me to do likewise. He had no idea what I was doing. I threw up my hands and shrugged my shoulders. "Habis!" I yelled out over the din of the ensemble, holding up the incomplete "Jagul" transcription for him to see while pointing at the blank staff lines at the bottom of the page. "There is no more."

Ketut laughed and shook his head, but he would not stop playing. He broke away from "Jagul" and started something new. To my ears, it sounded like he was improvising. I sat back and enjoyed the virtuosic display, but next thing I knew he was frantically gesturing for me to join him. "*Main, main,*" he called out. "Play, play." Play what? I wondered.

I hadn't a clue. Now Ketut played a long and complex passage, then paused and pointed his mallet at me. Apparently I was supposed to repeat what he had done, but I was completely at a loss. It was too much. I couldn't get it. I didn't even know where to begin.

Ketut persevered for a while, but my dumbfounded incompetence eventually won out. Mercifully, he signaled the ensemble to stop playing and asked me what was the matter. I told him that I was simply not clever enough to do what he wanted me to, that I would love to learn whatever it was he was trying to teach me, but that I would only be able to if I could write the music down, section by section, bit by bit. "I know this seems strange to you," I said, "but if you will let me do it this way I think I can learn well."

Ketut stared at me with a quizzical grin, leaned forward, and opened the manuscript pad to a fresh page. I pulled a pencil out of my bag and readied myself to transcribe, and at that moment an important precedent was set—one that would prove to have profound implications relative to the intercultural and interpersonal connections, confusions, negotiations, misunderstandings, and revelations that would ultimately emerge out of my musical relationship with this most outstanding musician, a relationship to which we will return in much greater detail in the later chapters of this book.

My debut lesson with Pak Ketut ended abruptly with an announcement by the wedding party host that it was time for the musicians to eat. I gratefully accepted the host's invitation to join the group for their meal, which featured a delicious *lawar* of shredded pork, vegetables, and chili peppers; various meats served *saté* style on skewers with peanut sauce; and, of course, a heaping portion of steamed rice.

After eating, the other musicians and I returned to the shade of the balé to relax and drink sweet coffee. I sat down with Ketut and the young man with whom he had arrived, whom Ketut introduced as his younger brother, Gedé Yudartha. (The two are actually cousins, as I would later discover.) I asked Ketut to tell me his full name. "It's I Ketut Sukarata," he stated, "but you can call me Tutnang, because that's what my friends call me, and you are my friend." I then asked him if he was from Seminyak. "No, I'm from Denpasar," he replied, explaining that his wife was originally from Seminyak, and that was why he was here at the wedding.

I was excited to hear that Tutnang lived in Denpasar. Up to this point in my research, my primary work had been with groups in other areas, Ubud (1989) and Kintamani (1990) in particular. My desire now, though, was to move my focus to the center of the kreasi beleganjur world, to Denpasar and the LBPB, and this chance meeting with Tut-nang seemed auspicious. My teacher, Pak Suweca, was an exceptional drummer and a Denpasar native and resident as well; but, as he himself was the first to acknowledge, he was not an *ahli beleganjur,* or "bele-ganjur specialist." Suweca had actually told me earlier that it was time for me to move on to intensive studies with one of the main Denpasar beleganjur teacher/composers, and although the name Sukarata was not familiar to me, my instincts told me that fate had likely led me to an ideal mentor and research consultant. This sense intensified all the more as my conversation with Tutnang turned to the subject of competitive beleganjur in Denpasar. He appeared to be very knowledgeable, so much so that I could not help but think that he must be centrally involved.

But when I asked Sukarata about his own beleganjur-related activi-ties, it seemed that my intuitions had been wrong. He claimed not to be an ahli beleganjur, and to have had only limited experience teaching and preparing sekehes for beleganjur contests. I was of course discour-aged by this news.

I told Sukarata about my research project in some detail now, ex-plaining that if I were to complete it successfully I would become a doctor of music, and would then be qualified to teach at a university music school in the United States—an institution like STSI, in other words—where I might someday direct my own gamelan group. I also told him that the doctoral degree I was working toward was the same type as that held by I Madé Bandem, the dean of STSI at the time. "This project is very, very important for me," I explained to him, "and to do it right I need a very good teacher, someone like you but with a deeper involvement in the Denpasar beleganjur scene. Can you recommend someone? Maybe someone you know, who you could introduce me to."

All of a sudden, Sukarata was transformed. "I am the teacher you need," he proclaimed boldly, backing up his assertion with a most im-pressive list of credentials and achievements. Three times, he stated— in 1986, 1988, and now 1992—groups under his direction had been crowned champions in the most prestigious of beleganjur contests, and even the non-champion sekehes he had coached over the years had al-ways finished near the top of the rankings. He claimed to be a most prolific beleganjur composer, noting that he had probably created "more pukulans than anyone else." Throughout Bali, he continued, he was known as one of the island's great drummers; he had played with all the best musicians, Suweca among them, and he was the son of the most revered master of them all, Pak Beratha. Then, finally, there was the matter of the conservatories: "I do not teach at STSI or SMKI," Sukarata informed me in a prideful tone, "but many of the best students from those schools, they come to my home, to study with me, many just to learn beleganjur, to know my style."

And then Sukarata told me that I too had to come study beleganjur with him. This was not presented as an invitation but rather as a command. Tomorrow, he explained, he would be back in Seminyak for the conclusion of the ceremony; we could have another lesson then, and after that my studies would continue at his home in Denpasar. In the upcoming months, he added, he would be preparing a sekehe for the LBPB. I was welcome to take part in that as well, to document the process and assist him. This, he said, would be very good for my project. Sukarata grabbed my journal, opened it to a blank page, and drew a map with directions to his home. Then he handed it back and shook my hand vigorously. "Sampai besok," he said. "Until tomorrow." He left the balé, jumped on his motorcycle, and rode away.

As I watched Sukarata drive off, I was stunned and more than a little confused by what I had just witnessed. Who was I to believe? The humble and modest Tutnang, who claimed only nominal involvement and limited competence in kreasi beleganjur; or the self-promoting and supremely confident Tutnang, whose achievements and renown in the competitive beleganjur world were apparently second to no one's? The more brazen of the two had delivered his résumé monologue with great assurance and conviction; it was hard to imagine that his impressive claims were mere fabrications. Yet if he was who he claimed to be, why had I not heard of him? Why was his name not listed on the cassette boxes of commercial beleganjur recordings? Why had he initially claimed to have little expertise or involvement in kreasi beleganjur? And why had he switched personas so rapidly and radically in the middle of our conversation?

As I came to know Sukarata and his situation, such questions became less mystifying. I had not heard of him because I had done little work in Denpasar, and outside of Denpasar it seemed that the composers and groups represented on beleganjur recordings were always the ones mentioned in connection with the vaunted Denpasar style; obviously, Sukarata did not belong in this category.

With respect to the shifting modes of self-representation, the issues were more complicated. Sukarata was who he had claimed to be in the self-assertive guise of the latter part of our conversation—the beleganjur champion and master composer/teacher, the heir to Beratha's legacy, the virtuoso drummer—but he was also the humble and unassuming individual he had been during the first part of our encounter. The more modest persona was consistent with core Balinese cultural values. Self-aggrandizement is strongly disapproved of in Bali; to sing one's own praises is categorically inappropriate in most any social situation.

Meeting me, however, posed the exception to the rule, for the simple reason that I was incapable of understanding what I ought to have been able to. It was my ignorance and cultural insensitivity, I believe, that ultimately compelled Sukarata to transform himself from a modest gentleman into an aggressive self-promoter. I failed to figure out on my own that he was the teacher I needed, and so he was forced to tell me, blatantly, in a quintessentially un-Balinese way.

And Sukarata felt that he needed me too. In his eyes, I was not the bumbling graduate student I conceived myself to be; I was, rather, "Doktor Michael" (as he soon took to calling me), an icon of the powerful cultural institutions of the West upon which Bali's own modern musical society has been largely modeled by the esteemed Dr. Bandem and his associates, the most high-ranking of whom are distinguished within the elite ranks by the graduate diplomas from American universities hanging on their office walls.

Sukarata, for all his defiantly anti-establishment sentiments, deeply desired acceptance and recognition among Denpasar's government-affiliated musical elite, as would become ever more clear through the course of our work together. He viewed me as a potential bridge between his world and that of the dominant establishment, which had at so many levels seen fit to shut him out. I fit the mold of the conservatory culture's internationalized reflection, and yet here I was, studying not at STSI but with him, Tutnang, the unappreciated, uneducated seniman alam, the heart of the *real* musical culture of Bali. I would make the others see how great he was; my book would be about him, not about them—about his beleganjur music, not theirs. Because of me, he hoped, they would have to listen. I would be Tutnang's honorary degree, his stamp of legitimacy. As he would tell me one day in 1995, some three years after our first meeting, "I know how they think of me; you know, 'He never went to school,' 'He's not clever like so-and-so,' 'He only composes beleganjur, nothing else,' and all those things. But in my music they can hear the true heroic quality of beleganjur. They know that's me and that I am a good Balinese person."

Sukarata was committed to making them hear and to making them see, and his first instinct about me and what I represented was that I could help to make this happen. And so he was compelled to let me know—directly, in a way that he could be sure I would understand— who he really was and how much I needed him. If this meant a momentary lapse in social grace and proper etiquette, so be it. I had fallen into his life serendipitously, as he had into mine, and he was not going to let me slip away. From the start, Sukarata and I liked each other, and we shared an immediate sense of musical connectedness that would grow over time; but the two of us were also drawn together by more self-centered motivations.

I Ketut Gedé Asnawa

I first met Asnawa just five days after meeting Sukarata. Again, it was a chance encounter. I was at a musik kontémporér concert at the Art Center in Denpasar and happened to run into the composer and ethno-musicologist Michael Tenzer following the show. Tenzer pointed out a slim man with a rather serious-minded, dignified look about him sitting on stage with some of the performers; he told me that this was Asnawa.

I walked up to the stage and introduced myself. I told Asnawa about my beleganjur project and asked him whether he might be kind enough to meet with me for an interview sometime.

"When would you like to meet?" he asked in perfect English.

"At your convenience," I responded.

"We can begin tonight. Come with me to my house," he said. He then hopped off the stage and walked quickly toward the exit, gesturing for me to follow him. The invitation surprised me—it was already after ten o'clock—but I was more than happy to accept.

About fifteen minutes later, we arrived at Asnawa's small, modest home in his family's house compound in Kaliungu Kaja. The house was dwarfed by a much larger, more luxurious one next to it belonging to his older brother, I Komang Astita, a composer and high-ranking administrator at STSI. I had actually visited Astita here for an interview a week earlier. At that time he had told me about his "little brother Tutdé" (Asnawa's nickname) and had encouraged me to seek him out. "He is really the one to talk to about beleganjur," Astita had remarked.

By this point in my research, Asnawa's name had been mentioned in several other contexts as well. I knew of him as the composer of "Beleganjur Angga Yowana" and as an important figure in the kreasi beleganjur world, but I was not yet aware of just how central he had been to the genre's origin and development. I did not realize that he had been a driving force behind the original 1986 LBPB and the principal author of its *Kreteria Lomba,* nor that the current shape and dimensions of contest beleganjur music and its culture were in large measure directly attributable to his multiple contributions and innovations as a composer, teacher, administrator, and adjudicator.

My interview with Asnawa that first night lasted for over three hours. At its conclusion, it was clear that we had barely even scratched the surface of all that he had to offer. Each question I asked generated a response longer, more informative, and more insightful than the last. No one else with whom I had spoken about beleganjur had even approached this level of knowledge and detail. I had only asked Asnawa for a single interview, but about forty-five minutes into the session it became clear to me that the present conversation would likely prove to be but the first installment of a much more extensive dialogue. Asnawa was excited by this project; he liked the idea of someone doing in-depth research on beleganjur, a genre to which he had contributed so much. He wanted to be involved, not superficially but deeply, and I was of course delighted at the opportunity of working with him intensively.

We finished our session at about 1:30 A.M., and Asnawa asked me what time I would like to come back the next day to continue. I told him that my morning would be taken up by a lesson with Sukarata, but that the afternoon was free. Asnawa seemed curious, perhaps even a bit surprised. He asked me what kind of work I was doing with Sukarata, and I explained that I was studying beleganjur drumming with him. Asnawa paused for a moment; he seemed a bit pensive. "Okay," he said. "You work with Tutnang on drumming in the mornings, and then at two o'clock you come here and work with me for beleganjur history and theory, for the *akadémik.*"

And that's how it was. Every morning I would meet with Sukarata for three to five hours, take a quick lunch break, walk the two blocks to Asnawa's house, and work with him for another three or four hours. My evenings were mainly spent either participating in or observing rehearsals of different Denpasar beleganjur groups. I would usually return home at about eleven o'clock at night, spend some time with Marilyn and our new puppy, Kajar, then work another two or three hours organizing and recopying transcriptions and notes after they had gone to bed. Four or five hours' sleep, and it was back to Sukarata's house to begin the routine again.

The schedule was grueling, but the work was rewarding and stimulating, and I felt fortunate to have fallen into the care of two such outstanding teachers who complemented each other so well. Sukarata, the seniman alam, taught me to drum and to be a performing beleganjur musician; Asnawa, the credentialed academic and composer, taught me beleganjur history and theory, and helped me to understand the music's place in traditional Balinese ritual life and in the modern sphere of Indonesian cultural nationalism. Their respective contributions to my project were clearly marked and delineated from the beginning, not because I tried to set things up that way, but rather because that was the way they both wanted them to be.

Life History

I Ketut Gedé Asnawa, or Tutdé (short for "Ketut Gedé"), as he is known to his friends, was born on 26 December 1955 in Banjar Kaliungu Kaja. He is married to Putu Oka Mardiani, an ASTI dance graduate and accomplished gamelan musician in her own right (see chapter 6). Putu is a *memindon* of Pak Beratha: Beratha's mother was a sister of Putu's grandmother. In marrying Putu, Asnawa thus became a relative of Beratha, bringing formality to a kinship-like bond that already existed in their close relationship of musical mentor and protégé.

Asnawa and Putu have three daughters: Ayu Putu Nias Tarika, who was born in 1983, and "the twins," Ni Madé Nias Yunirika and Ni Nyoman Nias Yonitika, born in 1992. In 1995, they moved from their small house in the family compound at Kaliungu Kaja to a newly built, larger one in the northern "suburbs" of Denpasar. The purchase of this home marked a major upward step in terms of socioeconomic status, though not one devoid of consequences. Mid-level Balinese conservatory instructors, despite their high social status and renown, receive quite small salaries. But Asnawa has lived thriftily, saved money earned during overseas teaching and performing engagements, and managed his money wisely. He is now able to provide for himself and his family some of the "luxuries" normally reserved for members of the Balinese upper middle class: the new home, a good automobile, a computer.

As he has discovered, however, the cost of ownership often far exceeds—and outlasts—the initial price of purchase. Asnawa has managed to find ways to cover the payments on his house and vehicle, but exorbitant utility bills, car-repair costs, and other such expenses have proven overwhelming. Like many in the growing class of upwardly mobile young professionals in Bali, Asnawa perceives himself, at least to some extent, as less a beneficiary than a victim of modest financial success.

"The tires on my car are completely bald," he complained to me in

1995. "It is very, very dangerous to drive, but even for a decent used set of tires it is about one million rupiah [or five hundred dollars]. This is several months' salary for a *dosén* [conservatory instructor]. I am Balinese, but I must live in an American world with these Western things and their American prices. It's bad enough to save so long to buy the car, but now I can't drive the car because the tires are no good. How can I buy new tires when they cost so much?"

Asnawa's comments on his car-tire dilemma reflect a tone of ironic paradox that pervades much of what he has to say about his life history and situation. An outsider's résumé-based perspective may affirm that he has achieved status as a success of "the system," as an insider of the musical establishment elite, but Asnawa himself contends that his successes have as often as not been partial, mitigated, hard-won, and painful, not only in his adult professional career but throughout his life.

Asnawa was born into a large family. He was the eighth of ten children: four boys and six girls. (One of the girls died while still a child.) His father and mother, I Ketut Degur and Ni Wayan Taman, were rice farmers, but Degur was a talented musician and dancer as well. He performed in Kaliungu Kaja's gamelan club and *arja* folk opera troupe.[4]

The gamelan was directed by Asnawa's uncle, I Nyoman Gebyuh, a wealthy architect and music instrument craftsman. Gebyuh recognized Tutdé's exceptional musical talents early on and took an active role in nurturing the boy's musical development. Together with his older brother Komang (Astita) and cousins I Wayan Sadra and I Wayan Yudana (Gebyuh's son), all of whom are now recognized as being among the leading Balinese composers of their generation,[5] the youthful Tutdé would hone his formidable musical skills in the stimulating environment of Gebyuh's fine Kaliungu Kaja gamelan group.

At an even earlier stage, though, it was another of Tutdé's uncles— I Ketut Geria, the trompong player with the Kaliungu Kaja ensemble— who began to shape the boy's burgeoning musical abilities with impromptu music lessons. The two would sit together under the shade of a eucalyptus tree, Geria singing trompong melodies and Tutdé listening attentively. Before the evening gamelan rehearsal, Tutdé would walk down to the balé banjar and work diligently at transferring the melodies he had heard onto the trompong; then he would stay around and "listen to the old men play."

When he was only seven or eight years old, Tutdé asked Geria if he could join the gamelan club. He became the group's youngest member. (Komang, five years his senior, had held the distinction up to that time.)

Even more remarkably, he "auditioned" with the sekehe on trompong, an instrument normally reserved for highly skilled and experienced players. Initially, the older musicians laughed when Geria plunked little Tutdé down behind the long row of trompong kettle gongs, but the child had taken his studies seriously, and he played so well that he was appointed assistant *juru trompong* to his uncle.

The one person who found the whole situation a bit annoying was Komang. "He was a little jealous of me," Asnawa recalls, laughing. "But soon he was moved up to the kendang, so then it was okay. We were always competing, Komang and I. We still are, you know, in our careers and all" (pers. comm., 1995).

A complex mix of competition and camaraderie has been an enduring theme in Asnawa's relationship with his famed older brother. "I'm still always competing with Komang," says Asnawa. "But it's very healthy. I like him so much. Often we're on panels together, juries, whatever. I'm very proud of that. It's hard to find that kind of relationship, even with a brother. A lot of brothers are in—what do you call that—a feud. But not us. And we still play [music] together. . . . He is, I think, my favorite drumming partner.

"But Komang and I are different. Komang is more ambitious. He has many different kinds of jobs: composing music, administration, and on and on. I'm not like that. I want things more steady. If you're always doing important work for the government and such, I think you risk losing something. For example, Komang is the head of the beleganjur group of Kaliungu Kaja, but he almost never has time to really work with the group because he's so busy. You lose the little things when your life is like that. I want to be there from the bottom up. . . . I want the benefits of the government-related things . . . but I don't want to have to go after them. Maybe I'm a little shy, or a little slow . . . but the main thing is I don't want to lose touch with the common people. I think there's a danger of that happening.

"The people who are so busy with the government, they tend to lose contact with the regular people. The job creates a distance with the people of the banjar. Komang doesn't want to ignore the banjar, but the demands on him are so great from the government side that it can happen sometimes. But of course it is people who approach life in that way who become famous. Me, I'm just famous here in the local area. That's different. Life is like a car tire. It keeps spinning around and around and sometimes you find yourself on top, other times on the bottom" (Asnawa, pers. comm., 1995).

Asnawa's first public performance with Komang and the Kaliungu Kaja group took place at a PNI (Indonesian Nationalist Party) political rally in 1963. He was only eight. This was a turbulent time in Bali's history. As Adrian Vickers explains, "Bali in the early 1960s was, according to those who lived through it, a place of tension and continual political rallies. Everyone was pressured to take sides in the growing split between the PNI and the PKI [Indonesian Communist Party]. . . . All the parties organised numerous public meetings, and stepped up pressure on all members of society to become involved in politics. Violence erupted at many of these meetings" (1989, 169). This climate of tension, in Bali and throughout Indonesia, foreshadowed the fall of President Sukarno and his ill-fated "Guided Democracy" regime. Bali would soon erupt in horrific violence during the "Communist massacres" of 1965–66, which accompanied Sukarno's demise (see Vickers 1989, 170–72; and Robinson 1995, 17–18, 181–272) and the ascent of Indonesia's quasi-totalitarian New Order (Orde Baru) under President (and formerly General) Suharto.

The tense state of Bali in the early 1960s seems to resonate at a microcosmic level in Asnawa's recollection of his musical debut at the 1963 PNI rally. Facing an audience of over a thousand PNI supporters and opponents, the precocious little trompong player lost his composure. "I was nervous," he recalls. "I smelled the food, saw everyone eating; it distracted me, and I lost my place in the music. I lost my concentration and had to stop playing, right there in front of so many people. It was terrible. Later, after the *gong,* I found my place again. But I never forgot that experience. I'll remember it forever" (Asnawa, pers. comm., 1995).

Asnawa's story is perhaps nothing more than a sad account of a little boy's first encounter with stage fright, but it is not unreasonable to speculate that it contains deeper levels of metaphorical significance. As Rodgers, Pospos, and Radjab (1995, 1) have argued, "Indonesian historical memory and personal memory are both animated by certain closely related key scenarios and social images, and societal histories and personal narratives interpenetrate. They also draw on each other's storehouses of aesthetic richness and emerge as deeper, more meaningful social texts because of that." Viewed in this light, Asnawa's autobiographical account of a young musician becoming overwhelmed and falling apart before a politically charged mob may be interpreted as a chronicling not just of the event itself, but of the anxious and uncertain sentiment of a volatile time.

Young Tutdé survived the humiliation of his unhappy musical debut and became an increasingly important and prominent member of the Kaliungu Kaja group through his later childhood years. He was afforded opportunities to play numerous types of gamelan music during this period, but mostly he played beleganjur. There were, of course, the cremation processions and other traditional ritual occasions requiring the music, but there was also now this plethora of political parades and rallies. As the nation spun out of control amid the chaos of Sukarno's declining years, and as Bali herself suffered through a series of calamitous natural disasters—including the devastating eruption of Mount Agung in 1963 and a severe famine in 1964—state pageantry flourished as the government endeavored to divert public attention away from these bitter and terrifying realities. Grand processions, most anchored in the powerful sound of beleganjur music, became the order of the day.

"Eventually we played beleganjur a lot because Sukarno used to promote lots of parades," Asnawa told me in 1995. "I played reyong when we would do beleganjur. Because I was just a young boy and my arm was so small, the reyong would cut into the arm [in which I held the instrument]. During the parades, I would cry all the way from the pain. That I'll never forget either."

When he was thirteen, Tutdé was promoted to the position of drumming partner to Komang in the Kaliungu Kaja group. With its abundance of talented, dedicated young musicians and the clever guidance and generous sponsorship of Pak Gebyuh, the sekehe was becoming increasingly active and its repertoire ever larger and more diversified. In addition to playing the standard pieces for banjar ceremonies, they took it upon themselves to learn the most demanding of newer pieces, especially the modern kebyar masterpieces of Pak Beratha, some of which Komang had learned directly from the master composer himself as a student at KOKAR.

Beyond their community-centered musical activities, Kaliungu Kaja gained increasing prominence as a professional musical organization in the late 1960s, largely in connection with a popular new theatrical genre known as *drama gong*. *Drama gong* was "invented" in 1965 by Anak Agung Gedé Raka Payadnya (Bandem and deBoer 1995, 146), who built upon older forms such as *stambul* and *arja* to create a new type of melodrama with musical accompaniment. Kaliungu Kaja's *drama gong* troupe established itself as one of the leading organizations of its kind in Bali. They were constantly in demand, and their busy schedule of all-night performances proved very taxing for a teenaged Asnawa committed to balancing his musical life with school and other daytime responsibilities. Sometimes, the balance could simply not be maintained.

"One time, the day after Galungan [a holiday]," Asnawa told me in 1995, "I stayed up all night playing *drama gong* until morning. The next day, all the boys in the village were invited to a picnic. It was a big deal and I was really looking forward to it. We were all to get dressed up in our party clothes and everything. But I overslept and missed the picnic because I had been up so late playing. I was crying because I lost my time, and it was all because of the gamelan."

As Asnawa advanced into his teenage years, Pak Gebyuh took over from Pak Geria as his principal musical guide and sponsor in the banjar community. "He was always trying to improve my knowledge of gamelan," says Asnawa of Gebyuh. "On important occasions, he would always invite a topéng dancer to perform in the banjar. We Balinese believe that you must learn about music from the dancer. Playing [drum] for topéng taught me how to respond to the body movements of the dancer. Sometimes the performance is dominated by the dancer, other times by the fixed form of the music. Playing for dance-drama, I always gained experience. The dancer would cue me for different angsels, different moods and manners, different movements, and so on. Here in Bali we believe that you have to learn that way. So I was successful with the topéng [dancer] Pugra, a dancer who was so famous that a whole style of topéng dance, Topéng Pugra, is named after him. I was about fifteen when I first performed with Pugra." [6]

It was around this time also that Gebyuh decided to hire a well-known music teacher from outside the banjar, I Wayan Konolan of Kayumas, Denpasar, to work with his talented and ambitious Kaliungu group. Konolan served for many years as a principal staff musician at Bali's RRI (Radio Republik Indonesia) station in Denpasar. His children include STSI faculty members I Wayan Suweca and Ni Ketut Suryatini, one of Bali's leading female gamelan musicians (see chapter 6). "We invited Pak Konolan to teach us lelambatan and topéng," Asnawa says, "but for the kreasi baru [kebyar pieces] we would just work things out on our own. Komang and I would figure things out. We would copy off cassettes, develop our own arrangements, whatever."

Under Konolan's tutelage, the quality of the Kaliungu Kaja group continued to increase, and so too did their popularity. They were hired for more and more performing engagements, both in the vicinity of Denpasar and in other areas of Bali. Unfortunately for Asnawa, all-night *drama gong* performances continued to be their stock-in-trade. "I got sick because I played the drum every night from nine at night until the next morning with the *drama gong,*" Asnawa told me in 1995. "It wasn't just in Denpasar, either. We traveled all over—to north Bali, everywhere. This is when I was an SMP [junior high school] student. I developed a case of chronic bronchitis which lasted for a long time. Each time I would have an attack I would have to go for a series of twenty-five injections, one per day for twenty-five days! I got sick because I was playing all night then going to school all day. I was stupid, very stupid."

In 1971 Asnawa was accepted into KOKAR. He quickly distinguished himself as a stellar student, becoming a protégé of Beratha and working closely with two of the school's other esteemed music instructors, I Nyoman Rembang and I Wayan Sinti. For over three years Asnawa had aspired to become a KOKAR student. His intense desire to gain admittance into the elite school was ignited one evening in 1968, when he happened to be in attendance at a rehearsal of a gamelan group preparing to represent Badung in an upcoming inter-regency gong kebyar competition.[7] The ensemble featured an all-star cast of Badung's finest musicians. Beratha and Sudhama were the two kendang players, and Sinti was on trompong. Rembang played as well.

"I had never heard gamelan played like that before," Asnawa remembers. "I went there every night to listen. It was so incredible. They played a [kreasi] lelambatan piece by Beratha, and 'Palguna Warsa,' another piece by him; that was the kebyar piece. They also did 'Legong Keraton,' 'Teruna Jaya.' I was so surprised and impressed at how great they were. I started going to tourist performances every day. Those guys and the other KOKAR teachers would all play at those performances. I decided I had to go to KOKAR so I could study with them. In those days, it was very cheap to go to KOKAR. It was highly selective.[8] If you got in, just about everything was paid for. That was very important to me since we had no money. I auditioned and I got in. Pak Beratha, Pak Rembang, and Pak Sinti became my gurus."

Even within the exclusive, competitive environment of KOKAR, Asnawa stood out among his peers. He normally learned music much more quickly than the other students, and thus he became a kind of unofficial teaching assistant for several of his instructors. In his second year, he was assigned by Beratha to play kendang with the KOKAR kebyar ensemble, despite the fact that the drummers were supposed to be third- or fourth-year students, according to the school's curricular guidelines.

Asnawa's instructors were also impressed by the young musician's serious interest in more archaic Balinese gamelan traditions, and especially by his fascination with the classical gamelan gambuh. "I was interested in learning gambuh because it was more difficult [than other musical styles]," he recalls. "When the faculty presented a gambuh workshop, I was the only student chosen to perform. I played gong.[9] That was good for me. It's difficult to keep your mind, to not get lost, and you have to know the drumming patterns. So from that experience, I was able to move to playing the drum. It was good for me. Playing the gong can be a nightmare. If you make a mistake, it's the worst. You can be sitting back there and just lose it."

Asnawa graduated from KOKAR in 1974. Following a special six-month teacher-certification course with Beratha and Rembang, he was appointed by the Ministry of Education and Culture to serve on the school's faculty as an assistant music instructor. Concurrent with the commencement of his teaching career at KOKAR, he enrolled as a student at the ASTI conservatory. He successfully completed his degree requirements in 1979, but did not take the final comprehensive examinations until a year later. "I didn't take the exams until 1980 because I didn't like to dance and I had to take a final dance exam, so I avoided it," he explained to me. "Also," he added, laughing, "I was busy with *pacaran,* with going out on dates and having fun, so I took my time finishing."

It was during his tenure at ASTI that Asnawa began to develop into a fine composer. He wrote his first major composition, "Sekar Kemuda," for his graduation recital in 1979. The piece was well received and ultimately became a standard work in the modern gong kebyar repertoire. The recital also featured "Ketug Lindu" (Earthquake), his first work in the experimental musik kontémporér vein. In 1979 Asnawa also began touring internationally with Balinese music-and-dance troupes; between that year and 1981 he performed in Singapore, Hong Kong, Italy, France, Poland, and the United States. In 1981, he was promoted to a full-time appointment as Instructor of Traditional Music/Karawitan (Gamelan) at SMKI (as KOKAR was renamed in 1976). Two years later, in 1983, he was made an adjunct instructor at ASTI as well, and later that same year he was sent to Yogyakarta, Java, to pursue graduate studies in composition at the Indonesian Institute of the Arts (ISI), receiving Indonesia's highest arts degree (S.S.Kar.) in 1985.

While at ISI, Asnawa composed the piece for which he is perhaps best known, the outstanding musik kontémporér work "Kosong."

"Kosong" received its premiere performance at the 1984 Jakarta Young Composers Festival (Pekan Komponis Mada Taman Isma'il Marzuki, Jakarta). Its acclaimed reception at the festival led to its being selected for performance at the International Gamelan Festival of the 1986 World Exposition in Vancouver, Canada.

The word *kosong* means "empty," and in the work's title refers to the "emptiness" of Nyepi, the Balinese New Year. In "Kosong," Asnawa created an abstract and impressionistic musical-theatrical collage of the noisy and festive period leading up to Nyepi, culminating with the arrival of the Day of Silence itself. The performers move between playing instruments, singing, acting, dancing, and miming. As Bandem and deBoer explain, they become involved in theatrical recreations of "such activities as chopping meat, decorating the houseyard, marching in procession with musical instruments, carrying the large effigies [seen in processions], and coming suddenly to the abrupt silence of Nyepi, when the entire island becomes quiet and public areas are deserted" (1995, 141–42).

A variety of unconventional instruments are employed in "Kosong," including stones (lithophones), metal plates, and a hair comb. The sound of gamelan beleganjur, which is of crucial importance to numerous pre-Nyepi ceremonies, is evoked through the prominence in the musical texture of several pairs of cengceng. The crash cymbals are played both in the traditional manner and in unorthodox ways. At different points in the piece, they are struck against the ground, played with the back ends of reyong mallets, even played with broom handles. The vocal element of "Kosong" also combines traditional and experimental aspects, ranging from the conventional singing of sacred *kidung* verses to the execution of jarringly unusual vocal sound effects. Similarly, the choreography combines a traditional Balinese dance vocabulary with experimental sequences of movement.

Certain experimental techniques used by Asnawa in "Kosong" in 1984 inspired his employment of similar devices in the new kreasi beleganjur context some two years later. For example, in "Beleganjur Angga Yowana" (1986), as in "Kosong," the cengceng players occasionally depart from conventional playing techniques, striking their instruments against the ground in some sections and tapping out interlocking rhythmic patterns with the back ends of reyong mallets in others (CD #33); and, according to Asnawa, the unique form of choreography, or gerak, that has become idiomatic of kreasi beleganjur grew directly out of "Kosong" as well. In certain parts of "Kosong," Asnawa experimented with having the performers execute set choreographic sequences while playing beleganjur-derived cymbal patterns and marching in processional style. When he composed "Angga Yowana," he decided to build on this concept, creating elaborate choreographies for the musicians of his Kaliungu Kaja beleganjur group. This, in turn, inspired him to include such choreography as a prescribed, compulsory element of contest beleganjur performance in the *Kreteria Lomba* for the original 1986 LBPB, setting a basic precedent for the genre's subsequent development.

With the international acclaim of "Kosong," a prestigious degree from ISI, central identification with the highly successful new musical genre of kreasi beleganjur, and numerous other achievements and contributions at several levels—local, national, and international—Asnawa's rank in the hierarchy of elite Balinese musical artists rose dramatically in the mid- to late 1980s. In recognition of his accomplishments, he received joint sponsorship from the Indonesian government and the United States–based Asian Cultural Council in 1989 to pursue graduate studies in ethnomusicology under Mantle Hood at the University of Maryland, Baltimore County (UMBC). He received the Master of Arts degree in 1991, writing an excellent thesis on the complex art of gambuh drumming (Asnawa 1991), and also directed the university's Balinese gamelan performance program throughout the course of his studies. Upon completion of his degree, Asnawa returned to Bali to resume teaching full-time at SMKI and part-time at STSI (ASTI until 1988). He was once again sent overseas for the 1993–94 academic year, teaching gamelan at the University of Montreal and the Eastman School of Music in Rochester, New York. Upon returning to Bali, he helped bring great honor to the recently established capital-city administrative district of Kodya Denpasar, coaching Kodya's entry in the 1995 Bali Arts Festival gong kebyar competition to its first-ever victory in that prestigious event.

"The Same All the Time Now": Caught between Worlds

Asnawa's more recent professional accomplishments and impact on his own musical community in Denpasar/Badung and on the musical culture of Bali at large have been highly significant and influential. As a composer, educator, administrator, and international emissary of Balinese arts, he has continued to make major and profound contributions. But when he speaks of what he has done of late, he does so with little of the enthusiasm or passion he conveys when recounting earlier events and episodes from his musical life history; rather, he adopts a calm, passive tone that seems to reside somewhere between a state of comfortable acceptance and one of barely suppressed frustration.

"My life is the same all the time now," says Asnawa. "Staying home with my family, teaching, directing groups, writing pieces for festivals. I am always trying to make people love making music. I often get invited to work in villages [teaching groups and preparing them for festivals and other performances]. Often I don't get paid, but I can't say no. It's my civic duty *(tugas)* to do that kind of work."

In many ways, Asnawa now finds himself caught between two worlds: torn between the values of his youth in the banjar and the more Western-oriented, less communal priorities that prevail in his new "yuppie" neighborhood; between the desire to devote his energies to cultivating artistic developments at the local, grassroots level and an ambition to seek increased status, prestige, and material gain both through further musical and educational pursuits at an international level[10] and through deeper involvement in high-level government arts-administration ventures in Bali; between acceptance of his current position in the highly stratified Balinese musical establishment and a drive to climb ever higher within it.

Asnawa's ambivalence concerning his present situation surfaces often—when he speaks about his new home and neighborhood, for example. He is proud to own a nice house in a relatively affluent neighborhood, and appreciates the comforts and conveniences that his new lifestyle has afforded him and his family. Yet his new way of life is in some ways a source of unhappiness. "In this neighborhood I feel isolated," he complains. "There are no artists around here. I like the quiet, but sometimes when I get bored, I just go to Printing Mas[11] or to the banjar (Kaliungu Kaja) to be with my friends; just to be with many people, where they're all just talking" (Asnawa, pers. comm., 1995).

The "luxuries" of residential privacy and "peace and quiet" valued in the West and by Balinese advocates of adapted Western lifeways have brought dubious advantages to Asnawa. He has bought into a kind of Balinese-appropriated rendition of the American dream, one that has gained great currency among upwardly mobile urban Balinese in recent years. He misses what he has at least in some measure left behind, however; he still yearns for the crowdedness, the noise, and the communality that were part and parcel of domestic life in the banjar.

Yet Asnawa will not—and likely cannot—return to where he came from, nor even truly revisit there. In his personal and social affairs, and especially in his professional life, it seems that he is compelled to continually pursue the trappings of a brand of material and symbolic success that does not readily conform to his inner sensibilities. He is driven to such pursuits by the desire to promote and ultimately justify his right to a certain position within the Balinese musical hierarchy, one that, for all of his accomplishments and accolades, he sees himself as having not been granted. Asnawa may appear to be an "insider" of the Balinese musical establishment's upper echelon from the perspective of a marginalized artist such as Sukarata, or even from the viewpoint of a foreigner such as myself. However, because of a variety of complicated personal, bureaucratic, and political conditions and circumstances that cannot be addressed in the present discussion, he perceives himself as someone who deserves a higher position than he actually holds. Furthermore, he knows enough about how the system works to realize that a solution to his predicament is likely beyond his control, regardless of his merits or how effectively he is able to display them. At times he is resigned to accepting this dilemma, but more often I have observed that he is driven to find ways to demonstrate his entitlement to that which he considers his due, even if this means having to struggle and endure considerable frustration in the process. The appearance of effort is carefully and artfully concealed in most situations, but there are times when it cannot be effectively contained, when the emotional scaffolding peeks through from beneath the smooth outward countenance.

My first glimpse of this occurred quite early on in my relationship with Asnawa, when I knew him only as a "success of the system" and had no inkling of the formidable complexities and challenges he faced in his professional life on a daily basis. He had been assigned to develop and teach a new course on ethnomusicological theory and method at STSI and requested my help in preparing the syllabus. One of the lesson units we devised was entitled "Insiders' and Outsiders' Perspectives in Ethnomusicological Research," or something to that effect. In discussing how this unit might be approached, I mentioned that issues of "insiderness" and "outsiderness" applied not only between foreign ethnomusicologists and indigenous representatives of the music cultures they studied, but between individual members within a given music culture as well—between different prospective "informants," as it were.

Asnawa seemed interested in this idea and asked me to clarify my point with an example. I made a disastrous choice.

"Say we wanted to look at the modern music culture of Denpasar," I began. "Both you and Tutnang are 'insiders,' because you both come from here and live here. But the perspective is different. Because of your education, because you work for the government—this kind of stuff—maybe you have certain opportunities and experiences that he doesn't, so maybe you know different things and understand things differently. If we want to know about Denpasar, *including* the schools and the government's involvement with music contests and all that, you are more of a cultural insider and Tutnang is more of a cultural outsider, even though both of you are from Denpasar."

There was a long silence. Asnawa stared at me icily, indicating that my "example" was neither welcome nor appreciated.

"You call me an insider," he said coldly, "but what do you know about that?"

Asnawa was offended by my essentializing characterization of him. What did I know about that? Clearly, not much. For me, his indictment was a painful but important lesson in the dangers of ignorance, a crash course in the potentially damaging impact of my insensitivity rooted in naiveté. It was also, though, a revelation. I had inadvertently opened a window, one through which I was able to see a glimpse of a very different Asnawa than the one I had known. Perhaps more than any other single experience of my fieldwork, the reproach forced me to take a more complex view of not only him and his situation, but of the situations of my other Balinese friends and colleagues as well. It had profound implications for my subsequent research, compelling me to see, like anthropologist Unni Wikan, that the actions and communications of Balinese individuals, despite the characteristic brightness and poise that normally appear at the surface of Balinese social life, emerge from "a world of effort, struggle, perhaps even covert desperation, not one of tranquility" (1990, xvi).

1. Cremation procession
beleganjur performance

2. Memukur procession

3. Memukur: throwing the effigies out to sea

4. Cengceng section choreographic maneuver, beleganjur contest

5. Reyong section of the championship beleganjur group from Meranggi, Denpasar

6. Carrying the gongs: beleganjur contest, Kintamani, 1990

7. Young women preparing to lead the procession before a beleganjur contest performance

8. Crowd control

9. I Ketut Gedé Asnawa

10. I Ketut Sukarata

11. I Wayan Beratha

12. I Ketut Suandita (*right*)

13. Cengceng section in rehearsal, Kencana Wiguna women's sekehe beleganjur of Kehen

14. Ni Madé Puspawati (*left*)

15. Starting off young

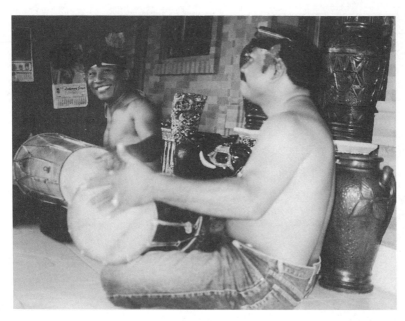

16. I Wayan Jaya (*left*) drumming with Sukarata

17. The author performing in a beleganjur contest, Kintamani, 1990

Part Three

Pengawak

Five

The High Stakes of Competition

In formal interviews and public encounters with musicians, teachers, ensemble directors, contest administrators, and government officials, I was told time and time again that beleganjur competition rankings were not terribly important, that the main priority of the contest experience was participation itself, with all its inherent contributions to communal spirit and cultural tradition. In less formal, less public moments, however, I learned that most of these people actually cared a great deal about who won and who lost beleganjur contests. They were also very much concerned with the whys and hows of competitive success and failure, especially in relation to the sekehes to which they belonged or by whom they were represented.

"Maybe they *say* that they do not care who wins, but I think they do care," I Wayan Dibia explained to me with candor in 1992. "Between the villages, it is very competitive. One group always wants to show that it is better than the group from a neighboring community. It has been like this for a very long time in Bali. You are right that the *most* important thing is actually taking part in the contest, and that is why we [who work at the conservatories and government arts agencies] encourage as many groups as possible to participate, which is good for the culture.[1] But I think the musicians, the villages, they always want to win, even if they act to you like it is not such a big deal."

The more deeply I became involved with beleganjur contest culture and with particular sekehes, the more clearly I came to see that winning was indeed "a big deal," despite a preponderance of public statements to the contrary. Furthermore, fear of losing emerged as a powerful deterrent against contest participation, preventing a great many sekehes from daring to take part in lombas at all. I observed that many inexperienced sekehes and all former championship groups shunned the glare of the competition spotlight (albeit for different reasons; see below), forgoing the pleasures of contest participation and the potential honor and rewards of competitive success so as to ensure avoiding the humiliations of defeat. Despite the government's concerted efforts to encourage beleganjur contest participation by "as many groups as possible," a conspicuously small percentage of eligible banjars were actually represented in most lombas; even among sekehes who seemingly possessed the necessary resources for a strong contest bid—motivation, personnel, funding, access to a quality teacher—only a select few would typically register to play in any given lomba. Moreover, withdrawals by one or more of the groups who did ultimately choose to register were very common.

Former winners never returned to contests in succeeding years to defend their championships, not because they were barred from doing so,[2] but because the risks were perceived as too great. "What if we do not win this time? Then we are not champions anymore," one member of a former LBPB championship sekehe explained to me in 1992, responding to my query about why his group had elected never to register for the event since their victory several years ago. The rank of champion was to be preserved and protected, not defended, he continued. His comments, like those of so many others I had encountered, implicitly undermined the widely promoted ideal of participation for its own sake.

The choices and attitudes of non-championship groups, from novice sekehes with no contest experience to former legitimate contenders, also seemed to contradict the espoused priorities of participation-centered ideals. Beleganjur groups, at least those I had the opportunity to observe between 1989 and 1995, played to win, and typically refused to play at all in instances where they perceived their competitive prospects as less than favorable. Granted, the concept of "winning" proved to connote different levels of achievement for different groups: for some it meant claiming the contest championship outright; for others, just beating out a rival sekehe from a neighboring village. Regardless of the specific competitive objectives, though, the decision of a sekehe to compete was almost invariably predicated on a will to triumph, and on a strong sense of confidence in its ability to do so. To participate with honor was not enough, and I would venture to suggest that the frequent comments stressing the importance of participation and the relative unimportance of contest results were in actuality indicative of how *much,* not how little, winning and losing truly mattered: studied indifference was employed as an antidote to the abject fear of humiliating defeat.

This last assertion was supported by my observations of a highly consistent and uniform pattern of post-lomba behavior demonstrated by representatives of the contest beleganjur groups with whom I had the opportunity to work most closely. The lag time between the conclusion of a lomba beleganjur and the public release of contest standings varies greatly from one contest to the next; the results of the judges may be known within fifteen minutes, or they may be withheld for up to three weeks. Regardless of the duration of the wait, however, members and supporters of the various competing sekehes normally express little if any interest in knowing the outcome; they appear sincerely indifferent right up until the moment the standings are announced.

But at that moment, a dramatic shift in attitudes becomes readily apparent—although, notably, only on one side of the win-loss divide. Those associated with defeated groups normally reveal no discernible change in stance: who wins and who loses, they steadfastly maintain, is unimportant, inconsequential; participation is what counts, and there is pride to be taken in that alone. Occasional hints of disappointment may slip through to the surface, but they are usually subtle and transitory.[3] The celebration of participation, a socially sanctioned virtue, becomes ever more the focus now. But is such behavior really an attempt to divert attention from the hurt and frustration of defeat? The actions and attitudes of the beleganjur champions in the aftermath of a lomba victory strongly suggest that this is so. They also reveal that the usual dictum of participation for its own sake in contrast to competitive ambition is something of a facade, a deception. The news of a contest triumph engenders a radical transformation in the collective persona of the winning group's members and backers. They may become uncharacteristically brazen and boastful, celebrating the victory by singing their own praises and unsympathetically ridiculing, even cruelly lambasting, the deficiencies of their vanquished competitors. An intense competitiveness soars to the surface, although it should be noted that its expression is concealed (at least publicly) from those who have suffered defeat, and in fact rarely exceeds the confines of the sekehe membership itself and the closely interwoven banjar community around it.

An incident that occurred shortly after the beginning of my third visit to Bali, in 1992, first focused my attention on these behaviors, which I now believe represent broad, socially sanctioned patterns that Balinese individuals and groups employ to deal with experiences of both victory and defeat in competitive situations. In 1990 I had participated for the first time as a performer in a major lomba beleganjur, playing cengceng for a group from the village of Batur Tengah in a regional contest in

Kintamani. Taking part in the contest was a great thrill, and after it was over I was anxious to know how "my" sekehe had fared. For days I pestered the group's lead drummer, I Nengah Jejel, with incessant queries about the contest's outcome, but he claimed to neither know nor care who had won. The same was true for all the other Kintamanians with whom I spoke. I grew tired of nagging—my questions seemed to annoy people—and when other research commitments forced me to leave the area about a week after the contest, I still had no pertinent information.

I did not see Jejel again until 1992, almost two years later. I found him at the exclusive Kartika Plaza Hotel in Kuta Beach, where he was now working as a bellboy by day and a dancer in tourist performances by night. He greeted me at the hotel entrance with a radiant smile and a hug and complimented me on having become fat since the time of our last meeting. He then held up his right index finger and shouted out "Number one! Number one!" in English. He was obviously very excited about something, but I had no idea what that something might be. "Number one!" he exclaimed again. I shrugged and shook my head. "Batur number one: champions. Kintamani," he now stated, slowly and deliberately.

I finally understood. The Batur Tengah group had won the Kintamani beleganjur contest championship back in 1990, and for some mysterious reason it now apparently mattered a great deal to Jejel that we had. He explained to me that he had never doubted we would win. After all, he boasted, the other groups had been "so primitive"; unlike us, they had lacked the "Denpasar style" and could not even play a basic "Jagul." We had stood head and shoulders above the competition, and by virtue of the novelty advantage my presence had provided, our victory had been all but assured from the outset.

As I listened, I could not help but think that this new Jejel bore little resemblance to the young man I had known two years earlier in Kintamani. What had happened to the Jejel who had spoken modestly of the "many good groups" against which ours had competed, and who had insisted that "winning is not so important anyhow" every time I had asked him about the contest's outcome? At first, I surmised that his new-found cockiness and braggadocio might be just for my benefit, that Jejel had appropriated an "American"-type competitive persona to gratify me. But I was wrong. Jejel was being quintessentially "Balinese" at this moment, acting in a manner that would become increasingly familiar to me as my acquaintance with numerous other representatives of champion groups in beleganjur contests grew and intensified through the course of my subsequent research.

Competing Views: The Problem of "Cultural Talent"

As I have argued, the stakes of competition in the contest beleganjur world are high: winning matters, and a great deal. It should be noted, however, that such a claim contradicts not only the more formal utterances of most of my Balinese associates, but prevalent Western notions concerning the motivations behind Balinese agency as well. With regard to the latter, some exploration of this disparity is in order.

Balinese gamelan performance organizations have long been driven by intense desires to garner the rewards of competitive success in musical battles against their rivals. The fanatical competitive zeal of village kebyar groups in the early 1900s (see Lendra 1983, 65) and of royal court gamelans during precolonial times (see De Zoete and Spies [1938] 1973) confirms that the modern competitive priorities evident in domains such as the lomba beleganjur are by no means novel. The structure of the modern lomba, with its formalized evaluation criteria and quantified grading scheme, may bear the indelible marks of Western influence, but the goal-directed competitive fervor exhibited by participants in modern Balinese music contests is "indigenous."

Yet at least since the time of Margaret Mead's influential research on Bali over a half century ago (to which we will return shortly), the competition-driven agency of Balinese people has rarely been acknowledged, either in the ethnographic constructions created by scholars or in the broader Western public imaginings resulting from such constructions. "The Balinese" have more often than not been essentialized as a people possessed of a prodigious "cultural talent" (my term) for emphasizing the process over the product, the means over the ends. The West's abiding fascination with Bali has in large measure stemmed from our attraction to a culture made to appear appealingly non-goal-oriented, or, more precisely, from our attraction to a particular people's talent for caring more about the doing of things than the end results of their endeavors.

The attribution of this specific talent to "the Balinese" is in actuality but one example of a broad-based ethnographic phenomenon: the identification and highlighting of cultural talents in portrayals of the ethnographic Other. Before focusing on the particular Balinese case, it will therefore be helpful to define what is meant here by "cultural talent" at a more general level.

A cultural talent is an abstraction, embodied in specific practices and behaviors, that is thought to define the distinctively unique "essential character" of a particular cultural group. In ethnography, manifestations of cultural talent are most often identified and reified in activities and objects of "artistic" or ritual endeavor. It is in such contexts that what separates the Others of our studies from ourselves normally comes most conspicuously and intriguingly into view, and it is at the level of emphasizing *interesting difference* that cultural talent takes on great significance in how cultures are represented ethnographically.

The significance of cultural talent relative to ethnography may be likened to the significance of individual talent relative to biography. In large measure, the marketability of a biography depends not on its accuracy or quality, but on the public's interest in some recognized and exceptional talent ascribed to the subject: the person whose life the book portrays. If Michael Jordan were not a great basketball player, most of us would not know, care, or read about how he lives his life, how he thinks, or what he believes in. Justly or unjustly, the way Jordan plays basketball is what defines the essence of who he is for the vast majority of people, even for those who have never seen him play. Basketball talent is what draws us into Jordan's lifeworld; it is the initial source of our fascination, wherever that fascination may ultimately lead us in our quest to "know" Jordan or to "be like Mike" (the catchphrase for a series of popular Gatorade commercials). Jordan is human, just as we are, but his talent distinguishes him as somehow different, even otherworldly. It is this inherent dichotomy between his Selfness and Otherness relative to our own conceptions of who and what we are that captivates our interest, whether in watching his games, seeing his television commercials, or reading about his "life story" in biographical accounts.

The individual subjects of biographies and the cultural subjects of ethnographies, I would argue, are often rather similar with respect to how "talent" influences modes of representation and perception. Talent, whether ascribed to a single person or to an entire culture, is the quality that renders Others not merely different but compellingly different. We might look for examples of this to the Kaluli's capacity for seeing and hearing human voices, bird songs, and the rainforest as a single integrated whole (Feld 1990), or to the Yoruba's penchant for "coolness" (Thompson 1973). Cultural talents such as these, which we identify as talents precisely because they symbolize vast distance from that which we have experienced and from that which we think ourselves *capable of experiencing,* become the cornerstones of our "understandings" and "appreciations" of who the Kaluli or the Yoruba are, much as Jordan's basketball skills become our primary index of who he is. We are drawn to that which impresses us, and we are impressed by that which seems at once beyond us yet profoundly human. This is the province of talent, and it is therefore not surprising that the talents assigned to foreign cultures, as manifested in the most intriguing and awe-inspiring symbols that distinguish Them from Us, are often the lifeblood of ethnographic inquiry and representation. These are the characteristics that most unfailingly lay claim to our interest, for better or for worse.

The core substance of a cultural talent often resides in close proximity to that of a cultural stereotype. The main distinction between the two derives from two factors: how symbols of Otherness are perceived and represented, and by whom. Stereotypes normally serve to marginalize through tactics of implicit essentialization (often involving "humor"); by means of stereotypes, cultural Others are made to appear inferior—or at least not quite right or not quite normal—because they act, create, think, or believe in "different" ways. To say that "African music is all about rhythm and drumming" is to propagate a stereotype; beyond being descriptively inadequate and grossly imprecise, the statement carries with it broader negative implications of the musical—and by extension cultural—"primitivism," "simplicity," and "lack of sophistication" that were used by Westerners to marginalize and disenfranchise the essentialized "African" for centuries.

For most academics and for others who oppose stereotype-based worldviews (at least publicly), cultural stereotypes are regarded as the province of the ignorant, the misinformed, the narrow-minded, the reactionary; they are insidious and categorically destructive. In their efforts to counter the deleterious effects wrought by cultural stereotypes, thinkers of scholarly- and liberal-minded persuasion have long relied on the allure of cultural talents in constructing cultural Otherness. Cultural talents reify the distinctive character and qualities of the Other, celebrating and often idealizing cultural difference in the process. The Other is represented in a manner that commands not only interest and respect, but awe and admiration as well. The conception of "African rhythm" outlined earlier is turned on its head: beyond debunking the fallacy that

African rhythm is "all about rhythm and drumming," the advocate of cultural talent highlights the exceptional rhythmic skills and abilities of musicians in specific African cultures. Rhythm now becomes a door opening onto the beauty, power, and complexity of African musical forms and styles, a locus of distinction at which "African music" remains in sharp contrast to "Western music," but in ways that render the former meaningful, impressive, and enlightening rather than "primitive" or "unsophisticated."

Through ethnographic emphasis on cultural talents, anthropologists and ethnomusicologists have defined their boundaries of Selfness and Otherness, not only by identifying and describing compellingly unique attributes of cultures distant from their own, but also by identifying these attributes as manifestations of cultural difference that reveal the shortcomings and fallacies of Western cultural ways and presuppositions. The scholarly study of the Other becomes "a form of cultural critique for ourselves. In using portraits of other cultural patterns to reflect self-critically on our own ways, anthropology [like ethnomusicology] disrupts common sense and makes us reexamine our taken-for-granted assumptions" (Marcus and Fischer 1986, 1; see also Bohlman 1991, 142–43). The beautiful, complex, and culturally meaningful rhythms of a West African Akan drumming performance now become not only indices of the Akan's cultural talent, but reference points for the Westerner's critical reexamination of criteria for assessing beauty, complexity, and meaning in all music, including Western music.

According to Marcus and Fischer, Margaret Mead, more than any other scholar, was responsible for introducing the reflexive mode of cultural critique into the ethnographic canon: "It was Mead who developed the strategic juxtaposing of a foreign perspective, gained from firsthand fieldwork, to disassemble for Americans their sense that their own customs were 'natural' and immutable" (Marcus and Fischer 1986, 127). In creating her challenging and strategic cultural juxtapositions, Mead depended on the power of cultural talents to make her points. Extreme manifestations of difference evident in the practices and values of Others (Samoans, New Guineans, Balinese)—in domains such as sexuality, emotional expression, and the role of the arts in social life—were highlighted and idealized in her ethnographic portraits. In foregrounding dramatic contrasts between the cultural ways of people from faraway places such as Bali and their Western (especially American) counterparts, Mead endeavored not only to describe and interpret the cultures she studied, but also to question powerful Western cultural assumptions and ideals in the process, and to challenge her readers to embrace, perhaps even adapt, ideals and practices of the Others about whom she wrote (see Pollmann 1990).

In her own articles and in the works on Bali she co-authored with Gregory Bateson, most notably *Balinese Character: A Photographic Analysis* (Bateson and Mead 1942), Mead's "Balinese characters" turned conventional Western wisdom upside down; Bali, the island where babies did not cry, was made to appear a quite rational place, prompting the Western reader to question just how natural and inevitable the frequent crying of their own infants was after all.

Mead was by no means alone among scholars in treating Bali as both a quintessential test case for the study of alternative cultural realities and an ideal foil for a cultural critique of the West, as is evidenced by the following passages from the introduction to Mantle Hood's *The Ethnomusicologist,* excerpted from a section called "Society and Its Scale of Values":

> For the sake of comparative illustration, we might look briefly at two contrasting examples with the assumption that the attitudes of all other societies fall somewhere between these two extremes: the United States and the island of Bali in Indonesia. . . . Viewed as a total society, the United States regards the arts as nonessential, low on its scale of values. The hero of the day is in orbit in outer space or tunneling into the bowels of the earth or exploring the ocean floor. The poet, the painter, the musician, the dancer, the writer, the actor manage a tolerable acceptance as nonessential members of an affluent society. . . . The island of Bali, to the best of my knowledge, has more artists per capita than any other society. Here, where religion pervades every aspect of living, the creation and performance of music, dance, various forms of theater, sculpture, painting, and decoration are such an indispensable part of religious devotion that the arts, too, have become a way of life. Within the communal organization of Balinese society, the artist and his products are regarded as absolute essentials in the functioning of the community. . . . There is no word in the Balinese language for "art"; the arts are such an organic part of living that there appears to be no need for such an abstraction. (Hood 1971, 10–15)[4]

Returning again to Mead, a fundamental aspect of the Balinese culture she constructed in her writings is to be found in her depiction of "the Balinese character, with its preoccupation with activity for its own sake and its studied avoidance of climax and of identification" (Mead [1942] 1970b, 343; see also Bateson [1949] 1970 and Geertz 1973c, 403–4). In her 1942 essay "Community Drama, Bali and America," Mead idealized Balinese cultural dispositions toward "activity for its own sake" and "studied avoidance of climax" in order to critique the opposite inclinations she observed in Western cultural disposition. Mead's attractive images of the Balinese "delight in the art of acting rather than in the play, in the way in which the music is played rather than in the music" ([1942] 1970b, 343) were employed to support her claim that, for the Balinese, "[n]othing is ever finished. There is no goal toward which an individual or a group work intensively, sinking into anticlimax when it is attained. The Balinese, whether they be musicians or actors or carvers, are primarily interested in the process, not in any fixed result" (342). Taking more explicit aim at the relative shortcomings of Bali's American cultural counterparts than did Hood in the passages from *The Ethnomusicologist* quoted earlier, Mead concluded her article with several practical suggestions of "various lines along which those who lead the community arts movement [in the United States] might work" to improve their organizations by adapting Balinese-inspired practices and values (348–49).

Mead's depiction of Bali as a process-over-product culture enhanced development of the construct of cultural critique and provided relevant insights into the values of certain Balinese in certain situations. As was suggested earlier, however, it did not convey an accurate view of the multiple and complex dimensions of Balinese agency, and evolved perhaps as much through exclusion of what did not "fit" as through inclusion of what did. Balinese people have been competitive and goal-directed in a great many ways and contexts long before, during, and since the period when Mead did her field research. But their frequent concern with "the fixed result," with recognized achievement rather than with communal participation alone, has perhaps seemed too familiar and unremarkable to warrant the attention of many Western scholars and of others who have consciously or subconsciously sought interesting cultural difference in Balinese lifeways. Alan Merriam, for example, in the *Anthropology of Music,* was content to accept Mead's theories unquestioningly, summarily reporting that "the rehearsal process in Bali tends to be almost of more importance than performance, thus stressing an attitude toward music which differs from our own" (1964, 160).

At least until quite recently, the ascribed Balinese cultural talent for privileging "activity for its own sake" was widely accepted and essentially absorbed into the fabric of received wisdom about Bali (see Wikan 1990 for a notable exception). It has remained the basis of an attractive and enticing essentialized cultural image, one that holds appeal for Westerners and Balinese alike in their representational strategies.[5] But the image commonly projected and accepted bears little resemblance to the Balinese worlds I encountered through my engagements with certain inhabitants of contemporary beleganjur musical culture. It is to this very different realm that we now turn our attention.

High Stakes and Hidden Battles

The notion that winning is very important in the contest beleganjur world may not seem especially surprising, even if it is contradicted by the majority of Balinese public statements on the subject, as well as by the theories and claims of many who have written about Bali. After all, kreasi beleganjur was created specifically for competitive musical display, and the lomba beleganjur is an institution whose social, cultural, and ideological messages and meanings are inextricable from a formalized system of comparative evaluation in which music groups representing larger sociopolitical entities—whether neighborhood organizations (banjars), villages, districts, schools, businesses, or entire Balinese regencies—are ranked according to a rigid system of hierarchical ordering.

The lengths to which some beleganjur competitors will go to *gain* competitive advantage, however, can be rather surprising; at least they were to me through the earlier phases of my field research, when I was inclined toward unquestioningly accepting what my Balinese consultants told me during interviews about their attitudes toward competition and the like. Accumulated observations and experiences eventually compelled me to recognize that the beleganjur contest, an event rooted in a music traditionally associated with battle, is not only the forum for healthy and productive competition it is purported to be, but also a battleground for bitter and complex wars raging beneath the surface. Behind the exterior of an institution publicly devoted to promoting communal participation and community solidarity through positive competitive endeavor, antagonists confront one another on a multiplicity of issues, using the contest event as an opportunity to settle—or, more accurately, to further complicate—a variety of scores, ranging from long-standing interpersonal and inter-village rivalries to cultural and ideological conflicts of broad, even national, scope and impact.

The "hidden battles" of beleganjur contests may lead to extreme instances of competitive action and behavior: to instances where unbridled, competition-driven aspirations motivate agents of particular groups or other institutions to exceed the normal (or what are publicly espoused to be the normal) bounds of propriety. Two such instances—in particular, two beleganjur contests whose quality and integrity were significantly diminished by "corrupt" actions undertaken to aid the competitive prospects of certain sekehes—will serve as the primary focal points of discussion through the remainder of this chapter. The analysis of the first contest will be fairly brief, that of the second more extensive. In examining these two events, I am interested in exploring what is at stake and what is at issue at certain levels located beneath the surface of beleganjur competitive endeavor.[6]

My decision to focus on events that may fairly be described as dysfunctional or atypical is not an arbitrary one. As anthropologist Michael Jackson has astutely observed, "Any theory of culture, *habitus*, or lifeworld, must include some account of those moments in social life when the customary, given, habitual, and normal is disrupted, flouted, suspended, and negated. At such moments, crisis transforms the world from an apparently fixed and finished set of rules into a repertoire of possibilities. To borrow Marx's vivid image, the frozen circumstances are forced to dance by us singing to them their own melody" (1996, 22). In cultural analysis, it is often the cracks beneath the smooth surface that reveal the most telling insights into individual agency and its broader social, cultural, and political implications.

Playing to Win: The Breakdown of a Beleganjur Contest

Today was going to be a good day, I thought to myself, gazing out the car window onto a gorgeous vista of terraced rice paddies. Asnawa and I were on our way to a small regional beleganjur contest in Gianyar. The weather was exquisite: cooler than usual, breezy, and partly cloudy. It was a perfect day for a lomba, and I had been looking forward to this one for quite some time. Asnawa had attended the inaugural version of this event a year before and had mentioned to me on several occasions how impressed he had been with both the quality of the groups that had competed and the energy and spirit of the audience. He had explained to me that this would be a smaller, more intimate affair than other contests we had attended of late, offering better opportunities not only for viewing and listening, but for photography and sound recording as well.

We arrived at the contest site just minutes ahead of the scheduled starting time. Immediately I sensed that something was wrong. The audience was unusually small, even compared to other events on this scale I had attended, and the festive air I had come to expect at beleganjur contests seemed entirely absent. The chief organizer of the contest, a conservatory music instructor named "Guban"[7] whom I had met on a couple of occasions, appeared anxious and distressed. A depressed, disturbed energy hung over the grounds like a heavy blanket; everything seemed out of sync.

The contest itself did nothing to improve matters. Only four sekehes competed. (Every other lomba I had attended had included at least eight.) None of the groups played especially well, and the dark mood of the audience proved consistent with that of the musicians themselves, who for the most part seemed to be doing little more than going through the motions during their performances, and fairly incompetently at that.

Within this field of mediocrity, the first two groups, from Banjar "Jeruk" and Banjar "Leong," were the best, "Jeruk" being the more polished of the two. The last of the four sekehes to play was truly awful, presenting the worst beleganjur contest performance I had ever heard. They did at least bring some life to the otherwise listless audience, however, prompting both taunting laughter and angry jeering with their endless mishaps—from botched entries to hopelessly sloppy ensemble playing to the dropping of a mallet by one of the reyong players. Most of the audience had already left in disgust by the time they finished, bringing this altogether ignoble event to a dismal if fitting conclusion.

After about a half hour, the jury rankings were announced over a crackling, distorted public address system. By this time the contest grounds were completely deserted save for the musicians who had played, members of the jury, contest organizers, a few straggling spectators, and Asnawa and myself. The announcement that Jeruk had won the championship brought almost no response, not even from the group's members. It was a bizarre situation, the likes of which I had never encountered (and have not since).

As I packed up my equipment, Asnawa came over and apologized for having dragged me to this debacle. He told me he was very confused. Last year, he explained, there had been ten groups, all good and some outstanding; the audience had been a good five times larger than this one and had been extremely enthusiastic from start to finish. He was clearly embarrassed; he seemed to be in a state of disbelief.

On the way back to the car, Asnawa and I ran into Guban. It was an awkward meeting, since Asnawa and Guban were friends and neither seemed to know what to say to the other in the wake of what had just transpired. Asnawa managed a gracious exit from the situation, telling Guban that he needed to speak to a friend of his on the jury who was just then leaving. Thus I was left standing alone with Guban, wishing I could congratulate him on a successful contest but knowing I could not.

Thankfully, Guban broke the painful silence, and in a most unexpected manner. First, he apologized for the poor quality of the event; it was unfortunate, he said, that an "honored guest" such as myself had had to endure something like this. Then came the surprising part. With stark candor, Guban explained to me how the contest had been "sabotaged" by the winning group from Jeruk, which had broken contest rules by employing several accomplished musicians from other villages, including some who were conservatory music students. (As a rule, STSI- and SMKI-affiliated musicians, whether students, faculty, or alumni, are banned from participating as musical performers in beleganjur contests island-wide.)[8]

That Jeruk was planning to use "ringers" was common knowledge throughout the district well in advance of the day of the contest, according to Guban; virtually everyone in the area knew of the situation, and members and supporters of several other registered groups had lodged formal complaints, threatening to withdraw from the event if the Jeruk ringers were allowed to play. But the main sponsor of the contest, "Wayan"—the wealthiest and most powerful man in the district—was from Jeruk; moreover, he was the administrative director (klian) of the Jeruk ensemble. When a member of the contest organizing committee, "Nyoman," a lifelong rival of Wayan, visited him to warn that Jeruk would be expelled unless the ringers were removed, Wayan countered by threatening to completely withdraw his sponsorship of the contest if any such action were taken. He did this knowing full well that without his aid the event would have to be canceled, and that a cancellation would bring unbearable disgrace upon those in charge, including Nyoman himself. Even a tarnished contest, Wayan strategically surmised, would be deemed better than no contest at all. The organizing committee would privilege the maintenance of an appearance of normalcy above all other considerations. The deck was stacked in his favor, in more ways than one.

Wayan's gamble worked; it was decided that the contest would be produced with the "fortified" Jeruk group intact. About a dozen sekehes had originally registered to compete, but most were so infuriated by the news of what had happened that they withdrew, leaving just Jeruk and three other groups. Frustration and anger spread throughout the broader community too, Guban continued, prompting most people who would have attended as spectators to avoid the event altogether and thwarting whatever enthusiasm may have existed among those who did come.

And now insult had been added to injury. Wayan and the Jeruk group had not only destroyed the integrity of the contest, they had been crowned champions in the process. And according to Guban, the cruel irony was that their victory had been virtually a foregone conclusion precisely because they had refused to play fair. On account of the distinct advantage provided by the ringers, Jeruk had entered the contest in a very favorable position. And because their performance had ultimately been sanctioned by the contest's producers—never mind the underlying circumstances—Jeruk, like all of the other groups, had been assessed "objectively" on the merits of its performance alone. With conscious disregard of the muck and mire surrounding the contest, the jury had awarded Jeruk the championship it "deserved." A modicum of rightful order and propriety had been maintained, paradoxically enough, by granting Jeruk the victory.

"We will not stoop to their level," Guban told me, casting aspersions on Wayan and his Jeruk charges while speaking with tentative self-righteousness on behalf of the lomba's organizing committee. This appeared to be the lone salvageable shred of dignity available to him in the aftermath of the fiasco. Guban, Nyoman, and all the others who would have opposed Wayan, given the chance, had been checkmated. It was a no-win situation, and Guban was doing what he could to save face.

But why had Wayan forced his hand so strongly? It is a question I never had the opportunity to take up with Wayan himself (I never met him, and must concede that my knowledge of what occurred is limited to Guban's unverified information). But the available evidence would seem to suggest three possible motives: first, Wayan wanted Jeruk to win the contest, for the simple reason that winning is important; second, he resented any challenge to his authority, especially one delivered by a rival of his such as Nyoman; and third, he was intent on demonstrating just how powerful he truly was, even if this meant essentially destroying the integrity of an event he was sponsoring and thereby diminishing the value of Jeruk's claim to championship status in that event. Wayan was not just bent on winning a championship for Jeruk; he was also committed to delivering a message: don't mess with me or I will destroy you, even at my own expense. This was more than an innocent beleganjur contest, more even than a corrupted one. It was a battle of wills. Wayan was letting everyone know who was boss, and who was not (i.e., Nyoman in particular).

As will be explored in the discussion that follows, actions and strategies such as those exercised by Wayan in connection with this one small beleganjur contest find parallels in other contexts where the stakes of power and privilege are considerably greater. In New Order Indonesia, where to a "remarkable extent . . . a rhetoric of culture enframes political will, [and] delineates horizons of power" (Pemberton 1994, 9), while a rhetoric of democracy only superficially veils the authoritarian martial command of President Suharto and his GOLKAR (Golongan Karya) party administration,[9] the potential political ramifications of beleganjur contests, and the manipulative use of such contests for political ends, can be extensive, high-reaching, and revealing at a number of levels.

New Orders and the New Order: The GOLKAR Contest

Shortly after my arrival in Bali in June of 1992, I was frustrated to discover that the largest Bali-wide beleganjur contest ever held had taken place just a few weeks earlier. Disappointed at having missed such an important event, I resolved to compensate by documenting it as thoroughly as possible after the fact.

It was during an interview with Pak "Bucu," a prominent Denpasar musician, that I first heard of the contest. I asked him what occasion had inspired the event.

"Oh, it was for the election," he told me, referring to the recent Indonesian general election of 1992, in which Suharto and GOLKAR had scored the latest in a long series of landslide victories. As part of its election campaign, Bucu explained, GOLKAR had sponsored a grand beleganjur contest featuring top groups from all over Bali. He had been a member of the contest jury. There had been more groups and bigger prizes than in any previous lomba beleganjur, and the island-wide scope of the event had brought championship groups of district and regional contests from all eight Balinese regencies together in head-to-head competition for the first time.

"So who won?" I asked. Bucu's answer surprised me.

"I don't remember," he said, the uncharacteristic edge in his voice prompting me to wonder whether I had inadvertently said or done something wrong. "Why don't you ask somebody else about that," he continued. "Let's talk about something else."

A few days later, the subject of the "GOLKAR contest" came up again during an interview with Pak "Julat," a leading figure in the Balinese arts community and a prominent GOLKAR official. Julat informed me that he had been the chairman of the contest jury, and proudly announced that the group from his own native village, "Kelabu," had won the championship. I noted this in my journal, along with a wealth of other information about the contest and its outcome that Julat was kind enough to share.

A week later I was enjoying a meal with my friend Pak "Petala," director of the Banjar "Sirsak" gamelan club in Denpasar. He asked me whether I had heard about the "big beleganjur contest" held during the election campaign. I told him I had, then asked whether his group had competed. He seemed perplexed by the question.

"Of course we competed," he said, seemingly a little agitated. "We won. Didn't you hear?"

I told him I had heard otherwise, that Julat had told me Kelabu had won. Petala laughed and shook his head. Sirsak had won, not Kelabu, he maintained.

Three days later, I was on my way to a wedding ceremony in Gianyar with Bucu's brother, Pak "Curam." Conversation turned to the subject of beleganjur contests, and I asked Curam if he had attended the recent GOLKAR event. He informed me that he had served on the jury.

"Who won that contest, anyhow?" I asked. I was completely unprepared for what happened next.

"That contest was just politics, not music!" Curam exclaimed, gesturing angrily with his right hand and nearly causing the car to swerve off the road. "It was not a good contest. I don't even like to talk about it." He paused, regained his composure, then added quietly, "I think they still don't know the results." Shaking his head in apparent disgust, Curam fell silent. Startled by the uncharacteristic outburst, I resolved to let the matter drop once and for all.

A month later, however, I was drawn back to the GOLKAR contest once again, when Pak "Gesit," a music instructor at one of the conservatories, mentioned to me during an interview that the beleganjur group from *his* native village in northern Bali, "Mangga," had been crowned the contest's champions. This group, I recalled, had been credited as the *second*-place finishers on Julat's original list.

What was going on here? How could such a simple question—who won the contest—yield such a bewildering array of responses? According to Julat, Kelabu had won; Petala insisted that the championship had gone to Sirsak; Bucu claimed not to remember the results, despite having been on the jury; and Curam would have me believe that the outcome had not even been determined yet. Now, here was Gesit stating in no uncertain terms that Mangga had been victorious.

"So Mangga won the contest?" I asked Pak Gesit incredulously. He nodded. "What about Sirsak? Where did they finish?" I asked. There was an awkward pause.

"Well, they also placed first," Gesit finally responded.

"So it was a tie?"

"Not exactly."

"Then how were there two first-place champions?"

Gesit shifted and fidgeted. "Well, you see," he began hesitantly, "there were actually three champions." The contest, he went on to explain, had consisted of three separate subcontests, with North, East, and West Bali, respectively, represented. Mangga had won the North, Sirsak the West.

Putting the pieces of the puzzle together quickly in my mind, I determined that Kelabu must have won the East. If so, all the troublesome contradictions of my data would be resolved. All versions of the contest results presented—Julat's, Petala's, and Gesit's—would be revealed as equally (that is, partially) "true." I surmised that the different versions of the contest results all followed a consistent pattern: acknowledge one champion—that of the reporter's native village—and omit mention of the other two. This was a seemingly simple method of privileging the "home team" and highlighting its accomplishments, a selective and strategic approach to reading and accounting for the actual facts of the contest's outcome. As David Harnish has observed, such compromises—where several things are simultaneously true and no one is telling "the truth"—occur frequently in Bali (pers. comm., 1997). (One need look no further than the multiple, often profoundly different accounts of the origins of kecak or gong kebyar for evidence of this.)

Fully anticipating being able to finally tie up the loose ends of my research data on the GOLKAR contest, I asked Gesit who had won the East division. I posed the question more as a formality than as a genuine query; after all, I was quite certain of what his answer would be. In fact, I was so certain that I could not resist scribbling "Kelabu" in my notebook even before he replied.

"Logam," Gesit stated matter-of-factly.

"Logam?" I blurted out, unable to believe what I had just heard.

"Yes," Gesit confirmed.

Somewhat desperately, I implored Gesit to consider the possibility that his recollection might be inaccurate. I told him of how Pak Julat had listed Kelabu as *the* contest champion, a designation that made perfect sense provided that Kelabu had at least been *a* contest champion.

"No," Gesit replied with firm conviction. "Pak Julat is wrong. He must have forgotten."

In an instant, my newfound optimism, my conviction that I had finally found the missing piece of information that would solve my dilemma, that would convert chaos into cultural formula, was summarily destroyed. Rather than becoming discouraged, though, I became ever more determined to get to *the* truth—the single, objective truth—of the contest's outcome. I attempted in vain to obtain permission to see government documents pertaining to the contest. I also pursued a second meeting with Julat—maybe he had just "forgotten" the actual standings, as Gesit suggested—but my telephone calls went unanswered.

Finally, two weeks after my conversation with Gesit, I succeeded in securing an appointment with the ever-busy Julat. He stood up to greet me when I entered his spacious office. I thanked him for taking the time to speak with me, then told him why I had been so persistent in pursuing this meeting. Since our last interview, I had run into a rash of contradictions relating to the GOLKAR contest, I explained, and now I needed help sorting things out.

I began by asking whether the contest had been, in essence, "three contests in one" rather than a single event; he confirmed that it had.

"So then," I asked, "who were the three first-place champions?"

"Kelabu in the East, Mangga in the North, and Sirsak in the West," he replied without hesitation.

Mangga and Sirsak were thus confirmed as champions, but the Kelabu versus Logam roadblock still stood. Exasperated, I decided to cut to the chase. I confessed that the contest was becoming an albatross around the neck of my study, as there was still one glaringly ill-fitting piece to the puzzle: the discrepancy between his account of the contest's outcome and that of another of my trusted informants, who insisted that Logam, not Kelabu, had won the East division championship. I implored Julat to help me iron out this one remaining wrinkle.

Julat leaned back in his huge reclining chair, locked his thin, elegant hands behind his head, and stared pensively at the ceiling for a moment. Then, quickly and energetically, he snapped forward, pounded his fists on the desk, and smiled at me.

"Yes, I can," he said. "You see, officially, Mangga, Sirsak, and Logam were the three champions of the contest, but this did not entirely correspond with the standings determined by the jury, which, as you know, I was the chairman of. After the contest, the jury met and decided the winners on the basis of the judges' grades. For the East division, Kelabu was chosen as champion. Logam came in second. I submitted these results to the government officials, who decided to wait until *after* the results of the election were in, and then to announce the winners of the beleganjur contest at a GOLKAR victory celebration. When the results were finally announced, they turned out to be a bit different than what we had submitted. Logam had been put into first place in the East, and Kelabu knocked down to second place. There were some other changes like this as well. The reason for the changes had to do with the results of the election. Since GOLKAR had sponsored the contest, they felt that the winners should be groups that represented districts which had given the strongest support to GOLKAR in the election. They consulted the election results for each of the areas represented in the contest and took these into account in assessing the contest standings I had submitted on behalf of the jury. The area represented by the Logam group had given GOLKAR nearly unanimous support, with almost 100 percent of voters voting for them. Kelabu, on the other hand, came up with only a slim majority vote in favor of GOLKAR. When the [GOLKAR] party officials discovered this, they decided to overturn the jury's decisions and to give the first prize to Logam instead of Kelabu. Does that answer your question?"

The Politics of "Culture"

Actually, Julat's disclosure of government tampering with the contest results answered certain questions while raising other ones. The basic scenario seemed clear: villages represented in the event who had voted strongly in favor of GOLKAR had been rewarded; those whose support had been weak had been punished. But why had the GOLKAR officials bothered to meddle with the contest in the first place? And what did they achieve by doing so, given that the election had already been won anyhow? In addressing such questions, it will be helpful to revisit and expand upon John Pemberton's earlier-cited assertion, and to consider how not only the rhetoric but also the *practice* of culture enframes political will and delineates the horizons of power in contemporary Indonesia.

The Indonesian government's abiding concern with mediating, controlling, and nationalizing "local" manifestations of cultural expression is central to a fundamental New Order political imperative identified by Clifford Geertz: how to "prevent regional, ethnic, linguistic, and religious differences from taking on political force" (1990, 79). Official endorsement of Indonesian cultural diversity has far less to do with a genuine interest in the promotion and display of symbols of distinctive cultural difference than with a hegemonic agenda rooted in the construction of what Pemberton, citing Foucault, identifies as an Indonesian "culture effect: the production of a knowledge, that called 'culture,' as certain of its own assumptions as it is devoted to recovering the horizons of its power by containing that which would appear otherwise" (1994, 9). "Culture," *kebudayaan,* serves New Order political agendas well so long as it models the existence of a world-as-it-ought-to-be mutuality between localized values and national priorities. Where such an impression is created, as in the vast majority of beleganjur contests (see chapter 2), "culture" can be exploited for political ends while appearing apolitical; it is used to make the empowered elite's political agendas appear "natural" rather than forced, organic rather than imposed.

What of a situation such as the GOLKAR beleganjur contest, however, where "culture" and politics fell out of step with one another, the "cultural event" failing to correctly model political and social order to the satisfaction of the powers that be? As Geertz has observed, in Indonesia "[a] sharp distinction is made, propagated, and indeed enforced between the realm of 'custom' (folklore, faith, costume, art) . . . and that of the struggle for power, where any intrusion of such matters in any form at all is feared as a prelude to general upheaval" (1990, 79). Beleganjur champions hailing from villages not sufficiently loyal to GOLKAR in the election did not present the right image, distorting—implicitly mocking—the fundamental and crucial distinction between "custom" and power noted by Geertz. The desired "naturalness" of "culture's" correspondence to the power status quo failed to emerge of its own volition, so such "naturalness" had to be created through other means.

The particular incident might be seen as a microcosm of larger processes at work in Indonesian politics, processes that are perhaps most clearly evident within the institution of the Indonesian general election itself, where the notion of "culture" enframing political will takes on special significance. As scholars of Indonesian politics, including Benedict Anderson, have noted, beneath (or within) the public rhetoric of Pancasila (the official national philosophy), Indonesian political ideology builds from a fundamental premise that power justifies itself, and that the primary responsibility of the ruler is not to his citizenry but to the cultivation of his own strength and invulnerability. "The welfare of the collectivity depends not on the activities of its individual components, but on the concentrated energy of the center. The center's fundamental obligation is to itself. If this obligation is fulfilled, popular welfare will necessarily be assured" (Anderson [1972] 1990a, 63).

The Indonesian gloss on "democratic elections" reflects such a worldview. As Pemberton suggests, national elections in New Order Indonesia have been centered far more on ritualizing democratic process than on involving the general populace in a democratic system (1994, 5). The goal of elections has been to produce national celebrations of "political stability"—which is generally understood to equate with the unchallengeable dominance of the present political order— rather than to provide the Indonesian public with opportunities to take part in national referendums on how the country should be run or by whom.

With no apparent sense of irony, the general election is known as Pesta Démokrasi, that is, the Festival of Democracy;[10] it is a form of *upacara nasional,* or national ritual (Pemberton 1994, 5). As President Suharto himself has explained, "With one and only one road already mapped out, why should we then have nine different cars? The General Elections must serve the very purpose for which they are held, that is, to create political stability. Only these kinds of elections are of value to us" (quoted in Schwarz 1994, 32).

The designated "car" is Suharto's own. Elections function to prevent those outside of the Suharto/GOLKAR circle from gaining access to real power or prominence in the governing of the nation. "Successing"—Pemberton's translation of the Indonesian term *mensukseskan*— which involves fixing election results or otherwise tampering with and manipulating the electoral process, is a method used to achieve this goal. As Pemberton explains, it is "the government's campaign imperative to *mensukseskan* the elections (to 'success' them), which means, in essence, to secure a victory already scored" (1994, 4–5).

Successing is justified as a means toward the desired end of political stability. That Suharto and GOLKAR will win is assumed. Nonetheless, the margin of victory must be overwhelming to ensure the proper image of political stability; political challengers can be allowed to garner only enough electoral support to maintain the public illusion that due democratic process has been served. As Adam Schwarz explains, "If 'only' nine hundred members of the People's Assembly voted for Soeharto [Suharto] . . . that would imply the existence of another 'power' to whom one hundred members owed their loyalty. This would be seen by Soeharto as a serious blow to his ruling mandate" (1994, 46). *Mensukseskan* practices are enacted precisely to militate against such blows.

While successing may be a standard, even acceptable practice in Indonesian politics, any particular instance of it tends to be undertaken covertly. This appears to have less to do with government concerns over ethics than with a fear on the part of officials about the possible exposure of poor political performance, or, perhaps more accurately, poor performance of politics. In a situation where political stability truly exists, successing is unnecessary. Therefore, an instance of *mensukseskan,* if brought to public attention, carries with it the inherent danger of becoming a symbol of weakness and vulnerability in the existing structure of power relations.

The decision of government officials to tamper with the results of the GOLKAR beleganjur contest was clearly made within the context of a larger successing agenda. The original results arrived at by the contest jury were broken; they therefore needed to be fixed. By implicitly equating musical excellence with political virtue—making villages loyal to GOLKAR into beleganjur champions—the "improved" results were better suited to the projection of the desired image in Indonesia's Festival of Democracy. But given that successing inevitably involves risk, it seems reasonable to ask why government officials would have deemed it worthwhile to tamper with something as ostensibly politically benign as a lomba beleganjur at all. The contest, like all such competitions, was presented essentially as a celebration of Unity in Diversity, highlighting the unique character of "Balinese culture" and the benevolence of a government committed to its support. On the surface, then, public perception of the event's success would seem unrelated to matters of partisan politics, given the purposefully apolitical nature of *kebudayaan:* its propagated separation from the struggle for power. An exciting, spectacular, well-produced, and well-attended beleganjur contest would seemingly have served GOLKAR's purposes adequately, regardless of the political leanings of the villages represented. If a correlation between contest standings and allegiance to GOLKAR were to emerge and could be publicized, so much the better. But why enforce it, especially when doing so might result in embarrassment?

Considering the effort and risk involved, GOLKAR's decision to success the contest suggests how firmly entrenched cultural events such as lomba beleganjur are in the negotiation of political power, despite official rhetoric to the contrary. For the contest to stand as a cultural symbol of national priorities and ideals was apparently not sufficient; in GOLKAR's view, the results had to reproduce the established order of power as well. In bending the contest to its will, it seems to me that GOLKAR used the event as a lesson in the privileges and consequences of political control at two different levels. To members of the public unaware of their meddling, the GOLKAR officials propagated a hegemonic ideal of distinguished achievement being a natural outcome of loyalty to the power elite, a world-as-it-should-be vision of a society committed to maintaining the status quo. Paradoxically, a similar if somewhat more complexly layered message was likely conveyed to those who did have knowledge of the politically motivated manipulation of the contest. Whether or not this select group was limited to the individuals who had served on the contest jury, for those in the know GOLKAR's actions were likely meant to be interpreted not as signs of weakness, but rather as signs of strength. The successing of the contest was a display of power, its arguably gratuitous employment serving to reinforce the premise that loyalty to GOLKAR is prerequisite to success of any kind in New Order Indonesia.

Partial Truths

Julat's "exposé" on the GOLKAR contest proved pivotal to my research at several levels. Beyond resolving the troublesome contradictions in my data and opening my eyes to a new understanding of just how profoundly "culture" was implicated in New Order political agendas, it helped me to see and comprehend a kind of cultural logic in the jumble of conflicting accounts of the contest's outcome. What had *actually* happened in the aftermath—what I had been struggling to make sense of—ultimately became less interesting to me than what my five consultants *told* me had happened; "the truth" as such became less intriguing than the myriad "partial truths" conveyed in my consultants' differing stories.

Hildred and Clifford Geertz, in their important 1975 study *Kinship in Bali,* identify a Balinese "culture pattern" that "is very general and flexible in form. Because its elements are global and imprecise, it is easily interpreted in different ways by persons with different points of view" (Geertz and Geertz 1975, 3). On the evidence of the different versions of the GOLKAR contest results I encountered, it seems reasonable to suggest that this culture pattern, or perhaps more precisely this cultural strategy of individual agency, may extend further, to domains where one (at least a Westerner such as myself) would expect little possibility for flexibility or imprecision. Even had I been privy to Julat's revelations from the outset (the truth of which I will at least provisionally assume, although I never managed to fully verify his information), I would never have anticipated that my seemingly straightforward question "Who won the contest?" would yield the diverse and seemingly incongruous "interpretations" that it did. In seeking simple facts, I found instead a complex web of partial truths, a collage of conflicting and adjustable reports that accounted as much for how particular individuals thought the contest should have come out as for how it actually did.

In this final portion of the chapter, I will attempt to untangle this web by exploring what may have motivated Julat, Gesit, Petala, Bucu, and Curam to report to me on the contest as they did, and by examining their motivations in terms of a proposed theory of how cultural priorities of self-identification guide Balinese people in their constructions of life events and situations. This theory will, I hope, provide insights into what renders the matrix of the divergent accounts of the contest not only culturally possible but culturally logical as well. Despite the seeming disparities contained in the various "stories" of the contest's outcome, all five of them appear to me to stem from similar personal motivations grounded in broadly cultural strategies used by Balinese individuals to make the world around them appear concordant with their idealized conceptions of their places within it. Personal identity, Balinese or otherwise, is a construct of individual will and imagination, composed of multiple aspects; it is grounded in a person's perceptions of the mechanisms and parameters of her or his culture. As I will attempt to illustrate, similar understandings of a culture's systems and rules held by different actors with different motivations may, paradoxically, pave the way for dissimilar renderings of "facts," because, as Unni Wikan observes, "interpretations of 'facts,' both facts of nature and social facts, proceed from particular viewpoints that are anchored in subjective experience" (1990, 132).

Multidimensional Selves, Personal Identity, and Culture

In his book *Self Consciousness: An Alternative Anthropology of Identity,* Anthony Cohen proposes that "any individual must be regarded as a cluster of selves or as a multi-dimensional self" (1994, 7). Building from this premise, I would posit that an individual's definition of her identity position in any situation evolves from an internal dialogue among her cluster of selves. These component identities are constantly engaged in dynamic processes of alliance and conflict, determining their primacy and subservience relative to one another. The ability of a person to effectively form alliances and resolve conflicts within her multidimensional self demands adherence to certain internalized identity hierarchies that facilitate productive decision-making strategies when matters of appropriate action, self-representation, or worldview are at issue.

The processes by which such identity hierarchies are structured and maintained are unique to every individual, but they are always directed and constrained in important ways by values and requirements defined in social contexts. Culture, an abstract entity with concrete implications, resides at the juncture of social life and individual agency. It functions to provide guidelines, both implicit and explicit, that aid the individual in determining what is needed, what matters, and what is possible in most any given situation.

When considering how culture and the individual intersect in the individual's lifeworld, it might be helpful to think of each component "self" within the cluster of selves that constitutes the individual (defined here as a culture-bearer distinguished from others by virtue of her personal identity) as a unique and changeable "product" encased by a more or less standardized "container." There are many such containers, each of which bears the name of some general category from within the individual's available cultural matrix—husband, mother, child, teacher, community leader, ethical individual, spiritual being, politician, patriot, rebel, scoundrel, and so on—and is accompanied by a set of instructions drafted and modified in accordance with the individual's experience throughout the lifelong process of enculturation.

Under the most ideal circumstances, the particular "self" represented by each container will be in sync and in harmony with all of the others, enabling the contents of the various identity categories to spill over into one another with positive reinforcing effects rather than negative consequences. In the absence of such a state of balance, however, where conflicts of interest arise (as is so often the case), certain containers must be stacked atop others; the priorities of one component identity must be privileged over those of its counterparts. The hierarchies manifest in the particular stackings that emerge reveal much about both the broader cultural templates that guide individual action and the distinctive improvisational strategies actors employ while moving within, around, and sometimes against these templates.

Among the many "containers" of culturally categorized components of personal identity that Balinese people carry through their life-worlds—the specific selves within the cluster, to again invoke Cohen's terminology—I will isolate three that help to inform an understanding of how certain broadly relevant cultural priorities and distinctive manifestations of individual agency came to be combined in the different accounts I documented in connection with the GOLKAR contest. These are (1) the individual as a member of his native banjar community; (2) the individual as an honorable and judiciously civil Balinese person; and (3) the individual as a professional motivated by career concerns.

In the following discussion, I will argue that in the ways they chose to reconstruct the contest's outcome for my benefit, my five consultants were endeavoring to make the best of a negative contest event by presenting *themselves* in the best possible light. Their attempts to salvage and/or maintain personal integrity in the face of a compromising situation (the tarnished contest) appear to me to have revolved around a fairly consistent pattern of prioritizing the three component identity constructs in the order listed above, with allegiance to the native banjar having especially great motivational force. "It is better, the Balinese say, to be wrong with the many than right by yourself. [The banjar] is our only support in the face of sickness, poverty or other calamity; with it we can live, without it we die" (Geertz and Geertz 1975, 115). This notion of the banjar as the core reference point of Balinese identity, as a locus of value that transcends all others, finds support in the evident priorities of the people discussed below. The approach presented here is highly speculative and represents only one of many possible interpretations. I believe, however, that it is sufficiently plausible to warrant serious consideration.

Motivating Priorities

The GOLKAR contest, unlike other lomba beleganjur, yielded no clearcut champion. The very structure of the event, with its three divisional subcontests and no unifying "final round" competition, generated inherent ambiguity. This ambiguity was in turn exacerbated by GOLKAR's alleged refashioning of the outcome, which brought additional confusion to the basic question of who had won the contest, while moreover tainting the event. In their desires to eliminate ambiguity and to restore a sense of dignity to the efforts they and those they represented had made on behalf of a flawed and misguided beleganjur contest, my five consultants each took unique and telling positions in regard to the "official" outcome of the contest, that is, the outcome after the adjustments made by the GOLKAR officials. This outcome was molded and transformed by my consultants in a variety of ways, each a manifestation of creative, motivated agency.

Petala and Gesit were the individuals whose personal interests in the contest fit most comfortably with its official rankings. The sekehes of Sirsak and Mangga, Petala's and Gesit's native banjars, respectively, were bona fide contest champions. This was irrefutable, so Petala and Gesit each told me matter-of-factly that his own village's group was *the* champion, rather than *a* champion, that is, one of three. For both these men, allegiance to the native banjar apparently justified a strategy of relating the contest standings to me in less than complete terms: by doing so, they were best able to promote the cause of their "home teams," conveniently constructing images of pure and absolute victory. Initially, neither felt compelled to make mention of the claim by the other's village to a portion of the championship, nor to Logam's. Failing to convey such information did not constitute a compromise of personal honor or integrity, since nothing *un*true was being related in either account; rather, the facts of the contest's outcome were merely being "edited" for my convenience—streamlined, as it were—in ways that happened to accord with Petala's and Gesit's idealized conceptions of things.

There was just one problem: Petala's and Gesit's stories proved to be in conflict with what I understood to be true about the contest results prior to my meetings with them. Thus, I was compelled in each case to question—and thus implicitly challenge—what they told me. In Petala's case, my challenge ultimately had no impact. He told me that Sirsak had won, I told him about Julat's claim that Kelabu had, and he was able to frankly refute this claim on solid technical grounds, holding firm to his original assertion. After all, according to the official results, Sirsak had achieved championship rank and Kelabu had not, neither in Sirsak's division nor in any other. No further explanation was required as far as Petala was concerned, since the official results, favoring his group, were all that mattered. (Furthermore, it is possible that Petala was not even aware of the political high jinks that allegedly led to Kelabu's demotion, since he, unlike the other four consultants, had not served on the contest jury.)

For Gesit, the situation was very different. My line of questioning essentially pressured him into revising his original declaration that Mangga had won the championship outright. In the face of my queries concerning Petala's and Julat's claims about Sirsak's and Kelabu's victories, he had little choice but to acknowledge Sirsak. They, like Mangga, had been official winners, and to deny this would have been to lie, a far more serious offense relative to basic cultural codes of honor and integrity than reporting a partial truth for the sake of native-village pride. Gesit was not willing to lie, so he conceded that the "GOLKAR contest" had in fact comprised three divisional contests rather than a single competition. This was a compromise. Mangga retained their championship rank in Gesit's expanded, more complete accounting of the standings, but the purity of the group's championship status suffered somewhat in consequence of that status's being shared with Sirsak and Logam. Attempting to balance his allegiance to Mangga with culturally defined standards of personal honor, Gesit had done what he thought was best in a less-than-ideal situation.

Perhaps the most intriguing aspect of Gesit's "revised" account of the contest results was his firm insistence that Logam, not Kelabu, had won the East division championship. According to the official contest results, Logam had been declared the winners, just as Gesit professed, but in maintaining that this was so even after I disclosed to him that Julat had told me Kelabu had won, Gesit put himself at risk professionally. Gesit, as a member of the contest jury presided over by Julat, almost surely knew that Kelabu had been the jury's original choice as East division champion. He also knew from what I had told him during our interview that Julat was still standing by Kelabu's claim to the championship. Given that Gesit was a full-time employee of Julat, and that Julat is a man of great power who is known to not take kindly to any perceived insubordination, Gesit's defiant assertions that "Pak Julat is wrong" and that "he must have forgotten [the actual results]" were not only startling, but potentially dangerous. To say such things on record was to question Julat's integrity (or at least his memory) and to publicly challenge his authority.

This was injudicious and seemingly out of character for Gesit, who had always struck me as a man of quintessentially *polos* character: modest, respectful, and painstakingly deferential to Julat. It was also seemingly unnecessary, since Gesit could have easily put himself in compliance with Julat by simply taking a less decisive stance on the matter of whether Logam or Kelabu had won. Julat obviously had an agenda in promoting Kelabu's cause, and it would have been prudent and in Gesit's professional self-interest to just refer me back to his boss for clarification on the matter of the East division contest rankings. After all, whether Kelabu or Logam were the champions of the East had no apparent bearing on Mangga's status as champions of the North; and furthermore, in a context that clearly sanctioned tacit non-acknowledgment of even the very fact that there were multiple champions in the contest, someone in Gesit's position need not have felt obliged to take a stand on behalf of Logam, Kelabu, or any other group whose prospects had no direct bearing on Mangga's own (and thus on his own). This was not a matter of protecting personal honor.

So why, then, did Gesit act as he did? Why did he risk offending Julat and enduring possible consequences when the advantage to be gained by doing so was by no means self-evident? These are difficult questions, and I can only speculate that prospective answers might again be sought in relation to the dominant identity priority of allegiance to the native banjar. Gesit had already been pressured to dilute the purity of Mangga's championship status by acknowledging the two other official champions. My mention of Kelabu likely made matters even worse, "reminding" Gesit of the corruption-tainted ambiguity hidden beneath the contest's favorable outcome. Through my interference, Mangga was quickly being reduced from the beleganjur champions of Bali to one of three victors in a marred and controversial lomba beleganjur. Such denigration was intolerable from Gesit's perspective, and further regression could be avoided only so long as the legitimacy of the official contest results was not permitted to come into question. Gesit was thus willing to stand in defiance of Julat, Kelabu, and his own professional safety, protecting Mangga's virtue by protecting the illusion that the contest had played out fairly. In doing so, he combatively pushed Julat's hand, setting up a situation where his boss would have to either acknowledge to me that Kelabu had lost to Logam or else blow the whole messy affair wide open by exposing the "foul play" that had converted Kelabu's earned victory into Logam's politically aided one.

In the end, Julat would not be outdone. His display of commitment to the imperative of native banjar allegiance proved greatest of all. As a high-ranking GOLKAR official, Julat's proper course of action would have been to confirm Logam's victory over Kelabu in order to resolve the glaring contradiction between his report of the outcome and Gesit's. He could have done this easily and without any sense of having compromised his *personal* integrity as a man of honor; all that would have been required to rectify the situation was a statement to the effect that the official outcome of the contest was undetermined at the time I first spoke to him, that now the results were in and Logam rather than Kelabu had been crowned champions of East Bali. As a native of Kelabu, however, Julat could not bring himself to take this seemingly safe and acceptable path of least resistance. For the sake of protecting the banjar's pride and honor, he was willing to expose an unsavory instance of politically motivated interference in the affairs of the ostensibly apolitical domain of "culture," to blow the whistle on GOLKAR and thus by implication on himself. His exposé brought unwanted attention to covert GOLKAR ploys, belittled the contest's significance, and posed at least a slight risk to his own political reputation. Apparently none of this mattered, or at least none of it mattered enough. Julat had to stand up for Kelabu's rightful claim to a piece of the championship regardless of the consequences, and in choosing to do so for the record, as it were, I suspect he took a certain satisfaction in sending a message of his own to his meddlesome GOLKAR cronies, something to the effect of "Play political games if you must, but don't play in my backyard."

Finally, we come to possible motivations underlying the accounts of two individuals without any partisan stake in the outcome of the contest: Bucu and Curam, jury members and brothers from a banjar whose beleganjur group did not compete. One might have expected these two men, with no specific obligations to their native village in this instance, to plainly account for the contest's structure and results, explaining the three-contests-in-one format and listing the three champions recognized in the official rankings: Sirsak, Mangga, and Logam. Politically and professionally, this would have been the most straightforward option.

Instead, both Bucu and Curam chose to evade the question of who won the contest altogether, Bucu by "forgetting," Curam by stating that the results were not yet known. Presumably there was not enough at stake to warrant a full exposé of the contest's messy underside, but on the other hand there was too much at stake to justify implicit compliance with GOLKAR's disreputable procedures. Bucu and Curam (especially Curam) were angered by what had happened, both as jury members whose professional integrity had been assaulted by GOLKAR's disregard for the rankings they had arrived at and as ethical individuals repulsed by the blatant, crass politicization of a music contest that had become something else. By claiming ignorance, each in his own way, Bucu and Curam washed their hands of an event with which they no longer wanted to be associated. The "untruth" of their supposed non-knowledge was deemed preferable to the partial truth of a politically manipulated, insidious officialdom.

Six

Agendas of Gender

For me, watching a woman play that music is like watching a beautiful
woman driving a big truck.

I Wayan Dibia

Bali, mid-May 1995: before my body-surfing accident, before the calamitous encounter with Doggie the dog. I arrive, exhausted, at Ngurah
Rai Airport after a grueling flight from Florida. Thankfully, Asnawa is
there to meet me as planned.

"Anything new or interesting going on in beleganjur these days?"
I ask him.

"There is one thing," he replies. "Suandita is preparing a women's
beleganjur group for the opening parade of the Bali Arts Festival next
month. They're rehearsing this evening in Kehen. Maybe you'd like to
go." A women's beleganjur group? What on earth?

No news could have come more unexpectedly, or been more intriguing, than this. Upon completing my dissertation fieldwork some three
years earlier, I had left Bali with many lingering questions, and as I
embarked on this latest research expedition I was intent on answering
as many of these as possible. If there was one thing about which I was
certain at this juncture, however, it was this: beleganjur, a musical embodiment of Balinese masculine identity, would never be a women's
music. In a series of formal interviews and informal conversations in
1992 with Asnawa, Beratha, Rembang, and a number of other leading
beleganjur authorities, in which issues of beleganjur's future prospects were addressed at length and from a variety of perspectives, I
had been told over and over again that despite the considerable progress and increased prominence of women's groups in the area of gong
kebyar performance,[1] "women's beleganjur" would never—and could
never—develop. The very idea of such a thing, I was assured, was

mustahil: impossible, out of the question. Summing up the consensus position on the matter with succinct clarity was the esteemed Beratha: "Beleganjur is music for men, not for women," he told me during an interview at his home, leaving no doubt in my mind that this was not only the way things were, but the way they would remain.[2] I was wrong.

A Masculine Territory

Beleganjur has always been a music associated with and exclusively performed by men. It is, in Suandita's words, "the most masculine of Balinese genres." Indeed, more than any other Balinese ensemble, the gamelan beleganjur defines a "masculine territory" on Bali's musical landscape (S. Willner [1992] 1996, 11). It is emblematic of the qualities of boldness and bravery *(keberanian),* heroism *(kepahlawanan),* and forceful strength *(kekerasan)* that dictate the core terms of an essentially masculine valor demanded of Balinese men who engage in battle, whether such battle is real or symbolic and whether it is waged against human or spirit adversaries.

Whether performed in contests or for cremations, in patriotic parades or purification rituals, with solemn seriousness or satirical irreverence, beleganjur manifests masculine energy and style. A variety of factors, including the music's intense and aggressive character, its historical connection with warfare and other predominantly male-defined domains of culture, and such "practical" considerations as the heavy weight of certain instruments (especially the large gongs and drums) and the high levels of physical exertion and endurance demanded of performers, have solidified beleganjur's position at the male extreme of gendered Balinese musical identity.

Balinese women have not necessarily been forbidden from playing beleganjur in the past; it is just something that women have not done, and have likely not thought much about wanting or having reason to do.[3] Against the backdrop of Balinese cultural convention, women playing beleganjur defies commonsense logic. In my conversations with Balinese women and men from various walks of life (especially middle-aged and older individuals), even as late as 1995 mention of the term "women's beleganjur"—*beleganjur wanita*—often met with perplexed or amused reactions. For many people I encountered, "women's beleganjur" appeared to be an oxymoron.

Yet, as I was to discover in 1995, Balinese women have been playing beleganjur since at least 1994, and have been doing so in increasing numbers and with growing frequency since that time. The musical arrangements played by the new women's groups are much simpler than those played by men; tempos are relatively slow and there is little if any choreography; the groups are taught and supervised by men and typically perform only in special demonstrations, rather than in competitions or in traditional ritual contexts. It is men, too, who normally compose the music for the women's groups and who carry the heavy gongs in processional performance, since, even within this radical context, women carrying gongs is viewed as too great a departure from conventional gender norms.

Existing at the margins of the broader beleganjur scene and Balinese musical culture generally, women's beleganjur stands as a small but intriguing aspect of contemporary Balinese musical life. It owes its existence not to processes of change and development emerging from within Balinese culture, but to the priorities of a specific program of New Order ideology: the official promotion of *emansipasi,* or women's emancipation, as a symbol of the Indonesian nation's modernization and progress. It is the very incongruity posed by the formerly mutually exclusive categories "women" and "beleganjur" that both empowers and problematizes women's beleganjur as a symbol of emansipasi values.

Questions, Issues, and Perspectives

This chapter examines women's beleganjur as a controversial musical phenomenon of Balinese culture implicated in the emansipasi ideological formula of patriarchal Indonesian nationalism. I will explore what is at issue and what is at stake for women who play beleganjur and for others—both women and men—who care whether or not they do. Materials drawn from interviews I conducted in 1995 with two "types" of individuals—female gamelan musicians (ranging in age from their late teens to their mid-thirties) and highly positioned male representatives of the Balinese arts establishment (ranging in age from their mid-twenties to their mid-seventies)—formed the core of the study.

My analyses and interpretations reflect the particular viewpoints and biases of my consultants, but also evidence the influence of a substantial body of scholarly literature addressing gender-related topics pertaining to Indonesian and other Southeast Asian cultures across a diverse range of subject areas. Building from theories proposed by other scholars, I argue that cultural symbols such as women's beleganjur, ostensibly designed to project images and reflect values of women's empowerment in modern Indonesia, are in actuality used to promote stereotypes, or sociocultural myths, that reinforce the stability and durability of male-dominated structures of power, the legitimacy of which depend on widespread public assumptions of women's marginality.

Examination of this central issue unfolds around a number of questions: How does women's beleganjur engage or defy conventional conceptions of gender in Bali? How is it employed as a hegemonic instrument of New Order emansipasi ideology, and in this respect, how does it compare to other emansipasi-directed forms of musical and cultural expression? Does it reinforce, reshape, or undermine "prevailing mythologies" (Douglas 1980, 179) about women's abilities and deficiencies in conventionally male domains? To what extent does it advance or diminish women's access to social and political rights, opportunities, and power in contemporary Bali (and Indonesia more generally)? And finally, how do the expressed attitudes and opinions of particular Balinese individuals reflect, challenge, subvert, or even transcend the ideological agendas and cultural moorings of the women's beleganjur phenomenon?

With respect to this last question in particular, it is important to consider that the Indonesian government's strategic employment of women's beleganjur as an ideological tool does not negate the music's significance as a medium of expression for its practitioners; nor does ideological usage fully dictate the limits of the genre's representational significance. As I have tried to emphasize throughout this book and will stress ever more emphatically in its concluding chapters, what music means in the lives of its makers is always important. It is crucial for us as scholars never to forget this, regardless of how far our analytical and interpretive forays may take us from direct engagement with the expressions and actions of musicians whose worlds we endeavor to understand.

From Oxymoron to Reality:
The Emergence and Development of Women's Beleganjur

In 1994, the first all-women's beleganjur group premiered on Bali's main stage of cultural display: the opening parade of the annual Bali Arts Festival (Pesta Kesenian Bali). Elegantly attired in matching, traditional-style ceremonial outfits, the women, ranging in age from their late teens through their mid-thirties, performed before a stunned and titillated audience numbering in the thousands.[4] Lacking the vigorous masculine energy and flashy musical and choreographic virtuosity of men's beleganjur, the nascent women's style exhibited was nonetheless notable for its uniquely restrained character and understated dignity. The performance's impact on the audience, however, reportedly had little to do with the quality or character of the music or its presentation. What alternately shocked, impressed, enthralled, and amused the huge crowd was the simple yet unfathomable fact of women playing beleganjur. In the blink of an eye, the crash of a cymbal, "women's beleganjur" had been transformed from impossibility to actuality, from oxymoron to reality.

This groundbreaking performance was ultimately revealed as more than a peculiar, isolated event when later in the same year a second ensemble, the Suandita-directed Kehen-based group referred to at the beginning of this chapter, was formed in response to a government request for a women's beleganjur performance at PORDYA (Pekan Olah Raga Kodya Denpasar), Denpasar's annual sports fair. The group formed was a beleganjur subdivision of a larger music performance organization, the women's division of Sekehe Gong Wanita Kencana Wiguna, the recently crowned champions of the Bali Arts Festival women's kebyar competition. While the kebyar group had featured female performers exclusively, the beleganjur division's debut at PORDYA 1994 was led by two male drummers. "I decided to use the boy drummers because they only gave me ten days to prepare the whole thing," Suandita told me in 1995. "That's not enough time to teach girls to drum."

Following the success of their PORDYA demonstration, the Kencana Wiguna beleganjur group received the invitation for their 1995 Arts Festival opening-parade performance. On this occasion all of the musicians, including the drummers, were women. The performance not only advanced Kencana Wiguna's own status and fame, but also helped to solidify the claim of an emergent women's beleganjur phenomenon to a niche in the contemporary Balinese musical culture.

By the end of my 1995 stay in Bali, it was clear that women's beleganjur, or *beleganjur wanita,* was a fast-growing phenomenon, with new groups being formed in Kuta (Badung), Pengosekan (Gianyar), and other locations. Individuals who in 1992 had categorically dismissed even the idea of such a thing were now becoming actively involved with it. For example, Asnawa, formerly a staunch opponent, was in 1995 talking about "liking the idea of it, women playing beleganjur," and even mentioning the possibility of producing a special women's beleganjur competition in Denpasar.[5]

Since that time, women's beleganjur has continued to develop. "Now, in 1995 and 1996," notes Sarah Willner, "more and more *gamelan wanita* are playing *beleganjur* . . . , though not in ritual contexts" ([1992] 1996, 11). The following posting of 9 June 1996 on the GAMELAN listserv (gamelan@dartmouth.edu) by Rucina Ballinger suggests that even in the realm of ritual, the impact of women's beleganjur has begun to be felt, and in remote areas far from the Denpasar urban hub from which the form emerged:

> Friends: I went to a Barong ritual north of Bitra a few nights ago and lo and behold, the baleganjur accompanying the Barong consisted of all women, not even a male drummer in sight. They played for a few hours, while waiting for another Barong from Bangli to arrive, through all the trancing and then a bit in the temple. Apparently the government is trying to encourage women's gamelans throughout the province. I was surprised to see this in such a small, isolated village. It's great!

Emansipasi or Hegemony?

Women's beleganjur has been hailed as great by some, as grating by others. Its controversial status is not unrelated to the inherent ambiguity of emansipasi itself, the ideological foundation upon which this new musical phenomenon essentially rests. Although locally conceived and developed in Bali, beleganjur wanita is a direct product of Indonesian government efforts to promote emansipasi, a nationalist version of "women's emancipation" that walks a fine line between appropriations of Western models of gender construction, a host of tenaciously persistent traditional views of the statuses and roles of women in Indonesian societies, and a rhetorical merging and conflation of gender, culture, modernity, and the national interest that is paradoxical and uniquely Indonesian.

The glossy exteriors of emansipasi rhetoric and symbolism only partially conceal the fragile entanglements of their underlying scaffolding. Public opinion, political discourse, and certain scholarly perspectives (see, for example, Lev 1996; A. R. Willner 1980; C. Geertz 1973b, 417–18 n. 4; and Geertz and Geertz 1975, 56) have collectively contributed to Indonesia's reputation, both internally and internationally, as a relatively progressive nation where matters of gender are concerned. Yet, as Julia Suryakusuma observes, "Beneath the superficial 'modernism' of 'national development,' gender and sexual discrimination has at

once become more acute and yet more subtle" (1996, 118). The out-
wardly modern, liberated women of idealized New Order imagination
and ideology, Suryakusuma asserts, are in truth valued "as appendages
of and companions to their husbands, as procreators of the nation, as
mothers and educators of children, as housekeepers, and as members of
Indonesian society—*in that order*" (101; italics mine).

Enframed by such paradoxes of nationalized gender construction
and perception, by the complexities of Bali's own traditional custom-
derived (i.e., *adat*-derived) norms and conventions of gender,[6] and by
the tensions and conflicting interests that animate the relationship of
New Order nationalist imperatives and "local attempts to protect local
autonomy and identity" (Guinness 1994, 284), beleganjur wanita has
been alternately promoted and contested. Its status as a potent but problematic symbol of both the advancement of Indonesian womanhood and
the "elevation" of traditional Balinese culture has contributed to the
controversy that surrounds it.

Women's Beleganjur, Balinese Culture, and the Emansipasi Agenda

In the following comments from a 1995 interview I had with him, Suandita eloquently captures the spirit of the official, government-promoted
perspective on women's beleganjur:

> It's important to have [women's beleganjur]. It's an experimental
> thing, a symbol of emansipasi. If women can play beleganjur, it
> really shows something, because it's the most masculine of Bali-
> nese genres. It's a new idea. It captures attention and it says some-
> thing important about how our society is changing. It's exciting to
> be involved with this. It's exciting and satisfying [for me] to be a
> part of it. . . . [Balinese society] has to be emansipasi. Girls and
> boys have to be treated on the same level. We need to make new
> forms to reflect this equality, like the women's beleganjur.

Suandita's enthusiastic endorsement is compelling, but the officially
sanctioned virtues of women's beleganjur he champions are not embraced by all. Critics, including Beratha and Dibia, attack beleganjur
wanita as a development that threatens established gender norms in dangerous ways, presenting not only formidable but also unfair challenges
to the delicate balance of *tradisional* (traditional) Balinese and *progrésif* (progressive) nationalist values that modern Balinese people

attempt to maintain as they negotiate and reinvent their culture within the political context of New Order Indonesia. Sarah Willner's characterization of women's beleganjur as an "inroad into more traditionally masculine territory" ([1992] 1996, 11) is certainly accurate, but perhaps understated. For some Balinese, at least, beleganjur wanita is seen not as an inroad into, but rather as an inappropriate and unwelcome invasion of, the musical territory of this most masculine of Balinese genres, an invasion that shakes the tenets of Balinese cultural propriety to their roots.

As Beratha asserts, "the proper spirit of [beleganjur] music is masculine and courageously bold *(berani)*, and to have girls play it both cheapens the music and puts the girls in an awkward and inappropriate situation." This notion affirms anthropologist Unni Wikan's assertion that among Balinese it is believed that "men should be brave *(berani)*, a quality unfitting in women" (1990, 71).

The following comments by Dibia (from an interview I conducted w.th him in 1995) express a similar sentiment in more expanded form:

> For me, beleganjur is like looking at rock music. I don't think I would enjoy women playing beleganjur. Once I saw it, and I thought, "This is too much." I guess I'm conservative, but I have my reasons. With gong kebyar, the women are still seated. There's still the grace and beauty of femininity. But to have women marching on the street, playing that loud [beleganjur] music is too much. . . .
>
> I reject the idea of developing women's beleganjur. . . . [F]or me, watching a woman play that music is like watching a beautiful woman driving a big truck. . . .
>
> The way [women's] beleganjur is developing now is not satisfying. What is happening in Bali doesn't always fit with modernity. Pushing things beyond hurts the quality of our cultural expression.

For both Dibia and Beratha, as for many like-minded Balinese, beleganjur wanita's violation of the integral connection that exists between Balinese conceptions of gender and Balinese conceptions of tradition is profoundly unsettling. "[W]ho bears more responsibility for being 'traditional' than women[?]" asks political scientist Daniel Lev rhetorically, "and what could be more uncomfortable, even destabilizing, than women redefining themselves as something other than the wives and mothers they [have] always been?" (quoted in Sears 1996b, 30).[7]

Whether women who play beleganjur are in actuality redefining themselves or are being redefined by others (i.e., by men), and whether or not their activities as musicians have any bearing at all on their values and priorities as wives and mothers, are relatively inconsequential matters at this level. The image—women performing beleganjur—is, in Lev's terminology, "uncomfortable, even destabilizing" regardless. In broader contexts, however, the matter of who actually controls women's beleganjur and defines its intended purposes does take on great significance. The perceived consumption of a Balinese cultural form by nationalist political interests has inspired resentment in certain quarters. As Barbara Hatley has observed, "Government cultivation of traditional, regional art forms [in Indonesia] has been seen to exacerbate the distancing of local communities from their own cultural expression, as performances are appropriated to new settings and 'developed' in accordance with outside values" (1994, 218).[8] Concerns over such distancing and appropriation processes are clearly evident in the above comments of Dibia. Implicit in his specific complaint about women's beleganjur—his criticism that "pushing things beyond" hurts the quality of Balinese cultural expression because "what is happening in Bali doesn't always fit with modernity"—is a much broader, more general critique of government-instituted programs and policies that impose nationalist values of modernity on localized forms of cultural expression in inappropriate ways.

By way of contrast, implicit in the official pro–women's beleganjur stance articulated in the comments of Suandita cited above is the notion that a national imperative of progress and modernization necessitates challenges and modifications to traditional beliefs and values at the localized, cultural level, even in instances where the departures from convention appear inappropriate to the people most directly affected by them. Change may hurt, but time and culture march on, and in New Order ideology the emansipasi imperative is cast as a fundamental component of Indonesia's drive toward modernization and progress.

On the surface, both the terms of the debate and the expression of those terms appear straightforward enough: Balinese cultural conservatism, as manifested in the archetypally masculine identity of beleganjur music and its world, versus Indonesian cultural nationalism, as manifested in the emansipasi symbolism of women's beleganjur. This specific opposition reflects a broader conflict of culture and ideology that exists within the Balinese women's gamelan world at large, one whose central dilemma is well articulated by Sarah Willner: "The structures of Balinese society and their interaction with modern Indonesian and international influences both encourage and discourage women playing [gamelan] music" ([1992] 1996, 1). This inherent tension of Balinese women's gamelan, in turn, reflects even broader sociohistorical Indonesian realities. As Guinness (1994, 270) explains, "Throughout the history of the Indonesian peoples local traditions and expressions of social and cultural autonomy have been pitted against external pressures for change."

With women's beleganjur in particular, however, the disparity between priorities of cultural autonomy and external pressures for change is extreme and unusually conspicuous. As we shall see later in our discussion, the stakes involved in choosing to encourage or discourage women's musical activities in the beleganjur sphere are probably higher than they are in the women's kebyar sphere. As a result, highly divergent opinions on the subject of women's involvement in beleganjur performance are common. Beleganjur wanita is Bali's musical manifestation of genderized "symbolic inversion" par excellence, seemingly possessing the power to "invert, contradict, or negate categorical distinctions" of gender constructs and thereby "furnishing a framework with which to comment upon or question the accepted order of things" (Roseman 1987, 145). The quintessential maleness of beleganjur music renders it an ideal vehicle for symbolically inverting gender distinctions, for reifying the *progrésif* ideal that in Bali, in the words of female musician Ni Madé Puspawati, "anyone can do anything, boy or girl."

But does beleganjur wanita even truly promote the progressive, egalitarian agenda for Indonesian womanhood that its symbolism and the rhetoric of its advocates imply it does? There is reason to suspect that it does not, and if this is the case, then a "traditional culture versus progressive ideology" opposition fails to do justice to the ideological complexity of beleganjur wanita's situation. A substantial literature encompassing approaches and perspectives of scholars from a variety of disciplines—and addressing topics ranging from women's activities and opportunities in music and other arts to their involvement in the Indonesian political sphere—suggests the need for a critical approach in the study of beleganjur wanita's purported intentions and ideological implications. Scholarly works concerned with women's issues in Indonesia, several of which will be discussed, compel the cultural analyst to view the women's beleganjur phenomenon not only in relation to the claims and counterclaims of its proponents and critics, but also through the lens of a critical theory orientation that frames beleganjur wanita as a hegemonic instrument of considerable power.

Processes of Marginalization

As was discussed previously in relation to Clifford Geertz's theories on New Order ideology, the challenge of how to prevent regional, ethnic, linguistic, and religious differences from taking on political force (Geertz 1990, 79) largely dictates the terms of an Indonesian nationalist agenda rooted in the construction and control of "culture." The work of Stephen Douglas, Barbara Hatley, Aline Scott-Maxwell, and other scholars suggests that this challenge extends beyond the domains of ethnicity, language, and religion to encompass gender as well; the proudly displayed cultural symbols of Indonesia's professed emansipasi ideals have frequently been revealed as contributing more to women's marginalization in political, social, and even musical spheres than to the purported empowerment of women in these areas. Cukier, Norris, and Wall (1996, 249) are correct in noting that "gender is a cultural phenomenon and, in consequence, modification of gender relationships require[s] changes in culture." Gender relationships and culture alike, however, can certainly be made to appear more enveloped in processes of change than they truly are.

In his revealing study "Women in Indonesian Politics: The Myth of Functional Interest," political scientist Stephen Douglas observes that despite "an absence of norms that severely proscribe the opportunities and status of women" (1980, 152), more subtle forms of institutionalized marginalization serve to ensure that women are "relatively inactive and have few opportunities for political expression" in Indonesia (176). Nonetheless, according to Douglas, "[a]lmost all public pronouncements on this topic by individuals of both sexes are reaffirmations of the myth that women do not merely have equal opportunities in politics but that they actually wield about as much political power and influence as do men" (178). This myth is strongly reinforced by the inclusion and prominent display of women at high-profile events such as political exhibitions and receptions. Through this systematic tokenism, the image projected, though illusory, is generally perceived as real. "The point is not merely that most Indonesians feel that both sexes should be accorded equal treatment and respect," claims Douglas. "The more interesting (and mythical) feature of popular thought on this topic is the belief that Indonesian women do in fact have opportunities for extensive and meaningful political activities and, further, that they have exploited these opportunities" (153–54).

The gulf between practical reality and public perception identified by Douglas is recognized in a different context by Barbara Hatley: "Viewed from different perspectives, a woman's position vis-à-vis that of men may be interpreted as either dominant or subordinate: ideological prescription and actual social practice are seemingly frequently at odds" (1990, 179). "[A]pparently egalitarian conceptions of gender relations in fact embody assumptions that are far from egalitarian in nature" (182).[9] In popular Javanese dramatic forms such as *kethoprak,* writes Hatley, even the ostensibly emancipated, modern, independent-minded heroines, that is, the *branyak/kenès* heroines, "are dramatically important only in their relationships with key male characters," their self-assertion occurring only "in regard to their relations with men" (204). In modern Javanese drama, as in modern Indonesian life generally, the "enhanced prestige of female concerns" invoked in the rhetoric of emansipasi is counterbalanced by a "greater female dependence on men" (205).[10]

Aline Scott-Maxwell, in "Women's Gamelan Groups in Central Java: Some Issues of Gender, Status, and Change" (1996), locates manifestations of similar patterns in a specific musical domain, noting that a "lack of *fundamental* change in the role and status of women in modern-day Indonesia finds correspondence in [Central Javanese] women's gamelan groups and perceptions of them in the community at large. While new, these groups are not seen as radical or as overturning social conventions" (226; italics in original). Countering possibilities for substantial change in the gender arena is what may be described as an indigenous theory of women's musical marginality that is strongly propagated, widely supported, and generally presumed true by members of Javanese society, whether male or female.[11] The musicianship and musical potential of Javanese women are discredited on account of a characteristic lack of "technical proficiency" and "aesthetic quality" among the women's groups (Scott-Maxwell 1996, 223, 226); their reliance on "visual appeal" rather than musical quality for the achievement of public recognition and popularity (228); and a notable lack of self-reliance in women's music-learning processes (226) that necessitates dependence on the guidance of male teachers and often the assistance of "two or three men who play the more difficult instruments" (224). "In the wider Javanese community," Scott-Maxwell asserts, "women's gamelan music is seen as an extension of other women's activities: a harmless interest that also provides an opportunity for socialising and acquiring a new outfit" (226).

Two fundamental and interrelated processes of women's marginalization, inferred from a review of Douglas's, Hatley's, and Scott-Maxwell's essays, appear to direct and define hegemonic appropriations of emansipasi ideals across a broad range of social, cultural, and political institutions in modern Indonesia. In the first process, cultural symbols of gender equality and women's emancipation—prominent displays of celebrated women at political events, assertive theatrical heroines, women's gamelan ensembles—are essentially turned upside down, coming to function less as reflections of than as substitutes for substantive advances in women's rights and opportunities. In the second process, both patriarchal control over the institutions of women's emansipasi and a host of "prevailing mythologies" (Douglas 1980, 179) that direct and distort public perceptions of the statuses and abilities of women in certain domains are seen to further diminish emansipasi's real potential to challenge established gender hierarchies that marginalize women.

In the discussion that follows, Balinese women's gamelan will be explored as a musical phenomenon rooted in these two basic processes of marginalization. The primary focus will be women's beleganjur, although we will begin with and frequently return to that genre's close relative and direct antecedent, women's kebyar *(kebyar wanita)*. The purposes of this examination are twofold: first, to identify how gamelan performance by Balinese women paradoxically reinforces myths of female marginality while purporting to advance the cause of emansipasi; and second, to illustrate that beneath the observable complex of practices and dispositions that relegates women's gamelan to the margins of Balinese musical culture lies a rather broad range of subject positions that alternately empower, challenge, and problematize the hegemonic authority of status quo conceptions of women's subordinate status.

Women's Kebyar: A Brief History

Women's kebyar, the dominant Balinese development of an otherwise Java-centered women's gamelan movement, became an established cultural institution in the 1980s. Its roots, however, date back to the early 1960s, when Beratha and Rembang began offering mixed-gender classes in gamelan performance at KOKAR. The purpose of the classes was to provide female dance students an opportunity to deepen their practical knowledge and understanding of the standard dance music repertoire.

Though the coeducational KOKAR groups did not perform publicly, they did influence future developments in important ways. According to Dibia, "The KOKAR classes with mixed gamelan set a precedent where people got used to seeing women playing gamelan. Before that, people would reject the idea of women playing drums and things like that. But that set a precedent. Because Beratha and Rembang were essentially endorsing the idea of women performing gamelan music, even some people in the villages picked up on the idea." Most notable among the village groups alluded to by Dibia was a pioneering women's ensemble formed in the village of Sidang, in Badung regency, around 1970.

The precedent set by the KOKAR classes also led to the formation of an all-women's kebyar group at the school in the late 1960s and indirectly fostered the eventual emergence of a highly significant women's group, Sekaa Gong Wanita Puspasari, over a decade later. In retrospect, the KOKAR all-women's group, which was organized by Beratha, likely had relatively little direct impact on the broader Balinese society, since the ensemble only performed once a year at the school's anniversary celebration. It was the formation of Puspasari that truly heralded the arrival of women's gamelan on the cultural stage of Balinese society.

Sekaa Gong Wanita Puspasari was co-founded by I Wayan Suweca and his sister, Ni Ketut Suryatini, now one of the two leading female musicians in Bali (the other being her Puspasari drumming partner, Ni Desak Madé Suarti Laksmi [Desak]).[12] In 1980, Suweca returned from a two-year teaching engagement in the United States, during which he, Michael Tenzer, and Rachel Cooper had co-founded Gamelan Sekar Jaya in California. Inspired mainly by the high levels of talent and ability exhibited by certain of his American female gamelan students—and additionally by the growing popularity of Javanese women's gamelan groups at that time—Suweca became curious about the potential musical abilities of Balinese women and decided to form a women's kebyar club, which rehearsed at his family home compound in Kayumas, Denpasar. Most of the group's personnel, including Suryatini, were veterans of the mixed or women's groups at KOKAR. At the time, many of them were dance majors at the ASTI conservatory. Two members, Rachel Cooper and Lisa Gold, were Americans who had studied with Suweca during his tenure with Sekar Jaya in California.

The most important event in Puspasari's short-lived career—the group as such survived for just over a year—was a performance on Indonesian national television, which was reportedly seen by millions of viewers throughout the country. "After that," recalls former Puspasari member Ni Putu Oka Mardiani (Asnawa's wife), "the group just kind of dissolved." Its legacy, however, did not. The attention generated by this pioneering women's ensemble largely influenced the government's eventual decision to add a women's kebyar division to the annual gong kebyar competition of the Bali Arts Festival.

Since its founding in 1985, the Arts Festival women's kebyar contest (Festival Gong Kebyar Wanita Seluruh Bali; see Yasa et al. 1993, 89) has been the defining institution of the Balinese women's gamelan movement, and has provided "the major incentive for the formation of women's groups in Bali" (S. Willner [1992] 1996, 12).[13] Through its first decade, the contest was largely dominated by a succession of women's kebyar groups representing Badung regency.

Badung won its first championship in 1986. The winning group (representing the civil service corps, KORPRI Denpasar) was composed mainly of former members of Puspasari, Suryatini and Desak among them. It also included two of the principal informants for the present study: Mardiani and Ni Nanik Kormaniati. While all of the performers in the ensemble were women, all of the teachers and coaches were men. In 1987, a nearly identical group represented Badung in the contest but did not win, finishing second to a strong ensemble from the small island of Nusa Penida (the representatives for Klungkung regency, in eastern Bali). From 1988 on, most of the women who had performed for the Badung groups in the 1986 and 1987 competitions were banned from the contest, when a regulation disallowing participation by arts conservatory students, alumni, and faculty was instituted.[14] In spite of this setback, Badung groups continued to be the dominant force in women's kebyar through the mid-1990s, winning five Arts Festival contest championships between 1988 and 1995.

Obstacles and Myths

In 1993, Badung's celebrated women's kebyar tradition became the basis of the first book-length scholarly study of Balinese women's gamelan, titled *Kehidupan dan Repertoire Gending Gong Kebyar Wanita di Denpasar* (The Life and Musical Repertoire of Women's Gong Kebyar in Denpasar; hereafter cited as *Kehidupan*). This important

180-page work (Yasa et al. 1993), written by a five-member committee of esteemed Balinese scholar-musicians, was published as a Research Committee Report (Laporan Penelitian Kelompok) by STSI Surakarta, Java, under the auspices of the Indonesian government's Ministry of Education and Culture.[15] Its contents reveal much about the ideological underpinnings of the Balinese women's gamelan movement.

In Sutton's terms, *Kehidupan* can be seen to represent a "crystallization" of the Balinese women's kebyar movement. Crystallization occurs when a particular arts genre or tradition undergoes "processes of objectification, formalization, and definition that are associated by Indonesians with a fine art tradition" (Sutton 1986, 118). "[T]he existence of a book, objectifying the tradition, a visible symbol of permanence" (122) stands as a certain indication that a crystallization process has occurred.

In the case of *Kehidupan,* what is crystallized is not the "fine art tradition" of gong kebyar itself, but rather the sanctioning of women's active involvement in that tradition. *Kehidupan* legitimizes the Balinese women's gamelan movement with reifying force, establishing women's kebyar as an integral feature of a modern, progressive, emancipated Balinese musical culture. The study legitimizes something else as well, however—namely, the same double-edged marginalization protocol observed in the Indonesian political, theatrical, and musical domains analyzed by Douglas, Hatley, and Scott-Maxwell, respectively: an imperative of patriarchal authority underscored by marginalizing assessments of female ability and character.

On the issue of male authority, an eleven-page appendix (Yasa et al. 1993, 147–57) listing all teachers and coaches *(pembina* and *pelatih)* employed in 1991 and 1992 rehearsals of Badung groups in the Bali Arts Festival women's kebyar contest is most revealing: not one woman's name appears among the dozens of individuals listed. Also noteworthy is the fact that while two of the three principal informants consulted in the *Kehidupan* study itself were women (Desak and Ibu Ketut Arini), all five co-authors of the report were men. Thus, in the making of music and in its study alike, the "voices" of female gamelan musicians are seen to be directed, mediated, and controlled by men.

A rationale for this evident subordination of female musical expression to male authority can be inferred from the one-page abstract *(Abstrak)* of *Kehidupan* (Yasa et al. 1993, viii). The abstract begins with a preamble in which "[t]he emancipation of women that was ignited by Raden Adjeng Kartini in the nineteenth century and that developed rapidly during the twentieth century" is hailed as a proud achievement of the Indonesian nation.[16] The accomplishments of celebrated Indonesian women in a variety of professional areas are cited in support of the position that emansipasi has in large measure already been achieved. Mention is made of female doctors and professors, a university president, the national government's Minister of Social Affairs, a foreign ambassador, and even an astronaut.[17]

Next, Indonesian emansipasi's debt to the Western "women's liberation" movement is acknowledged, but the use of the word "radical" *(radikal)* in connection with that movement—a term with pejorative connotations in Indonesia—suggests a subtle condemnation of the extremity of Western views: "Overseas, the form of women's emancipation has been known for a long time as Women's Liberation," write the authors. "Certainly they are sufficiently radical, that is: [there are] equal rights between women and men in a broad range of areas, as well as equality in professions, careers, and economic power."

Following the preamble, the discussion turns to the subject of the women's arts community of Denpasar (Badung), which, we are informed, was formerly limited to involvement in "the arts of dance, weaving and painting," but which has more recently come to encompass musical activity as well through the formation of approximately eighteen active gamelan clubs, "in which all of the instruments in the gong kebyar ensemble are played by women."

This development, however, has not occurred without considerable challenges. "The journey of women's gong kebyar has not been as smooth as that of the men's gong kebyar," write Yasa and his colleagues. "Certainly it is widely known that the obstacles as well as problems that have interfered have been complex enough. Several among them are: the busy schedules of women, where Hindu religious obligations have rendered establishment [of the women's gamelan movement] difficult;[18] a view held by society that the women's community still constitutes a weak community; [and] ethical problems of propriety and impropriety *(pantas/tidak)*."

These three major "obstacles" and "problems"—practical constraints on women's time and freedom, the relative lack of self-sufficiency and solidarity of the women's arts community, and issues of propriety relating to women's crossing over into men's domains— are identified at the outset by Yasa et al. with specific reference to Balinese women's gamelan. Through the remainder of the study, they serve as foundations for the rationalization of a seeming paradox: the marginalized status of women in an ostensibly emancipated musical world. They in turn come to support and to be supported by broadly held "commonsense" notions that (1) Balinese women lack the inherent capacity to play gamelan with anything approaching the competence of men and (2) whatever musical potential Balinese women do possess in the area of gamelan performance will not likely be fully realized without the direct guidance and assistance of men.

Thus, the case of women's kebyar appears similar to that described by Scott-Maxwell in connection with Javanese women's gamelan groups. It is not change in the role and status of women, but lack of such change that is fundamentally reinforced in the women's kebyar world. As in Java, the newness of the form does not imply a form of radicalism or the overturning of social conventions (see Scott-Maxwell 1996, 226); on the contrary, women's kebyar symbolically supports long-accepted beliefs in women's inferiority in traditionally male domains and justifies the authority of patriarchal institutions over women's emansipasi-defined activities and programs. In these ways, women's kebyar supports the dominant position of Balinese cultural traditionalists and Indonesian cultural nationalists alike, legitimizing the appropriateness and "naturalness" of sociopolitical hierarchies in which women's empowerment and liberation are celebrated in symbolic life while being carefully limited, monitored, and controlled by a male-dominated order.

Beleganjur Wanita: Unjustifying Gender's Margins

With respect to the ideological functions it serves, the overall profile of women's beleganjur closely resembles that of women's kebyar, and Javanese women's gamelan as well. In all three cases, the deference of women to patriarchal authority is deemed justifiable by the power of prevailing mythologies to codify the status of women as marginal. But while the generalities are the same, beleganjur wanita's specific dimensions render its position in the women's gamelan world unique.

Paradoxically, by placing women at the most extreme reaches of a male-dominated and male-defined musical terrain, women's beleganjur strengthens the case for Balinese women's musical marginality while at the same time threatening the established sociocultural order within which the terms of gender are constructed and negotiated. On the one hand, the definitive masculinity of beleganjur's character essentially ensures that women who play the music will be perceived as less competent and less convincing in their performances than their male counterparts. Even female musicians who may in fact possess the inherent capacity to achieve levels of musical force and physical robustness comparable to those that define the proper style, energy, and aesthetic of men's beleganjur cannot *afford* to fully realize their potential in these areas, since to do so would be to violate the most basic norms of appropriate female decorum, to cross lines that are not to be crossed even in the most "emancipated" of cultural frameworks. In order to protect the integrity of their womanhood, women who play beleganjur must do so with less force and bravura than men; and since force and bravura are essential components of good beleganjur performance, women's beleganjur cannot avoid assessments of inferiority. The symbolic impact of this situation strengthens public perceptions (or misperceptions) that women are unable to function equally with men in formerly gender-exclusive domains, and thus reinforces belief in the need for men to oversee women's musical activities. The case is similar in the kebyar world, but beleganjur magnifies more glaringly the appearance of a fundamental disparity between male and female musical aptitude.

On the other hand, beleganjur wanita groups, merely by virtue of the brash defiance of gender expectations they embody, *are* radical and *do* overturn social conventions, perhaps in ways that the kebyar and Javanese groups do not. Scott-Maxwell has observed that within the constraints of their marginalized status, Javanese women's groups challenge and redefine "certain images and meanings of gamelan performance that are perpetuated by the essentially male, *[sic]* mainstream of the gamelan tradition" (1996, 228). The same might be said of women's kebyar groups.

In women's beleganjur, though, the transformation of conventionalized, male-defined gamelan-related images and meanings appears to go beyond the level of challenge and redefinition, to the point of bordering on subversion. For example, the involvement of women in kebyar instrumental performance can be seen as representing a radical departure from gender conventions, but it can alternatively be viewed as no more than an expansion — albeit a rather significant one — of preexisting gender roles. As dancers and singers, women have long had a direct and intimate connection with kebyar music; in one sense, for them to play the musical instruments of the gong kebyar ensemble is merely an extension, or alternate manifestation, of their long-established involvement with the genre.

In beleganjur, there is no real precedent for women's involvement in musical performance.[19] Moreover, turning again to dance aspects of presentation, the choreography of the modern kreasi beleganjur, with its warlike postures and masculine images, is completely out of character with any culture-grounded Balinese aesthetic of appropriate female demeanor. Bali's historical and mythological histories do include legacies of female warriors (e.g., the warrior-heroine Srikandi of the *Mahabharata,* wife of Prince Arjuna), but even female warriors are not idealized in terms of the kinds of martially heroic masculine values of character embodied in beleganjur's symbolic universe. On account of its greater distance from a perceivable connection to established cultural precedents, women's beleganjur treads closer to a subversive position relative to foundational conventions of gender in Bali than does women's kebyar. This perhaps helps to explain the serious concerns of critics such as Beratha and Dibia, who appear to conceive of women's beleganjur not only as a somewhat awkwardly constructed symbol of emansipasi, but as a genuine threat to Balinese cultural integrity.

To paraphrase Margaret Wiener (1995a, 489), the women's beleganjur phenomenon, as a product of nationalist discourse, harnesses Balinese ethnicity and tradition through the symbolic potency of beleganjur sound and image, using a text of the past (beleganjur) in a new text indexical of the present (women's beleganjur) to serve the interests of the modern state and its projects (emansipasi). Such a form of discourse, Wiener notes, "does not recreate and rework the past in order to understand more richly and act more effectively in the present; rather it evokes the past in order to subvert it, transforming it into a manipulable object" (ibid.). Subverted past and mediated present collide in beleganjur wanita's world, exacerbating tensions at the border of culture and nation and unjustifying the established margins of gender. The core of beleganjur has come somewhat unraveled in the face of a women's performance medium, generating enthusiasm countered by derision, opening new doors while galvanizing efforts to keep the old ones firmly shut, and creating confusion—at least in the minds of certain men in the upper echelons of the Balinese arts community—over whether Balinese women are beneficiaries or victims of nationalist emansipasi agendas.

Balinese Viewpoints: An Interpretive Perspective

Beleganjur wanita's unlikely and uneasy synthesis of a Balinese cultural symbol (beleganjur) and a national ideological agenda (emansipasi) exposes disparities between the purported intentions and underlying motivations of an ideologically grounded musical phenomenon. How do individuals at various levels of the women's beleganjur world define the genre's complex, multilayered musical and ideological terrain? Through an interpretive examination of the expressed views and opinions of female gamelan musicians, male teachers and coaches of women's groups, and high-ranking members of the Balinese arts community, the following discussion explores how particular people negotiate conventional constructs of gender—gender myths, as it were—in relation to the ideological and cultural implications of a musical phenomenon that largely confounds such myths.

Following Douglas (1980, 153), I employ the term *myth* here "not in the sense of an erroneous belief, but rather in the sense of a belief widely enough shared and highly enough valued that it helps integrate the political culture," or in this case, the musical culture. In their implicit engagement of certain gender myths and certain modern musical realities within particular frameworks of ideas and perceptions, the individuals discussed below address the following questions: Is it proper *(pantas)* for women's gamelan groups to use men's musical performances as models for their own aesthetic and stylistic priorities? Do women have the inherent capacity to play as well as men? Do they possess the strength of character to be as musically self-reliant? How much impact does the issue of "visual appeal" have on public attitudes toward female musicians and on the reception of their music?

What emerges from the ensuing discussion is a composite "dialogue," in which the views of certain Balinese individuals toward women's beleganjur (and women's gamelan more broadly) are contextualized within a set of culture-grounded gender constructs that guide and influence *but do not necessarily determine* personal attitudes, actions, and opinions. The distinction between influence and determination is an important one, since neither traditional assumptions nor modern ideologies can fully contain or account for the range of responses presented here.

The people whose voices are invoked on these pages speak within, around, and in some cases beyond the prevailing mythologies and hegemonic prerogatives that ideologically enframe women's beleganjur. As Ward Keeler notes in reference to Java, "Blanket characterizations of females do not constrain individuals' actions completely. Yet by the same token, no individual can really undercut these categorical statements, which constitute a system of gender constructs" (1990, 148). The accounts that follow suggest that the same is true in Bali's beleganjur wanita world.

Part I: Girls Will Be Boys? Issues of Appropriate Style in Beleganjur Wanita Performance

In 1995, the fundamental debate about women's beleganjur that I encountered concerned the basic question of whether or not it should even exist. While women's kebyar was by that time an accepted reality of modern Balinese musical life,[20] even among culturally conservative factions, women's beleganjur was not. This difference rested on more than the fact that women's kebyar had simply been in existence for many more years than women's beleganjur. Deeper matters were at stake.

While kebyar's legacy as a men's music is indisputable, its character and the circumstances of its origin have made it relatively amenable to adaptation as a vehicle of women's performance. The case is the opposite for beleganjur. Gong kebyar is an invention of the twentieth century that has essentially defined the terms of innovative, experimental musical modernity in Bali. Women's performance of kebyar music can thus be rationalized as an adventurous extension of a broadly experimental kebyar aesthetic. Furthermore, as has been noted, women were already intimately connected with kebyar, as dancers and singers, long before the advent of women's kebyar groups. No parallel links existed historically in beleganjur's world.

The inherent affront to conventions of feminine character and beauty posed by women's beleganjur presented problems not only for those individuals with whom I spoke who claimed categorically that the genre should not exist, but for those who acknowledged its right to a place in the Balinese musical pantheon as well. For the latter group, the fundamental dilemma posed by the huge chasm separating conventional femininity from conventional beleganjur was whether or not efforts should even be made to bridge that chasm: Should women who play beleganjur act like women when they perform or should they in effect act like men, emulating the musical and performance styles of men's ensembles to the best of their supposedly limited abilities? Given an awkwardly difficult choice of options, is it preferable for women to compromise the integrity of female character by appropriating the style and energy of a male performance aesthetic or, alternatively, for beleganjur's character to be compromised by the concessions to femininity implicit in the notion of a distinctive women's style? Such questions of propriety prompted disparate and sometimes ambiguous responses, disclosing beleganjur wanita's problematic status relative to an ideology that essentially conflates gender equality and women's marginality.

For Ni Madé Puspawati, who at eighteen performed as a drummer with the Kencana Wiguna beleganjur ensemble in the 1995 Bali Arts Festival opening parade, emulating male performance models unquestionably represents the proper aesthetic ideal for women's beleganjur, despite the "fact" that practical achievement of such an ideal is unattainable. According to her,

> We want to play like that, with all the flashiness and the moves of the boys. It's not that we're embarrassed [to play that way], it's just that we lack the ability. . . . We have to concentrate just on the playing. We can't think about doing [choreographed movement sequences like the boys do] and other things. You know, we can have more action and movement during [the less technically demanding] slow passages, but not in the fast sections.

Puspawati's principal teacher, Suandita, expresses similar views in the following interview excerpt:

> Bakan: If you could get the girls to play and move exactly like the boys [when playing beleganjur], would you?
>
> Suandita: Yes, of course. That is the ideal; that is the model. That's how it should be. But it's impossible. Maybe if I had a whole year to prepare [a women's group it would be possible]. But yes, that's the goal.
>
> Bakan: So you don't see a need for a distinct "women's style"?
>
> Suandita: No. Beleganjur is about masculine energy and style. That's what you strive for. That's the ideal. For boys or girls.

Suandita reported to me that teaching women to play beleganjur presented formidable challenges and was in many respects more difficult than teaching them to play kebyar. Especially problematic for him was trying to deal with the choreographic aspects of women's beleganjur performance:

> Suandita: [I]n beleganjur, you need more action [than in kebyar]; it's about heroic feeling and the playing has to be strong, too. You have to play with so much energy and move that way also to get that. But in kebyar, the music, if played right, sort of takes

care of itself more. Therefore, as far as style, energy, and action are concerned, it is much more difficult to teach girls beleganjur, even though teaching the music itself is easier. For the boys, it's easy to get that energy, that action, but for the girls, doing choreographed sequences [like those seen in men's beleganjur performances] makes them a little embarrassed, a little nervous. Because of that, I try to create special choreography appropriate for the girls.

Bakan: How is it different?

Suandita: Of course, men are very comfortable with being bold and strong *(keras)*. That's what it's like being a boy. For the girls, it has to remain feminine. The movement must be slower, and the music, too. If it's a little slower, it's more appropriate.

Ni Nanik Kormaniati, a government employee in her mid-thirties who is married, has two children, and has performed for Badung annually in the Bali Arts Festival women's kebyar contests since 1986 (as a drummer since 1988), is one of Bali's most accomplished and well-known female kebyar performers.[21] In 1994, she was the lead drummer for the government group that first introduced women's beleganjur to the Balinese public at the opening parade of that year's Bali Arts Festival. As the following passage indicates, Kormaniati's opinions on the matter of how women should represent themselves in beleganjur performance are complex, suggesting a certain degree of ambivalence:

Bakan: Why don't the girls dance like the boys when they play beleganjur?

Kormaniati: Because we lose our concentration. We can't play and dance at the same time like the boys can.

Bakan: But you would if you could?

Kormaniati: Oh, yes.

Bakan: And if you could do that, the style and energy [you would strive to achieve] would be the same as [that of] the boys?

Kormaniati: Well, it depends on the situation. Sometimes, it's embarrassing to be like that. Sometimes we need to be more feminine—more like women, to keep a more composed *(polos)* expression, to be more refined *(halus)*. Maybe in rehearsal, we can be more like the boys, but in front of a committee, or honored guests, we can't be like that. There are moments when we could probably perform with the energy of the men, just as there are in kebyar.

When we play *topéng keras,* it has that strong, masculine feeling, but generally, yes, the appropriate style is going to be a little different for women than it is for men.

From I Wayan Dibia's perspective, women's gamelan style not only should but must be different from men's style. As we saw earlier, Dibia considers beleganjur to be so fundamentally at odds with the basic qualities of feminine character that development of an appropriate women's beleganjur style is in his view highly unlikely. In the following remarks, he identifies the specific source of the basic problem, although in doing so he at least acknowledges some tentative, speculative possibilities for improvement.

"You have to give [women] more space to demonstrate what is special about women," Dibia explained to me in contrasting beleganjur with other Balinese art forms, such as kebyar and *wayang* (puppet theater), where he sees distinctive women's performance styles having been developed with far greater success. "This is why I reject the idea of developing women's beleganjur. There's just no room for that to happen. Maybe if they developed a form of beleganjur with smaller drums and smaller cymbals, and if they used a *slendro* [instead of *pelog*] scale, that would make it appropriate. . . . If it has to develop at all, it should be developing as something different that allows for the cultural expression of women to emerge, through its instrumentation, compositions, and so on." [22]

Even in the far more hospitable medium of kebyar, Dibia finds fault with an increasing tendency for women's groups to be pressured into appropriating unbecoming aesthetic goals based on the models of men's groups:

> [T]he problem is that [women] can't play fast. Some instruments— reyong, drum—they can't play well. [Interlocking melodic patterns] are also difficult for them—at least that was the situation during the early days—but now the tempos are almost like those of the boys, because the teachers are always pushing for that. But I disagree with that [tendency of the teachers to push the girls], because you lose the artistic expression. You lose the identity of the women's groups.
>
> If it's going to be like that, why not just have men play? Why bother with women's groups? It should be distinct. There should be a separate style of gamelan playing for women. They shouldn't

push the tempo of the music. New pieces should be created with women in mind: pieces with slower tempos, different ornamentation. Seeing women play so fast, it hurts my feeling because it's pushing the limits. Maybe that's sexist, but I'm concerned about the artistic expression. It's like watching women bodybuilders. You know they're women, but they don't have feminine identity. I don't like that they are subject to this pressure to play like the men. It is gong kebyar, but it is gong kebyar [performed] by women.

Asnawa also feels that the emulation of men's performance styles by women's groups is unsuitable. In contrast to the more skeptical Dibia, however, he sees real possibilities for the development of distinctive, appropriate women's styles not only in kebyar, but in beleganjur as well. For Asnawa, the fundamental problem resides less in the act of women playing beleganjur than in the limiting position, held by most Balinese, that the correspondence between beleganjur and masculinity is essentially an absolute one. Advocating the adoption of more flexible perspectives on beleganjur's representational parameters in the following passage, Asnawa offers an interesting view of how a more appropriate women's beleganjur style might be forged:

[T]he gamelan beleganjur does not only play the strong-character *(keras)* music. There are also softer styles, [even] in the traditional beleganjur music. We have to create music that is appropriate for the women. That is the challenge. I think if you take strong, masculine music and have women play that music, it's nonsense. It has to be appropriate. . . . We have to create appropriate forms and appealing presentations; the etiquette of how women carry the drum, how they walk, their costumes, these are important. The biggest problem is probably the carrying of the gong. How can you have women carrying gongs [and still being feminine]? I don't know. As for the costume, maybe it can be something "semi," between man and woman. That's going to take some work.

For the women's beleganjur, we can keep the form of beleganjur, but the theme should be different. The "heroic" theme is appropriate for the men, but for the women, we have Srikandi, the female warrior [of the *Mahabharata*]. She's an appropriate symbol for the women; still heroic, but heroic "women's style." . . . In terms of theme, I don't care. We can establish new ones [that are more consistent with appropriate images of women]; for example, [themes related to] beleganjur accompanying wedding processions or for dewa yadnya[-type ceremonies, such as temple festivals, where slower, less intense styles of beleganjur are played].

From Asnawa's viewpoint—problematic details of gong carriers and costumes aside—neither the integrity of Balinese women nor the integrity of beleganjur need be sacrificed for the sake of the other in beleganjur wanita, since, as the above passage suggests, the tradition of beleganjur itself is not nearly so monolithic in its aggressively masculine identification as conventional wisdom proclaims it to be. Alternate symbols, such as the female warrior Srikandi, and alternate "themes," such as different types of religious ceremonies that move beleganjur away from its usual assumed identification with martial heroism of the masculine type, can be employed to bridge the semiotic chasm between "women" and "beleganjur."

In Asnawa's view, women need not look out of place, inappropriate, or incompetent playing beleganjur; that they have tended to appear thus is a consequence of a lack of sensitivity and imagination on the part of those who have been responsible for beleganjur wanita's conception and development. A suitable "women's style," according to Asnawa's theory, should not be modeled on the aesthetic priorities of men's style; nor should it represent a caricature of such priorities. The key to appropriate beleganjur wanita is to be found in a more creative dialogue with beleganjur's own past, one that facilitates the avoidance of, or at least diminishes the centrality of, the fundamental dichotomy inherent in a forced integration of feminine character and masculine music.

Part II: Strength, Talent, and Marginality

As the above accounts illustrate, opinions concerning whether female beleganjur groups should strive to emulate men's groups in their performances are rather diverse. Opinions on whether or not they can actually do so successfully are far more uniform. Regardless of their views on other matters, my consultants, female and male, were generally consistent in asserting that women lack not only the ability but also the innate capacity to play as competently, as expressively, and with as much strength and power as men.

Female gamelan musicians, according to Puspawati, are simply "weaker than men. The difference is in the power and expression. Girls have less power; we cannot play very fast. But it doesn't matter. If I can't play strong or fast, it's still okay for me. I love playing gamelan."

"It's just different," states Mardiani, echoing Puspawati's position. "Boys are just stronger. They can move their hands faster. I think even if a girl started from a very young age, same as a boy, the boy probably would still be better. It's physical."

Even Kormaniati, whose musical proficiency clearly exceeds that of many Balinese male gamelan players, and who has performed kebyar both in Bali and abroad with government-organized ensembles otherwise composed of men, supports this marginalizing notion. When I asked her if gamelan competitions featuring mixed-gender groups might emerge in Bali's musical future, Kormaniati laughed, shook her head, and replied, "Not possible. We're too slow. We can't keep up with the boys."

Emiko Susilo, an American woman who has studied and performed Balinese gamelan extensively in both the United States and Bali as a member of Gamelan Sekar Jaya and other groups, contends that the issue of physical strength is actually secondary to that of *bakat*—that is, aptitude or inherent talent—in the consistently marginalizing assessments of women's gamelan performance that one encounters in Bali. As she explained to me during a 1995 interview,

> Everyone [in Bali] acknowledges that the women's groups are inferior, though there are some really bad men's groups. But the best women's groups are not even close to even the middle-level men's groups. I don't think they think of [the difference] as really being a matter of physical strength—although there is a big concern that women are not supposed to lift heavy instruments. I think they believe the central difference is a matter of bakat, that in the women's gamelan, there is simply less bakat.

Ironically, the musical talent and competence of accomplished Western female gamelan musicians, such as Susilo herself, Rachel Cooper, Lisa Gold, and Sarah Willner—whose abilities oftentimes equal or eclipse those of their male peers—have prompted some Balinese musicians to devise alternate theories to support their marginalizing opinions of Balinese women who play gamelan. For example, Susilo reports that Dewa Ketut Alit, a well-known Balinese musician who in working with the Sekar Jaya group was very impressed by the bakat of certain female members of the ensemble, has suggested that the inferiority of Balinese women musicians may have less to do with physiology or an inherent bakat deficiency than with attitudes rooted in the processes of enculturation they experience. In his view, Balinese women, in contrast to both Balinese men *and* American women, are not taught to be bold *(berani)* and therefore suffer from fears that "they shouldn't do things that men do, like playing gamelan."

Most exceptional among the individuals with whom I discussed the matter of women's putatively inferior musical attributes was Suandita, who takes the "nurture-over-nature" concept implied in Alit's gender "theory" one step further; he goes so far as to suggest, at least tentatively, that Balinese women may indeed possess the inherent potential to play as well as their male counterparts.

"I think the [family] lineage issue is more important [than gender]," claims Suandita. "If a girl comes from a musical family, growing up in that environment and starting to play from a young age, she could very well end up a better musician than a boy from a less musical family. But we don't have girls playing from a young age like that yet.[23] I don't really know how to answer the question [of whether women are innately less gifted as musicians]."

Against the backdrop of a seemingly near-universal societal presumption that Balinese women are categorically deficient in musical capacity, Suandita's willingness to express uncertainty and open-mindedness on the issue of women's bakat (because there is insufficient evidence at present to reasonably do otherwise) represents a progressive, even radical, perspective. As we recall from Hatley, however, apparently egalitarian conceptions of gender relations in Indonesia typically embody assumptions that are far from egalitarian in nature (1990, 182). Her assertion is substantiated by the following comments of Suandita:

> There is a big difference between teaching girls and boys. Teaching the boys is easier. You give them the piece directly. Teaching girls is different. They take a much longer time to learn, and they don't have the power [of boys]. . . . Another problem: for the girls, the teacher tries to make the arrangement of the music really easy, something simple they can play. How to make the music simple and good? That's a challenge and a problem. . . .
>
> If I'm teaching [girls], I have to be calm and gentle. The girls don't know the patterns [or] the arrangement. You have to be very patient. . . . You have to speak slowly and be calm.[24] The girls, when they start, are embarrassed. . . . You have to always be encouraging and comforting. Also, [in teaching the Kencana Wiguna women's group], I used several [male] assistant teachers, so there

> could be more one-on-one attention. It's very difficult to deal with
> twenty-four people when they're learning like that. With the boys,
> I just go straight in.

Despite his earlier-cited pronouncement that "[g]irls and boys have
to be treated on the same level," Suandita's views on the practicalities
of teaching suggest otherwise. The future is one thing, the present
another. One infers from Suandita's remarks that female gamelan players in the here and now must be treated with a certain patronizing benevolence, since they lack self-reliance and physical power and are both
slow to learn and easily embarrassed. Such assessments affirm that in
order for women to survive and thrive in the "emancipated" modern
world of Indonesian Bali—where ideology, if not practical perception, dictates that "anyone can do anything, boy or girl," even play
beleganjur—the guidance, direction, and wise counsel that only men
can reportedly provide is still deemed essential. The success of emansipasi, paradoxically enough, is depicted in such a view as dependent
on women's submission to a benevolent patriarchal authority, and the
structure of the women's gamelan world bears this out, nowhere more
clearly than in the beleganjur wanita realm.

With respect to the issue of musical ability and inherent capacity, the
myth of Balinese women's musical marginality is uniform and pervasive. What is rather remarkable to the outside observer is that it persists
so tenaciously in the face of abundant contrary evidence, evidence
emerging not only from beyond Bali's borders or in vague speculations
about possible future developments, but from within present-day Balinese realities as well. In the women's kebyar world, at least, leading
female musicians such as Suryatini and Desak play as well as or better
than many male musicians and have achieved prominent positions in
the music-teaching profession;[25] the top women's groups equal or sur-
pass in quality many mid-range men's groups; and, as Sarah Willner
notes, "the issue of strength is questioned after seeing [Balinese]
women construction workers carry[ing] 100 pound sacks of cement on
their heads" ([1992] 1996, 3).

The marginalizing stereotypes persist under the guise of a commonsense body of public gender knowledge not because they are necessarily
true but because they are enframed by a thick protective layer constructed from the raw materials of female essentialization. The flexibility of these essentializing materials assures their resilience. Keeler
notes a similar pattern in the employment of gender stereotypes in Java:

That such stereotypes do not prevent women from attaining fairly high rank in the bureaucracy follows from the very flexibility of the system; that such women do not challenge anyone's impressions of females follows from the resilience of its categories. If women achieve success, they are seen to possess those qualities usually thought lacking in women. No one need wonder at that, nor reconsider their stereotypes (1990, 148).

Part III: Objectification: The Matter of "Visual Appeal"

In Bali, societal acceptance of a gender-based mythology of disparate musical potential and ability supports and affirms broader structures of patriarchal hierarchy that exist at many levels, from family organization to village politics and national governmental affairs. Acceptance of this myth reinforces public faith in a system that defines sociopolitical change in the realm of gender as consisting of increased female involvement and prominence in conventionally male domains where women are still denied the opportunity to significantly alter their subordinate status.

Maintaining the prevalent notion that women cannot play gamelan as well as men is a social and political priority at the levels of both local Balinese and national Indonesian interest. Beleganjur wanita powerfully supports such a priority by placing women in a musical context that highlights gender disparity to a degree verging on the bizarre. While official rhetoric espouses the virtues of women's beleganjur in terms of its embodiment and projection of emansipasi ideals, public responses to performances, and to the phenomenon as a whole, focus far less on issues of musical quality or progressive symbolism than on beleganjur wanita's "strangeness" or on the peculiar attractiveness of women playing music that defies any logical association with femininity. Relative to the first type of response, Dibia states that "[w]e have a word, soleh, meaning 'strange.' Sometimes things that are soleh, like women's beleganjur, are used to attract people's attention. It's something unusual so people will take notice."

For Dibia, this soleh quality is cast in negative terms relative to women's beleganjur, which, he claims, panders to a prurient public fascination with things bizarre but offers little beyond such fascination. Asnawa sees women's beleganjur in a more positive light, but he too recognizes that the genre's achieved public popularity has had relatively little to do with its musical attributes. He cites novelty value and the visual appeal of women as beleganjur wanita's two strongest selling points. In the following comments, it is evident that Asnawa views these extramusical matters as keys both to the genre's own success and to its potential contribution to the revitalization of a somewhat stagnant beleganjur scene:

> The challenge now [in 1995] for creators of kreasi beleganjur such as myself is how to make beleganjur music more attractive and to give it more variation. I think the [men's] contest style kind of reached a plateau in the early 1990s; you know, [with] the [championship] groups like Sedang [in 1991] and Meranggi [in 1992]. Since that time, it's gotten a bit stale. In many cases, people are already bored. That's why we need innovation: use beleganjur to accompany dance, have women's beleganjur, mix the standard beleganjur instruments with other instruments like bamboo instruments, put beleganjur on stage rather than in a procession, things like that. . . . [With women's beleganjur] the audience doesn't just want to hear music, but also to see the beautiful women. That's [human] nature. So I think if we have women playing beleganjur, people will come to see [them].

Objectification of the female musician as a beautiful, sexually desirable, and/or strange physical presence devoid of real musical significance most certainly plays into the broader processes of marginalization that undercut emansipasi's ostensible aspirations for change in the status of Indonesian women. The consensus position of all women musicians with whom I spoke, however, was that emphasis on their visual appeal served as a form of empowerment, not marginalization. To be on stage, I was told—and especially to be there doing something as demanding of attention as playing beleganjur, where feminine beauty is highlighted by its juxtaposition to masculine musical sound—increased one's attractiveness greatly.

In Bali, where a young woman's perceived worth is gauged largely in terms of her marriage prospects, the practical advantages of such enhanced powers of attraction are considerable. According to Kormaniati, playing gamelan, whether beleganjur or kebyar, is an excellent way to assert one's desirability to prospective husbands. "That's a good reason for women who don't have boyfriends to play gamelan," she explained to me on one occasion, quickly qualifying her remark by adding, "Of course, I'm married. I have children."

Even for female gamelan musicians who already have boyfriends, playing gamelan can be a useful social asset. "It makes us more attractive to *everyone!*" exclaims Kormaniati's close friend and drumming partner Ni Nanik Sujati, a single woman in her late twenties who works for a bank in her native village just outside Denpasar. "And especially if there's someone special out there in the audience. When my boyfriend is out there, he sees me play and I think he gets a little jealous because he knows all the other boys are looking at me [laughter]."

Sujati's claim that playing gamelan increases a woman's attractiveness "to everyone" suggests possible parallels between the public image of the female gamelan musician and that of the *branyak/kenès* heroines of Javanese *kethoprak* theater mentioned earlier in the discussion of Hatley's work. *Branyak/kenès* characters are admired for being "glamorous and flirtatious, spirited and vivacious, direct and assertive of speech" (Hatley 1990, 188). The popularity of this image "can perhaps be explained in terms of its multifaceted appeal. For male audience members it affords glamour, flirtatiousness, and sexual daring; for women, dynamic assertion of a woman's perspective; for the modern-minded, suggestion of potential progressiveness" (ibid., 197). And yet, as Hatley pointed out, these heroines are dramatically important only in their relationships with male characters; their self-assertion becomes manifest only in their relations with men (ibid., 204).

"The Best It Can Be"

In Javanese *kethoprak* theater and in Balinese women's gamelan, one is presented with images of assertive, modern, emancipated women whose assertiveness, modernity, and emancipation are mediated by male control and valuation. As I have argued throughout this chapter, this central paradox is manifest in the specific instance of women's beleganjur and in the culturalized appropriation of emansipasi symbolism and rhetoric generally. Beleganjur wanita represents one of many examples of a prevalent emansipasi pattern, in which gender myths function to marginalize women and render them subordinate to patriarchal authority in contexts ostensibly designed to highlight and celebrate women's independence and liberation.

To overlook the sociopolitical manipulations evident in beleganjur wanita or to deny their hegemonic implications would be naive and irresponsible. To conclude this discussion without directly addressing how that which is at stake and that which is valued in beleganjur wanita's world may transcend these manipulations and implications, however, would be negligent. Women who play beleganjur (and other forms of gamelan as well) claim to derive real benefits and genuine pleasure from doing so; there is no reason to question the sincerity of their claims. Dilemmas of proper musical style and demeanor, assessments of inferior musicianship, prescribed dependence on the leadership and guidance of men, and the privileging of visual appeal over musical performance do not change the fact that women who play beleganjur take pride in the music they make and in the musical organizations to which they belong.

Regardless of what machinations and manipulations underlie women's beleganjur, compelling the critical theorist to "deconstruct" it, the genre possesses meaning, significance, and power—*real* meaning, significance, and power—for those who are most directly involved. In this era of critical ethnomusicological thought, it is crucial to remember that what musicians do, what they feel, and what they care about still truly matter.

"Since childhood, I had a feeling I really wanted to play [beleganjur] music," Puspawati told me one hot August afternoon. "I saw the boys playing and I thought, 'I really want to try.' But initially, the head of the village didn't allow it. 'Maybe wait a couple years and we'll make a [women's] group,' he would say." Eventually he did, and now Puspawati plays beleganjur. She enjoys it. The desire to play, she says, "comes from a feeling in myself. I did it for myself, but I wanted to play with good players, the best possible. The quality is important. It must be the best it can be."

Puspawati's sentiments are heartfelt and impassioned. It means a great deal to her both to play beleganjur and to have the opportunity to do so. Perhaps she is aware of the hegemonic agendas beleganjur wanita has been employed to serve; or perhaps she is not. In either case, for her, to play beleganjur is to do something that is both important and enjoyable. Fortunately, neither the agendas of politicians nor the analyses of cultural theorists can do much to change that.

It is possible that the power of "blanket characterizations" of gender to effectively confine women's rights, opportunities, and prospects in Bali (and throughout Indonesia) is significantly limited by the inability of such characterizations to "constrain individuals' actions completely" (Keeler 1990, 148). If women such as Puspawati enjoy playing beleganjur and find in the experience something that is meaningful in their lives and relevant to their personal desires and aspirations, perhaps beleganjur wanita has achieved some of its purported emansipasi goals in spite of itself. Perhaps the ramifications of marginalizing assessments of female musicality, and of the presumptions of a need for patriarchal control stemming from such assessments, are neutralized—even rendered irrelevant—in contexts where women express little concern about whether their music-making is taken seriously or whether they have autonomous control over the activities of their musical lives.

And finally, we should not too readily dismiss beleganjur wanita's potential power as a force of substantive social change. As Guinness reminds us, "Despite the New Order's intent to appropriate cultural meanings and symbols to the purposes of national integration . . . [the] government has found it difficult to manage all aspects of the social and symbolic order" (1994, 299). (The GOLKAR beleganjur contest fiasco discussed in the previous chapter would certainly seem to lend support to Guinness's claim.) If ideological prescription and actual social practice are seemingly frequently at odds, as Hatley suggests, one does not necessarily guide the other; their relationship is dialectical. If the experience of performing beleganjur brings strength, power, solidarity, or even just a sense of joy to the women who play it, that which is internalized will likely be projected outward as well. The image may become the reality; ideological symbol may inform a transformation of social and political practice, if only to the extent that women may eventually gain greater control over the creation and production of the music they make.

The radical incongruity of beleganjur wanita brings to the genre a power to effect change that is perhaps unequaled in other spheres of the women's gamelan world. Women's beleganjur is a phenomenon with no reasonable place in a well-ordered and sensible Balinese beleganjur culture, for the simple reason that beleganjur, on its surface and at its core, is generally conceived of as a categorically male form of expression and a formal expression of maleness. Beleganjur wanita is thus a musical reality that defies cultural logic in the eyes of most Balinese. As such, it is a destabilizing force operating in a rapidly changing culture, a conspicuous and compelling anomaly that exists among people committed to shaping and defining their identity within the context of a nation whose political future is by no means certain or secure.

"The significance of representations," writes Wiener, "depends far more on the way they are received than on the aims of their creators" (1995a, 497–98). Paradoxically, women who play beleganjur have been cast as both recipients and agents of the musical and ideological messages they deliver, but not as the creators of those messages; in its representational significance, women's beleganjur has primarily been a creation of the hegemonic aims of a male-dominated political order committed above all else to its own preservation and continued strength. Nonetheless, as public performers, female beleganjur musicians are active agents rather than passive recipients of their designated cultural and ideological roles. They therefore possess an inherent creative capacity to interpret and negotiate the received terms of their own representational significance, and in turn to influence the perspectives of others and to promote real change: musical, social, even political. Beleganjur wanita may have emerged out of the hegemony of patriarchal Indonesian nationalism and its underlying mythologies, but at this critical juncture in Indonesia's history, the prospect that it may help to promote new agendas of gender, informed and inspired by the values and expressive desires of women in their efforts to represent themselves, is by no means untenable.

Part Four

Pengecet

Introduction to the Pengecet

At the conclusion of her essay "The Ethnomusicologist, Ethnographic Method, and the Transmission of Tradition," Kay Shelemay writes: "Most of us are well aware that we do not study a disembodied concept called 'culture' or a place called the 'field,' but rather encounter a stream of individuals to whom we are subsequently linked in new ways." Citing Arjun Appadurai, she proposes that "human relations may be the most promising residue of a field once conceptualized as local, stable, and bounded. We can begin by teaching and practicing an ethnography that acknowledges a reality of sharing and interaction, one predicated on negotiated relationships" (1997, 203–4).

It is to such a form of ethnography—of musical ethnography in particular—that the remainder of this book is dedicated. In these final chapters, we begin to move away from the Balinese musical culture of beleganjur per se and into a specific intercultural space of beleganjur-centered musical experience shared by two drummers: I Ketut Sukarata and myself. It was through the medium of beleganjur drumming that Sukarata and I became linked as people, and it was through learning to drum with Sukarata that I gained some of the most important insights and understandings of my research. Beyond the sphere of beleganjur itself, our musical relationship revealed to me a great deal about how people learn, communicate, share, negotiate, and come to trust and connect with one another through musical experience: intraculturally, interculturally, and through creative means that sometimes appear to either bypass or transcend altogether the cultural identities of the individuals involved.

Experiencing and reflecting upon the world of beleganjur drumming Sukarata and I created and shared has compelled me to view ethnomusicology in a new light, one in which the researcher's own learning and performing experiences and musical encounters during the fieldwork process are themselves treated as important ethnomusicological data worthy of scholarly attention, rather than just as means toward a desired end of knowledge and understanding of the musical and cultural Other. The particulars of who we are when we begin, what we experience as we go along, and where we arrive at the provisional endpoints of our musical journeys with musicians whose worlds we endeavor to understand are essential components of ethnomusicological investigation and should not be marginalized, let alone ignored, in our writings.[1]

Seven

Learning to Play: Balinese Experiences

Although the primary issues to be addressed in these final chapters relate to the intercultural musical encounter comprised in my studies and experiences with Sukarata, the first concern will be to examine the more normative pedagogical context within which this encounter was framed: teacher-student interactions between Sukarata and his Balinese beleganjur drumming students (who ranged in age between fifteen and twenty-two). This examination, drawn to a significant extent from an earlier publication (Bakan 1993–94) and based mainly on live observation and videotape analysis of drum lessons taught by Sukarata during a three-month period in 1992, should prove useful on two levels: first, it offers a case study of Balinese *maguru panggul* pedagogy, the primary teaching method employed in kreasi beleganjur and in Balinese gamelan music instruction generally; and second, it provides a comparative basis for the reflexive analysis and interpretation of music-learning processes presented later in the book.

During my studies with Sukarata in 1992 and 1995, I was often compared—by him, by others, and admittedly by myself as well—to his other kendang students. Their work with him, like mine, was directed toward achieving mastery of the complex drumming parts in his kreasi beleganjur compositions. The broader purposes of our respective projects were different, however. I was a Western-trained percussionist engaged in ethnomusicological research; they were young Balinese musicians preparing for upcoming beleganjur contests.

At a fundamental level of shared *musical* aspirations, though, Sukarata's Balinese students and I inhabited a common ground, learning similar if not identical musical materials from the same teacher-composer over similar spans of time. The methods and techniques these other students and I employed in our efforts to achieve musical competence were at times closely related, but more often were vastly different. My musical and cultural background, together with the idiosyncratic larger goals toward which my beleganjur drumming endeavors were being directed, ensured that I would approach things differently than my

Balinese peers, and that I would be perceived as different from them regardless of how I actually played.

Not Seeming to Teach

In his 1954 essay "Children and Music in Bali," Colin McPhee paints an evocative portrait of a method of music instruction familiar to anyone acquainted with Balinese music pedagogy:

> The teacher does not seem to teach, certainly not from our standpoint. He is merely the transmitter; he simply makes concrete the musical idea which is to be handed on, sets the example before the pupils and leaves the rest to them. It is as though, in teaching drawing, a complex design were hung on the wall and one said to the students, "Copy that." No allowance is made for the youth of the musicians; it never occurs to the teacher to employ any method other than the one he is accustomed to use when teaching adult groups. He explains nothing, since for him, there is nothing to explain. (1954, 232–33)

Such teaching is known in Bali as *maguru panggul,* literally, "teaching with the mallet" (Asnawa, pers. comm., 1992). Maguru panggul is an oral/aural tradition approach. No music notation is employed, and the effectiveness of teaching is almost exclusively dependent on a holistic demonstration-and-imitation mode of transmitting musical knowledge from teacher to student (see also Herbst 1997, 151–56). The term *maguru panggul* refers specifically to the teaching of gamelan. A related term with broader applications is *nuwutin,* defined by Dibia as a "traditional teaching method emphasizing on [sic] imitating rather than analyzing" (1992, 383). *Nuwutin* can be used to describe traditional teaching methods employed in dance, theater, sculpture, and other arts, as well as music.

The terms *maguru panggul* and *nuwutin* themselves suggest what actually takes place in interactions between Balinese kendang teachers and students, and also offer insights into the pedagogical values and concepts underlying such interactions. The central role of the mallet as a transmitter of musical information implied by the notion of "teaching with the mallet," and the either/or distinction between imitation and analysis implied in Dibia's definition of *nuwutin,* provide important clues concerning basic differences between Balinese and Western conceptions of what it means to teach music. The Balinese teacher functions as a modeler of ideal music whose methods are decidedly anti-analytical. In the way he conveys musical information to the student and orients the entire learning process, there is a consistent aim to present the musical whole without drawing undue attention to the parts of which it is composed. This "holistic" orientation fundamentally distinguishes the Balinese maguru panggul teaching method from analytical and intervention-oriented Western pedagogical approaches, especially those involving music notation (see Bakan 1993–94, 4–5).

One-on-One

In the teaching of kreasi beleganjur groups (as in the teaching of gamelan in virtually all contexts outside of certain conservatory training environments),[1] maguru panggul is the standard pedagogical method employed. In general, beleganjur is taught and learned in the context of full-ensemble rehearsals. There is one notable exception, however. Because of the technical difficulties of the kendang parts and the ensemble leadership responsibilities of the drummers, drum parts are often learned in advance, during specially designated drum lessons.

The teacher may choose to work with just one of the drummers initially, or he may opt to instruct both at the same time; in either case it is usually the lanang player, the ensemble leader, who is the focus of his attention. While the lanang part is being taught, the wadon player, if present at all, will usually attempt to work out his part alone by means of a process of "filling in the spaces" between lanang strokes. Alternatively, the teacher may work privately with the lanang player, who is then assigned to teach the wadon part to his partner at some later time. Whichever method is employed, one-on-one instruction is emphasized in the beleganjur drum lesson, and since this was also the case in my own course of kendang beleganjur training with Sukarata, comparative perspectives are appropriate.

Imitation and Immediacy

"Teaching with the mallet"—maguru panggul—is a literal description that captures the essence of interaction between Sukarata and his students during beleganjur drum lessons. For the sake of illustration, let us investigate the maguru panggul process through a study of kendang beleganjur lessons involving Sukarata and an imaginary student, "Wayan." [2]

Sukarata's performance demonstration of the drum part to be learned (kendang lanang) is the only "score" available to Wayan as he attempts to come to grips with highly exacting and complex musical materials. Notation is not used, nor does any exist. Adding to the challenge (at least from a Western perspective) is the fact that Sukarata does not tailor his demonstrations to Wayan's specific learning capacities or limitations, as a Western music teacher might in an aural learning situation. Rather than beginning with short patterns and motives and building up from there in "call-and-answer" style, Sukarata plays an entire puku-lan for Wayan right away, in its complete form and at full speed. The demonstration may last a minute or longer. Nothing is broken down or simplified for Wayan's benefit; he must fend for himself. Like the arche-typal teacher of McPhee's description, Sukarata "simply makes con-crete the musical idea which is to be handed on, sets the example before the pupils and leaves the rest to them." [3]

So how does Wayan begin to make sense of a quantity of incoming musical information that would confound even the most talented West-ern music student? He begins by focusing on Sukarata's mallet. The mallet, or *panggul,* is the implement that connects drummer to drum, turning a dance of playing motion into musically patterned sound. More than the words he utters or the rhythmic patterns he produces, it is Su-karata's panggul that initially "tells" Wayan what to play. The path to technical competence and musicality begins with the student's ability to reproduce the motion patterns of the teacher's mallet.

From the moment the performance demonstration begins, Wayan fo-cuses his gaze intently on Sukarata's mallet. Almost immediately, he jumps in and attempts to play along with Sukarata, doing all he can to follow the guiding mallet's motion and reproduce it with his own. Mim-icking the motion of the teacher's mallet is the first and key element in a process that will see Wayan gradually move toward re-creating the entire kinesthetic-musical event being modeled. Mallet motion func-tions as a symbolic code containing visually discernible musical data. It is, in its own way, a form of musical notation. Thus, in the early stages of learning, rather than striving to capture the musical sound and struc-ture of what he hears, Wayan, like other Balinese music-learners, as-pires to effectively emulate the physical manner and expression of what he perceives in his teacher's playing *visually.*

As "the music" is transported from Sukarata's mind through his body, through his hands, and into his mallet, ultimately being brought to life by the kendang itself, it enters Wayan's body and mind through an inverse process. As his mallet motion begins to approximate Suka-rata's, first hands, then arms and body follow suit. Before Wayan can play anything that sounds even remotely like "the actual notes" of the music, he is in full command of a vocabulary of movement and a *style* of playing that capture the essence of the musical passage while lacking most of its structural and formal content.[4] The *gestalt* of the performance is intact before the specific notes and patterns begin to fall into place; Wayan's response to what he sees and hears being played is based, at least initially, on his perception of "a complete and unanalyzable whole rather than a sum of . . . specific elements in the situation." [5] Primary learning occurs as a product of direct kinesthetic imitation rather than through a step-by-step processing of incoming musical information.

Wayan's response is also notable for its immediacy. As was mentioned, he jumps directly into the act of drumming without first listening to what he is being instructed to play. In contrast to a schooled Western musician facing similar learning challenges, Wayan approaches his formidable task with little initial concern for knowing what the music is supposed to sound like before he attempts to perform it. To a Western observer, his approach may appear random and chaotic, disruptive to the teacher, even counterproductive. This was indeed my first reaction. Yet closer study revealed that "playing before thinking" is part of a systematic learning strategy that is characteristic of Balinese music-learning situations: simultaneous reception and attempted reproduction of the music performance model are part of standard practice. This has also been noted by Michael Tenzer in a comparison of Balinese and Western cognitive strategies for learning music: "Reading music," writes Tenzer, "is a process of translating symbols into sounds; Balinese musicians bypass this stage entirely and learn music by transforming a received musical gesture directly into the physical act of playing" (1991, 106).

From Mimetic Imitation to Conceptual Learning

As we have seen, the direct transformation of received musical gesture into physical act of playing described by Tenzer commences in the beleganjur drumming case with imitative mallet motion. This paves the way for a multistage learning process that enables students such as Wayan to convert purely imitative and "musically meaningless" physical actions into technically precise, stylistically appropriate, and expressive musical performances modeled on those of their teachers. As this process unfolds, imitative methods increasingly give way to more conceptual strategies of learning that yield the more precise details of musical content.

Throughout this evolving process, the teacher's role remains essentially unchanged: Sukarata "repeats" the performance demonstration for Wayan over and over again, as many times as is necessary.[6] With each repetition, though, Wayan moves to deeper levels of musical comprehension and competence. His progress appears to be more "choreographic" than musical over the course of the first few repetitions; he begins to *look* more and more in control of what he is playing, although it remains difficult to discern much structure in the *sound* of what he is producing. Eventually, a clear sense of the general musical style begins to come into focus in Wayan's playing, but command of the content of the music—that is, the correct notes, rhythms, stroke patterns, and the like—remains at an embryonic stage. What one hears is a kind of rhythmic rambling, analogous to the "expressive jargon" of infants who produce "a string of utterances that *sound* like sentences, with pause, inflections, and rhythms, but that are made up of 'words' that, for the most part, are nothing more than meaningless gibberish" (Papalia and Olds 1975, 92).

Full technical command of the pukulan does not develop until relatively late in Wayan's learning process, and it comes about in a seemingly haphazard manner. Mastery of the specific patterns of strokes and rhythms does not follow a linear progression. Rather, small, scattered "patches" of properly executed notes begin to emerge here and there amidst the semi-improvised, semi-imitative rhythmic ramblings. In each successive repetition, the patches of correct notes become a bit longer, and more of them start to pop out from the rambling texture, until finally the musical structure of the model begins to take shape and become recognizable in Wayan's playing.

It is noteworthy that at precisely the point in the learning process where correct patches begin to emerge from rambling, Wayan begins listening to Sukarata's demonstrations of the pukulan without trying to play along. This change in learning strategy clearly indicates a shift of attention from general musical shape and style to specific details of structure and form. It is here that Wayan's learning becomes more conceptual than imitative, more mental than physical.

In effecting this cognitive shift, Wayan is provided with little if any direct guidance by Sukarata. Verbal feedback from the teacher is rare, and does not usually exceed a blanket assessment of "pas" or "belum pas"—"correct" or "not yet correct"—in response to one or another of Wayan's attempts to re-create the drum part being illustrated. At most, Sukarata may nod his head animatedly, exaggerate his playing motions, or increase his dynamic level at some point during a demonstration to highlight a segment of the pukulan that Wayan has been struggling with or playing incorrectly. Such accommodations are implemented with reluctance, however. They are a last resort, since they necessitate compromising the inherent integrity of the demonstration model performance. The facial expressions that go along with them seem to carry a message: "What's wrong with you, Wayan?" or "Can't you listen, Wayan?" Sometimes such things are actually said.

Stock Phrases

In the process of converting rhythmic rambling into coherent drumming forms, kendang beleganjur students such as Wayan build from their knowledge of what I will refer to as "stock phrases." Stock phrases are here defined as standard, idiomatic kendang patterns and short forms that can be employed in many different compositions. They are recognizably distinct and transferable. Some are specific to pieces within a particular style, genre, or repertoire; others may span a wide range of different genres and repertoires. Like standard jazz licks or blues text formulas, stock phrases constitute a common resource pool of musical materials that can be recast and recombined in an infinite variety of ways in the creation of new musical works or new treatments of existing ones (and also in kendang improvisation, though this is beyond our present scope). In the kreasi beleganjur drumming context, anything from a short cadential angsel pattern to a lengthy passage of "Jagul" drumming may be identified as a stock phrase in a new beleganjur contest piece, for example, in one of the pieces composed and taught by Sukarata.

My research on kendang beleganjur has indicated that stock phrases provide the primary "handles" used by student drummers such as Wayan in their efforts to come to grips with new musical materials. How quickly and efficiently a student learns is directly related to the size of his store of stock phrases. In general, the more extensive a musician's repertoire is, the more stock phrases he will have in his memory bank; and the more stock phrases accumulated, the more quickly new pieces can be learned. Master drummers such as Sukarata and Asnawa often appear to learn the drum parts of even highly complex new gamelan compositions almost instantly, largely on account of their having internalized huge personal "data banks" of stock phrases that can be drawn upon at any given moment. For such musicians, the learning of new pieces becomes mainly a matter of ordering and arranging chunks of musical material that are already familiar, rather than one of starting from scratch.

Stock phrases, once they have been recognized and located within the form of a piece being learned, come to function as pillars that provide the student with a sense of shape, structure, and orientation from which to build the pukulan as a whole. Sections of the pukulan directly leading up to and away from these musical pillars tend to be mastered more quickly than others that are further away. A single pukulan may contain two, three, or even four stock phrases, and the later stages of learning involve the student in a strategic process of linking these phrases together with ever increasing accuracy and refinement. The stock phrases provide points of orientation and direction within the larger musical design, enabling a student such as Wayan to progress from mere mimicry of the teacher's motions to a combination of imitation and cognitive structuring strategies that help to gradually turn his early rhythmic ramblings into precisely executed extended drum forms. And since stylistic competence tends to precede technical mastery in the learning process, by the time Wayan finally links all of the pillars together and can play the entire pukulan correctly and precisely, he has already learned to play it "musically": with appropriate style and expression.

Engendering a Holistic Conception of the Music

Because Balinese music teachers tend to provide little in the way of explicit instruction, students such as Wayan must be extremely self-reliant and resourceful in order to be successful learners. As I observed Sukarata's teaching, it became evident that promoting self-reliance on the part of his students and presenting the music he teaches in as holistic and complete a manner as possible are key to his conception of what constitutes "good teaching." Techniques that involve breaking a musical work down into discrete, manageable segments, or that are premised on providing students with specific directions on how to solve musical problems they encounter—hallmarks of "good teaching" by Western standards—are totally foreign to Sukarata's pedagogical methods and sensibilities. He is categorically anti-analytical when working with Balinese students.

Analysis, by definition, draws attention to specific aspects of a piece of music rather than to the musical whole to which they belong. Since in Sukarata's view it is the whole rather than its parts that must be emphasized, any method that privileges the smaller picture over the bigger one is undesirable. Musical holism and flow are of highest priority, and are stressed at a variety of levels throughout the entire music transmission process.[7] Sukarata's strong preference for complete, unmodified demonstration performances is but one manifestation of his holistic teaching philosophy (and of the central philosophy underlying maguru panggul more broadly). Three other characteristics that are especially important are interlocking rather than playing in unison with students at the first possible opportunity; emphasizing complete run-through performances during lessons and rehearsals; and fostering "ensemble environments" in all learning situations, even "private" drum lessons.

Interlocking

Throughout this discussion, I have stressed the central importance of demonstration performance models in Sukarata's pedagogical method. What Sukarata actually plays in a demonstration, however, changes significantly from one "repetition" of a pukulan to the next. He constantly shifts between performing the drum part he is teaching (e.g., the lanang) and its complementary interlocking part (e.g., the wadon) over the course of a lesson.

The guiding principle underlying Sukarata's improvised decisions to play one part or the other at any given moment is his desire to provide as complete a picture as possible of the composite two-drum part at all times. Thus, he begins by modeling the lanang part for Wayan, but at every point where Wayan is able to join in with even a nominal degree of competence—however partial or fleeting—Sukarata switches immediately to the wadon part. He switches back the instant Wayan falters, and so on, back and forth.

As Wayan achieves greater command of his lanang part in successive repetitions, a seamless textural shift from lanang alone to lanang and wadon together is effected; unison playing by the two drummers is systematically avoided on account of Sukarata's part-switching technique. Thus, by the time Wayan can navigate his way through his own part, he has already learned to play it—and to hear it—in tandem with the other part. This is of crucial importance to Sukarata, since it ensures that Wayan will never be prone to conceiving of his own part as being in any way musically independent. In order for Wayan to play effectively, he must feel the lanang and wadon as one, not just as complementary but as completely interdependent. This sense must be reinforced from the earliest possible stage of the learning process. Once again, one sees in Sukarata's method a systematic avoidance of anything that would privilege the isolated part above the integrated whole.

Run-Throughs: Maintaining the Music's Formal Integrity

With respect to issues of large-scale linear musical form, similar priorities are in evidence. Not only are the component parts of a given pukulan essentially denied independent status in Sukarata's teaching, but the pukulan as a whole is likewise stripped of any claim to an autonomous identity. As soon as Wayan is able to play through a new pukulan with some semblance of competence, it is woven into the larger fabric of the piece to which it belongs. From this point on, it will not likely be played in isolation ever again; Wayan will only have opportunity to practice it in the context of run-through performances.

In all instances except those where new musical materials are being taught, Sukarata's drum lessons and the full-ensemble rehearsals he coaches are dedicated almost exclusively to run-throughs. It is rare for him to isolate and work on specific passages or problem spots in either context. Pieces are run from start to finish, or, in the case of compositions that are still being learned, from the beginning to whatever point in the piece has already been taught. They are always played at full speed (or as close to full speed as possible). If Wayan makes a mistake during a drum lesson, he is expected to simply recover and continue, without missing a beat. If the mistake is sufficiently serious to grind the performance to a halt, he must start again from the very beginning of the piece, regardless of what point he had reached when the mistake occurred. The same rules apply in ensemble rehearsals.

Because so much time and energy is spent on running through the complete piece, rather than on working in detail on selected sections, the entire multipart arrangement is eventually committed to memory as something more like a solid block of musical material than a sequence of distinct musical segments connected by transitions. Memory lapses are rare once the piece has been learned, and the achievement of proper musical flow and a sense of continuity is greatly facilitated by this run-through-based method.

The Ensemble Environment

Sukarata's holistic priorities as a kendang beleganjur teacher are further exemplified by his tendency to create "ensemble environments" in all teaching situations, even in contexts where one-on-one drumming instruction is the primary activity. Wayan's drum lessons with Sukarata are held at the balé banjar, where the village beleganjur group's rehearsals take place and where their instruments are stored as well. The balé banjar is an open-sided, out-of-doors pavilion in the center of town. During Wayan's lessons, members of the sekehe and other villagers congregate there to watch and listen. Rather than being mere passive observers of the lesson, the visitors often become active participants. At Sukarata's encouragement, beleganjur instruments are removed from the storage closet and used to "accompany" the lesson. Usually it is members of the sekehe who play, but even the non-members in attendance are welcome to take part, especially children who hope to join the ensemble some day.

The dynamic between Sukarata and Wayan is disciplined and highly focused, while that of the ad hoc aggregation of accompanying players is contrastingly informal. However, the observable disparity is somewhat deceptive. While little if any direct attention is paid to the "extra" players, their contribution is very significant from Sukarata's perspective. The presence of the additional instrumental parts they provide ensures that Wayan will not internalize the drumming as a distinct musical entity, that he will be compelled from the outset to hear the drumming in context, as one component of the greater musical whole to which it belongs. Even if only a *gong* player and a kajar player are present, the quality of the learning environment is enhanced considerably, and the more instruments that are played, the better. From Sukarata's perspective, the ideal is to create for Wayan an environment that is geared simultaneously toward a focused concentration on drumming and toward a diffusion of such concentration into the more comprehensive and inclusive musical feeling of an ensemble rehearsal situation. In contrast to the typical Western music lesson, there is no closing of the studio door, no attempt to create an isolated space where teacher and student can devote themselves to meeting their pedagogical objectives in an environment free of potential distractions. As John Blacking has written, "music is a social fact" (1980, 195). One might say that all music cultures are social, but some are more social than others.

Eight

Learning to Play:
An Ethnomusicologist's Experiences

> The failures and obstacles . . . are often as enlightening as the successes,
> provided one is able to step aside and observe oneself and others, analyz-
> ing the problems that arise from clashing assumptions, perceptions, de-
> mands, and capabilities, few of which are made explicit.
> Benjamin Brinner, *Knowing Music, Making Music*

The path I pursued in my efforts to gain competence as a kreasi beleganjur drummer was far removed from those followed by Sukarata's
Balinese kendang students. From the time of our first meeting in Seminyak in 1992, Sukarata and I established an unorthodox dynamic of
teacher-student interaction, by Balinese or Western standards. At the
moment I reached into my shoulder bag and pulled out drum transcriptions from my lessons with Suweca, any pretensions I may have har-
bored of someday being able to claim that I had learned to play kendang
beleganjur from a "cultural insider's perspective" (whatever that may
be) effectively vanished. Sukarata and I were destined to forge our relationship in a liminal space of beleganjur music-making belonging to
no "culture" in particular, neither his nor mine. The norms, rules, and
standards that ultimately came to guide our interactions were of our
own making; they were products of an ongoing process of negotiation
between us. In our efforts to understand each other and make music
together, we improvised, compromised, and often struggled through
conflicting personal agendas and frustrating miscomprehensions, musical and otherwise.

   This chapter and the one that follows it are about my relationship with
Sukarata and the musical world we created and shared as beleganjur
drummers in Bali. Whereas ethnomusicologists have normally treated
their own music-making and music-learning experiences in the field as
stepping-stones toward gaining knowledge and understanding of the
musical-cultural Other "from within," or from an "emic perspective,"

my purposes here are different. The focus and endpoint of this study are found in the intercultural musical encounter itself; it is an exploration of how two individuals were moved toward new approaches to music-making, new insights, and new understandings of their worlds and each other through musical experiences they shared in the context of an ethnomusicological research project. This constitutes a reversal of normative epistemological priorities, the privileging of a domain of music-making that has usually been muted or even ignored altogether in ethnomusicological publications. In this study, beleganjur music and the Balinese cultural world of which it is an integral part—the world of the Other that is the expected and assumed source of our scholarly interest—form the background, while a "contrived" musical relationship between a Balinese musician and a Western ethnomusicologist who drummed together is advanced to the foreground.

Prelude: Ethnomusicology and Music Performance— Understanding from Within?

In spite of the diversity of their methods and the eclectic goals of their research, ethnomusicologists, as practitioners of a discipline, are unified in their common desire to "understand" the musics they study. They are likewise unified by a belief in the primacy of fieldwork-based participant observation, and by a notion that learning to perform the musics they study—at least to some level of competence—constitutes an important dimension of the participant-observation enterprise. Music performance study has become a basic component of the modern ethnomusicological method, one that is thought to offer access to ways of understanding a music and the culture to which it belongs that would otherwise be elusive, even unattainable.

But what kinds of understanding are these? And from whence do they emerge? Benjamin Brinner, in what may be read as a contemporary refashioning of Mantle Hood's original dictum of "bi-musicality" (Hood 1960, 1963, 1982), provides a reasonable starting point from which to pursue such matters, expressing a view that is widely shared among ethnomusicologists today: "The most direct access to a different way of thinking and making music, one based on different assumptions and expectations about human action and sensation, is gained by making an intense, long-term effort to absorb those ways of music from within, attempting to get inside other peoples' heads and fingers" (1995a, 8).

One may infer from this passage that to "understand" a music is to understand it "from within," but it is likely not incidental that Brinner avoids actual use of the term "understand" in this context. Rather than speaking of understanding a music of another culture, he speaks of gaining "access to a different way of thinking and making music." Such terminological precision reflects an astute, arguably "postmodern" sensitivity on Brinner's part to the inherently problematic notion that an "outsider" can understand a music "from within" at all.

Timothy Rice (1994) and Paul Berliner (1994), as well as Brinner himself, have produced studies that illustrate in exemplary fashion how ethnomusicologists, through their intense and long-term efforts in performance-centered musical research, might productively approach the formidable challenge of getting inside other peoples' heads and fingers in order to gain access to different ways of thinking and making music. Their works have served to extend, refine, and contemporize earlier ethnomusicological notions of bi-musicality by problematizing a too often assumed association between deep performance competence and the understanding of a music "from within."

Applying an approach derived largely from the theories of Gadamer and Ricoeur, Rice identified the "new understanding" of Bulgarian bagpipe *(gaida)* ornamentation he developed by learning to play the instrument as "a provisional endpoint of a hermeneutic arc" that represents "neither an insider's (emic) nor an outsider's (etic)" perspective. Invoking Gadamer, he claims to have achieved by reaching this point a "fusion of horizons" with the understandings of Bulgarian musicians that has "important lessons to teach about music cognition, crossing musical barriers between cultures, and Bulgarian music itself" (Rice 1994, 72).

Berliner's approach to the study of jazz represents something of a reversal relative to the music-learning and performance aspects of ethnomusicological method. As part of a "formal effort to understand the concepts of others and thereby extend [his] own understanding" of jazz improvisation, Berliner consciously attempted to bracket out his own musical past in the interest of minimizing "impressions" and perceptions that might have arisen from his "personal experience as a jazz learner before studying ethnomusicology" (Berliner 1994, 5). Through this strategy, Berliner engaged in a systematic endeavor to prevent his own pre-understandings of jazz improvisation from interfering with his research findings. Rather than building from his background as a jazz trumpet player, he reinvented himself to the best of his ability as a new student of jazz improvisation, a tactic that had important methodological implications. According to Berliner, "Using myself as a subject for the study—training myself according to the same techniques described by musicians—offered the kind of detail about musical development and creative process that can be virtually impossible to obtain from other methods. So, too, did reflection during my own performance on the experiential realm of jazz" (10).

Berliner, like Brinner and Rice, is careful and meticulous in his construction of the relationship between practical experience as a learner/practitioner of a music and conception and representation of understandings of that music. Despite the very different challenges of their respective studies, Berliner, Brinner, and Rice each broach a similar methodological-epistemological dilemma: how to mediate between established ethnomusicological ideals of bi-musical performance, on the one hand, and the realization that to "understand a music from within" as a scholar is not really possible, on the other. Even for "native" ethnomusicologists who write from within their own cultures, processes of abstraction and distanciation are inevitably involved in ethnomusicological research, ensuring that all theories and representations concerned with "musical understanding," even those proposed by so-called cultural insiders, emerge from without as much as from within.

A Different Musical Understanding

As a student of Balinese drumming, my own situational response to the disparity between formerly held bi-musical ideals and current ethnomusicological sensitivities to the inherent limitations of musical understanding moved me in a rather different methodological direction than those that have been pursued by Brinner, Berliner, Rice, and others. While problematizing the notion of "musical understanding from within" in innovative and groundbreaking ways, Brinner's and Berliner's methods relative to music performance study nonetheless remain firmly dedicated to the pursuit of such understanding, to an emic way of thinking and of learning and making music. Even Rice, despite the deeply reflexive orientation of his writing on the Bulgarian *gaida,* ultimately pledges his principal commitment to an "understanding of the tradition" (1994, 72), rather than to what might be termed a more "localized" understanding of the intercultural, idiosyncratic musical world he and his *gaida* teacher Kostadin Varimezov invented, negotiated, and sustained over the course of Rice's studies.

It is this latter kind of musical world—the kind rooted in a specific musical tradition of a specific culture, but developed in the context of cross-cultural experimentation involving two musicians from very different backgrounds—that interests me the most here, and that I furthermore believe I am best qualified to explore. From the commencement of my beleganjur drumming studies with Sukarata, I was plagued by internal conflict. At one level, I felt compelled to approach the project in the traditional ethnomusicological manner, to attempt to learn as Balinese drummers learned and thereby move toward an understanding of beleganjur music "from within," or at least from somewhere in relatively close proximity to "within." At another level—a practical level—I viewed this idealistic aspiration as an impossible task. For reasons I will explain later, my original research plan had not included an intensive course of study in the complex art of kendang beleganjur. I eventually committed myself to such study, reluctantly, only because Sukarata insisted that I should. In taking on his challenge, though, I made significant compromises. If constraints of time and musical ability precluded the possibility of learning to drum beleganjur in the traditional way, as I believed they did, and if Sukarata insisted that I learn to drum in spite of this, I would have to devise some alternate way of learning. Though I was not necessarily conscious of it at the time, I instinctively adopted a new epistemological stance that defied the conventional wisdom of bi-musical ideals. Instead of dedicating myself to learning in the Balinese manner, I committed myself to a pragmatic approach to acquiring musical competence, one in which the ability to function adequately in music performance situations took priority over all other concerns. In turn, I was converted from an idealistic pursuit of musical understanding "from within" to a more practical pursuit of musical understanding as the mere ability to drum, however achieved. "Understanding" for me was equated with practical mastery of the task at hand.

My goals came to reside in playing the music competently and in context—with Balinese musicians in real-life performance situations—as soon, as often, and with as great a technical command as possible. If applying my training and background in Western music to the beleganjur context would enable me to move more quickly to a level of functional competence, then I would do it; if requesting Sukarata to teach me in ways that defied his usual pedagogical methods seemed advantageous, I would make such requests.

Musical understanding, I rationalized on the basis of my experience as a Western music performer, demanded musical experience, that is, "real" musical experience playing with expert musicians—musical "insiders," as it were. If willfully shedding the musical and cultural "baggage" I had brought to Bali in the first place would slow my progress toward functional musicianship as a beleganjur drummer, then willful pursuit of the musical understanding "from within" that would demand such shedding was contrary to my interests, to *my* goals of musical understanding under the constraints of my current situation. In approaching things as I did, perhaps I did not learn to perform "in the inverse order of the traditional manner," as Rice claims to have done (1994, 72), but I did learn in a radically unconventional way.

There are those in the ethnomusicological community who would claim that how I learned was thus "wrong," and that how I understand beleganjur music must therefore be wrong as well. An alternate epistemology of understanding, however, problematizes this facile deduction. As Edward Bruner has proposed, "participants in a performance do not necessarily share a common experience or meaning; what they share is only their common participation" (1986, 11), a premise supported by Blacking's criticism of theories of musical communication that "imply that there must be precise correlations between the feelings of two persons, fantasized or actual, for effective communication to take place" and that rely on "identity of interpretation and strict correlations between sound and meaning that must be shared by co-performers" (Blacking 1992, 307). In a related vein, Zygmunt Bauman, building on an idea from Wittgenstein, has asserted that "[u]nderstanding of meaning is to know how to go on in the presence of a word, an act or other object whose meaning we understand" (1978, 179), a notion that carries with it the implicit suggestion that the very act of knowing "how to go on" indicates an understanding of the meaning of what one is going on in relation to. Considered collectively, Bruner's, Blacking's, and Bauman's positions suggest that "understanding" need not occur within a context of shared conception of meaning in performative action. So long as multiple participants in a performance all *believe* themselves and each other to be functioning effectively, and so long as they are collectively meeting the objectives demanded of the performance, those participants are all operating, on some level at least, from a position of "understanding," even if such understanding lacks language-like criteria of mutual intelligibility.

Such an idea has profound implications for the study of music. The relative non-referentiality of musical sounds and structures facilitates considerable perception of "understanding" on the part of musicians playing together even in the absence of "a common experience or meaning" between them, certainly to a degree unparalleled in the domain of linguistic communication. Long before I was able to communicate verbally with Balinese musicians, I was able to play music with them. Musically, we did not require a common vocabulary in which "words" meant the same things to the various parties concerned in order to make music that sounded sensible, orderly, and for the most part, musical. In music, "words" and "sentences," that is, meaning-imbued syntactical structures of sound, need not be understood as having the same meaning in order for them to be communicatively effective and seemingly mutually intelligible.

Musical skills and forms of musical cognition are typically far more readily transferable and adaptable from one music culture to another than are their counterparts in language. In one sense, this situation provides distinct advantages for the ethnomusicological fieldworker who engages in applied music study and performance as part and parcel of field research method. As Blacking has noted, "It may be possible to tune into an alien musical expression without having to acquire all the cultural clutter of which it is a part, and perhaps through the music to gain a deeper understanding of some of the principles on which the social and cultural experience of its makers is founded" ([1977] 1990, 272). At another level, the employment of musical expression in the service of cutting through the "cultural clutter" may render problematic the very situating of music in culture at all, since the recognizable parameters and boundaries of "culture," a cognitive construct whose lowest common denominator so often appears to be located in the ability of a group of people to communicate in a common language,[1] may be obfuscated by the unique non-referentiality (perhaps more accurately, the unique capacity for multi-referentiality) of musical sounds and structures.

With respect to my own encounter with beleganjur music, my application of a practice-based conception of understanding meant that if I sounded convincing as a beleganjur musician to the ears of Balinese beleganjur musicians, I could assume I was operating from a position of musical understanding that was provisionally sufficient and acceptable. My goals as a performer were defined in such terms. My conception of beleganjur rhythms in groupings of eighth notes and sixteenth notes surely had little relation to Sukarata's cognitive map; my playing undoubtedly lacked a certain sensitivity to cultural values and symbols that largely defined musical meaning for my Balinese fellow musicians.

Still, I put faith in an instinctive belief that so long as I could play, there was value to what I was doing, to how I was learning, and that somehow I was moving toward a new kind of musical understanding that would ultimately prove significant and revealing.

Terms of an Intercultural Musical Experiment

By the time of my fourth lesson with Sukarata, he and I had determined that the main goal of our work together would be to perform and record a complete contest-style beleganjur piece. I would play the lanang drum part and he the wadon; the beleganjur group of Banjar Tatasan Kaja, which he and Pak Jaya had co-directed to the 1988 LBPB championship and other prestigious victories, would perform with us. The composition, specially composed by Sukarata to highlight his distinctive kreasi beleganjur style, would be about twenty minutes long. I would be required to play my part by memory, despite having used my own transcriptions to learn it. The overall project and its basic terms were worked out by Sukarata and me, with consultation from Jaya.

Paradoxically, this was "my" project, in that it was conceived and undertaken in direct relation to my 1992 dissertation field research, yet it was Sukarata rather than I who initiated it. As was mentioned earlier, upon coming to Bali in 1992, I had no intention of pursuing in-depth kendang studies. My two previous fieldwork ventures had convinced me that endeavoring to gain true competence as a beleganjur drummer would be impractical and unwise, given the limited scope and parameters of the dissertation project. Beleganjur drumming, at least the kreasi variety, seemed prohibitively difficult and complex, and despite my many years of experience as a professional percussionist—or perhaps because of them—I had resolved that the challenge was too great, that attempting to become even a reasonably capable beleganjur drummer would be counterproductive to my larger research goals as an ethnomusicologist. I had already achieved considerable competence on all of the other beleganjur instruments, especially cengceng and reyong, and had enjoyed a wealth of experience performing with various beleganjur groups in an array of contexts, from the 1990 Kintamani contest to numerous cremations and other ritualistic and ceremonial events. In short, at the level of music performance–based participant observation, I felt I was well prepared to meet my ethnomusicological objectives. Beyond perhaps attempting to acquire a rudimentary drumming facility, as I had begun to do during my brief course of study with Suweca, I did not see

further intensive performance study as necessary at the time I met Sukarata. Other research demands seemed more pressing.

Sukarata had a very different opinion. Regardless of what I thought
I had to do, he was resolutely certain that I needed to delve as deeply as
I possibly could into the intricacies of beleganjur drumming, and that
the only way for me to do this was to become a drummer, and a good
one at that. The heart of the music was in the drumming, he explained,
and indirect, *akadémik* knowledge—whether of technique, style, formal structure, or repertoire—was woefully inadequate. If I was training
to be some kind of an authority on beleganjur music—to be "Doktor
Beleganjur," as he liked to call me—I had to learn to drum, and he was
not going to have any part in my project if learning to drum was not on
my agenda. Furthermore, Sukarata told me that I possessed the talent to
be a beleganjur drummer: the rhythmic sense, the technique, the innate
musicality. Therefore, it logically followed in his view that it was my
duty to become one, and he promised to do all he could to help me
realize my potential and meet my "obligation," provided I was willing
to put in the hard work necessary to meet his expectations.[2]

As a drummer, I found Sukarata's arguments convincing, and his proposal that I become immersed in his musical world highly enticing.
How could I resist such an offer from such an exceptional musician?
But the scholar in me was wary and resistant. Accepting Sukarata's
drumming challenge would blow my carefully designed research plan
to pieces, stealing precious time from other research pursuits and potentially derailing my project in the process. Neither my dissertation committee nor the grant agencies funding my research would likely be
pleased. The cost of learning to drum seemed too great.

After a sleepless night of introspective deliberation, my "solution"
to the dilemma was to present Sukarata with a counter-proposal that
would demand compromise on both our parts. I told him that my ability
to become a beleganjur drummer within the constraints of my situation
would depend on his willingness to accommodate me through an unorthodox and experimental process of cross-cultural learning. The standard maguru panggul–type learning methods alone were not going to
work for me, I explained, but if I were to combine them with my tried-
and-true Western-derived techniques of absorbing musical material—
employing notation and reading from transcriptions, taking in each new
musical passage one small segment at a time—I was confident that I
could learn to drum beleganjur efficiently and with good results. Such
an approach, however, would have an effect not only on my way of

learning, but on Sukarata's way of teaching as well. Realizing this, I asked Sukarata for permission to instruct him on how to teach me. It was a peculiar request and he seemed perplexed initially, but after mulling things over for a few minutes, he told me that he would be willing to try things my way, provided that he retained the right to insist that I do things *his* way at any point in the process where he deemed that the "experimental" approach was not working. The terms of agreement were thus established; the foundation was laid.

The Experimental Method

The basic precedent for the experimental pedagogical method Sukarata and I developed through the early period of our relationship was actually set by the end of my first lesson with him, at the wedding in Seminyak discussed in chapter 4. On that occasion, Sukarata attempted to teach me a rather difficult jejagulan drum variation in the standard maguru panggul way: he performed the entire lengthy variation at full speed and tried to get me to imitate what he was doing, and when I did nothing in response he repeated his demonstration. But this technique did not work. At first I was not even aware I was being taught, and then I was overwhelmed and ultimately disheartened by the impenetrable complexity of the drum rhythms I was hearing. Coming from where I did, musically *and* culturally, learning something this difficult in this way seemed categorically out of the question. But I did want to learn, and I sensed that Sukarata sincerely wanted to teach me. So I asked him to indulge me, to help me to learn by letting me "write down" the music I was hearing before trying to play it. Sukarata, who had never worked with notation, appeared skeptical, but was curious enough to play along.

Hunching forward over my drum to reach the tattered manuscript pad laid out on the floor in front of me, I readied myself to begin transcribing. I asked Sukarata if he could play just one short segment of the pukulan he had been demonstrating, at a slow tempo. He smiled and nodded his head. I gestured for him to begin, and he proceeded to perform the entire pukulan, from start to finish, at the very same breakneck tempo he had been playing at all along. He completed the demonstration, then looked at me and grinned quizzically, as if to ask, "Did you get it all?" I had gotten none of it. Clearly, I had to find a better way of conveying what I had in mind here.

Apologizing for my ineptitude, I told Sukarata that I would need to hear the pukulan again. I asked him if he would play it "even slower" this time, and also whether he might consider approaching the demonstration in a different manner for my sake. I requested the following of him: play from the beginning over and over again, but stop each time I raise my left hand in the air and wait for me to give a cue before starting again. Sukarata laughed and shook his head. He found my request absurd, or at least comical, but decided to indulge me a bit more nonetheless.

I took pen in hand and indicated I was ready. Sukarata started playing. Again, the tempo was fast, but it was slightly slower than before. About two measures in, my left hand shot up, and to my surprise and delight, Sukarata immediately stopped. I scribbled away frantically, then tapped out the transcribed rhythm with my pen. Sukarata stared down at the page with evident curiosity. I gestured for him to proceed. This time he got about four measures into the pukulan before my hand went up again. He waited patiently as I added on to the transcription.

After about five such starts and stops, I had transcribed one complete gilak cycle, comprising eight measures of music. I asked Sukarata which drum part this was: the lanang or the wadon. He told me it was the lanang (although he was playing on the wadon drum). I put down my pen, adjusted the position of the drum in my lap, and began to play back what I had written. Immediately, Sukarata joined in with me, but playing the interlocking wadon part rather than the lanang part he had been demonstrating. Our parts fitted together correctly. Apparently the transcription was accurate. Sukarata seemed impressed, and a little surprised. He smiled warmly and gave me a hearty thumbs-up. "Bagus!" he exclaimed. "Good!" The musicians of the Seminyak beleganjur ensemble, who had been observing all the while, laughed and nodded approvingly, as though reacting to a clever card trick.

Rather than having Sukarata proceed further into the lanang part, I asked him to first take me through the wadon part up to the point we had reached, using the same play-and-stop method as before. He told me that this would not be necessary, since the wadon part was actually "the same" as the lanang. At the time, I did not possess sufficient knowledge of how kendang interlocking theory worked to be able to "abstract" a wadon part from its lanang counterpart. To me, the two sounded quite different indeed. Apologizing once again for my lack of competence, I explained that even if the two parts were in fact the same, as he claimed, I would still need to be taught both separately, at least for now. Sukarata allowed himself a momentary expression of impatience before quickly regaining his composure and accommodating this latest strange request. Segment by segment, he demonstrated the wadon part for me as he had the lanang, pausing each time I raised my hand in the air and patiently waiting for me to jot down what I had heard before repeating and extending the passage. Over the course of a little more than an hour, I managed to transcribe both drum parts for the entire pukulan using this method. I would take down one gong cycle of the lanang part, play it back to check for accuracy, repeat the process for the wadon, then proceed to the next gong cycle. Once the transcription process was completed, Sukarata and I played through the full pukulan a couple of times alone, then a few more times with the whole ensemble accompanying. Eventually, Sukarata integrated the new pukulan into a little arrangement that also featured the other, more basic pukulans I had studied in my earlier lessons with Suweca.

The play-and-stop protocol Sukarata and I worked out during our initial encounter in Seminyak became the foundation for a more refined and systematic pedagogical method that we developed over time. On the surface, not much changed at all. I took to gently tapping Sukarata on the knee with my mallet rather than flailing my hand through the air to cue him to stop, and there were certain other changes along these lines as well; but aside from such relatively minor procedural details, our basic mode of interaction remained remarkably consistent. What did change significantly was our degree of efficiency, and concomitantly, our level of comfort working together in an unconventional pedagogical framework. Sukarata proved to be not only highly accommodating but also exceptionally adept at adapting his usual teaching methods to my unorthodox requests. He came to be at ease demonstrating small musical segments at slow tempos rather than lengthy passages at full speed. Meanwhile, my skills at transcribing relatively long musical chunks in a single hearing increased, and I learned how to determine wadon parts on the basis of the lanang part's structure, which saved us much time. Our sessions, which were held at either Sukarata's home or Jaya's (both in Denpasar), became ever more productive for a period, and as I learned one difficult pukulan of Sukarata's evolving new kreasi beleganjur showpiece after another at an unusually quick pace, he was pleased to acknowledge that the experimental method we had devised was indeed far more effective than he had initially thought it would be. He became most generous in his praise of my progress.

Showing Off

While I enjoyed the compliments, one aspect of my "success" that proved annoying was Sukarata's predilection for showing me off. When guests or other students of his would come to visit, I would invariably be asked to play for them. The odd spectacle of a gawky, bearded Westerner whizzing through a challenging sequence of Sukarata drum variations while staring down at a pad of paper served as a source of amusement and intrigue. The guests would pore over my transcriptions in apparent wonderment, carefully scrutinizing the documents for clues that would help them decipher the incomprehensible code of dots, lines, and squiggles that enabled me to re-create Sukarata-style drumming.

Meanwhile, Sukarata would wax enthusiastic about my cleverness and the ingeniousness of my notation system. He would describe me as an "American professor" and a "music doctor," even though I was neither at the time, and proudly tout my "book" (which was then nothing more than a dissertation-in-progress), in which I had chosen to focus on his beleganjur style rather than those of his more erudite peers on the conservatory music faculties. I grimly tolerated such displays out of respect for Sukarata, but they always made me uncomfortable. I often felt like a prize monkey in a variety show, and I was embarrassed at the attribution of professional credentials I did not yet hold.[3]

Far more unpleasant, though, was being put on display during the drum lessons of Sukarata's Balinese students, which I often attended. If a certain student was having problems mastering some passage that I had already learned, Sukarata would sometimes call on me to provide a "demonstration." Then, after I had played, he would glare disdainfully at the student, shake his head, and quietly comment on how odd and disappointing it was that an American could play this pukulan while a Balinese boy could not. This "motivational strategy" actually proved quite effective on the few occasions it was used, but I found it disturbing to be implicated in others' humiliation.

Learned Misconceptions

Through the first two weeks or so of my studies with Sukarata, what was most surprising to me was that I did indeed learn considerably more quickly than his Balinese students, or so it seemed. The traditional maguru panggul method I observed in their lessons appeared highly inefficient; their haphazard efforts to emulate Sukarata's performance models were painful to watch. I was shocked to discover that the path to basic technical competence followed by these drummers was so slow and arduous. In fact, seeing the maguru panggul process in action during drum lessons shattered certain illusions of mine.

Prior to working with Sukarata, my observations of beleganjur drummers had always occurred in contexts of full-ensemble rehearsals or public performances. In such situations, they had almost invariably appeared extremely competent, in full command of the musical materials at hand. As a drummer, I had often been in awe of them, sharing the sentiment of so many Westerners who have admired Balinese people doing things well, and who, like Gregory Bateson in a famous analogy, have witnessed the grace and poise of Balinese and wondered, "How does one feel empathy for gazelles?" (see Wikan 1990, xv). But now the laborious effort beneath the smooth surface was being revealed; I was beginning to see, through the medium of drumming, that the renowned "natural" grace and effortlessness of Balinese public endeavor were at least in some instances products of hard toil, struggle, frustration, and occasional humiliation.

And now, through an ironic twist, I came to be viewed by Sukarata and his students and friends in idealized terms, as an essentialized embodiment of the unique "natural" cultural attributes of the Western individual. I do not suspect that anyone mistook me for a gazelle, but the efficiency of my transcription-based learning methods did generate a kind of mystique, reifying the stereotypical "clever Westerner," whose command over sophisticated technologies (in this case music notation) begets distinct advantages where speed and productivity are at issue.

Alas, this illusion was ultimately dispelled when the assumed depth of my learning was exposed as a fallacy. What Sukarata and others in his circle had failed to see early on was that my transcriptions, not my musicianship, were primarily responsible for my prodigious accomplishments. Even I was not fully aware of the extent of my notation-boundedness until first logistical and then cognitive barriers began to interfere with my ability to continue to progress at the quick pace I had established initially. My problems started to surface toward the end of my second week of study with Sukarata. Each of my lessons commenced with a complete run-through of the piece I was learning, up to the point I had learned. If the run-through went well, we would move on to new material. Through our first few sessions, the run-throughs were easy for me; I would simply lay out my two or three or four pages of transcriptions and read them in sequence.

As the piece expanded and became more complicated with the addition of numerous new sections, however, the number of pages upon which my notations were scrawled became unwieldy. The straight read-through approach was rendered impossible, both on account of the sheer quantity of pages amassed and an eventual inability on my part to document Sukarata's ever evolving composition in a logical, sequential order. The source of my difficulties was that the piece was not set. It comprised a new arrangement of existing pukulans from earlier contest pieces created by Sukarata over a period of six years. He was basically "composing" the work in the process of teaching it to me, and with the addition of just about every new passage the arrangement of the *preceding* materials was subjected to significant changes.

Every night I would spend hours diligently recopying the newly transcribed materials from that morning's lesson onto fresh sheets of manuscript paper, and in addition trying to create a readable score of the overall arrangement for the next day's session. By the end of the second week, however, the amount of music and Sukarata's unending transformations of the arrangement had overwhelmed me. My "performance score" was reduced to a confusing and cumbersome maze of arrows, asterisks, repeat signs, codas, and cut-and-pastes, and I became unable to read through it from start to finish without either losing my place or interrupting the performance to rearrange pages. In addition, navigating my way through the labyrinth of notation, even when I was nominally successful in the effort, demanded so much concentration that it detracted from my ability to play musically, with the ironic consequence that my playing started to become more stiff and mechanical-sounding with each lesson. An abiding obsession with "the notes" caused me to lose sight of the music, to forget about playing with style and to neglect the importance of creating a groove with Sukarata.

From my perspective, such obstacles were annoying, but they did not concern me greatly. I had faith that I was still on task; if I could just muddle through to the end of the transcription process and end up with accurate notations for all of the different pukulans, I would then be able to create a clean, well-organized, complete score from which I would in turn be able to memorize the piece. Then, with both Sukarata's guidance and recourse to his playing as a performance model for my own, I would learn to play with appropriate style and musicality. Once I had the transcription in hand, I surmised, mastery of my part would be achieved through more or less the same learning process that I had used effectively for many years as a percussionist in the Western "art" music tradition: first learn the notes, then worry about playing them musically. Basically, I felt that I was on track to meet the objectives Sukarata and I had established at the outset.

Sukarata, however, saw the situation in a very different light. He became disappointed with me and confused. As a musician whose learning and teaching processes had always been grounded in the maguru panggul method, he could not help but perceive what was happening to me as ludicrous. Compared to me, his Balinese students appeared to be slow learners at an early stage; but what he did not realize was that the appearance was deceptive, for unlike me, they essentially *knew* a piece of music and were able to perform it musically from the moment they achieved the requisite technical competence to play through it for the first time. Memorization and stylistic competence were acquired during the initial learning process rather than in its aftermath, as was discussed in the previous chapter. Sukarata initially assumed that I was learning in this same way—or, more precisely, at this same level of depth, only faster. He did not realize that my use of notation had caused me to appear much more musically competent than I actually was. Nothing in his prior experience had prepared him to comprehend someone like me, who could play through a given musical passage with perfect or near-perfect technical accuracy while possessing little if any recognizable sense of the overall structure of the piece to which it belonged, nor of how to play with appropriate musical expression or style. My Western predilection for approaching the learning of a piece of music as a series of discrete tasks rather than as a holistic process of absorption defied the inherent logic of Sukarata's musical worldview. As the composition grew in length and complexity, his only way of measuring my progress was to monitor how well I was able to play, and as my playing became increasingly disjointed in response to the ever growing logistical and cognitive challenges I faced, he heard only disintegration. Our formerly impressive experimental method, as well as my own "talent," began to appear as little more than smoke and mirrors. What had initially seemed to him an unorthodox yet surprisingly effective alternative approach to learning his music now looked more like a clever trick devoid of substance, and he did not want to continue to be party to this charade.

My efforts to convince Sukarata that the difficulties evident in my playing were less problematic than they appeared to him had little impact. He decreed that in order for us to continue with the project, he would have to exercise his prerogative to fundamentally alter our approach. I could continue working with the transcription-based method I had devised, but from now on, he would no longer indulge my desire to learn large quantities of new material at almost the same rate I was able to accurately transcribe them. Rather, he would only teach me as much on any given day as he thought I could truly learn. Unless I could demonstrate mastery of what I had already been taught by playing the entire piece with him up to the endpoint of my transcription—musically, at full tempo, with no stops or significant errors, and, most importantly, by memory—he would not be willing to proceed with the teaching of any new material.

These proposed amendments to our established pedagogical protocol were certainly reasonable. I dedicated more of my late-night work time to memorization and less to recopying and reorganizing transcriptions. Even though I had been relying on the transcriptions, I soon realized that in the process of notating and practicing, I had actually memorized most of the material I had learned. Problems came to bear at the level of integration. While my command of individual segments of the piece was quite solid, my retention of transitional passages and the overall sequence of pukulans within the evolving arrangement was less secure. Unlike Sukarata's Balinese kendang students, I conceived of the piece as a sequence of connected but independent musical segments. This conception made me vulnerable to memory lapses even after I had studiously committed myself to meeting Sukarata's challenge of memorizing everything as I proceeded through the learning process.

It was my memory lapses that mystified and frustrated Sukarata more than any of my other learning idiosyncrasies. After his determination that I had to memorize everything he taught me on a daily basis, he was initially pleased with my ability to quickly make the transition from playing with notation to playing without it. Once again, however, his satisfaction with my progress diminished in short order in the face of a learning deficiency problem that was completely incomprehensible to him: I could memorize music well enough, but my ability to recall what I memorized was disturbingly inconsistent. One day I would arrive at my lesson and perform the entire piece up to the point studied without error. Sukarata would reward me by teaching me a new pukulan. The next day, I would try to play through the piece, only to falter and have a memory lapse—not during the new, untested section, but at some point early on in the arrangement that I had been playing perfectly for over a week. Where a memory lapse might occur during any given performance was anyone's guess (including mine). Transitional sections and points in the arrangement where Sukarata had introduced changes in the form of the piece certainly presented the greatest risks, but there was no assurance that I would successfully navigate my way through even the most familiar and well-learned passages. In fact, I was just about as likely to go blank or fall apart during an easy section that I knew well as during a difficult one that had been taught to me only recently.

My unpredictable memory difficulties distressed Sukarata greatly. How could I play something perfectly one day, completely forget it by the next morning, then play it correctly later that afternoon, only to have a lapse in some other section that had been totally under my control an hour earlier? Such random failures of memory made no sense to him. Sometimes, I even sensed that he suspected I was playing a practical joke, feigning memory lapses just to annoy him. He seemed at a loss regarding my problem; it was beyond his range of comprehension.[4] His response was to monitor my progress even more rigorously. Now, before he would teach me anything new, I would have to play the entire arrangement up to the point learned three times nonstop by memory rather than just once, which slowed me down quite a bit but did ultimately lead to vast improvement in my memorization skills.

Pak Jaya

While Sukarata was by no means sparing in his criticisms of my memory problems and other musical shortcomings, his critical assessments were usually softened by a gentle graciousness and words of encouragement. Such was his nature. His longtime drumming partner, best friend, "sponsor," and alter ego Pak Jaya, who attended most of my lessons and was never shy about commenting on either my musical skills or deficiencies, was less diplomatic in his judgments, more severe and extreme.

Jaya was integrally involved in my program of study with Sukarata at every stage and in many ways. His interconnectedness with Sukarata at multiple levels—musical, social, professional, business, and more— ensured that this would be the case. As I would eventually come to realize, the vast majority of Sukarata's professional activities, musical and otherwise, were undertaken in direct association with Jaya. Jaya was not just Sukarata's friend and associate; he was also his patron, and I came to be encompassed within the domain of his patronage.

When I moved to Denpasar to pursue studies with Sukarata after meeting him in Seminyak, the first thing he did was to take me to meet Jaya at his luxurious home in northern Denpasar. After making the proper introductions, Sukarata explained to me that Jaya would be the principal "teaching consultant" and "sponsor" for our project, and that it would be Jaya's esteemed beleganjur group from Tatasan Kaja (Jaya's native banjar), that would work with us when I reached the level of competence necessary to perform with an ensemble. Whenever possible, we would hold our lessons at Jaya's house, so as to be able to take advantage of his valuable input. As Sukarata explained to me, Jaya knew the music I would learn "better than anyone," since he, as Sukarata's own drumming partner in the Tatasan Kaja ensemble, was the musician for whom a great many of the pukulans had been created in the first place. The kendang lanang part I would learn was "Jaya's part," and his insights into how to play it were thus invaluable.

Jaya took his dual role as teaching consultant and sponsor very seriously. He was supportive of me and committed to my musical development. He was kind, generous, and helpful in many ways, but his support came with high expectations. As I would eventually come to understand, it was extremely important to him that I achieve success as a beleganjur drummer. For Jaya, as for Sukarata, I was a potential source of legitimization, a "distinguished Westerner" who could send an important symbolic message to Denpasar's cultural elite, who he believed had been guilty of unduly disrespecting him for years. Beyond being an accomplished musician, Jaya was a wealthy and successful businessman (mainly in the area of real estate), but he, like Sukarata, perceived himself as a victim of marginalization. He attributed this to both his lack of formal education and his controversial status as a maverick businessman with an "unconventional" lifestyle operating outside the accepted channels of government employment and government-endorsed business institutions.

My decision to work with Sukarata served as "proof" to Jaya that his friend's artistry and worth had been grossly underappreciated by the government-centered elite. If I, the prestigious "American professor" and "music doctor," had chosen to study with Sukarata, then clearly Sukarata was the great artist that Jaya had always maintained he was. And by extension, Jaya himself would also be great, and deserving of a measure of respect and legitimacy long denied him. In order for my "message" to have the proper impact, however, it was essential that I become an outstanding drummer. If I was to make Sukarata and Jaya appear impressive in the eyes of others, Jaya explained to me on numerous occasions, I would have to be impressive to them myself, not merely by virtue of who I already was when I came to Bali, but also by virtue of what I had become and what I had accomplished as a protégé of Sukarata and himself.

Such high stakes certainly accounted to a large extent for Jaya's consistently tough scrutiny of my progress, although I suspect that in more than a few instances his criticisms were steeped in a spirit of competitive one-upmanship resulting from his perception of me as a rival. Whatever his motivations may have been, Jaya was nothing if not candid. His denouncements of my inadequacies were as direct and pointed as were his aggrandizements of my attributes, and his lessons, while often hard to take, taught me much about what is valued and considered meaningful in Balinese drumming.

Jaya the Critic

Like Sukarata, Jaya found my proneness to memory lapses more irksome than anything. As one might expect, he was much more demonstrative than Sukarata in expressing his displeasure. Whenever I had memory problems, he would yell at me and laugh mockingly, then plead for me to provide an explanation for my stupidity. Such behavior was intended to motivate me to do better, but it often had the reverse effect.

Jaya's two other pet peeves concerning my playing were my sound and my tendency to play in a manner that lacked sufficient expressiveness. By his explanation, the weakness of my sound—especially my left-hand "pak" stroke—was an inevitable consequence of my cultural identity. Westerners, Jaya asserted matter-of-factly, were simply incapable of producing a powerful, focused left-hand stroke such as Sukarata's or his own. To illustrate his point, he would sometimes grab my drum in the middle of a lesson and slap the left-hand head hard several times, producing an impressive "pak" sound. "Strong!" he would exclaim, placing my right hand over his muscular left forearm; then he would grab my left arm forcefully, chuckle, and proclaim "Not strong!"

The matter of my musical expressiveness was more complicated for Jaya to rectify. His general inclination was to believe that a Westerner like myself would naturally lack even the capacity to play Balinese music in a properly expressive manner—that this too was a matter of "culture" or "ethnicity"—but he was willing to acknowledge that I might be something of an exception to this "rule," albeit a frustrating one. Both he and Sukarata were actually highly complimentary of my *ability* to play expressively from early on in my studies, but they were perturbed by the fact that as often as not I failed to do so (for reasons explained earlier in the chapter).

It was Jaya rather than Sukarata who devised a pedagogical solution to this "problem." In observing my lessons, he was intrigued by the odd way I sometimes moved when drumming. I would roll my shoulders up and down and rock my head from side to side in rhythm, smiling with my eyes closed all the while. This was a profoundly un-Balinese way of playing. First Jaya and then Sukarata took to impersonating my antics, which they found to be alternately amusing and disturbing: amusing because they were so unorthodox, disturbing because they were so at odds with the proper, upright kendang playing posture *(agem).*

At first they discouraged me from moving in my odd, distinctive way and told me to sit up straight, but this changed after Jaya arrived at the conclusion that I played in an appropriately expressive manner only when I *did* move in my unique fashion. Jaya noted that whenever I sat up straight and did not move freely (as was my habit when concentrating hard on some new or difficult passage with which I did not yet feel secure), my playing became stiff, unexpressive. He thus posited a direct correlation between my playing body language and my ability to play expressively, and in an effort to remedy my tendency toward performing without proper feeling, he developed a tactic that proved quite effective. At the first sign of my slipping into an unmusically "mechanical" mode, he would shout out "Éxprésif!" in order to get my attention, then put on a silly grin and rock his head back and forth, at once impersonating me and prompting me to loosen up and flow naturally with the music. This technique produced good results; it was helpful to me as a kind of feedback mechanism. Sukarata soon started using it as well.

One area of my musicianship that both Sukarata and Jaya found to be consistently praiseworthy was my *mat.* The term *mat,* as used by Balinese musicians, is difficult to translate. Perhaps the closest correlate is what is known among jazz musicians as "time." If a jazz drummer is described as having "good time," the assessment encompasses a cluster of attributes relating to the rhythmic/temporal domain of musical performance: steady tempo-keeping ability, a good swing feel, a talent for making the music groove,[5] a strong intuitive sense of place relative to the music's formal structure and beat, an aptitude for responding sensitively to the time-feelings of other musicians, and a host of other subtle elements best described as "intangibles."

Like "beat," "time" in jazz belongs to what Berliner has identified as "that category of intangibles made comprehensible by being properly envisaged or accurately inferred from their effects upon other things" (1994, 150). The same might be said of *mat* in the Balinese context. "Good *mat*" comprises far more than just basic competence in keeping a steady beat and playing rhythms accurately, though these skills do indeed represent its foundation: the ability of a drummer to interlock precisely with his partner, to execute all rhythms exactly, and to set, maintain, and change tempos fluidly while leading the ensemble are fundamental requirements. But there are more subtle, intangible elements to "good *mat*" as well—the elements that define musical time-sense as an expression of feeling and a point of human connection.

Drumming partners in Bali with whom I spoke often identified "a shared sense of *mat*" as the foundation of their musical bond. The Balinese drumming partnership may represent a lifelong commitment and may be characterized by an intensity akin to that which exists between brothers, or between a husband and wife.[6] In actuality, brothers often do form deep and enduring drumming partnerships, and in reflecting on what unifies them as brothers at a *musical* level, the members of these partnerships frequently mention *mat*. For example, Asnawa refers to his older brother Komang Astita as his "favorite drumming partner," and traces the strength of their musical relationship to a deep sense of rhythmic synchrony. "We call it *kawin*—married—when the drummers are in sync," he explained to me. "If the balance is off, or the rhythm is off, it's not *kawin*. The *mat* must be right. To be called *kawin* is a high compliment. Komang and I have that quality together when we play" (Asnawa, pers. comm., 1995).

Sukarata described his musical bond with his late older brother, Wayan Sudhama, in a similar way. "He was the best for me. When we would drum together, it was as though our heart was one. With me and Sudhama, the *mat,* it was exactly the same, like one player."

Sukarata told me on several occasions over the course of our work together that it was my *mat* that had initially inspired him to want to work with me, that it was this "unteachable" aspect of my musicality that gave him great confidence in my potential. Whatever social, professional, or economic motivations may have actually been involved in his decision to commit so intensively to my musical development, Sukarata always insisted that he was driven by a sincere desire to share with me in the experience of making music, and that the key to our capacity for sharing musically in a meaningful way was that our sense of *mat* was "the same."

From my perspective, too, it was a common sense of "time" that seemed to link Sukarata and me together as musicians with a shared sense of what playing music was about, despite my limitations and deficiencies as a beleganjur drummer and our profoundly different musical and cultural backgrounds. *Mat* was the intangible property that allowed me to trust implicitly in my ability to communicate with Sukarata as a musical partner and co-creator, not just as a student and researcher studying a specific musical tradition of a foreign culture. Whatever happened between us, whatever obstacles we encountered, I always knew that we had the ability to "entrain" with one another, to experience "the process that occurs when two or more people become engaged in each other's rhythms, when they synchronize" (Hall 1983, 177). When we were really drumming well together, Sukarata and I created a sense of rhythmic groove and in-syncness that I have never experienced with any other musician in any context, and while I would never presume to suggest that the feeling was mutual, certain things he said to me indicated that he too perhaps recognized a special chemistry between us. "You are my brother," he told me one day following an especially good lesson. "I know this because of your *mat.* It is the same as mine. Even with Balinese drummers, the *mat,* it is not always like this. This is special because it means we are the same."

Jaya too was normally complimentary of my *mat,* but it seemed to cause him a certain discomfort, perhaps on account of the easy musical rapport between Sukarata and myself that it appeared to facilitate. It was always my impression that Jaya brought to his musical relationship with Sukarata a streak of possessiveness. He proudly proclaimed that Sukarata was the only kendang player with whom he would perform, and in my experience this was indeed shown to be true.[7] His exclusivity in this regard, however, was likely premised as much on practical concerns as on his pride at being integrally associated with Sukarata as a drumming partner. Possessing excellent technique, a powerful sound, and considerable charismatic flair as a performer, Jaya was a drummer whose abilities commanded respect. His *mat,* however, was somewhat idiosyncratic—one might even say unique—and as a result, he found it difficult to play with many kendang players, and they with him. Sukarata was the exception; his extraordinary musicianship and flexibility enabled him to effectively accommodate Jaya's different time-sense, even to exploit it in a manner that increased the overall quality of musical expressiveness in their performances.

Jaya justly regarded himself as superior to me in most every way as a kendang player; *mat,* however, was an area where he was apparently prone to some self-doubt, and Sukarata's generous praise of my *mat* did not always sit right with him. This became most evident to me during a lesson at which I played unusually well, prompting Sukarata to enthusiastically proclaim that "not even Pak Jaya's *mat* is as solid as yours, Michael." Jaya graciously smiled and joined Sukarata in commending me on my performance, but the wounded look in his eyes was more than enough to ensure that Sukarata would never again make such a comment in his presence. Jaya wanted for me to become an excellent beleganjur drummer, but not at the expense of his own regard as such. From the time of that lesson onward, he scrutinized my *mat* with unprecedented vigor. At the slightest hint of any rhythmic insecurity in my playing, he would quickly jump up and run toward me. "*Mat! Mat!*" he would shout in my ear, clapping loudly and flashing an inimitable, superior grin.

Nine

Playing to Learn: Toward New Understandings

> To reach an understanding with one's partner in a dialogue is . . . a transformation into a communion, in which we do not remain what we were.
> Hans-Georg Gadamer, *Truth and Method*

Tuning In

Earlier I cited a passage from an essay by John Blacking, a portion of which bears reconsideration here. "It might be possible," he wrote, "to tune into an alien musical expression . . . and perhaps through the music to gain a deeper understanding of some of the principles on which the social and cultural experience of its makers is founded" ([1977] 1990, 272). Blacking's notion of "tuning in" is intriguing, since it appears to connote something very different from the modes of observing, documenting, analyzing, and even interpreting that are usually encompassed within the domain of ethnomusicological method.[1] It suggests to me a process by means of which ethnomusicologists might more productively engage what are often their most direct and subjective experiences of the "alien musics" they study, the experiences of music-learning and performing, and in so doing move toward new and deeper musical and scholarly understandings.

In different ways and to varying degrees, most if not all ethnomusicologists rely for their understandings on a process of tuning in to the musical expressions of the music-makers they study. Tuning in is basic to the ethnomusicological research encounter, but in our writings we are often inclined to tune out our tuning-in experiences. Why is this so? Perhaps because tuning in demands a self-reflexive acknowledgment of the ways in which we are affected by the musics we study, of how particular musical sounds and occurrences make us feel, think, act, and react. Acknowledging the impact of tuning in explicitly grounds the researcher's claims to knowledge and understanding in subjective responses to experience, and in so doing places her in an epistemological territory that has traditionally been viewed as dangerously suspect. This is territory worth exploring, however.

It was through a process of tuning in as a drummer to Sukarata's musicality that I believe I was able to gain my most telling insights into the foundations of his musical lifeworld, and that I was eventually able to comprehend some of the deeper lessons he was trying to teach me— lessons that were not about music alone but about music as a vehicle for understanding the deep importance of trust. The pivotal tuning-in moment in my learning process occurred during the final drum lesson of my 1992 field research project, which took place a few hours before the first of the recording sessions with the Tatasan Kaja group that marked that project's official conclusion. By this point in my studies, Sukarata's composition had grown into the complex work of some twenty minutes' duration he had envisioned from the outset several months earlier. He was pleased with the piece's comprehensiveness as a kind of musical compendium of his kreasi beleganjur style, a "concert suite" centered on the LBPB championship–winning "Beleganjur Padma Mudra" of 1988 but including diverse pukulans from his various other contest creations of the past several years as well.

I had managed to learn my part (the kendang lanang) well, and both Sukarata and I (and also Jaya) were pleased—and relieved—that we had managed to accomplish as much as we had. Despite the many problems and challenges I had struggled with in the months following my "honeymoon period" of rapid early progress, I had somehow managed to learn and memorize the entire piece, and while I was still not immune to memory lapses nor to other performance-related problems that had plagued me, I had proven on a few occasions that I was capable of playing through from start to finish without any major errors. In the weeks leading up to my final lesson, Sukarata and Jaya had noted that I had become "clever" again, though seemingly in a deeper way than before. I was commended for not only learning material quickly, but also for being able to retain it and play it with proper expression and musicality, at least most of the time. Even I was surprised by how much easier it had become for me to learn, retain, and integrate new music in this latter period of my training, but I had neither the time nor the inclination to ponder why I was learning more effectively. I assumed that I had simply become a more efficient and competent student in general, which was fine with me.

During those final weeks of lessons with Sukarata, things actually seemed to me to be much as they had been earlier on. Each of our sessions would begin with a full run-through of the piece up to the point I had learned, with me always playing by memory. If I made a serious mistake (minor errors were acceptable so long as I was able to recover without stopping) or had a memory lapse, we would start again, and so on until I got it right. Typically, we would repeat this process the prescribed three times, although as the piece got longer and I proved my memory to be at least more reliable than it had been before, Sukarata became a bit more lenient in his enforcement of the three-run-through policy.

The review portion of the day's lesson would usually take between one and two hours, sometimes longer, after which we would take a break for tea or Sprite and bananas. Then, for an additional one to three hours, Sukarata would "dictate" a new pukulan or two, I would transcribe the new material, and we would play through it together several times (with me reading from my notation) before concluding with a final run-through of the now-expanded piece.

While this basic process came to seem completely routine to me, it was actually undergoing a gradual but significant transformation over time, a transformation I was unaware of until several months after its occurrence. Throughout the entire course of my work with Sukarata, I was convinced that the play-and-stop experimental method we had originally devised had remained basically intact in spite of the important modifications to it implemented by Sukarata at key points along the way. While I had never viewed this method as an ideal one from an ethnomusicological standpoint (it was, after all, founded mainly on the appropriation of Western pedagogical approaches), I accepted it for what I saw it to be: a concession to practical demands deriving from a particular set of research objectives, constraints, and circumstances.

One possibility I never considered was that my method of learning might inadvertently become more "Balinese" through the course of my development as a beleganjur drummer, that with neither intention nor effort I might arrive at a process of learning in a maguru-panggul-like way, or at least something resembling one. Yet this is precisely what I observed happening when, back in my Los Angeles apartment working on my dissertation, I began to carefully analyze and compare videotapes of my own drum lessons with Sukarata and those of several of his Balinese students.[2] I had consciously resisted learning by their methods because I was convinced they could not work for me in my situation, but as I was surprised and intrigued to discover while watching the tapes, I had gradually come around to something resembling their way of doing things in spite of myself.

How this transformation occurred is still largely a mystery to me, but I suspect that at least two major factors were involved: first, whatever explicit claims I may have made to the contrary—whether to Sukarata, Jaya, or myself—at a subconscious level I must have realized that my Western-based learning methods were failing me; and second, although I tried to convince myself that all that really mattered for my study was transcribing Sukarata's piece and being able to play it well enough to produce a representative recording to accompany the dissertation, deep down what I was really after *as a musician* was to play like Sukarata, and at some intuitive level I think I knew that to sound like him I had to learn in his way.

Signs of Change: The Transcription Process

In my analysis of the observable changes I underwent over time as a kendang student, monitoring my evolving approach to the transcription process was revealing. On the videotapes of my earlier lessons, I noted that I would (as I would have predicted) always listen to Sukarata play a small musical segment first, write down what I had heard, follow the same process for the remaining segments of the phrase (usually one complete gong cycle), and only then play back what I had written. But as I proceeded through the tapes, I observed that the original transcription protocol was gradually transformed into something quite different.

The first signs of this transformation were subtle and sporadic, but by the sixth week of study it was clearly evident that my approach to transcribing had been dramatically and fundamentally altered. Now, upon first hearing Sukarata demonstrate a new passage, I would attempt to play it back directly, before rather than after attempting to notate it; and, moving even further from my Western roots, I would sometimes not even take the time to listen to the full demonstration before I began to play. Like the Balinese students, I began to watch Sukarata closely from the moment he started playing and would try to play along with him immediately, getting a visceral feel for the rhythmic patterns in my hands before concerning myself with the particulars of "the notes," let alone with how they might be inscribed in notated form. Another noteworthy alteration of procedure I detected was that in my later lessons, I would try to take down longer and longer segments of music in a single hearing. Eventually I went from transcribing in one- to two-measure chunks to sometimes transcribing complete gong cycles, and in certain instances even longer passages.

On account of these modifications in my procedures, the videotapes of my later lessons and those of the Balinese students at similar stages in the learning process came to resemble each other far more closely than the tapes of our respective lessons at earlier stages. As I was becoming more advanced as a drummer, I was also evidently becoming more "Balinese-like" in learning orientation, despite having no conscious awareness that this was happening.

Reading versus Feeling, Discipline versus Freedom

A gradual change in my approach to *relating* to my transcriptions as a music reader was also evident in the lesson videotapes, though in this case observing the tapes served mainly as a reminder of certain mental transformations I had consciously experienced in the process of learning to drum. Shortly after Sukarata decreed that I would henceforth be required to memorize everything I learned before he would teach me anything new, I began, strangely, to experience unprecedented difficulties when trying to read from my musical transcriptions. I did not allow this mysterious development to concern me much at the time, since the ability to play by memory had become the near-exclusive focus of my attention anyhow. Although being forced to perform without recourse to my transcriptions initially felt like trying to walk on a broken leg without crutches, I found the experience oddly liberating. Perhaps I had appeared more competent and in command (even if deceptively so) during my early "clever" period, when my ability to drum was completely dependent on my ability to read music, but upon having the option of reading taken away from me, I immediately began to feel more musical and musically interactive when playing. Without my transcriptions in front of me, I was a more expressive drummer, and I found myself able to lock in with Sukarata's groove in ways that previously I had not. Alas, the liberating moments of flowing groove were rare and elusive for quite some time, and tended to dissipate quickly when tentative mastery of my part or problems with my sound or technique interfered; but the excitement and release I felt at such moments were enough to compel me to always want to play without aid of notation, even independent of the fact that this was what Sukarata had in mind for me.

With practice and experience, my memory playing skills got better and better, but at the same time my reading skills became progressively worse. Eventually this odd regression became a real problem, since I was still dependent on my transcriptions to get me to the point of being able to play by memory in the first place. I felt as though I were losing my ability to read music rather than just moving away from a reading-dependent approach to performing it, and I knew neither why this was happening nor what to do about it.

The primary symptom of this unanticipated onset of what I can best describe as a kind of music-reading attention deficit disorder was a lack of ability to maintain focused attention on my performance score. Without meaning to, I would momentarily look away from the page or close my eyes while trying to play a pukulan that I was still in the process of learning. Often I would find my attention fixed on Sukarata's hands as he played, rather than on my notation; at other times I would suddenly open my eyes with the realization that I had been playing with them shut. Somehow, I would still be playing—just how I could not understand—but then I would panic as I scrambled to find where I was in the transcription, sometimes succeeding and being able to continue, more often failing and being forced to stop.

Sukarata, already perplexed by the recent revelation of my fallible memory, found this new problem even more puzzling. At least in the area of music reading—my stock-in-trade, as it were—he had thought he could assume a consistent level of competence from me. Now this was disappearing, too? I had no ready answers, neither for him nor for myself. That I had developed a taste for playing without notation did not logically preclude my ability to remain a competent performer when reading from my own score.

I struggled to stay on task when called upon to be musically literate, but the harder I tried to keep my focus on the score, the more I tended to be drawn away from it. Sometimes I would end up just staring at the page blankly in mid-performance, finding nothing comprehensible in notation patterns that would normally have been completely familiar. In my search for explanations, I began to wonder if Sukarata himself might be at the center of my problems. On the basis of disturbing intuitions alone, I came to suspect that I was caught in the middle of some absurd game of tug-of-war between him and my transcriptions, and that the two were quickly becoming mutually exclusive where I was concerned. If I concentrated on my score, I could not really listen to Sukarata play as I wanted to, but if I allowed myself to be drawn into his performance, I could not help but lose my place and thus my ability to continue playing. It was a catch-22. Part of me wanted to give in to Sukarata, to forget about the score altogether and just have fun and see where the experience led me; but the more rational self always prevailed, instructing me to do everything I could to maintain a disciplined sense of order, to force myself to concentrate and pay attention to the score when I needed to, regardless of my distracting impulses to do otherwise.

Eventually, through discipline and perseverance, I managed to gain enough control over the problem to enable me to learn through to the end of the piece. But after meeting the basic demands of note-learning and memorization involved in that pursuit, I was confronted with what seemed like a new manifestation of the same old malady. Even when playing by memory, I became increasingly torn by inner conflict. My disciplined, rational self held to a firm conviction that intensive focus on my drum part was the key to successful performance. There was, however, a strong alternative impulse that would occasionally catch me off guard, spinning me for fleeting moments into a performance mode in which I would lose conscious awareness of my part and try to play by instinct. Again, I determinedly fought irrational impulse with focused discipline, but again I was confused and frustrated by the need to engage in such a fight at all.

What confused me the most was that there appeared to be a basic contradiction between what Sukarata told me verbally and what I felt being communicated to me through his drumming. When we played together, he often made me have a nearly uncontrollable urge to just be free and play by feel, without regard for the consequences of such a reckless approach. I began to suspect that he actually wanted me to play this way. But this made no sense. When he spoke, Sukarata, just like Asnawa, Suweca, I Nyoman Wenten,[3] and the other Balinese teachers with whom I had worked, consistently stressed that precise, disciplined technical command constituted the essence of good drumming, and that proper musical expression and feeling would flow naturally and inevitably from the performer who possessed such command. The words commonly used by Balinese to describe excellence in musical performance implicitly supported such a position: *adung, lengat,* and *nabuh, incep* and *resik*—all of these terms of praise essentially meant "precise"; and when I asked Asnawa in 1992 to elaborate on the meaning of the highly complimentary term *ngelangenin,* which he had translated for me as "the effect of everything that is good in music," he responded by telling me that this effect was the product of technical perfection.

On account of all of this, it was logical for me to infer that in endeavoring to drum proficiently, my exclusive focus should be on the technical aspects of performance, on playing my part with accuracy and exactness. The rest would take care of itself. There was no margin for error here; playing music as difficult as this with the required technical precision demanded total, disciplined concentration. Playing "by instinct," as I was wont to do, had no rightful place. This was no touchy-feely New Age drum circle; this was serious musical—and ethnomusicological—business, and it demanded to be treated as such.

Final Lesson, 1992: A Transformative Moment

> The idea of aesthetic appreciation in Tantric teachings has to do with a special kind of perception, of paying full attention to whatever is before one at the moment. One is taught to strive constantly to be in the present, not mentally reliving the past or rehearsing the future; to be mindful of every moment; and to see, hear, taste, smell and touch without preconceptions, without the interfering overlay of the memory of all one's past sensory experiences. To see things as they are, to hear music as it is, without precognition or judgmental overlay, is to perceive aesthetically.
>
> Judith Becker, *Gamelan Stories*

I arrived at Sukarata's house for my final drum lesson with clearly defined objectives, a strong determination to meet them, and a good deal of anxiety. I knew exactly what I needed to do: record and videotape a clean, precise, technically accurate performance of the complete drum parts for the piece I had learned. This was a reasonable goal, but achieving it would be no easy task. The piece was long and difficult to play, and it would have to be recorded in a single take; punch-ins and overdubs were not available options. After months of hard work, the critical moment had arrived: my last opportunity to get the drumming right and record it properly, for purposes of documentation, analysis, posterity, and a sense of pride and accomplishment that Sukarata and I would hopefully always be able to share, even at the distance of thousands of miles that would soon separate us. Yes, there were still the upcoming recording sessions with the Tatasan Kaja ensemble, but in facing the prospect of recording a twenty-one-piece gamelan with only a Pro Walkman analog recorder in a less-than-ideal environment, while at the same time trying to perform one of the lead musical parts, I knew better than to approach those sessions with anything beyond rather modest expectations.[4] It was this lesson, not the large-scale recording sessions to follow, that offered the best and only opportunity for me to produce an accurate, representative record of what had been at the heart of this project all along: kreasi beleganjur drumming in the distinctive Sukarata style, performed by him and me together.

My realization that much was riding on this one particular lesson made me nervous. Sukarata would play with his usual consummate artistry—nothing to worry about there—but my confidence in my own ability to live up to my potential, to play my part from beginning to end without making any mistakes (at least significant ones) was shaky. I knew I had the capacity to accomplish my goal; I had done this before, though unfortunately never while recording. The problem once again was consistency. I was still vulnerable to memory lapses, and to moments of poor technical execution when my rhythmic accuracy or my sound (or both) would suddenly disintegrate; and there was of course the lurking potential for one of my "spacing out" episodes, when I would lose my disciplined concentration and play "by instinct" to deleterious effect. Finally, there was the question of stamina. Playing the piece was mentally and physically exhausting for me. On the basis of previous experience, I knew that if I could not play it right within the first two or three run-throughs, I would not likely be able to play it right at all, especially given that this was a high-pressure situation for me in the first place. In short, I had found much to worry about, had identified many things that might well go wrong. I thus approached the lesson with trepidation, although I had to admit that the fact that Pak Jaya would not be able to attend provided some comfort. I regarded Jaya as a great supporter and friend, but given the way I was feeling at the moment, the last thing I desired was his unsparing critical scrutiny.

I placed the video camera in its usual place on the tripod and set it to the remote function, then positioned my tape-recorder microphone in front of the drums at the appropriate distance and engaged the record/pause buttons on both machines. Sukarata and I took our customary playing positions, facing each other cross-legged with our drums in our laps. He smiled at me warmly and asked if I was doing all right; apparently, my anxiety was showing through. I told him I was fine, that I just needed to get started to work off a bit of unwanted adrenaline. I attempted a confident smile, turned on the camera with the remote control, released the pause button on the tape recorder, and gestured that I was ready to begin.

We started to play, but it was immediately evident that my nerves were getting the best of me; I was not able to play well. My left-hand stroke was pitifully weak, and I found myself stumbling through passages that normally posed no difficulties. After several failed attempts to get the performance up and running, my worry level had increased substantially, and the negative energy seemed to be rubbing off on Sukarata. At one point he himself actually lost track of the arrangement and had to stop, an occurrence unprecedented in our months of work together. One aborted take followed another as I found a way to mess things up again and again. Each time this happened, Sukarata would suggest we take a break in order that I might regain my composure. I kept insisting that I was fine, that I would get it right the next time around, but I was wrong. Finally, Sukarata put his drum down and leaned back against a column directly behind him on the verandah. His wife arrived with two glasses of tea for us. I told Sukarata I was ready to try again, but he just shook his head and smiled at me peacefully.

"No," he said. "Your head is too full. You know the piece, but you won't let it play. Drink some tea first."

I was impatient. I didn't want any tea. I was ready to play. But Sukarata would not budge. He took a deep breath and looked upward to the sky. Suddenly, he seemed removed, detached, as though he had gone off to some other place in his mind. He had left me alone to find a way to relax and pull myself together.

I turned off the video camera and the tape recorder, leaned back, closed my eyes, and breathed deeply. Sukarata was right. My head was too full. I had to calm down. Otherwise, I was going to experience nothing but further anxiety, frustration, and ineptitude. I sipped my tea slowly and tried to clear my mind of distractions. Gradually, a calm and quiet mood settled over me.

Sukarata remained silent and seemingly distant for some ten minutes. Then, quite suddenly, he sprang forward, placed his kendang on his lap, and smiled. It was a smile of blissful unconcern; his expression conveyed that everything was now going to be just fine.

"Okay," he said energetically, "now we can try again."

I reset the video camera and tape recorder and we began, and as soon as we started I knew that my playing was "on." I was totally focused on my part; nothing could distract me. Even when I faltered momentarily during a tricky transitional passage about halfway through the arrangement, I was able to quickly recover and push through to the end without further incident.

When the performance was over, I let out a huge sigh of elation and relief. I checked to make sure that everything had recorded; thankfully, it had. The tension poured out of my body. I felt like an athlete at the successful conclusion of a trying and long-anticipated match. Indeed, even the performance itself had somehow seemed athletic.

I had done what I needed to do. I had the recording I required. Sukarata had of course played beautifully, and I could live easily with the one error I had committed and the few other minor glitches that separated what I had done from the idealized technical perfection of my fantasies. The performance had been good, better in fact than I could have realistically hoped for, and I was content to leave it at that. Now I could go home and rest up for the evening recording session in Tatasan.

I smiled at Sukarata. "Bagus?" Was that good? I asked, seeking confirmation that things had in fact gone as well as I thought they had. He smiled and gave me a thumbs-up sign, but there was a sense of hesitation and uneasiness in his demeanor that surprised me.

"Bagus," he said finally, but with a marked lack of enthusiasm. It seemed as though he wanted to tell me something but was afraid of hurting my feelings. I could not begin to fathom what he might be thinking. There was a long, tense silence, and then the tension was broken by the arrival of Nyoman, Sukarata's youngest daughter, who came out of the house with a tray of tea and bananas for us. This usually signaled that the lesson was over.

After finishing my tea and fruit, I stood up and began to pack up my equipment. Then Sukarata did something I had not expected. He gestured for me to leave everything set up, placed his drum on his lap, and suggested that we try the recording one more time. He did not say why. Although I was tired, I figured I had nothing to lose by running through the piece again. Given the success of the last take, I could afford to relax on this one. If it came out better, great; if not, nothing would be lost.

I checked the battery in the video camera, reset the tape recorder, and got into playing position, but just as I was about to release the pause buttons, Sukarata held up his hands and told me not to begin yet. There was something he needed to tell me.

"This time, you must not worry," he said, staring directly at me with an eerily serious expression. "Just play. You don't have to try. If you listen, you will not forget. I play and you play. It is the same. Then it is good. Then the feeling is good."

Sukarata's remarks struck me as unusual. They were uncharacteristically "philosophical" for him, perhaps even a bit enigmatic. He had always assessed my playing in starkly clinical terms: my rhythmic execution was either correct or incorrect, my sound strong or not yet strong, my performance expressive or not expressive enough. Further commentary and explanation were rarely provided, and talk of "the feeling" between us and the like was rare indeed. Why the sudden implicit addressing of deeper and more subtle aspects of the dynamics of our musical interaction? I was not sure, but clearly Sukarata felt compelled to convey something to me that he considered very important. His message was delivered with the intent of making an impact, and I would do my best to heed it wisely and follow the "prescription": just play and don't try, don't think too much, let go. It was an invitation to follow a path that my musical instincts had been directing me toward for a while, but that judicious reason had prevented me from exploring. Now was my chance to give free rein to those "irrational" impulses I had fought so hard to suppress. I already had the recording I needed, and now I had Sukarata's encouragement to "just play" in addition. It was time.

As soon as we started, I felt something unusual in Sukarata's playing. There was a power and gravity to it that was truly exceptional, even for him; it pulled me in more strongly than ever before. His part and mine began to feel so deeply integrated that I felt as though I were not even playing at all. True to my past inclinations, however, my initial instinct was to resist, to hold on to my distinct perspective on the music and keep track of my own part. I was still fighting not to lose my concentration, but the pull was too powerful, too overwhelming. I was going under and there was nothing to be done about it, but I still felt frightened.

And then I recalled Sukarata's words of just moments before. They echoed through my swirling mind with a new power and relevance. *Play. Listen. Don't try.* Sukarata *wanted* me to let go. He wanted me to give in to this strange desire I had so stubbornly resisted, to lose track of where I was in the music, of the part I was playing, of my body . . . of my self.

Whoosh! Into the undertow I crash, into the roar of waves of rhythm and sound, a roar completely familiar yet now profoundly new. Brief terror followed by giddy exhilaration as the rhythms crush down upon me and shoot me back to the surface. And I emerge, still playing, but differently than before. Not hearing myself. Not hearing him. Just this delicious perpetual motion of sound. Floating over it. Weightless. Nothing to worry about anymore, for Sukarata is with me, and so the music can play itself, and it does. And then, it is over.

I sit unable to move. My heart races; my hands and arms buzz with electricity. A shiver runs up my spine. I become aware of seeing again as Sukarata's drum comes into focus. For a long time I feel paralyzed. I just stare at the drum. Then, looking up, I catch Sukarata's eyes, and am snapped back to consciousness by his mysterious, penetrating stare. Suddenly I am self-conscious, confused, even scared. I don't feel like talking but force myself to say something to break the silence.

"Bagus?" I ask sheepishly, my eyes still locked in his stare.

More silence. And then Sukarata's face bursts into smile.

"Ngelangenin!" he exclaims: the highest of compliments. And suddenly I know that for one brief moment, at least, I have been able to move to some deeper place; into the experience of a more profound musical awareness than I had known or known existed; to a musical realm where the technical, the precise, the well-wrought, the beautiful, have become something other than what they seemed: reflections and embodiments not of themselves, but of a deep commitment and trust, of a transformation into a communion where we do not remain what we were before.

Drumming and Understanding: Some Speculations on Trust

The experience of that lesson with Sukarata caused me to see beleganjur drumming, our relationship, and many other things in a new light. Most significantly, I have come to believe after much thought and reflection that for Sukarata, meaning and value in drumming are located not so much in the playing of music itself as in the precious achievement of a trusting partnership realized and represented in that playing. I have also come to believe that Sukarata was intent on teaching me this valuable lesson about drumming and trust from the time of our first meeting in Seminyak. My stubbornness of will, however, together with my personal insecurities and my insensitivity to the unspoken messages of his musical communications, prevented me from seeing this until the last possible moment.

What makes matters complicated and problematic from a research perspective is that these inferences concerning Sukarata's views on drumming and trust are not based on anything he has explicitly told me. Neither formal interviews nor informal conversations during our encounters prior to or since that enlightening drum lesson have confirmed or disproved my speculations. My inferences have been drawn mainly from musical experience itself: from drumming with Sukarata and also from seeing and hearing him drum with others (especially Jaya) during subsequent visits to Bali. And they have furthermore been substantiated by my observations of the kind of person Sukarata is in nonmusical situations. I have noted his unshakable devotion to Jaya, who he claims has always proved worthy of his trust, and to his late brother Sudhama, who was always there for him when others were quick to judge. I have witnessed the hurt he has suffered and the bitterness he feels toward people who he believes have betrayed or abandoned him, or who have not cherished the dedicated friendship he tried to offer them. I have observed his frustration with those who have failed to accept that he is a virtuous and honorable man. And I have benefited from his dedication to my personal growth, from his persistent commitment to making me understand, feel, and treasure the true essence and meaning of trust, whether in drumming or anything else.

Sukarata wanted me to trust him, to feel as one with him in something approaching the way that Balinese drummers who share deep musical partnerships feel as one with each other. This was not something he could simply tell me to do in words, however, for he realized that no one ever truly comes to trust another by being told to do so. His medium for communicating both the deep importance of trust and his wish that I should place my trust in him was drumming. Drumming, after all, was what he did best, and it was the domain of experience where we stood to share the most.

Indeed, two-drum styles of Balinese kendang playing, with their dazzlingly complex interlocking structures and total interdependence of parts, offer a cogent symbol of trusting connection idealized in sound. To drum in the absence of one's partner, or, just as importantly, in the absence of an abiding *faith* in one's partner, is not to drum at all; the notion of private practice on one's instrument, the presumed foundation of musical competence among Western musicians, is deemed absurd by all the Balinese drummers I have known. Good drumming is premised on trust, and is in a very important sense *about* trust. Trust is both the cause and product of the technical precision of execution highlighted in verbal descriptions of Balinese drumming excellence. Individual drum parts, and by extension individual drummers, are like threads in a cloth. Alone, each is lifeless, meaningless, a directionless strand of material. But as the different strands are woven together in a balanced and integrated way, each gains significance and purpose as a unique but ultimately indistinguishable part of something greater. The thread does not sacrifice its individuality to the cloth into which it is woven. Rather, it gains its identity in the process of moving toward its own eventual absorption into a fabric shared with trusted others, where it can finally be recognized not for what it was alone but for the whole of which it has become an integral part.

On the basis of a nonverbal musical understanding of a kind that "often exists in the absence of verbal explanations of it" (Rice 1997, 115), I "understand" that there is an integral connection between the experience of Balinese drumming and the experience of trust between partners with a willingness to become more than they were alone through each other. I understand this as one musician who has learned from another musician.

Musical Experience, Reflexivity, and Musical Understanding

I realize that the above exploration of my musical relationship with Sukarata is a partial and imbalanced one. It is a tale of my personal struggle for competence and understanding in the musical world he and I shared rather than a balanced account of the dialectic of interpersonal, interculturally mediated communication and experience that emerged from within that world. Here I admit to having positioned myself as the central figure in a drama rather than as the "bit player" of Jeff Titon's preferred vision (1993, 6). What I have presented might certainly be described as an example of the oft-maligned autobiographical narrative ethnography (ibid.), and might also be described as highly self-absorbed. I do not, however, feel a need to apologize for this, for as Rice has suggested, "personal experience is . . . the place where understanding begins and in some sense remains located" (1994, 10).

My story of learning to drum with Sukarata represents a provisional endpoint, the first step in what I hope will prove to be a long and continuing journey toward deeper understandings and insights. In presenting it, I have attempted to demonstrate by way of example that explicitly acknowledging and engaging with one's own experiential path through the interpersonal encounters of fieldwork is of scholarly relevance, *whether or not* the particular experiences explored ultimately lead beyond themselves and the ostensibly "fabricated," "artificial" spheres of intercultural musical interaction from which they originated.

Tuning in to Sukarata through the direct musical experience of drumming has enabled me to think in ways that I otherwise would not have, to ask questions I had not considered before, and even to challenge formerly held assumptions concerning what ethnomusicology is and what it should rightly comprise. Drumming with Sukarata, and reflecting upon that experience, have been critically important in the evolution of understandings and perspectives I have been developing throughout the process of my research on beleganjur. Insights I have gained through the experience have been key to my efforts to disentangle certain perplexing contradictions with which I have struggled along the way: contradictions between what I have been told by my Balinese teachers and what I have seen and heard them do in the moment of making music; between the outward appearances of Balinese music-learning processes and the results they yield; and between what I have read and heard about Balinese music and culture in the scholarship of others and what I have felt and experienced of Balinese music and culture in my lived interactions with Balinese people.

And tuning in to Sukarata as a drummer, most especially in the transformational moment of my final lesson with him in 1992, also taught me that to open oneself to knowing and understanding in new ways demands letting go. This has been important to me not just as a musician but as an ethnomusicologist as well, for it is largely on account of what happened to me as a drummer working with Sukarata that I have ultimately felt compelled in writing this book to let go of certain methodological, epistemological, and writing conventions that have long defined the basic parameters of appropriateness and acceptability in the field of ethnomusicology.

"The measure by which the worth or truth of any view is judged must be a worldly one," Michael Jackson has written. "Whether one calls upon correspondence to the facts or force of personal conviction in claiming merit for one's point of view, such invocations indicate ways we construct, contest, and experience our worlds; they are not notions which can be arbitrated decisively, or regarded as arguments that can be won" (1996, 1).

The ways we construct, contest, and experience our worlds determine what we understand and how we understand. They also direct and define the understandings of those who read what we write, hear what we say, speak with us about what we think, and see what we do. We can only truly believe in that which we have felt, and belief, as much as knowledge, is central to our "understanding." Drumming with Sukarata has led me to understandings of drumming, of beleganjur, of music, of trust, and perhaps even of "Balinese culture" that I consider important. These understandings are certainly not rooted in verifiable facts; they are not even grounded in anything approaching what might normally be categorizable as substantive ethnomusicological data. They have emerged instead from that odd class of "vivid, deeply moving, often unarticulated inner experiences" of music that so often remain hidden from view in ethnomusicological writings (Rice 1994, 3). Yet they are of integral importance to this study and reflect what and how I think to a profound degree. I believe that they also reflect, at least to some extent, what Sukarata believed was important for both myself and others to know.

I therefore see it as my responsibility as a scholar to communicate these understandings and, in the process, to communicate from whence they came to the best of my abilities. Music *is* philosophy. It reflects upon itself in ways that may only be accessible to those who participate actively in its creation, that is, to the music-makers. As music-makers—not just as scholars—ethnomusicologists have a responsibility to address their experiences and the insights that issue from them. These experiences and insights deserve to be considered as important issues of scholarship rather than as marginalized prerequisites to the understanding of things other than themselves. If we fail to address our own musical lives as ethnomusicologists, we eliminate the possibility of engaging potentially stimulating and revealing forms of understanding that could open new vistas in the study of music not only in or as culture, but between, across, and around cultures as well.

If we continue to subscribe to the inherent limitations of epistemological perspectives that frame our fieldwork musical interactions as primarily dictated by the respective statuses of "insiders" and "outsiders," and continue to cling to the hierarchical and exclusionary position that "understanding the music from within" ought to be the only proper goal of our musical efforts as researchers, we will continue to negate the ethnomusicological value of the reflexive study of musical experience as a significant form of intercultural dialogue in which all who participate, including the researcher, are relevant contributors to meaningful music-making.

As Jackson has explained, what makes fieldwork vital and meaningful is not that it guarantees "certain knowledge of others," but that it "brings us into direct dialogue *with* others, affording us opportunities to explore knowledge not as something that grasps inherent and hidden truths but as an intersubjective process of sharing experience, comparing notes, and finding common ground. In this process our social gumption and social skills, as much as our scientific methodology, become measures of the limits and value of our understanding" (1996, 8).

For most ethnomusicologists, music-making constitutes a core intersubjective process of sharing experience, finding common ground, and entering into direct dialogue with musicians whose music we endeavor to understand. It is time for us to stop avoiding the issue of what happens when we interact musically with people we "study" for fear that explicit attention to such issues might distract us from a focus on the "more important" and central quest for knowledge and understanding of "the Other"; or perhaps for fear that open and honest reflection might reveal our fieldwork methods and subsequent musical understandings as less noble than we would like them to appear to others. Conceiving of and explicitly addressing what we experience as music-learners and musicians in the field can broaden "the boundaries of *what we are able to think*" (Turino 1993, 6), and can thereby enhance the richness of ethnomusicological thought. Attempting to "get inside the heads and fingers" of the musicians we study in part through our own studies with them need not preclude the effort to get inside our own heads and fingers as well, as we move—albeit sometimes erratically, unpredictably, clumsily, and circuitously—toward the particular forms and levels of musical understanding that inevitably shape our thinking and our perspectives.

In the musical relationship Sukarata and I shared through bele-ganjur drumming, every success and failure, every effective strategy employed, every misguided decision and mishap, every joy and frustration, accommodation, misunderstanding, incomprehension, acceptance, rejection, reflection, and disorientation had meaning, and each contributed to the realization of a musical understanding and the construction of a shared musical world. There was value and purpose even in my long resistance to opening myself to what I am now convinced he was trying to communicate to me for quite some time. When Sukarata finally *forced* me to trust him, first telling me things I should have been able to perceive from the music alone and then drawing me into his world with the consuming passion of his drumming, the depth of my understanding of what trust meant to him and should mean to me became far greater than it would have had my resistance to his will not been so strong. By sheer power of musicality and strength of will, Sukarata compelled me to see what made his music live. He wrenched me from a musical place where I had been determined to remain and showed me that true musical experience is the experience of trust, that only when we learn to trust one another, to dissolve in the realization of our shared humanity, will the music finally play.

Notes

Introduction

1. This translation was provided by I Ketut Gedé Asnawa. *Bala* is an Old Javanese (Kawi) term for a soldier or warrior ("military personnel" is perhaps a more accurate translation); *ganjur* means "to walk in an ordered manner" and also "crowded." (*Ganjur* is also an old term used in Java to refer to certain strong-toned, fast-vibrating gongs and *kempuls*. See Kunst 1949, 1:141, 149.) Koichi (1995, 9–10) offers an interesting alternative interpretation, relating the *bala* portion of *balaganjur (beleganjur)* to *kala,* one of several types of Balinese evil spirit beings.

2. "I" before a Balinese name indicates that the individual is a male; "Ni" indicates a female.

3. Throughout the book, the abbreviation "pers. comm." (personal communication) is used in reference to information conveyed to me by my teachers and other consultants during lessons, conversations, and interviews. My interviews and conversations with Asnawa, and also with I Wayan Dibia, I Madé Bandem, I Komang Astita, I Wayan Suweca, I Wayan Rai, and I Madé Lila Arsana, were typically conducted in English (sometimes partially in English and partially in Indonesian), while those with all the other Balinese consultants were in Indonesian. Most of the quotations and other references to personal communications included in the text were drawn from transcripts of tapes (audio and video) recorded in the field. In those cases where recordings were not made, I have relied on the documentation contained in my field journals. I am indebted to Arsana and Dibia, and most especially to Asnawa, for their assistance in translating interviews and other materials. Any mistranslations, misquotations, or misrepresentations are fully my responsibility.

4. In some cases, the body has already decayed prior to the cremation as a result of its having been buried underground for a lengthy period of time. If only the bones remain when the body is finally exhumed, these are burned during the cremation ceremony.

5. The ngaben and memukur rituals will be discussed in more detail in chapter 1.

6. Alternate spellings include *baleganjur* (DeVale 1990; Bakan 1993, 1993–94), *balaganjur* (several commercial recordings; see the discography), and *belegandjore* or *balagandjoer* (McPhee n.d.).

7. Two excellent, comprehensive books on the different forms and styles of Balinese gamelan are Colin McPhee's *Music in Bali: A Study in Form and Instrumental Organization in Balinese Orchestral Music* (1966) and Michael Tenzer's introductory text *Balinese Music* (1991). McPhee's semi-autobiographical *A House in Bali* ([1947] 1991) is worthy of mention on account of both its informative and evocative descriptions of music-making events in Bali and its narrative style, which foreshadowed the narrative approaches represented in many contemporary music ethnographies. (See the bibliography for other McPhee publications on Balinese music as well.) Edward Herbst's *Voices in Bali* (1997) is an important study of Balinese vocal music forms and practices (see also Wallis 1980). *Balinese Music in Context,* edited by Danker Schaareman (1992), is an outstanding collection of essays by some of the foremost Balinese, European, and North American scholars in the field. Mantle Hood, best known among Indonesianists for his writings on Javanese music, has made important contributions to Balinese music studies as well (1982, 1990). Other works on Balinese music–related topics include Aryasi 1985; Asnawa 1991; Bandem 1980, 1983; Barkin 1990; Brinner 1995b; DeVale 1990; DeVale and Dibia 1991; Dibia 1992, 1996; Harnish

1995; Keeler 1975; Lendra 1983; Ornstein 1971; Rembang 1985; Sanger 1985, 1988; Schaareman 1980; Seebass 1978; Toth 1975; Vitale 1990; S. Willner [1992] 1996; and Yasa et al. 1993. Some additional works that contain important information on different aspects of Balinese culture relating to musical activities include Bandem and deBoer 1980, 1995; Barth 1993; Belo [1949] 1966, 1970; Covarrubias 1937; Daniel 1981; de Zoete and Spies [1938] 1973; A. Hobart 1987; Hobart, Ramseyer, and Leemann 1996; Lansing 1977, 1979, 1983; McKean 1973, 1979; Mead [1939] 1970c, [1940] 1970a, [1942] 1970b; Picard 1990; Ramseyer 1986; and Zurbuchen 1987. Balinese periodicals and scholarly journals such as *Wreta Cita* and *Mudra,* both published by STSI Press, include articles on music-related subjects by leading Balinese scholars; STSI student theses (see Rai 1992) are another important resource for scholarship on Balinese music and culture.

8. For example, iron-keyed *gamelan selonding* instruments, bamboo-keyed *gamelan joged bumbung* instruments, and wooden-keyed *gamelan gambang* instruments. Note that only the percussion-based gamelan types are being discussed here.

9. See Warren 1993 for a comprehensive study of the banjar/desa system and its complex interactions with Indonesian political institutions. It should be noted that all levels of government above that of the desa are controlled by local bureaus and ministries of the national government of Indonesia, the ruling party of which is GOLKAR (Golongan Karya).

10. As Annette Sanger has convincingly argued, despite the theoretical equality of all sekehe members, inequalities articulate intra-sekehe social relations at many levels (1985, 51).

11. Barz and Cooley 1997; Berliner 1978, 1994; Blacking 1973; Bohlman 1997; Brinner 1995a; Burnim 1985; Chernoff 1979; Feld 1990; Friedson 1996; Gourlay 1978; Herbst 1997; Keil 1979; Lindsay 1996; Lortat-Jacob 1995; Nettl 1995; Quigley 1988; Rice 1987, 1988, 1994, 1997; Seeger 1987; Shelemay 1991, 1997; Suanda 1982; Titon 1988, 1993, 1997; Turino 1993; Waterman 1990; and Ziporyn (see Bamberger and Ziporyn 1992) represent important ethnomusicological contributions in this area. Earlier writings by McPhee and Hood are among the works foreshadowing current reflexive ethnomusicological approaches. Works by scholars in other disciplines that have been influential in the current reflexive, dialogical approaches in ethnomusicology include Abu-Lughod 1991, 1993; Bakhtin 1981; Bourdieu 1977; Clifford 1986; Clifford and Marcus 1986; Crapanzano 1980; Dumont 1978; Dwyer 1982; Gadamer [1965] 1975; C. Geertz 1973b, 1983, 1984, 1988; Heidegger 1962; Husserl 1970; Jackson 1996; Marcus and Fischer 1986; Merleau-Ponty [1960] 1964; Newman 1965; Rabinow 1977; Ricoeur 1981; Riesman 1977; Rorty 1989, 1991; M. Rosaldo 1984; R. Rosaldo 1989; Schütz 1951; Stoller and Olkes 1987; Sudnow 1978; Turner and Bruner 1986; and Wikan 1990.

12. A revised version of the essay was published in the book *Shadows in the Field.* See Titon 1997.

13. An earlier version of this definition was employed in my dissertation, in which I defined ethnomusicology as the study of "how music lives in the lives of the people who make it, and how people live in the music they make" (Bakan 1993, xvii).

14. This is in contrast to most other forms of Balinese gamelan, where the principal movement is typically the pengawak. See chapter 3.

15. In terms of internal formal structure, the gamelan gong and beleganjur versions of a pengecet have little in common, but they share a likeness in terms of musical character. See chapter 3.

Chapter 1

1. See Kartomi 1990 for discussion of Indonesian musical instrument classification.

2. Where both a female *(wadon)* and a male *(lanang) gong* are employed, their alternate strokes usually mark the beginning/endpoint and the midpoint of each formal cycle, respectively.

3. See DeVale and Dibia 1991 and Eiseman 1989, 11–24, for further discussion. Semiotic research on gamelan music and music instruments (both Javanese and Balinese) has been extensive and important. See DeVale 1977, 1989, 1991, 1992; Becker 1979, 1980, 1988, 1993; and Becker and Becker 1981. DeVale's "Death Symbolism in Music: Preliminary Considerations" (1990) is especially relevant to the present study, since it concerns the gamelan beleganjur specifically.

4. Technically, the term *gong* should be used only in reference to the two *gong ageng:* the male *gong lanang* and the female *gong wadon.* Smaller gong-type Balinese instruments, which likewise exhibit the curved rim, tiered surface, and bossed center *(moncol* or *pencu)* construction characteristic of the gong ageng, have different names: *kempur, kempli, kempluk,* and *kelenang,* to provide a few examples. Melodic sets of gong-type instruments go by names such as *ponggang, bonang, trompong,* and *reyong.* Smaller variant forms of the gong ageng "prototype" include the *bendé* and the *kajar,* on which the *pencu* is sunk down into the instrument. As was mentioned earlier, in this book the italicized word *gong* refers specifically to the gong ageng, while the un-italicized words "gong" and "gongs" shall be understood to potentially encompass any of these instruments of gong-type construction.

5. See Vickers 1989, 11–76, for a concise account of the volatile, war-ravaged history of pre-colonial Bali.

6. Eiseman 1989; Hobart, Ramseyer, and Leemann 1996; Phalgunadi 1991; and Hooykaas 1973 are recommended sources for information on such religious rituals and ceremonials, which will for the most part be discussed here only with specific reference to their employment of beleganjur music.

7. It should also be noted that all three beleganjur ensemble configurations represent what might be described as ideal types. Even today, outside of formal contest and demonstration contexts, beleganjur is sometimes played by makeshift ensembles; the full complement of players and instruments is not always available for every ritualistic occasion. Prior to the advent of kreasi beleganjur, which has reportedly had the effect of standardizing beleganjur instrumentation throughout Bali to a considerable degree, the instrumentation was likely more variable and flexible than it is today. Photographic evidence from the 1920s and 1930s, for example, indicates that beleganjur or beleganjur-like ensembles were sometimes limited to just five or six players (see Kunst and Kunst–van Wely 1925, 46, 223; McPhee n.d., folder 37).

8. This ensemble should not be confused with a similar processional ensemble, the *gamelan batel bebarongan,* which accompanies sacred Barong (Bebarongan Sakral) performances (CD #1), employs just one kendang rather than two, and differs from the beleganjur bebatelan in other aspects of its instrumentation as well *(kemong* used instead of bendé, no gong ageng). Like the music of the beleganjur bebatelan, the music of the batel bebarongan is based on the batel colotomic form. Sometimes the ensemble is referred to as simply *gamelan batel.* Adding a further layer of potential terminological confusion is a third and quite different type of ensemble, the *gamelan batel gendèr wayang,* which is also sometimes referred to in abbreviated form as just *gamelan batel;* it is used to accompany *wayang Ramayana* and *wayang wong* performances (see Bandem 1980).

9. Besides Bandem, at least two other Balinese scholars, I Komang Astita and I Wayan Rai, have conducted research on the gamelan gong bheri. Unfortunately, I have thus far been unsuccessful in my efforts to gain access to their writings on the subject.

10. Kunst (1949, 1:150) notes the existence of a Javanese gong called *gong bèri* (bheri), which is defined as "a small, often knobless gong" that "is never found in any gamelan, but serves exclusively as a signaling- and war-cymbal."

11. For further discussion of Adi Merdangga, gong bebonangan, batel bebarongan, and other ensemble relatives of the gamelan beleganjur, see Bakan 1993, 138–47. On the subject of Adi Merdangga, see also Suartaya 1993.

12. Other names used for this same ensemble include *gamelan bebonangan, gamelan bebonang,* and *gamelan bonang* (see McPhee 1966).

13. In more experimental musical contexts, the cengceng may be played with beaters as well. Two pieces composed by Asnawa that will be discussed in later chapters, "Kosong" (1984) and "Beleganjur Angga Yowana" (1986), make use of this effect.

14. This method of classification was developed by Javanese musicologists (including Sindu-sawarno [Sindoesawarno] and Martopangrawit; see Sumarsam 1995, 154) but is also used by Balinese musicologists. The discussion here of the beleganjur ensemble in terms of irama and lagu instruments is derived from an explanation provided for me during a 1992 lesson with Asnawa.

15. *Pengisep* is from the word *ngisep,* meaning "to take a breath."

16. The situation might be compared to that described by Herbst in connection with *wayang lemah,* a ritual form of puppetry often required for ceremonies. "It is uncommon," notes Herbst, "to hear Balinese saying 'That was great (or terrible) *wayang lemah,* because people do not judge it by common artistic standards. It is cherished because it fulfills an aspect of the religious ceremony" (1997, 95).

17. The colotomic gong punctuations of other tabuh, such as *tabuh telu* and *tabuh batel,* are occasionally heard in beleganjur performances, especially in beleganjur arrangements of compositions adapted from other gamelan repertoires (see chapter 2) and in the more experimental modern contest-style pieces. The tabuh telu colotomy is identical to that of gilak except that in tabuh telu there is no gong ageng stroke at the midpoint of the cycle.

It should also be noted that gilak is a common colotomic form beyond the specific domain of beleganjur, being associated with *baris* and *topéng* dance compositions and with *lelambatan* pieces, among others.

18. Note that in the figures included in this chapter, the gong wadon is always shown to mark the beginning and end of each gong cycle (gongan), while the gong lanang stroke always falls at the cycle's midpoint. According to Asnawa, this represents the correct order of *gong* strokes in the pattern of gilak beleganjur. In practice, however, the order of *gong* strokes is often reversed; in many live and recorded beleganjur performances I have heard, it is the lanang that commences and concludes each gong cycle, while the wadon marks the midpoint. This variant form is illustrated below (CD #7).

$\sqrt{}$ = 48-196

| Gong wadon | Gong lanang | Kempur | Bendé | Kempli | Kajar (or Kempluk) |

19. As has been discussed in numerous publications on Indonesian music, such stratification of rates of rhythmic density is characteristic of gamelan music generally. It is in no way unique to beleganjur.

20. The characteristic unison texture in beleganjur involves the kendang wadon, the eight cengceng, and the four reyong kettles all being struck together, with each unison stroke being anticipated by a single stroke on the kendang lanang. In this texture the reyong players strike the edges *(lambé)* of their kettles with the wooden tips of their mallets rather than striking the central boss with the cord-wrapped part of the shaft.

21. See McPhee 1966, 33, for a more detailed organological description of Balinese kendang.

22. During rehearsals and in non-processional performance contexts, the kendang are usually played from a seated position, the drummers sitting cross-legged with their drums laid across their laps, as in other non-processional types of gamelan performance.

23. In gong kebyar, these roles are typically reversed; the wadon is usually the lead drum.

24. Note, however, that while convenient, the reduction of interlocking cengceng rhythms to a single line of rhythm, as represented in many of the transcriptions, fails to reflect the timbral complexity and richness of the interlocking texture.

25. According to Bandem and deBoer (1995, 95), the elaborate rhythmic structures heard in women's rice-pounding music (which may feature upwards of two dozen performers) "are considered by many Balinese musicians to be the source for the patterns used by the Cak chorus accompanying the Sang Hyang Dedari dances" (ibid., 10–15, for further discussion of sanghyang dedari;

128–31, for further information on kecak). Those patterns, in turn, are believed by some scholars to represent the direct antecedents of the kilitan cengceng (Dibia, pers. comm., 1992).

26. A commoner-caste priest specializing in mortuary rituals, the *balian konteng,* may also perform these ritual duties (I Nyoman Wenten, pers. comm., 1997).

27. My discussion here focuses on ngaben as a ritual dedicated to the cremation of one person. In many cases, however, the ngaben is a multiple affair, involving the cremations of several individuals in one very large event. Often, a wealthy and/or high-caste family conducting cremation rites for one of their own will also serve as the "sponsor" for the cremations of people from less well-to-do, commoner families with which they are associated.

28. Schaareman mentions the gamelan beleganjur in passing in the introductory paragraph of his article; see Schaareman 1980, 465.

29. As was noted earlier, if the body has been buried for a lengthy period prior to the ngaben, as often occurs in nonwealthy or commoner-caste families, it may consist of little more than exhumed skeletal remains.

30. The particular form of sarcophagus is determined by the caste of the deceased. See Eiseman 1989, 118.

31. If the home banjar of the deceased is located far from the sea, a local stream or river will often suffice. Nowadays, the family may elect to reach the sea by automobile or truck rather than by foot (Eiseman 1989, 124).

32. According to Eiseman (1989, 126), *mamukur (memukur)* is the term used for wealthy, high-caste ceremonials, while *nyekah* refers to the more modest ceremonials of the commoner caste. For the most revered and wealthy (kings, princes, etc.), lavish memukurs requiring months of preparation and involving hundreds of thousands of people may be produced; these are known as *maligia.*

33. Once again, if there are distance or other logistical problems, the procession may culminate at a local river or stream.

34. At one large memukur I attended in Kesiman in 1995, two gamelan angklung were played.

35. Although cooking on Nyepi is forbidden, Balinese are permitted to eat food cooked beforehand. Fasting is encouraged, however.

36. *Barong* refers to a very important category of Balinese masks attached to large and elaborate regalia. Taking the form of a particular animal (dog, wild boar, cow, tiger, monkey) or supernatural being (especially the Barong Ket, a "dragon-like lion"; see photo in Bandem and deBoer 1995, 132), a Barong is typically animated by two dancers positioned one behind the other underneath the costume. Barongs play a critically important role as protector spirits in Balinese communities. See Bandem and deBoer 1995, 144, for a listing of types of Barongs; and also Belo's classic study, *Bali: Rangda and Barong* ([1949] 1966).

37. "Pak," short for "Bapak" (Father), is a term of respect used in reference to a man; "Ibu" (Mother) is the equivalent term for a woman. (The abbreviation "Bu" is sometimes used.)

38. This happens to have been the contest described in the introduction.

Chapter 2

1. The new women's *beleganjur* groups that began to originate in the mid-1990s pose a conspicuous and controversial exception, as will be discussed in chapter 6.

2. See Sutton 1991, 185, for a discussion of the lomba phenomenon in Java.

3. Although the Republic of Indonesia achieved nationhood in 1945 under Sukarno, a struggle with Dutch forces trying to reestablish control after the Japanese occupation of 1942–45 continued through 1949. See Robinson 1995, 95–180, for detailed discussion of the political, economic, and social instability in Bali during this period.

4. The Ngurah Rai Airport is located outside the city limits of Denpasar in the southern part of Badung, close to the tourist enclaves of Kuta.

5. Alternatively, a fifth reyong kettle tuned to pitch *ding* was reportedly added by some groups.

6. Hobart, Ramseyer, and Leemann translate *puputan* as "until the last," "until the bitter end" (1996, 238 n. 2).

7. The 1908 puputan of the Balinese kingdom of Klungkung is the subject of an excellent study by Margaret Wiener (who claims that the common depiction of puputan as a form of "mass ritual suicide" is incorrect and misleading). See Wiener 1995b.

8. See Clifford Geertz's *Negara: The Theater State in Nineteenth-Century Bali* (1980) for a fascinating (and controversial) study of Balinese society during the historical period preceding Dutch colonization.

9. Beyond being the original chief administrator of the LBPB, Ebuh has many other distinguished achievements to his credit in the sphere of competitive beleganjur. He was the administrative director *(klian)* of the beleganjur group from his native banjar, Pandé Sumerta Kaja, which won the 1989 LBPB championship and a 1990 Bali-wide beleganjur championship, and which was featured on the first (and to date only) kreasi beleganjur recording to receive international distribution, *Balaganjur of Pande and Angklung of Sidan, Bali* (KICC 5197), released by Japan's King Record Company in 1995 as part of their World Music Library series.

10. Raden Adjeng (Ajeng) Kartini is regarded by Indonesians as a national heroine. *Letters of a Javanese Princess* (Kartini 1920), which was published after her death, became a defining icon of both the Indonesian struggle for national independence and the Indonesian women's movement.

11. PORSENI stands for Pekan Olah Raga dan Seni, meaning "Week of Sports and Arts."

12. In exceptional cases, someone who is related to one of the families of the banjar but is not himself from there may be granted permission to perform in a contest.

13. The one partial exception was when I was allowed to play with the beleganjur group from Banjar Tatasan Kaja (Denpasar) in a kite-flying competition at Ketewel in 1995. Even though the different beleganjur performances in this event were graded (contributing to the overall grade of each participating banjar's kite-flying presentation), this was not a lomba beleganjur per se.

14. In the aforementioned kite-flying contest featuring beleganjur groups, the group with which I performed was sponsored by Coca-Cola. Our costumes featured red T-shirts with the Coca-Cola logo and slogan emblazoned (in Indonesian) across the back.

15. Only those teachers who are native to or reside in the village of a participating group are normally eligible to perform with that group.

Chapter 3

1. For further discussion of the kebyar musical style, see Mack 1992; McPhee 1966, 328–51; Ornstein 1971; Keeler 1975; Lendra 1983; Tenzer 1991, 77–81 and elsewhere; and Vitale 1990.

2. The literal translation of *pukulan* is "beat" or "stroke," and the term can have several implied meanings depending on context. It may refer to a single stroke on a percussion instrument (such as a drum or gong), or to a specific pattern played on that instrument, or to an entire segment of music played by one instrumentalist. In the present discussion, however, *pukulan* shall be understood in the broader context implied by Asnawa's statement, that is, in reference to the individual "variations" or "mini-compositions" contained within a *demonstrasi*'s larger form.

3. Subtle changes and variations in the two-toned core melody ostinato of the ponggang may occur as well, but usually these result from alterations that allow the ponggang to follow the melodic direction of the reyong, rather than the reverse.

4. I use the term "essentially nonmetric" here because there is frequently an implied sense of metrical organization in passages of an awit-awit.

5. Some kreasi beleganjur composers have in recent years moved even further in the direction of kebyarizing beleganjur by replacing the drum prelude altogether, opening the piece instead with a virtuosic, kebyar-like reyong introduction. Such pieces have come to represent a substyle within kreasi beleganjur: *beleganjur kekebyaran* (Asnawa, pers. comm., 1992).

6. The kawitan may alternately be referred to as the *pengawit*. McPhee translates *pengawit* as "a holding in readiness" (1966, 94 n. 10). According to Asnawa (pers. comm., 1995), *kawitan* is by far the more common designation in the kreasi beleganjur context.

7. While not a beleganjur kekebyaran opening per se, this opening foreshadowed that later development.

8. There is still one more "surprise," however: the sequence of gong lanang and gong wadon strokes is reversed at the eleventh measure after "E".

9. It is perhaps worth mentioning that *penyelah* is also the name of the largest pair of cengceng kopyak (McPhee 1966, 237–38), although this would appear to have no particular significance to the present discussion.

10. In fact, musical materials and passages from the kawitan of a demonstrasi are often heard again in the pengecet. It should also be noted that the pengecet movements of all but the final demonstrasi of a contest performance may be rather brief in duration, to the degree that their status as independent "movements" is debatable in some pieces.

11. The adaptation of the Jagul-based drumming form into the kreasi beleganjur context in 1986 was actually the result of a three-phase process. It was directly inspired by a Jagul-type drum feature section that had been incorporated into a gamelan Adi Merdangga composition by the ASTI conservatory's Adi Merdangga ensemble earlier that same year (see Bakan 1993, 143–46, for discussion of gamelan Adi Merdangga). The Adi Merdangga version was in turn inspired by another adaptation of Jagul-style drumming four years earlier, in I Wayan Beratha's popular 1982 kreasi lelambatan composition "Minaing Segara." (See Bakan 1993, 290–91, for further discussion of this history.) It is possible that Beratha himself created the particular drumming form that has become so widely used in kreasi beleganjur and other modern styles in the process of adapting the original lelambatan piece (see Vitale 1996, 12).

12. Despite the tendency toward such resistance, however, recent years have seen an increasing interest on the part of many Balinese and other Indonesian composers in the implementation of more stringent copyright regulations for original compositional works.

13. The avant-garde experimentalism of Balinese *musik kontémporér* compositions poses something of an exception. As Asnawa explained to me in 1995, however, even in this more radical sphere of creative musical production, he and most other Balinese composers aspire to maintain a tangible sense of continuity and connection with the Balinese musical past.

14. The occasional appearance of dyads within the single-line texture results from the reinforcement of certain main-melody tones by consonant partner tones. These dyads are representative of a kind of "harmonization" procedure that is common in Balinese gamelan music. See Vitale 1990 on the subject of *empat* for further discussion.

15. Proper pitch correlations between melodic instruments and colotomic punctuating instruments — especially the two gong ageng — are of great importance. See Bakan 1993, 132–34. Also note that throughout the Pengawak movement, the bendé is tacit.

16. Suandita is not credited on the commercial cassette box as the composer of Kehen's 1990 championship-winning piece, "Gita Kencana Jaya"; Wayan Raka is listed as the piece's *penata tabuh,* or composer. By his own account, however, and those of several other reliable sources, including Asnawa, Suandita was the principal creator of the work.

17. See Manuel 1988, 213–18, for an introductory discussion of jaipongan music; and Manuel and Baier 1986 for a more detailed study.

18. In jaipongan, the kendang player uses the heel of his foot to raise, lower, and bend the pitch of the main drum.

19. A dance-like element is also present in performances of kebyar groups, especially in the choreographed movements executed by drummers, *jegogan* players, and *ugal* players during kebyar competitions. The choreographic element has not been as extensively or as formally developed in kebyar as in kreasi beleganjur, however—likely on account of the fact that kebyar performers are seated when they play, whereas beleganjur performers stand and can move freely.

Other instances where a blending of the performative roles of "musician" and "dancer" occurs include the solo dance part in "Kebyar Trompong," in which the dancer's performance on a *trompong* gong-chime is integrated into the dance (Bandem and deBoer 1995, 75–76); kecak, where members of the gamelan suara, or vocal gamelan, are also featured as dancers and actors (and sometimes as props as well) (see Dibia 1996; Bandem and deBoer 1995, 128–31; Bakan 1998a, 43–62; and McKean 1979); and gamelan Adi Merdangga, which features actual dancers but

involves in addition a somewhat rudimentary form of kreasi beleganjur–like choreography performed by the musicians as they play. Gerak sequences performed by the musicians in Adi Merdangga and in related forms such as *gamelan okokan* and *gamelan grumbyungan* have actually
been influenced by developments in kreasi beleganjur choreography in recent years.

20. Genres in which such clowning is prominent include *wayang, janger, prembon, drama
gong,* and *topéng.* For a rather graphic example, see Herbst 1997, 71–72.

Chapter 4

1. This was one of the groups with which I worked closely during my 1992 field research.

2. I Madé Murna was the composer and musical director for the highly acclaimed sekehe
beleganjur from Banjar Pandé Sumerta Kaja, which won the 1989 LBPB (as well as a major Bali-
wide contest in 1990 produced in conjunction with the Bali Arts Festival).

3. Sutton's comments (1986) on the importance of commercial recordings in Indonesian processes of musical "crystallization" are of particular relevance here.

4. See Dibia 1992 for an excellent comprehensive study of *arja;* Bandem and deBoer 1995,
79–82, for a concise overview description. While the principal dancers were traditionally men,
today women characteristically perform in the lead roles.

5. The work of Sadra, one of Indonesia's best-known composers of experimental music internationally, is well represented on the Lyrichord recording *Karya: Compositions of I Wayan Sadra*
(New Music Indonesia, vol. 3, Lyrichord LYRCD 7421). Yudana is known for his adventurously
unconventional works in the musik kontémporér and kebyar genres. His innovative kebyar composition "Lebur Seketi" (1993) was Kodya Denpasar's championship-winning piece in the 1995
Bali Arts Festival gong kebyar competition.

6. Asnawa's involvement with topéng has extended to the realm of scholarship as well; see
Asnawa 1995.

7. This may have been the first such contest to be held under government sponsorship in Bali.

8. Asnawa believes that entrance standards have become somewhat less rigorous in recent
years.

9. Asnawa must have meant the kempur when he referred to playing the gong, since the actual
gong (i.e., gong ageng) is not used in the gamelan gambuh orchestra.

10. Among other ambitions, Asnawa has an interest in pursuing a doctorate in ethnomusicology at an American university.

11. Printing Mas is a highly regarded Denpasar-based gamelan club consisting of accomplished musicians from different areas of Bali. Asnawa serves the group in the capacity of a kind
of musical director/consultant. The group formed the nucleus of Kodya Denpasar's championship
sekehe in the 1995 Bali Arts Festival gong kebyar contest.

Chapter 5

1. Dibia speaks here as a representative of the Balinese arts establishment. At the time of this
conversation, he was the associate dean of STSI. Since that time he has been promoted to the
position of dean.

2. The rules of many contests, including the LBPB, stipulate that not only the first-place champions, but the second- and third-place finishers as well are ineligible to take part in the competition
for a subsequent period of three years. Even after the imposed three-year absence, however, no
LBPB champion has ever returned to "defend" its championship.

3. On a few occasions, close friends of mine who had competed in contests and lost were
candid in expressing their disappointment to me during private conversations. I cannot recall a
single instance where such grievances were expressed in a public setting, however.

4. The passages from the original 1971 edition of *The Ethnomusicologist* quoted here also
appear in the new edition of the book (Hood 1982, 10–15). The "Bali Update" section included
in the introduction to the latter (ibid., xix–xx), however, in which Hood bemoans the destructive

impact of "tourism and great commercialization" on Balinese society, suggests a change in his perspective relative to these earlier cross-cultural comparisons.

5. This warrants comparison to another (and I believe related) long-ascribed cultural talent that over time led to the pervasive and misleading characterization of Balinese society as "essentially harmonious and apolitical" (Robinson 1995, xii). Recent historiographical studies on Bali by scholars such as Robinson (1995) and Vickers (1989) have largely overturned the formerly presumed validity of such characterizations. Also of relevance in this regard are writings by Boon (1977, 1990) and M. Hobart (1986).

6. My approach here has been influenced by Kingsbury 1988.

7. Here, as in subsequent sections of a sensitive nature, pseudonyms are employed. All names that first appear in quotation marks are pseudonyms.

8. This is to ensure that the contests remain essentially "amateur" events focused on community-based musical organizations. Generally, rules pertaining to performance eligibility are strictly enforced, especially in major contests such as the LBPB. In exceptional circumstances, conservatory-affiliated musicians have been granted permission to perform in certain contests, but this has only been deemed allowable in instances where permission has been secured in advance from the contest adjudication or organizational committee.

9. Some of the many publications that have directly or indirectly examined the employment of culture as an ideological tool of the New Order are Anderson 1990, 1991; Anderson and Kahin 1982; C. Geertz 1990; H. Geertz 1991; Hill 1994; Hobart and Taylor 1986; Holt 1972; Jackson and Pye 1978; Pemberton 1994; Pye 1985; Robinson 1995; Schulte Nordholt 1991; Schwarz 1994; and Vickers 1989. Among writings that have specifically addressed gamelan music relative to issues of modern Indonesian politics and ideology are Becker 1980; Pemberton 1987; Ramstedt 1992; and Sutton 1986, 1991. Also noteworthy here is Sumarsam's *Gamelan: Cultural Interaction and Musical Development in Central Java* (1995), which explores political implications of Javanese gamelan from a historiographic perspective.

10. Pemberton prefers the translation "Formal Democracy Reception" (1994, 5).

Chapter 6

1. See S. Willner [1992] 1996 for a concise but informative discussion of the women's kebyar phenomenon in Bali. See Yasa et al. 1993 for a more detailed historical account that focuses primarily on the development of women's kebyar organizations in Badung. (Yasa et al. also briefly discuss the legacy of Balinese women performers on the *gendèr,* a keyed metallophone used in the accompaniment of shadow puppet plays [1993, 52]). For studies of women's instrumental music performance traditions in Java, see Scott-Maxwell 1996, 1993 and Soedarsono et al. 1987–88 on the modern women's gamelan movement in Central Java; Weiss 1993 on Central Javanese female *gendèr* players; and S. Williams 1995, 1997 on Sundanese *gamelan degung* of West Java and other forms. For perspectives on historical relationships between women and gamelan in Indonesia, see Vickers 1985; Sumarsam 1995, 27, 60; and Perlman 1998.

2. The impetus for my interest in "women's beleganjur" was actually a men's beleganjur contest I attended in Denpasar in 1992, in which the musical personnel of one of the groups included three women. Though the women played only "easy" instruments (ponggang and kempli, the instruments sometimes played by women in gamelan Adi Merdangga performances), did not participate actively in the choreography, and were stationed at the very back of the performance area, their involvement shocked the audience and drew a great deal of attention.

After the contest I questioned Asnawa, Beratha, Rembang, and some of my other consultants (all of whom, it should be acknowledged, were middle-aged and older men with high positions in the Balinese musical establishment) about whether this surprising performance may have heralded things to come, in particular a nascent interest in the development of a women's beleganjur performance tradition in Bali. Without exception, I was informed that there was no possibility of such a development.

3. The situation is perhaps comparable to that among the Munda people of India. Referring to

"male" music instruments used by the Munda, such as the flute and the kettledrum *(nagara)*, Carol Babiracki notes that "[t]here was no taboo against women playing these instruments, and no penalty for doing so, but women normally didn't" (1997, 128).

4. The group was organized by and represented Pemda Badung (Pemerintah Daerah Badung), the Badung regency division of the Indonesian government.

5. However, email correspondence with Asnawa revealed that no such contest had been produced or even scheduled as of October 1997.

6. See Guinness 1994 for an informative discussion of how *adat* (traditional custom, traditional law) functions as a force of mediation between the localized cultural beliefs and expressions of specific Indonesian societies (e.g., Bali) and nationalist appropriations of such beliefs and expressions in terms of New Order ideology. See Geertz and Geertz 1975 and Wikan 1990 for detailed studies that address the implications of Balinese *adat* for women's lives in Bali from quite different perspectives.

7. Lev is speaking of gender issues in Indonesia generally rather than in Bali specifically.

8. See Sutton 1991 and Becker 1980 for insightful discussions of the complex relationships that exist between government cultural development programs and gamelan traditionalism and regionalism in Java.

9. Writings by C. Geertz (1973b, 417–18 n. 4) and Geertz and Geertz (1975, 56) on Bali and by A. R. Willner on Java (1980, 189) present rather different interpretations in implying a basic consistency between ideology and social practice where matters of gender equality are concerned. Keeler (1990) in a sense mediates between the different perspectives of Hatley and these authors in engaging the complex dialectical tension of social practice and ideology implicated in Javanese constructions of gender. Such complexity is further explored from a variety of points of view and in relation to the particular circumstances and conditions of a diverse array of gender-defined cultural situations in the essays of *Fantasizing the Feminine in Indonesia* (Sears 1996a). Other volumes of collected essays (which I have not cited elsewhere in this book) offer additional contributions to this dialogue: Ong and Peletz 1995; Berninghausen and Kerstan 1992; Stivens 1991; Alexander 1989; Van Esterik 1982; Hainsworth 1981; and Tétreault 1994.

10. This paradoxical relationship of female prestige and female dependence has been addressed in several ethnomusicological studies of Javanese musical traditions. In addition to Scott-Maxwell's work, which receives considerable attention in the present chapter, Weiss 1993 is especially notable on account of the author's insightful analysis of how mythical and historical representations of women function to elevate the musical status and artistic freedom of the female *gendèr* player, while simultaneously reinforcing and legitimizing the prevalent notion that it is impossible for women "to be active participants in the hierarchies of male society except through association with the power of the men in their lives" (26). The prestige versus dependence dialectics/dichotomies faced by Indonesian female musicians have also been addressed in studies focusing on vocalists; see, for example, Sutton 1984, 1987; S. Williams 1995, 1997; and W. Williams 1991, 110–15.

11. The one notable exception is the performance domain of *gendèr wayang*, where, according to Weiss (1993), the musical abilities of female *gendèr* players are often more highly esteemed than those of their male peers, largely on account of the emotional depth attributed to women's playing and their sensitivity to the direction of the puppeteer's *(dalang's)* performance. Such esteem, however, is paradoxically linked to prevailing myths concerning the essentially weak character of women, especially to the notion that women, unlike men, largely lack the capacity to control their emotions.

12. Both Suryatini and Desak are now employed as college music instructors *(dosén)* at STSI. As of 1995, they were the only Balinese women to hold such positions and to have achieved a professional status in musical careers. Some other female musicians (such as Nanik Kormaniati) have achieved what Sarah Willner ([1992] 1996) terms "semi-professional status" by virtue of their prominent participation in the Bali Arts Festival women's kebyar contest over many years, but these women receive little in the way of remuneration (usually the equivalent of about five dollars per month) for their musical efforts.

13. It should be noted that prior to the first Arts Festival women's kebyar contest in 1985, a small number of women's groups other than Puspasari were already active, including ensembles in Krambitan (Tabanan) and Nusa Penida (Klungkung). A kebyar group directed by I Gusti Bagus Suarsana was also formed in Jakarta, Java; this group, like Puspasari, was featured in a television broadcast (in 1983). See S. Willner [1992] 1996.

14. Since that time, many of these women, along with current conservatory students, have continued to play intermittently as members of a government-sponsored women's gamelan group operating out of STSI under the musical direction of Suryatini and Desak.

15. See Soedarsono et al. 1987–88 for a study of Central Javanese women's gamelan conceived along similar lines.

16. All quoted passages from *Kehidupan* represent my translations of the original Indonesian-language text.

17. The content, style, and spirit of this section of the abstract of *Kehidupan* bear a strong resemblance to those of a work published forty years earlier: *Wanita di Indonesia*, by Datoe Toemenggoeng (1953).

18. Between family responsibilities, professional obligations, and the time-intensive tasks of making offerings for and taking part in a multitude of ritual and ceremonial events, Hindu-Balinese women (and even girls) are left with precious little time for "nonessential" activities such as playing in a gamelan club. While performing gamelan has traditionally been an integral part of the Balinese male socialization process, this has not been the case for women. Critics (women and men) accuse women's gamelan organizations of promoting an indulgent, superfluous cultural activity that occupies too much time and energy, preventing women from devoting sufficient attention to both their mandatory duties and more "worthwhile" and "appropriate" optional pursuits, for example, studying dance.

19. The involvement of female performers in gamelan Adi Merdangga performances, noted earlier, may be seen to represent a partial exception to this claim.

20. In 1998, for the first time since its inception in 1985, the women's kebyar contest of the Bali Arts Festival was not held. The reasons for its "cancellation" and the future implications for women's gamelan in Bali were not clear at the time this book went to press. Nonetheless, I feel compelled to acknowledge that this turn of events places in question my former beliefs concerning broad societal acceptance of women's kebyar.

21. In addition to her high-profile performance activities with women's groups, Kormaniati is one of the few women to have performed with government-organized gamelan groups consisting mainly of men, including one that toured Korea in 1991 and another that toured the United States and Canada in 1997.

22. I do not know whether Dibia's advocacy of a slendro rather than a pelog tuning for women's beleganjur had specific aesthetic implications or was merely presented as an example of how contrast between men's and women's forms might be achieved.

23. Since the time of this interview, an STSI children's gamelan club including both daughters and sons of faculty members has been formed.

24. Remarks made to me by Mardiani suggest that the gender-biased mode of pedagogy evident in Suandita's comments regarding teaching women represents a continuation of earlier practices. Recalling her experiences in the KOKAR women's kebyar student groups in the 1970s, Mardiani spoke of how Beratha "was much nicer when he taught the girls, not like when he taught the boys, where he was very tough."

25. See S. Williams (1997, 8) for discussion of a similar situation in the Sundanese musical culture of West Java.

Introduction to the Pengecet

1. Ethnomusicological publications that have offered important contributions in this area include Berliner 1978, 1994; Blacking 1973; Burnim 1985; Chernoff 1979; Feld 1990; Friedson 1996; Herbst 1997; Koskoff 1993; and Rice 1994.

Chapter 7

1. Even at the STSI and SMKI conservatories, teaching and learning of music with the aid of notation is not very common; oral/aural methods of music transmission continue to represent the norm.

2. "Wayan" represents a composite of the several students of Sukarata whose lessons I observed in connection with this research.

3. Another work by McPhee on children's music-learning processes in Bali is *A Club of Small Men* (1948).

4. One is reminded of Timothy Rice's observations of a Bulgarian boy learning to play the *gaida* (Bulgarian bagpipe) under the tutelage of his grandfather, a master bagpiper named Grivnin. "The boy understood, or was trying to understand, the total sound of the instrument, not just the melody and rhythm. What he saw were rapidly moving fingers; what he heard was a dense succession of sounds; and he tried to reproduce both. His mind and fingers had grasped, or were close to grasping, the essence of ornamentation, but he had not yet integrated his aural and visual understanding of the total sound with whatever understanding of melody and rhythm he may have had" (Rice 1994, 66–67).

5. *Webster's New Twentieth-Century Dictionary of the English Language,* 2d ed., s.v. "Gestalt psychology."

6. As will be discussed later in the chapter, what is actually performed during successive "repetitions" changes as Sukarata switches between playing the lanang part he is teaching Wayan and the wadon part with which it interlocks.

7. Despite this "holistic" pedagogical ideal, however, practical constraints are understood to exist and are accommodated. While Sukarata will often demonstrate the drum part of a lengthy pukulan in its entirety from the outset of the teaching process, he will not normally demonstrate the complete drum part for, say, a full five-minute-long beleganjur contest demonstrasi.

Chapter 8

1. Blacking himself poses a convincing challenge to my generalization concerning language's normative status as a lowest common denominator of cultural identification. There "are no necessarily one-to-one relationships between languages and cultures," he writes, "as is illustrated by the variety of cultures of English- and German-speaking peoples and the common cultures shared by the speakers of different Chinese languages" ([1977] 1990, 275).

2. Rice (1994) and Burnim (1985) similarly discuss how they were guided in their pursuits as musical performers in the field by a sense of duty to their teachers and to other members of the musical communities in which they conducted research.

3. Again, the situation bears striking similarities to that described by Burnim (1985, 441), who relates that "[n]ot infrequently, I was referred to as 'Dr. Burnim,' despite my constant admonitions that the degree was yet to be conferred. This . . . was particularly stressful and disconcerting for me."

4. This is not to say that Indonesian musicians do not experience memorization problems, only that they are different in kind and degree. See Brinner's work on musical memory among Javanese (1995a) and Balinese (1995b) musicians.

5. The book *Music Grooves* (1994), by Charles Keil and Steven Feld, offers many important insights into the concept of groove as it pertains to the performance and perception of various kinds of music.

6. As was noted earlier, the male and female drums of a kendang pair are symbolically married in performance.

7. The only context in which I ever witnessed Jaya drumming without Sukarata was during Barong performances (which he identified as his area of specialization as a drummer), where just one drummer rather than two is employed.

Sukarata, in contrast to Jaya, performs with many different drumming partners in an array of musical contexts. In spite of this, however, the range of his musical activities is determined to a remarkable degree by his dedication and commitment to Jaya. Outside of playing for banjar functions in his native Belaluan Sadmerta and performing in special performances produced under the auspices of government arts and culture agencies (competitions, festivals, international tours), Sukarata rarely participates in musical events that do not involve Jaya in some central role, either musical (usually as Sukarata's drumming partner) or administrative.

Chapter 9

1. Although Blacking does not cite Alfred Schütz's work relative to the concept of "tuning in" in this article, a passage from Schütz's 1951 essay "Making Music Together: A Study in Social Relationship" would seem to suggest the connection. Schütz (1951, 79) writes of "what might be called the 'mutual tuning-in relationship' upon which alone all communication is founded. It is precisely this mutual tuning-in relationship by which the 'I' and the 'Thou' are experienced by both participants as a 'We' in vivid presence." Schütz's influence on Blacking in this instance seems especially likely in light of Reginald Byron's claim that in Blacking's work, Schütz's "ideas were always present between the lines, simply taken for granted. . . . To Schutz, he owed the idea that shared experience depends critically on *intersubjectivity,* the phenomenon of meaningful mutual intelligibility, and of its interpretive and expressive schemata, signs, and symbol systems" (1995, 20–21).

2. I videotaped most of my own lessons with a remote-controlled, tripod-mounted video camera. Some of the lessons were videotaped by Marilyn Campbell.

3. Wenten was the director of the Balinese gamelan at the University of California at Los Angeles during the period of my studies there.

4. These recording sessions were held at the balé banjar in Tatasan Kaja, the reverberant acoustics of which were not conducive to producing a high-fidelity recording with the equipment available to me.

Glossary

Agama Tirta   Balinese Hinduism; literally, "the religion of holy water"

agem   Correct, upright playing posture in Balinese drumming

ahli   Specialist, expert

angsel   In the beleganjur context, a cadential closing figure or accent articulated by the ensemble at the end of a phrase

angsel bawak   Regular (short) form of angsel heard in a beleganjur performance

angsel lantang   Long form of angsel heard in a beleganjur performance

arja   A type of Balinese folk opera

ASTI (Akademi Seni Tari Indonesia)   *see* STSI

awit-awit   Drum prelude of a beleganjur performance

bagus   Good, well done

bakat   Aptitude or inherent talent

balé banjar   Community center of a banjar, where gamelan rehearsals and performances are held

banjar   A Balinese neighborhood organization; village ward or hamlet

Baris Cina   "Chinese Baris," a rarely performed sacred dance accompanied by the gamelan gong bheri

Barong   "Mask" depicting some form of animal or supernatural being, the best known being the dragon-like lion creature Barong Ket. Processions featuring Barong may be accompanied by the gamelan batel bebarongan.

batel   Musical form (tabuh) based on a four-beat gong cycle; heard in certain styles of beleganjur music and in other repertoires

batu-batu   Drumming form heard in beleganjur featuring improvisation in one of the drum parts; employed in both traditional and kreasi styles of performance

Bebarongan Sakral   Sacred Barong ritual

bedug   Large, barrel-shaped drum used in the gamelan gong bheri

beleganjur (baleganjur, balaganjur)   Music played on the gamelan beleganjur

"Beleganjur Angga Yowana" (1986)   The first kreasi beleganjur composition to be released on a commercial recording; a classic of the genre that has been widely influential. Composed by I Ketut Gedé Asnawa and premiered by the sekehe beleganjur of Kaliungu Kaja.

"Beleganjur Padma Mudra" (1988)   LBPB championship–winning composition of the Tatasan Kaja beleganjur group, composed by I Ketut Sukarata

beleganjur wanita   Women's beleganjur

bendé (bebendé)   Clangy-toned, sunken-bossed hanging gong used in the gamelan beleganjur

berani   Brave, bold, courageous

Bhinnéka Tunggal Ika   Unity in Diversity, the national slogan of Indonesia

bhuta   Evil spirit being

bonang   The proper name for the beleganjur instrument more commonly known as *reyong*. Also the name of an important Central Javanese gong-chime instrument.

bossed gong   A gong with a protruding central "knob." This is the standard type of gong in Indonesian gamelans.

bukur Tower in which memukur effigies are carried to the sea (see plate 2)

cadence Closing figure of a musical phrase or section of a piece of music; similar to an angsel in Balinese music

cadenza Virtuosic display section in a musical performance, usually nonmetric

cedugan Technique of drumming used in beleganjur, in which the right-hand drum head is played with a mallet (panggul) and the left-hand head is played with open palm strokes

cengceng kopyak (cengceng) Crash cymbals used in the gamelan beleganjur and in the ceremonial gamelan gong repertoire. Usually, eight pairs of cymbals are used, on which are performed both interlocking and unison rhythmic patterns.

colotomic structure (colotomy) The foundational cyclic structure of gong tones in a gamelan piece (or section of a piece)

dalang Shadow puppeteer

demonstrasi Demonstration; in particular, a graded demonstration portion of a beleganjur contest performance

Denpasar Capital city of Bali; birthplace of the modern beleganjur contest (lomba beleganjur) and the beleganjur contest musical style (kreasi beleganjur)

desa (desa adat) A Balinese "village," usually comprising an association of related banjars

dosén College or conservatory instructor

drama gong A popular Balinese theatrical genre developed in the 1960s; may be described as a melodrama with musical accompaniment

emansipasi Women's emancipation; Indonesian women's emancipation movement

epistemology Philosophical study of the nature of knowledge, of ways of knowing

gambuh (gamelan gambuh) Ancient Balinese court dance-drama featuring a gamelan in which the melody is performed by several large suling flutes and a two-stringed spike fiddle (rebab)

gamelan (gambelan) An Indonesian ensemble, usually composed mainly of percussion instruments. The gamelan beleganjur is one of over twenty distinct types of Balinese gamelan.

gamelan Adi Merdangga Massive "traditional Balinese drumband." The music is derived primarily from beleganjur but also exhibits Western marching band influences. Adi Merdangga was developed at ASTI in 1984.

gamelan angklung Four-toned gamelan in a slendro tuning that features small-sized instruments, including a number of four-keyed metallophones. Often played processionally, for example in ngaben and memukur processions.

gamelan batel bebarongan An ensemble used to accompany Barong processions; its instrumentation closely resembles that of the gamelan beleganjur

gamelan beleganjur The Balinese "gamelan of walking warriors," a processional orchestra of gongs, drums, and cymbals used in ritual and ceremonial contexts and in special music contests (lomba beleganjur). The standard modern form is the gamelan beleganjur bebonangan; antecedent forms are the beleganjur bebatelan and the beleganjur peponggangan.

gamelan gambang An ancient gamelan featuring wooden-keyed idiophones that is associated mainly with ngaben ceremonies

gamelan gong Any of three large types of gamelan featuring gong ageng: the gamelan gong gedé, gamelan gong (a specific ensemble form in this context), and gamelan gong kebyar

gamelan gong bebonangan A non-processional gamelan beleganjur to which are added metallophones: *penyacah* and *jublag*

gamelan gong bheri A form of gamelan that is unique to the village of Renon, in Sanur district. The gongs are flat rather than bossed, and a large, barrel-shaped drum (bedug) is used instead of a pair of kendang. The music of gong bheri exhibits strong similarities to beleganjur, suggesting historical ties between the two.

gamelan gong gedé Grand court ceremonial gamelan, only a few of which still exist today; identified with the core ceremonial lelambatan repertoire

gamelan gong kebyar The dominant form of gamelan in modern Balinese musical life; used for the performance of modern concert and dance-accompaniment repertoires as well as for traditional musics

gamelan joged A gamelan featuring bamboo-keyed idiophones that is used to accompany a popular social dance called *joged*

gamelan krawang Any gamelan featuring bronze gongs and/or bronze-keyed metallophones

gamelan luang (gamelan saron) An ancient form of Balinese gamelan played for memukur ceremonies

gamelan pegongan Forms of gamelan that feature the gong ageng, or "great gong(s)." Other than the gamelan beleganjur, all belong to the ensemble category of gamelan gong.

gamelan selonding An ancient gamelan with iron-keyed instruments that is associated with the Bali Aga people of the village of Tenganan

gamelan Semar pegulingan A classical ensemble that was prominent in the royal courts of precolonial Bali; employs a distinctive seven-pitch tonal system

gamelan suara A "vocal gamelan" of the type heard in kecak

gaya laki-laki Masculine energy and style

gegedig Open strokes (on the reyong in beleganjur)

gendèr Metallophone with bamboo resonators. Usually, the name is used with specific reference to the *gendèr wayang*, which accompany shadow puppetry (wayang kulit).

gendèr wayang The main melodic instruments used to accompany Balinese shadow puppetry; unlike other Balinese metallophones, they are played using a difficult, two-hand mallet technique

gerak The choreography of kreasi beleganjur; literally, "movement"

gilak Eight-beat cycle, or form (tabuh), marked by a specific sequence of gong punctuations that provide the foundation, or colotomic structure, for numerous Balinese gamelan pieces, including most beleganjur pieces

gilak beleganjur Gilak form as employed in the beleganjur musical context

GOLKAR (Golongan Karya) Ruling political party of the Indonesian government

gong ageng *(gong)* "Great gong." The higher-pitched, male form is gong lanang; the female form is gong wadon. The shape of the gong ageng, which is the prototype for most of the other gong-type instruments in a Balinese gamelan, features a protruding central boss, or "knob" *(moncol* or *pencu),* a bent-down rim *(bibih,* lit. "lip"), and a tiered surface *(awak,* lit. "body").

gongan Gong cycle. In beleganjur and other pegongan repertoires, the simultaneous start and endpoint of a gongan is articulated by a gong ageng stroke.

gong-chime A set of tuned gongs in a gamelan, such as the reyong in beleganjur. Gamelans and other types of melodic percussion ensembles found throughout Southeast Asia are sometimes referred to as gong-chime orchestras.

guru Teacher, mentor

halus Refined

hocketing Technique used in Western music in which a melody or rhythm is divided among two or more instrumentalists or vocalists; similar to certain forms of interlocking in Balinese music

HSR (Himpunan Seniman Remaja) Badung Young Artists' Association (now defunct). This was the organization that produced the original Lomba Beleganjur Puputan Badung in 1986.

irama Rhythm; rhythmic and temporal aspects of the music; rhythmic and colotomic punctuating instruments (all instruments other than reyong and ponggang in beleganjur)

ISI (Institut Seni Indonesia) Indonesian Institute of the Arts

Jagul ("Tabuh Pat Jagul") A classic lelambatan composition

"Jagul" Drum feature section heard in most kreasi beleganjur contest performances. The drumming form is derived from the classic lelambatan composition of the same name.

jaipongan Popular social dance form of Sunda (West Java). The jaipongan music and dance styles have become popular throughout Indonesia, including Bali.

jamu Traditional medicines and herbal remedies

jejagulan   Newly invented variations based on the standard "Jagul" form

jejalanan   "Walking music" that a beleganjur group plays as it proceeds from one judging station to the next during a contest

juara   Champion. The first-, second-, and third-place finishers in a beleganjur contest are referred to as Juara Satu (Juara I), Juara Dua (Juara II), and Juara Tiga (Juara III). The fourth- through sixth-place finishers receive honorable mention *(harapan)* recognition.

juru *or* **tukang**   Musical performer; literally, "skilled worker"

juru kendang lanang   Lead drummer and musical director of a beleganjur ensemble

kabupaten   Administrative regency of Bali, of which there are eight: Badung, Bangli, Buleleng, Gianyar, Jembrana, Karangasem, Klungkung, and Tabanan. Since 1993, the capital-city region of Bali, Kota Madya Denpasar (Kodya Denpasar), has had kabupaten-like political autonomy.

kajar   Sunken-bossed hand-held gong that marks the tempo in beleganjur; may be substituted for by a kempluk

kala   Evil spirit being

karawitan   Theory and practice of gamelan music

kawin   Married; in two-part Balinese drumming, partners who play exceptionally well together may be described as *kawin*

kawitan   The first main section, or movement, of a beleganjur contest demonstration (demonstrasi), consisting of an ensemble introduction (opening rangkep) and a series of pukulans; may be referred to as *pengawit*

keberanian   Bravery

kebudayaan   Culture; in this book, it refers specifically to the officialized culture of Indonesian cultural nationalism

kebyar   Modern (twentieth-century), virtuosic style of music associated with the gamelan gong kebyar

kebyarization   The application of kebyar-derived stylistic, technical, and aesthetic devices to other gamelan repertoires. The transformation of traditional beleganjur into kreasi beleganjur was largely a product of kebyarization.

kecak (cak)   A dance-drama based on the Hindu epic *Ramayana*, in which the musical accompaniment is provided by a large "vocal percussion" orchestra (gamelan suara). The interlocking rhythms of kecak are closely related to those of beleganjur and have influenced developments in kreasi beleganjur.

kekerasan (keras)   Forceful strength

kempli   Tempo-marking hand-held gong used in the gamelan beleganjur

kempluk   Bossed hand-held gong that marks the tempo in beleganjur; may be substituted for by the kajar

kempur   A hanging gong heard in the gamelan beleganjur and in other Balinese gamelans

kendang   Drum. In beleganjur, as in most other types of Balinese gamelan music, two drums, the male lanang and the female wadon, are played in a complex interlocking style.

kepahlawanan   Heroism, in particular relating to a masculine heroic ideal emphasized in beleganjur contest performances

kesenian tradisional   Traditional arts, usually "elevated" in accordance with cultural nationalism priorities

kethoprak   A form of popular Javanese drama

kidung   Sacred form of sung poetry

kilitan cengceng   Interlocking rhythmic patterns of the cengceng cymbals

kilitan telu   Set of three core rhythmic patterns involved in cengceng interlocking textures *(megbeg, nyandet,* and *ngilit)*

klasik   Classic, as in classical music, dance, and theater forms of Bali (gambuh, lelambatan, Semar pegulingan, etc.)

klian gong   Administrative director of a sekehe gong

KOKAR (Konservatori Karawitan Indonesia)   *see* SMKI

KORPRI   (Korps Pegawai Republik Indonesia)   Indonesian civil service corps

kotekan   Interlocking elaborating parts, most specifically those of pemadé and kantilan metal-lophones, but the term is used in reference to the interlocking of other instruments as well. One player performs the polos part, the other the sangsih.

kreasi   Creation. The kreasi genres of music, dance, and theater typically are modernizations of traditional artistic forms.

kreasi baru   New creation. An original composition representative of one of the kreasi styles.

kreasi beleganjur   The modern contest style of beleganjur music, developed since 1986

kreasi lelambatan   A neo-traditional Balinese musical genre featuring modern gamelan gong kebyar arrangements of classic lelambatan pieces

Kreteria Lomba **(Contest Criteria)**   An official document outlining the evaluative criteria and regulations of a contest, such as a beleganjur contest

kris   Sacred dagger

kuburan   Cremation ground and temporary burial ground for those awaiting cremation

kul-kul   Large wooden slit-drum

kuno   Traditional, ancient (as in *beleganjur kuno*)

lagu   Melody; melodic aspects of the music; melodic instruments (reyong and ponggang in beleganjur)

lagu pengawak   Pengawak melody; in particular, the reyong melody in a pengawak beleganjur

lambé   Strokes played on the edge of the reyong kettles, usually with the wooden ends of the mallets

LBPB   *see* Lomba Beleganjur Puputan Badung

legong (legong keraton)   Classical Balinese dance featuring three young female dancers accompanied by gamelan

lelambatan   Core ceremonial repertoire of the gamelan gong, formerly played on the gamelan gong gedé but now most often heard on the gamelan gong kebyar

leyak   Evil spirit being

lomba   A contest, usually produced under some form of government sponsorship. Lombas take place throughout Indonesia.

lomba beleganjur   Formal beleganjur contest

Lomba Beleganjur Puputan Badung (LBPB)   Beleganjur Contest in Commemoration of the Puputan Badung; the original formal beleganjur contest, which was first produced in Denpasar in 1986

maguru panggul   The conventional method of Balinese gamelan music pedagogy; literally, "teaching with the mallet."

main   To play; for example, to play music

malpal   Highly energetic section of a beleganjur arrangement characterized by driving rhythms

mat   Musical beat; musical time-sense

meancung   The act of cremation

mecaru   Hindu-Balinese rituals devoted to the appeasement and exorcism of evil spirits; often involve beleganjur music

melis (mekiis)   Hindu-Balinese ceremony devoted to honoring deities and deified ancestors. Melis processions are accompanied by beleganjur music.

memukur   Hindu-Balinese mortuary ritual in which the soul of the deceased receives final rites of purification. Beleganjur music is performed during memukur processions.

mensukseskan   *see* successing

musik kontémporér   Indonesian "contemporary music"; specifically, experimental art music, often combining Balinese traditions and instruments with Western avant-garde musical devices and influences. The kontémporér genre has been developed in the Indonesian arts conservatories, including those of Bali.

ngaben   Hindu-Balinese cremation ritual. Beleganjur music is performed during ngaben processions and during other parts of the ceremony.

nganyut Final rite of a memukur ceremony, in which the effigies are thrown out to sea (see plate 3)

ngawit To alert, prepare beforehand

ngelangenin A term of high praise. When used in relation to a musical performance, it means, according to I Ketut Gedé Asnawa, "the effect of everything that is good in music."

ngerupuk Exorcistic ritual held the evening before Nyepi

ngilehin caru Final part of an exorcistic mecaru ritual, during which the evil spirits are driven away by loud sounds, often including beleganjur music

nuwutin Traditional Balinese teaching method in which imitating rather than analyzing is emphasized

Nyepi (Hari Raya Nyepi) Balinese New Year's Day, the Day of Silence. Grand exorcistic purification rituals the day before Nyepi feature beleganjur music prominently, and numerous beleganjur contests are typically held during the preceding weeks.

odalan Hindu-Balinese temple festival

ostinato A recurring figure, rhythm, motive, or melody that is repeated throughout a musical performance or a section thereof

Pancasila The Five Principles, the official national philosophy, or ideology, of the Republic of Indonesia

pandé Metalsmith; gamelan instrument maker

panggul Beater or mallet

pedanda Hindu-Balinese high priest

pekaad Closing section (coda) of a kreasi beleganjur or other gamelan performance

pelatih Coach or teacher (of a gamelan group)

pelog One of two main tonal systems employed in Javanese and Balinese gamelan music, the other being slendro. The system is based on a seven-tone tuning system, from which numerous five-tone "modes" are abstracted. The gamelan beleganjur uses a unique four-toned pelog-type scale.

pemadé and kantilan Mid- and high-registered metallophones, respectively, heard in the gamelan gong kebyar and other types of gamelan; they normally play interlocking elaborating parts, or kotekan

pemangku Village priest (commoner caste)

pembina Coach or teacher (of a gamelan group)

Pembina Tabuh Badung Honorary Council of Musicians

penata (penata tabuh) Composer or arranger

pengalihan *or* **pengiba** Transitional passage of music

pengawak beleganjur (pengawak) Slow middle movement of a kreasi beleganjur contest demonstration, in which melodicism in the reyong part is emphasized. Although called a *pengawak,* it does not conform to the usual formal criteria of pengawak movements in other Balinese gamelan repertoires.

pengecet Last main section, or movement, of a beleganjur contest demonstration

pengisep Section of a performance during which certain instruments are not played. In beleganjur, the absence of drums and cymbals indicates a pengisep section.

penyelah Second part of the pengawak movement of a kreasi beleganjur demonstration (and of the lagu pengawak in particular), in which the tempo and intensity are normally increased

penyuwud Closing piece performed by a gamelan at the end of a ceremony or other event

pepayasan Elaborative musical figurations, for example, those heard in the reyong parts of beleganjur pieces; more broadly, variations and musical developments in the kendang, cengceng, and reyong parts in beleganjur music

PKI (Partai Komunis Indonesia) Indonesian Communist Party (no longer exists)

PNI (Partai National Indonesia) Indonesian Nationalist Party

pokok "Core melody" of a Balinese gamelan piece. In beleganjur, this consists of a two-toned ostinato played on the ponggang.

polos Aspect of a kotekan that relates most closely to the core melody (pokok), usually involving predominantly "on-beat" rhythms

ponggang Core-melody (pokok) instrument of the gamelan beleganjur, consisting of two kettle gongs tuned approximately a semitone apart

PORDYA (Pekan Olah Raga Kodya Denpasar) Annual Denpasar sports fair

propinsi Province of the Republic of Indonesia (e.g., Bali, Java)

pukulan "Mini-composition" or variation within one of the larger formal sections of a beleganjur piece; may also mean a stroke or a pattern of strokes on a particular instrument

pura Temple

puri Palace

ramé "Crowdedness"; the quality of energetic busyness deemed desirable for most Balinese rituals, ceremonies, and public events

rangkep (rangkap) Section of a performance during which the entire ensemble plays

rebab Two-stringed spike fiddle

reyong In beleganjur, a gong-chime instrument (also known as bonang) consisting of four tuned kettle gongs that are played in an interlocking style. Normally, one player is employed for each of the four kettles. The gamelan gong kebyar version involves four players performing on a rack-mounted set of twelve kettle gongs.

reyongan Interlocking patterns (figurations) played on the reyong

RRI (Radio Republik Indonesia) Indonesian national radio station

rupiah Indonesian unit of currency

saih A "scale" or "mode" in Balinese music

saih selisir A five-tone pelog derivative heard in the gamelan gong kebyar and other Balinese gamelans. The four-tone beleganjur tonal system is derived from saih selisir.

sangsih The aspect of a kotekan that interlocks with the polos, usually involving predominantly "off-beat" rhythms

sekehe (seka, sekaa, sekaha) A voluntary organization or club, usually banjar-based, devoted to some particular activity or endeavor

sekehe beleganjur Beleganjur performance organization, usually a subdivision of a larger gamelan club

sekehe gong Gamelan performance organization

sekehe teruna Banjar youth club

sembahyang Group prayer ceremony

seniman alam "Natural artist"; an artist (musician, dancer, actor, etc.) without formal training

slendro One of two main tonal systems employed in Javanese and Balinese gamelan music, the other being pelog. The system is based on a five-tone tuning system, in which the intervals between successive tones tend to be nearly equidistant.

SMKI (Sekolah Menengah Kesenian Indonesia) Bali's government high school of the arts; known as KOKAR until 1976

STSI (Sekolah Tinggi Seni Indonesia) Bali's government college of the arts; known as ASTI until 1988

successing Anthropologist John Pemberton's translation of the term *mensukseskan,* which relates to manipulation of the Indonesian electoral process

suling Bamboo flute

tabuh Musical form defined by a specific colotomic structure, such as gilak or batel; can also refer to a composition

tabuh telu Musical form whose colotomic structure is nearly identical to that of gilak, except that there is no *gong* stroke in the middle of the eight-beat cycle. This form is sometimes used in beleganjur performances.

taksu Force underlying a charismatic, compelling performance; often explained in terms of divine inspiration

Taman Puputan Badung   Park in central Denpasar; location of the original Lomba Beleganjur Puputan Badung

tektekan   Form of gamelan featuring bamboo slit-drums; also the name of the slit-drums themselves

tetekep   Damped strokes (on the reyong in beleganjur)

tirta   Holy water

topéng   Literally, "mask"; term used in connection with a variety of different masked dance forms accompanied by gamelan music

trimurti   The trinity of supreme Hindu deities: Brahma (the creator), Wisnu (the protector), and Siwa (the destroyer); collectively the "three shapes" of God

trompong   a gong-chime instrument consisting of ten kettle gongs arranged in a single line; the lead melodic instrument in performances of traditional music (e.g., lelambatan) played on the gamelan gong

Ubud   Arts and culture center of Gianyar regency and the "cultural tourism" center of Bali

wadah *or* **badé**   Cremation tower

wanita   Woman

wayang kulit   Shadow puppetry, featuring leather puppets

wayang wong   "Human puppetry," in which human actors rather than puppets are used to enact the drama

Selected Beleganjur Discography (Annotated)

Recordings Available Internationally

Balaganjur of Pande and Angklung of Sidan, Bali. Features Sekehe Gong Kumala *[sic]* Budaya of Banjar Pandé, Desa Sumerta, Denpasar. 1995. World Music Library/King Record Company KICC 5197.

The first internationally distributed commercial recording devoted primarily to beleganjur music. Features the championship sekehe of both the 1989 Lomba Beleganjur Puputan Badung (LBPB) and the 1990 Festival Kreasi Beleganjur (Bali-wide competition), from Banjar Pandé Sumerta in Denpasar, performing a version of their prize-winning kreasi beleganjur showpiece "Jaya Sakti," composed by the group's musical director, I Madé Murna. The recording is also valuable for its inclusion of a selection entitled "Balaganjur Kuno," which exemplifies beleganjur performed in a more traditional-style musical context.

Bali. Volume 35 of the series Traditional Musicians: A Suite of Tropical Music and Sounds. 1995. WDR/Westdeutscher Rundfunk. Produced by Wolfgang Hamm and Rika Riessler. Frankfurt. World Network.

A sampler CD featuring various styles and genres of Balinese music. The eighth selection, "Cockfight—Trance in Paksabali & Kesiman—Gamelan Beleganjur," provides an excellent example of beleganjur being performed in ceremonial contexts.

Music of the Gamelan Gong Kebyar. Volume 1. Musicians of STSI Denpasar. 1996. Recorded by Wayne Vitale in 1991. Vital Records 401.

Features the Jagul drum form in a modern arrangement (by I Wayan Beratha) of the classic lelambatan composition "Tabuh Pat Jagul" (track 2), the source from which the "Jagul"-style drumming in kreasi beleganjur and Adi Merdangga was derived. An excerpt from this selection is included with permission on the CD accompanying this book.

Recordings Available in Indonesia

Gong Beleganjur. Features Sekehe Beleganjur Padma Kencana of Pejaten. 1980. Aneka 212.

The only commercially available recording of beleganjur music produced prior to the advent of kreasi beleganjur in 1986. An important musical document of pre-kreasi styles.

Kreasi Beleganjur. Features Seka Gong Kalingga Jaya of Banjar Kaliungu Kaja, Denpasar. 1987. Bali Record B 720.

Includes I Ketut Gedé Asnawa's kreasi beleganjur classic, "Beleganjur Angga Yowana," winner of the second prize in the original 1986 Lomba Beleganjur Puputan Badung (LBPB). Several excerpts from the digital master of this recording are included with permission on the CD accompanying this book.

Balaganjur: Juara I Kabupaten Badung 1987. Features Sekehe Gong Suta Dharma of Banjar Dauh Kutuh and Banjar Pemangkalan, Ubung Kaja, Denpasar. 1987. Maharani/Rick's Records (no catalogue number).

Includes a version of the 1987 LBPB championship–winning piece "Tabuh Jaya Suara," by I Wayan Sinti.

Kreasi Beleganjur Yadnya Swara. Features Sekehe Gong Dharma Santi of Banjar Kutri, Singapadu, Gianyar. [Late 1980s?] Bali Record Indonesia B 763.

Examples of "Gianyar style" kreasi beleganjur. Includes two compositions by I Nyoman Windha, one of Bali's most well-known composers.

Beleganjur. Features Gong Sandi Kumara of Banjar Tegal, Bangli. 1990[?]. Bali Record B 819.

Kreasi beleganjur from another regency of Bali, Bangli, is highlighted on this recording, which includes the championship compositions from the 1989 and 1990 Bangli lomba beleganjur.

Juara II, Festival Kreasi Beleganjur SE Bali '90. Features Sekehe Gong Teruna Mekar of Banjar Kebon, Singapadu, Gianyar. 1990. Bali Record Indonesia B 814.

This recording by the second-place finishers in the Bali-wide Festival Kreasi Beleganjur, which was held during the 1990 Bali Arts Festival, includes "Tabuh Kreasi Kesari Yuda" and "Tabuh Kreasi Semara Werdhi," both composed by I Wayan Darya.

Kreasi Baru Beleganjur Kapal—Badung. Features Sekehe Gong Puspa Werdi of Banjar Pemebetan, Kapal, Badung. 1991. Bali Record Indonesia B 833.

This fine recording includes kreasi beleganjur compositions by four different composers: Asnawa, I Gusti Ngurah Padang, I Ketut Budiasa, and I Wayan Rundu. It was produced under the direction of I Nyoman Cakra.

Balaganjur: Juara I Lomba '90–'91. Features Sekehe Gong Remaja Kencana Wiguna of Banjar Kehen, Kesiman Petilan, Denpasar. 1991. Maharani/Rick's Records (no catalogue number).

Includes a version of "Gita Kencana Jaya," the championship piece of the 1990 LBPB. This was the first in a series of three consecutive groups directed by I Ketut Suandita to win this prestigious contest.

Kreasi Beleganjur. Features Gong Kertha Yasa Budaya of Desa Sedang, Abian Semal, Badung. 1991. Bali Record B 838.

Includes Suandita's 1991 LBPB championship piece "Kertha Manggala Yudha," performed by a sekehe that some authorities (including Asnawa) consider to be the best kreasi beleganjur group ever. (Another version of the same material was produced on the Maharani/Rick's Records cassette entitled *Balaganjur: Juara I Lomba '91–'92.*)

Balaganjur: Juara I Lomba '92–'93. Features STT Yuwana Dharma Laksana of Banjar Meranggi, Kesiman Petilan, Denpasar Timur. 1992[?]. Maharani/Rick's Records (no catalogue number).

Another brilliant performance featuring prize-winning music by Suandita, this time the championship composition of the 1992 LBPB, "Wira Ghorava Cakti." Excerpts from the digital master of this recording are included with permission on the CD accompanying this book.

Balaganjur: Juara I Lomba Puputan Badung 1994–1995. Features Sekehe Gong Teruna Dharma Yowana of Banjar Bindu Mambal, Badung. 1995. Maharani Gamelan Series GS-015.

The 1994 LBPB champions performing music composed by I Wayan Gedé Arwana and I Wayan Griya.

Spesial Baleganjur.   Features Sekehe Gong Darma Semara of Banjar Tatiapi, Gianyar. 1988. Aneka Record 803.

Features an expanded, non-processional form of beleganjur ensemble (gamelan gong bebonangan) in which *penyacah* and *jublag* metallophones are added to the standard beleganjur instrumentation. In precolonial times, such ensembles were commonly heard during royal palace ceremonies.

Kreasi Baru Gong Kebyar: Badung dan Gianyar.   Features Sekehe Gong Kalingga Jaya of Banjar Kaliungu Kaja, Denpasar, and Sekehe Gong Remaja Tunas Mekar of Banjar Pengosekan, Ubud, Gianyar. 1991. Bali Record B 730.

Includes an Asnawa composition, "Beleganjur," that employs the expanded beleganjur instrumentation of the gamelan gong bebonangan described above. Also notable on account of the inclusion of works by the American composers Michael Tenzer and Wayne Vitale.

Adi Mardangga (Drum Band Tradisional Bali).   Kreasi Gong & Tari ASTI, volume 12. Features the Adi Mardangga (Merdangga) group of ASTI (STSI), Denpasar. 1992. Aneka 712.

Exemplifies the large "traditional Balinese drum band" style of beleganjur-derived music that originated in 1984 and in turn influenced the development of kreasi beleganjur two years later. The musical style combines beleganjur rhythms with Western marching band elements. The huge Adi Merdangga orchestras feature upwards of sixty kendang drummers and large contingents of the other standard beleganjur instruments as well. A large section of bamboo *suling* flutes is added to the expanded beleganjur-type instrumentation, and an elaborate dance is typically included in performances. Composers I Nyoman (Komang) Astita and I Nyoman Windha coordinated the performances on this recording, which was produced under the direction of I Madé Bandem.

Ogoh-Ogoh: Dasa Tembang Pop Bali.   Features popular songs by Okid, Yan Bero, Yan Stereo, Luh'tu Bintang, and Imam Tirta. 1991[?]. Maharani (no catalogue number).

Okid's "Ogoh-Ogoh," the title track of this Bali-pop music sampler, was a commercial hit in Bali when it was released in 1989. The song features a synthesized version of a gamelan beleganjur (employing digitally sampled instrumental sounds) in the context of a Western-influenced pop tune. Samples of kecak-style vocal textures are incorporated as well.

Unpublished Recording

"Kosong" (1984), by I Ketut Gedé Asnawa.

Copy of a live recording from the composer's private collection. This musik kontémporér composition, which is discussed in chapter 4, had an important influence on the development of kreasi beleganjur.

Bibliography

Abu-Lughod, Lila. 1991. "Writing against Culture." In Richard G. Fox, ed., *Recapturing Anthropology: Working in the Present,* 137–67. Santa Fe, N.M.: School of American Research Press.

———. 1993. *Writing Women's Worlds: Bedouin Stories.* Berkeley and Los Angeles: University of California Press.

Alexander, Paul, ed. 1989. *Creating Indonesian Cultures.* Sydney: Oceania Publications.

Anderson, Benedict. [1972] 1990a. "The Idea of Power in Javanese Culture." In *Language and Power: Exploring Political Cultures in Indonesia,* 17–77. Ithaca: Cornell University Press.

———. 1990b. *Language and Power: Exploring Political Cultures in Indonesia.* Ithaca: Cornell University Press.

———. 1991. *Imagined Communities: Reflections on the Origin and Spread of Nationalism.* 2d ed., revised and extended. London and New York: Verso. First edition published 1983.

Anderson, Benedict, and Audrey Kahin, eds. 1982. *Interpreting Indonesian Politics: Thirteen Contributions to the Debate.* Ithaca: Cornell Indonesia Project/Southeast Asia Program.

Aryasi, W. 1985. *Pengetahuan Karawitan Bali.* Denpasar: Departmen Pendidikan dan Kebudayaan/Proyek Pengembangan Kesenian Bali.

Asnawa, Ketut Gedé. 1991. "The Kendang Gambuh in Balinese Music." Master's thesis, University of Maryland, Baltimore County.

———. 1995. "Topeng Sidakarya." *Wreta Cita* 4 (2): 4–7.

Astita, Nyoman. 1993. "Gamelan Gong Gede: Sebuah Analisis Bentuk." *Mudra,* special edition, February 1993, 118–27.

Atkinson, Jane Monnig, and Shelly Errington, eds. 1990. *Power and Difference: Gender in Island Southeast Asia.* Stanford: Stanford University Press.

Babiracki, Carol M. 1997. "What's the Difference? Reflections on Gender and Research in Village India." In Gregory F. Barz and Timothy J. Cooley, eds., *Shadows in the Field: New Perspectives for Fieldwork in Ethnomusicology,* 121–36. New York: Oxford University Press.

Bakan, Michael B. 1993. "Balinese Kreasi Baleganjur: An Ethnography of Musical Experience." Ph.D. diss., University of California, Los Angeles.

———. 1993–94. "Lessons from a World: Balinese Applied Music Instruction and the Teaching of Western 'Art' Music." *College Music Symposium* 33/34: 1–22.

———. 1997–98. "From Oxymoron to Reality: Agendas of Gender and the Rise of Balinese Women's *Gamelan Beleganjur* in Bali, Indonesia." *Asian Music* 29 (1): 37–85.

———. 1998a. "Asian Traditions." In William M. Anderson and Marvelene C. Moore, eds., *Making Connections: Multicultural Music and the National Standards,* 43–66. Reston, Va.: Music Educators National Conference.

———. 1998b. "Walking Warriors: Battles of Culture and Ideology in the Balinese Gamelan Beleganjur World." *Ethnomusicology* 42 (3): 441–84.

Bakhtin, Mikhail. 1981. *The Dialogic Imagination.* Trans. Carol Emerson and J. Michael Holquist. Austin: University of Texas Press.

Bamberger, Jeanne, and Evan Ziporyn. 1992. "Getting It Wrong." *World of Music* 34 (3): 22–56.

Bandem, I Madé. 1980. "Wayang Wong in Contemporary Bali." Ph.D. diss., Wesleyan University.

————. 1983. *Ensiklopedi Gambelan Bali.* Denpasar: Proyek Penggalian, Pembinaan, Pengembangan Seni Klasik/Traditional dan Kesenian Baru, Pemerintah Daerah Tingkat I Bali.

Bandem, I Madé, and Fredrik Eugene deBoer. 1980. "Gambuh: A Classical Balinese Dance-Drama." *Asian Music* 10 (1): 115–27.

————. 1995. *Balinese Dance in Transition: Kaja and Kelod.* 2d ed. Kuala Lumpur: Oxford University Press.

Barber, Clyde. 1979. *A Balinese-English Dictionary.* 2 vols. Occasional Publications No. 2. Aberdeen: Aberdeen University Library.

Barkin, Elaine. 1990. "About Balinese New Music Concert Audiences: Background and Foregrounds and First Impressions." Unpublished ms.

Barth, Fredrik. 1993. *Balinese Worlds.* Chicago: University of Chicago Press.

Barz, Gregory F., and Timothy J. Cooley, eds. 1997. *Shadows in the Field: New Perspectives for Fieldwork in Ethnomusicology.* New York: Oxford University Press.

Bateson, Gregory. [1949] 1970. "Bali: The Value System of a Steady State." In Jane Belo, ed., *Traditional Balinese Culture,* 384–402. New York: Columbia University Press.

Bateson, Gregory, and Margaret Mead. 1942. *Balinese Character: A Photographic Analysis.* New York: New York Academy of Sciences.

Bauman, Zygmunt. 1978. *Hermeneutics and Social Science.* New York: Columbia University Press.

Becker, Judith. 1979. "Time and Tune in Java." In A. L. Becker and Aram A. Yengoyan, eds., *The Imagination of Reality: Essays in Southeast Asian Coherence Systems,* 197–210. Norwood, N.J.: Ablex.

————. 1980. *Traditional Music in Modern Java: Gamelan in a Changing Society.* Honolulu: University Press of Hawaii.

————. 1988. "Earth, Fire, *Sákti,* and the Javanese Gamelan." *Ethnomusicology* 32 (3): 385–90.

————. 1993. *Gamelan Stories: Tantrism, Islam, and Aesthetics in Central Java.* Tempe: Program for Southeast Asian Studies, Arizona State University.

Becker, Judith, and Alton Becker. 1981. "A Musical Icon: Power and Meaning in Javanese Gamelan Music." In Wendy Steiner, ed., *The Sign in Music and Literature,* 203–15. Austin: University of Texas Press.

Belo, Jane. [1949] 1966. *Bali: Rangda and Barong.* Monographs of the American Ethnological Society, vol. 16. Seattle: University of Washington Press. Original edition, New York: J. J. Augustin.

————, ed. 1970. *Traditional Balinese Culture.* New York: Columbia University Press.

Berninghausen, Jutta, and Birgit Kerstan. 1992. *Forging New Paths: Feminist Social Methodology and Rural Women in Java.* Trans. Barbara A. Reeves. London and New Jersey: Zed Books.

Berliner, Paul. 1978. *The Soul of Mbira: Music and Traditions of the Shona People of Zimbabwe.* Berkeley and Los Angeles: University of California Press.

————. 1994. *Thinking in Jazz: The Infinite Art of Improvisation.* Chicago: University of Chicago Press.

Blacking, John. 1973. *How Musical Is Man?* Seattle: University of Washington Press.

————. 1980. "Trends in the Black Music of South Africa, 1959–1969." In Elizabeth May, ed., *Musics of Many Cultures: An Introduction,* 195–215. Berkeley and Los Angeles: University of California Press.

————. [1977] 1990. "Some Problems of Theory and Method in the Study of Musical Change." In Kay Kaufman Shelemay, ed., *Garland Readings in Ethnomusicology: Musical Processes, Resources, and Technologies,* 6:259–84. New York: Garland Publishing.

————. 1992. "The Biology of Music-Making." In Helen Myers, ed., *Ethnomusicology: An Introduction,* 301–14. New York: W. W. Norton & Co.

Bohlman, Philip V. 1991. "Representation and Cultural Critique in the History of Ethnomusicology." In Bruno Nettl and Philip V. Bohlman, eds., *Comparative Musicology and Anthropol-*

ogy of Music: Essays on the History of Ethnomusicology, 131–51. Chicago: University of Chicago Press.

———. 1997. "Fieldwork in the Ethnomusicological Past." In Gregory F. Barz and Timothy J. Cooley, eds., *Shadows in the Field: New Perspectives for Fieldwork in Ethnomusicology,* 139–62. New York: Oxford University Press.

Boon, James A. 1977. *The Anthropological Romance of Bali, 1597–1972: Dynamic Perspectives in Marriage and Caste, Politics and Religion.* New York: Cambridge University Press.

———. 1990. *Affinities and Extremes: Crisscrossing the Bittersweet Ethnology of East Indies History, Hindu-Balinese Culture, and Indo-European Allure.* Chicago: University of Chicago Press.

Bourdieu, Pierre. 1977. *Outline of a Theory of Practice.* Cambridge: Cambridge University Press.

Brinner, Benjamin. 1995a. *Knowing Music, Making Music: Javanese* Gamelan *and the Theory of Musical Competence and Interaction.* Chicago: University of Chicago Press.

———. 1995b. "Recalling Complex Compositions: Some Perspectives on Musical Memory from Bali." Paper presented at the Annual Meeting of the Society for Ethnomusicology, Los Angeles.

Bruner, Edward M. 1986. "Experience and Its Expressions." In Victor W. Turner and Edward M. Bruner, eds., *The Anthropology of Experience,* 3–30. Urbana and Chicago: University of Illinois Press.

Burnim, Mellonee. 1985. "Culture Bearer and Tradition Bearer: An Ethnomusicologist's Research on Gospel Music." *Ethnomusicology* 29 (3): 432–77.

Byron, Reginald. 1995. "The Ethnomusicology of John Blacking." Introduction to John Blacking, *Music, Culture, and Experience: Selected Papers of John Blacking,* 1–28. Chicago: University of Chicago Press.

Chernoff, John Miller. 1979. *African Rhythm and African Sensibility: Aesthetics and Social Action in African Musical Idioms.* Chicago: University of Chicago Press.

Clifford, James. 1986. "On Ethnographic Self-Fashioning: Conrad and Malinowski." In Thomas C. Heller, Morton Sosna, and David E. Wellbery, eds., *Reconstructing Individualism: Autonomy, Individuality, and the Self in Western Thought,* 140–62. Stanford: Stanford University Press.

Clifford, James, and George E. Marcus. 1986. *Writing Culture: The Poetics and Politics of Ethnography.* Berkeley and Los Angeles: University of California Press.

Cohen, Anthony P. 1994. *Self Consciousness: An Alternative Anthropology of Identity.* London and New York: Routledge.

Covarrubias, Miguel. 1937. *Island of Bali.* New York: Alfred A. Knopf.

Crapanzano, Vincent. 1980. *Tuhami: Portrait of a Moroccan.* Chicago: University of Chicago Press.

Cukier, Judie, Joanne Norris, and Geoffrey Wall. 1996. "The Involvement of Women in the Tourist Industry of Bali, Indonesia." *Journal of Developmental Studies* 33 (2): 248–70.

Dahlan, M. Alwi, and Chris D. Walean. 1995. *Pancasila: An Introduction.* Jakarta: Kadin Indonesia Komite Amerika Serikat (KIKAS) (Indonesian Chamber of Commerce and Industry, U.S. Committee).

Daniel, Ana. 1981. *Bali: Behind the Mask.* New York: Alfred A. Knopf.

DeVale, Sue Carole. 1977. "A Sundanese Gamelan: A Gestalt Approach to Organology." Ph.D. diss., Northwestern University.

———. 1989. "Power and Meaning in Musical Instruments." *Concilium* 202 (2): 94–110.

———. 1990. "Death Symbolism in Music: Preliminary Considerations." *SPAFA Digest* 11 (3): 59–64.

———. 1991. "Musical Instruments and the Micro-/Macrocosmic Juncture." In Yoshihiko Tokumaru, ed., *Tradition and Its Future in Music: Report of SIMS 1990 Osaka,* 255–62. Tokyo and Osaka: Mita Press.

————. 1992. "Lions, Tigers, and Trees, Om Eye: Cosmological Symbolism in the Design and Morphology of Gamelan in Java." In Kathy Foley, ed., *Essays on Southeast Asian Performing Arts: Local Manifestations and Cross-Cultural Implications,* 54–95. Berkeley: Center for South and Southeast Asian Studies, University of California.

DeVale, Sue Carole, and I Wayan Dibia. 1991. "Sekar Anyar: An Exploration of Meaning in Balinese Gamelan." *World of Music* 33 (1): 5–51.

De Zoete, Beryl, and Walter Spies. [1938] 1973. *Dance and Drama in Bali.* Kuala Lumpur: Oxford University Press. Original edition, London: Faber & Faber.

Dibia, I Wayan. 1992. "Arja: A Sung Dance-Drama of Bali; a Study of Change and Transformation." Ph.D. diss., University of California, Los Angeles.

————. 1996. *Kecak: The Vocal Chant of Bali.* Denpasar: Hartanto Art Books.

Douglas, Stephen A. 1980. "Women in Indonesian Politics: The Myth of Functional Interest." In Sylvia A. Chipp and Justin J. Green, eds., *Asian Women in Transition,* 152–81. University Park and London: Pennsylvania State University Press.

Dumont, Jean-Paul. 1978. *The Headman and I.* Austin: University of Texas Press.

Dwyer, Kevin. 1982. *Moroccan Dialogues: Anthropology in Question.* Baltimore and London: Johns Hopkins University Press.

Echols, John M., and Hassan Shadily. 1989. *An Indonesian-English Dictionary.* 3d ed. Ithaca: Cornell University Press.

Eiseman, Fred B. 1989. *Bali: Sekala and Niskala.* Vol. 1, *Essays on Religion, Ritual, and Art.* Singapore: Periplus Editions.

————. 1990. *Bali: Sekala and Niskala.* Vol. 2, *Essays on Society, Tradition, and Craft.* Singapore: Periplus Editions.

Feld, Steven. 1990. *Sound and Sentiment: Birds, Weeping, Poetics, and Song in Kaluli Expression.* 2d ed. Philadelphia: University of Pennsylvania Press. First edition published 1982.

Friedson, Steven M. 1996. *Dancing Prophets: Musical Experience in Tumbuka Healing.* Chicago: University of Chicago Press.

Gadamer, Hans-Georg. [1965] 1975. *Truth and Method.* Trans. Garrett Barden and John Cumming. New York: Seabury Press/Continuum. Originally published as *Wahrheit und Methode,* 2d ed. (Tübingen: J. C. B. Mohr [Paul Siebeck]).

Geertz, Clifford. 1973a. "Deep Play: Notes on the Balinese Cockfight." In *The Interpretation of Cultures,* 412–53. New York: Basic Books.

————. 1973b. *The Interpretation of Cultures.* New York: Basic Books.

————. 1973c. "Person, Time, and Conduct in Bali." In *The Interpretation of Cultures,* 360–411. New York: Basic Books.

————. 1980. *Negara: The Theater State in Nineteenth-Century Bali.* Princeton: Princeton University Press.

————. 1983. *Local Knowledge.* New York: Basic Books.

————. 1984. " 'From the Native's Point of View': On the Nature of Anthropological Understanding." In Richard Shweder and Robert A. LeVine, eds., *Culture Theory: Essays on Mind, Self, and Emotion,* 123–36. Cambridge: Cambridge University Press.

————. 1988. *Works and Lives: The Anthropologist as Author.* Stanford: Stanford University Press.

————. 1990. " 'Popular Art' and the Javanese Tradition." *Indonesia* 50: 77–94.

Geertz, Hildred, ed. 1991. *State and Society in Bali: Historical, Textual, and Anthropological Approaches.* Leiden: KITLV Press.

Geertz, Hildred, and Clifford Geertz. 1975. *Kinship in Bali.* Chicago: University of Chicago Press.

Goris, R. n.d. *The Island of Bali: Its Religion and Ceremonies.* With photographs by Walter Spies. Java: The Royal Packet Navigation Company (K.P.M.).

Gourlay, Kenneth. 1978. "Towards a Reassessment of the Ethnomusicologist's Role in Research." *Ethnomusicology* 22 (1): 1–35.

Guinness, Patrick. 1994. "Local Society and Culture." In Hal Hill, ed., *Indonesia's New Order:*

The Dynamics of Socio-Economic Transformation, 267–304. Honolulu: University of Hawaii Press.

Hainsworth, Geoffrey B., ed. 1981. *Southeast Asia: Women, Changing Social Structure, and Cultural Continuity.* Ottawa: University of Ottawa Press.

Hall, Edward T. 1983. *The Dance of Life: The Other Dimension of Time.* New York: Anchor Books/Doubleday.

Hanna, Willard A. 1976. *Bali Profile: People, Events, Circumstances, 1001–1976.* New York: American Universities Field Staff.

Harnish, David. 1995. "Compositional Processes and Innovations in Bali." Paper presented at the Annual Meeting of the Society for Ethnomusicology, Los Angeles.

Hatley, Barbara. 1990. "Theatrical Imagery and Gender Ideology in Java." In Jane Monnig Atkinson and Shelly Errington, eds., *Power and Difference: Gender in Island Southeast Asia,* 177–207. Stanford: Stanford University Press.

———. 1994. "Cultural Expression." In Hal Hill, ed., *Indonesia's New Order: The Dynamics of Socio-Economic Transformation,* 216–66. Honolulu: University of Hawaii Press.

Heidegger, Martin. 1962. *Being and Time.* Trans. John Macquarrie and Edward Robinson. New York: Harper.

Herbst, Edward. 1997. *Voices in Bali: Energies and Perceptions in Vocal Music and Dance Theater.* Hanover, N.H.: Wesleyan University Press.

Herndon, Marcia, and Norma McLeod. 1980. *Music as Culture.* Norwood, Pa.: Norwood Editions.

Hill, Hal, ed. 1994. *Indonesia's New Order: The Dynamics of Socio-Economic Transformation.* Honolulu: University of Hawaii Press.

Hobart, Angela. 1987. *Dancing Shadows of Bali: Theatre and Myth.* London: Kegan Paul International.

Hobart, Angela, Urs Ramseyer, and Albert Leemann. 1996. *The Peoples of Bali.* Oxford: Blackwell Publishers.

Hobart, Mark. 1986. "Thinker, Thespian, Soldier, Slave? Assumptions about Human Nature in the Study of Balinese Society." In Mark Hobart and Robert H. Taylor, eds., *Context, Meaning, and Power in Southeast Asia,* 131–56. Ithaca: Cornell Southeast Asia Program.

Hobart, Mark, and Robert H. Taylor, eds. 1986. *Context, Meaning, and Power in Southeast Asia.* Ithaca: Cornell Southeast Asia Program.

Hobsbawm, Eric, and Terence Ranger, eds. 1983. *The Invention of Tradition.* Cambridge: Cambridge University Press.

Holt, Claire, ed. 1972. *Culture and Politics in Indonesia.* Ithaca: Cornell University Press.

Hood, Mantle. 1960. "The Challenge of Bi-Musicality." *Ethnomusicology* 4 (2): 55–59.

———. 1963. "Music, the Unknown." In Frank L. Harrison, Mantle Hood, and Claude V. Palisca, eds., *Musicology,* 217–326. Englewood Cliffs, N.J.: Prentice-Hall.

———. 1971. *The Ethnomusicologist.* New York: McGraw-Hill Book Company.

———. [1971] 1982. *The Ethnomusicologist.* New edition. Kent, Ohio: Kent State University Press.

———. 1990. "Balinese Gamelan Semar Pegulingan: The Modal System." *Progress Reports in Ethnomusicology* 3 (2): 11–20.

Hooykaas, C. 1973. *Religion in Bali.* Leiden: E. J. Brill.

Husserl, Edmund. 1970. *The Crisis of European Sciences and Transcendental Phenomenology: An Introduction to Phenomenological Philosophy.* Trans. D. Carr. Evanston, Ill.: Northwestern University Press.

Jackson, Karl D., and Lucian W. Pye. 1978. *Political Power and Communications in Indonesia.* Berkeley and Los Angeles: University of California Press.

Jackson, Michael. 1996. "Introduction: Phenomenology, Radical Empiricism, and Anthropological Critique." In Michael Jackson, ed., *Things as They Are: New Directions in Phenomenological Anthropology,* 1–50. Bloomington and Indianapolis: Indiana University Press.

Jensen, Gordon D., and Luh Ketut Suryani. 1992. *The Balinese People: A Reinvestigation of Character.* New York: Oxford University Press.

Kartini, Raden Adjeng. 1920. *Letters of a Javanese Princess.* Trans. Agnes L. Symmers. New York: Alfred A. Knopf.

Kartomi, Margaret J. 1990. *On Concepts and Classifications of Musical Instruments.* Chicago: University of Chicago Press.

———. 1995. " 'Traditional Music Weeps' and Other Themes in the Discourse on the Music, Dance, and Theatre of Indonesia, Malaysia, and Thailand." *Journal of Southeast Asian Studies* 26 (2): 366–400.

Keeler, Ward. 1975. "Musical Encounter in Java and Bali." *Indonesia* 19:85–126.

———. 1990. "Speaking of Gender in Java." In Jane Monnig Atkinson and Shelly Errington, eds., *Power and Difference: Gender in Island Southeast Asia,* 127–52. Stanford: Stanford University Press.

Keil, Charles. 1979. *Tiv Song.* Chicago: University of Chicago Press.

Keil, Charles, and Steven Feld. 1994. *Music Grooves.* Chicago: University of Chicago Press.

Kingsbury, Henry. 1988. *Music, Talent, and Performance: A Conservatory Cultural System.* Philadelphia: Temple University Press.

Koichi, Minagawa. 1995. *Balaganjur of Pande and Angklung of Sidan, Bali.* Booklet accompanying the compact disc recording. Trans. Oshima Yutaka and Matthew Zuckerman. World Music Library/King Record Company KICC 5197.

Koskoff, Ellen, ed. 1987. *Women and Music in Cross-Cultural Perspective.* New York: Greenwood.

———. 1993. "Miriam Sings Her Song: The Self and the Other in Anthropological Discourse." In Ruth Solie, ed., *Musicology and Difference: Gender and Sexuality in Music Scholarship,* 149–63. Berkeley and Los Angeles: University of California Press.

Kunst, Jaap. 1949. *Music in Java: Its History, Its Theory, and Its Technique.* 2 vols. The Hague: Martinus Nijhoff.

Kunst, Jaap, and C. J. A. Kunst–van Wely. 1925. *De Toonkunst Van Bali.* Weltevreden: Druk G. Kolff & Co.

Lansing, John Stephen. 1977. "Rama's Kingdoms: Social Supportive Mechanisms for the Arts in Bali." Ph.D. diss., University of Michigan.

———. 1979. "The Formation of the Court-Village Axis in the Balinese Arts." In Edward M. Bruner and Judith O. Becker, eds., *Art, Ritual, and Society in Indonesia,* Southeast Asia Series No. 53, 10–29. Athens: Ohio University, Center for International Studies.

———. 1983. *The Three Worlds of Bali.* New York: Praeger.

Lendra, I Wayan. 1983. "Kebyar Dance Genre: Continuity and Further Development of Balinese Dance." Master's thesis, University of California, Los Angeles.

Lev, Daniel. 1996. "On the Other Hand?" In Laurie Sears, ed., *Fantasizing the Feminine in Indonesia,* 191–203. Durham: Duke University Press.

Lindsay, Shawn. 1996. "Hand Drumming: An Essay in Practical Knowledge." In Michael Jackson, ed., *Things as They Are: New Directions in Phenomenological Anthropology,* 196–212. Bloomington and Indianapolis: Indiana University Press.

Lortat-Jacob, Bernard. 1995. *Sardinian Chronicles.* Trans. Teresa Lavender Fagan. Chicago: University of Chicago Press.

Mack, Dieter. 1992. "The Gong Kebyar Style of Pinda, Gianyar." In Danker Schaareman, ed., *Balinese Music in Context: A Sixty-Fifth Birthday Tribute to Hans Oesch,* 313–32. Winterthur, Switzerland: Amadeus.

Manuel, Peter. 1988. *Popular Musics of the Non-Western World: An Introductory Survey.* New York: Oxford University Press.

Manuel, Peter, and Randall Baier. 1986. "Jaipongan: Indigenous Popular Music of West Java." *Asian Music* 28 (1): 91–110.

Marcus, George E., and Michael M. J. Fischer. 1986. *Anthropology as Cultural Critique: An Experimental Moment in the Human Sciences.* Chicago: University of Chicago Press.

McKean, Philip Frick. 1973. "Cultural Involution: Tourists, Balinese, and the Process of Modernization in an Anthropological Perspective." Ph.D. diss., Brown University.

———. 1979. "From Purity to Pollution? The Balinese Ketjak (Monkey Dance) as Symbolic Form in Transition." In A. L. Becker and Aram A. Yengoyan, eds., *The Imagination of Reality: Essays in Southeast Asian Coherence Systems,* 293–302. Norwood, N.J.: Ablex.

McPhee, Colin. 1948. *A Club of Small Men.* New York: John Day.

———. 1966. *Music in Bali: A Study in Form and Instrumental Organization in Balinese Orchestral Music.* New Haven: Yale University Press.

———. [1954] 1970. "Children and Music in Bali." In Jane Belo, ed., *Traditional Balinese Culture,* 212–39. New York: Columbia University Press.

———. [1947] 1991. *A House in Bali.* Singapore: Oxford University Press. Original edition, London: Victor Gallancz.

———. n.d. The McPhee Collection. Ethnomusicology Archive, University of California, Los Angeles.

Mead, Margaret. [1940] 1970a. "The Arts in Bali." In Jane Belo, ed., *Traditional Balinese Culture,* 331–40. New York: Columbia University Press.

———. [1942] 1970b. "Community Drama, Bali and America." In Jane Belo, ed., *Traditional Balinese Culture,* 341–49. New York: Columbia University Press.

———. [1939] 1970c. "The Strolling Players in the Mountains of Bali." In Jane Belo, ed., *Traditional Balinese Culture,* 137–45. New York: Columbia University Press.

Merleau-Ponty, Maurice. [1960] 1964. *Signs.* Trans. Richard Calverton McCleary. Evanston, Ill.: Northwestern University Press. Originally published as *Signes* (Paris: Libraire Gallimard).

Merriam, Alan P. 1960. "Ethnomusicology, Discussion and Definition of the Field." *Ethnomusicology* 4 (3): 107–14.

———. 1964. *The Anthropology of Music.* Evanston, Ill.: Northwestern University Press.

———. 1977. "Definitions of 'Comparative Musicology' and 'Ethnomusicology': An Historical-Theoretical Perspective." *Ethnomusicology* 21 (2): 189–204.

Myers, Helen. 1992. "Fieldwork." In Helen Myers, ed., *Ethnomusicology: An Introduction,* 21–49. New York: W. W. Norton & Co.

Nettl, Bruno. 1995. *Heartland Excursions: Ethnomusicological Reflections on Schools of Music.* Urbana and Chicago: University of Illinois Press.

Nettl, Bruno, and Philip V. Bohlman, eds. 1991. *Comparative Musicology and Anthropology of Music: Essays on the History of Ethnomusicology.* Chicago: University of Chicago Press.

Newman, Philip L. 1965. *Knowing the Gururumba.* New York: Holt, Rinehart & Winston.

Ong, Aihwa, and Michael G. Peletz. 1995. *Bewitching Women, Pious Men: Gender and Body Politics in Southeast Asia.* Berkeley and Los Angeles: University of California Press.

Ornstein, Ruby Sue. 1971. "Gamelan Gong Kebjar: The Development of a Balinese Musical Tradition." 2 vols. Ph.D. diss., University of California, Los Angeles.

Panitia Peringatan Hari Ulang Tahun Puputan Badung. 1986. *Nama-Nama Sekehe Beleganjur.* Denpasar.

———. 1991a. *Juara Beleganjur Dan Angklung Dari Tahun 1986, 1987, 1988, 1989, 1990, 1991 Puputan Badung.* Denpasar.

———. 1991b. *Laporan Beleganjur Dari Tahun 1986, 1987, 1988, 1989, 1990, 1991 Puputan Badung.* Denpasar.

———. 1992a. *Daftar Nilai Lomba Beleganjur Dalam Rangka HUT Puputan Badung ke-86.* Denpasar.

———. 1992b. *Kreteria Lomba; Lomba Beleganjur Dalam Rangka HUT. Puputan Badung ke-86.* Denpasar.

———. 1992c. *Pembentukan Panitia Penyelenggara dan Tim Juri—Lomba Beleganjur Pada Peringatan Hari Ulang Tahun Puputan Badung ke-86.* Denpasar.

Papalia, Diane E., and Sally W. Olds. 1975. *A Child's World.* New York: McGraw-Hill.

Pemberton, John. 1987. "Musical Politics in Central Java (or How Not to Listen to a Javanese Gamelan)." *Indonesia* 44: 17–30.

———. 1994. *On the Subject of "Java."* Ithaca: Cornell University Press.

Perlman, Marc. 1998. "The Social Meanings of Modal Practices: Status, Gender, History, and *Pathet* in Central Javanese Music." *Ethnomusicology* 42 (1): 45–80.

Phalgunadi, I. Gusti Putu. 1991. *Evolution of Hindu Culture in Bali: From the Earliest Period to the Present Time.* Delhi: Sundeep Prakashan.

Picard, Michel. 1990. " 'Cultural Tourism' in Bali: Cultural Performances as Tourist Attractions." *Indonesia* 49: 37–74.

Pollmann, Tesse. 1990. "Margaret Mead's Balinese: The Fitting Symbols of the American Dream." *Indonesia* 49: 1–35.

Pye, Lucian W. 1985. *Asian Power and Politics: The Cultural Dimensions of Authority.* Cambridge, Mass.: Belknap/Harvard.

Quigley, Colin. 1988. "A French-Canadian Fiddler's Musical Worldview: The Violin Is 'Master of the World.' " *Selected Reports in Ethnomusicology* 7: 99–122.

Rabinow, Paul. 1977. *Reflections on Fieldwork in Morocco.* Berkeley and Los Angeles: University of California Press.

Rai, I Wayan. 1992. *Bibliography of Balinese Performing Arts.* Denpasar: Sekolah Tinggi Seni Indonesia.

———. 1996. "Balinese Gamelan Semar Pagulingan Saih Pitu: The Modal System." Ph.D. diss., University of Maryland, Baltimore County.

Ramseyer, Urs. 1986. *The Art and Culture of Bali.* Singapore: Oxford University Press.

Ramstedt, Martin. 1992. "Indonesian Cultural Policy in Relation to the Development of Balinese Performing Arts." In Danker Schaareman, ed., *Balinese Music in Context: A Sixty-Fifth Birthday Tribute to Hans Oesch,* 59–84. Winterthur, Switzerland: Amadeus.

Rembang, I Nyoman. 1985. *Hasil Pendokumentasian Notasi Gending-Gending Lelambatan Klasik Pegongan Daerah Bali.* Denpasar: Departmen Pendidikan dan Kebudayaan.

Rice, Timothy. 1987. "Toward the Remodeling of Ethnomusicology." *Ethnomusicology* 31 (3): 469–88.

———. 1988. "Understanding Three-Part Singing in Bulgaria: The Interplay of Theory and Experience." *Selected Reports in Ethnomusicology* 7: 43–57.

———. 1994. *May It Fill Your Soul: Experiencing Bulgarian Music.* Chicago: University of Chicago Press.

———. 1997. "Toward a Mediation of Field Methods and Field Experience in Ethnomusicology." In Gregory F. Barz and Timothy J. Cooley, eds., *Shadows in the Field: New Perspectives for Fieldwork in Ethnomusicology,* 101–120. New York: Oxford University Press.

Ricoeur, Paul. 1981. *Hermeneutics and the Human Sciences: Essays on Language, Action, and Interpretation.* Ed. and trans. John B. Thompson. Paris: Cambridge University Press/Editions de la Maison des Sciences de l'Homme.

Riesman, Paul. 1977. *Freedom in Fulani Social Life: An Introspective Ethnography.* Chicago: University of Chicago Press.

Robinson, Geoffrey. 1995. *The Dark Side of Paradise: Political Violence in Bali.* Ithaca: Cornell University Press.

Rodgers, Susan, P. Pospos, and Muhamad Radjab. 1995. *Telling Lives, Telling History: Autobiography and Historical Imagination in Indonesia.* Berkeley and Los Angeles: University of California Press.

Rorty, Richard. 1989. *Contingency, Irony, and Solidarity.* New York: Cambridge University Press.

———. 1991. *Objectivity, Relativism, and Truth.* New York: Cambridge University Press.

Rosaldo, Michelle Z. 1984. "Toward an Anthropology of Self and Feeling." In Richard Shweder and Robert A. LeVine, eds., *Culture Theory: Essays on Mind, Self, and Emotion,* 137–57. Cambridge: Cambridge University Press.

Rosaldo, Renato. 1989. *Culture and Truth: The Remaking of Social Analysis.* Boston: Beacon Press.

Roseman, Marina. 1987. "Inversion and Conjuncture: Male and Female Performance among the Temiar of Peninsular Malaysia." In Ellen Koskoff, ed., *Women and Music in Cross-Cultural Perspective,* 131–49. New York: Greenwood.

Sanger, Annette. 1985. "Music, Dance, and Social Organization in Two Balinese Villages." *Indonesia Circle* 37 : 45–62.

———. 1988. "Musical Life in a Balinese Village." *Indonesia Circle* 46 : 3–17.

Schaareman, Danker. 1980. "The Gamelan Gambang of Tatulingga, Bali." *Ethnomusicology* 24 (3): 465–82.

———, ed. 1992. *Balinese Music in Context: A Sixty-Fifth Birthday Tribute to Hans Oesch.* Winterthur, Switzerland: Amadeus.

Schulte Nordholt, Henk. 1991. *State, Village, and Ritual in Bali: A Historical Perspective.* Comparative Asian Studies 7. Amsterdam: VU University Press.

Schütz, Alfred. 1951. "Making Music Together: A Study in Social Relationship." *Social Research* 18 : 76–97.

Schwarz, Adam. 1994. *A Nation in Waiting: Indonesia in the 1990s.* Boulder and San Francisco: Westview Press.

Scott-Maxwell, Aline. 1993. "The Dynamics of the Yogyakarta Gamelan Music Tradition." Ph.D. diss., Monash University.

———. 1996. "Women's Gamelan Groups in Central Java: Some Issues of Gender, Status, and Change." In Brenton Broadstock et al., eds., *Aflame with Music: 100 Years of Music at the University of Melbourne,* 223–30. Melbourne: Centre for Studies in Australian Music, University of Melbourne.

Sears, Laurie, ed. 1996a. *Fantasizing the Feminine in Indonesia.* Durham: Duke University Press.

———. 1996b. "Fragile Identities: Deconstructing Women and Indonesia." Introduction to Laurie Sears, ed., *Fantasizing the Feminine in Indonesia,* 1–44. Durham: Duke University Press.

Seebass, Tilman. 1978. "A Note on Kebyar in Modern Bali." *Orbis Musicae* 9 : 103–21.

Seeger, Anthony. 1987. *Why Suya Sing: A Musical Anthropology of an Amazonian People.* Cambridge: Cambridge University Press.

Shelemay, Kay Kaufman. 1991. *A Song of Longing: An Ethiopian Journey.* Urbana: University of Illinois Press.

———. 1997. "The Ethnomusicologist, Ethnographic Method, and the Transmission of Tradition." In Gregory F. Barz and Timothy J. Cooley, eds., *Shadows in the Field: New Perspectives for Fieldwork in Ethnomusicology,* 189–204. New York: Oxford University Press.

Slobin, Mark. 1992. "Micromusics of the West." *Ethnomusicology* 36 (1): 1–87.

Soedarsono, R. M., et al. 1987–88. *Laporan Penelitian Karawitan Ibu-ibu, Satu Fenomena Sosio-Kultural Masyarakat Jawa pada Tengah Kedua Abad Ke-20.* Yogyakarta: Institut Seni Indonesia.

Stivens, Maila, ed. 1991. *Why Gender Matters in Southeast Asian Politics.* Monash Papers on Southeast Asia No. 23. Clayton, Victoria, Australia: Monash University Centre of Southeast Asian Studies.

Stoller, Paul, and Cheryl Olkes. 1987. *In Sorcery's Shadow: A Memoir of Apprenticeship among the Songhay of Niger.* Chicago: University of Chicago Press.

Suanda, Endo. 1982. "The Social Context of Cirebonese Performing Artists." *Asian Music* 13 (1): 27–41.

Suartaya, Kadek. 1993. "Drumband Tradisional Adi Merdangga: Kreativitas Seni Berdimensi Universal." *Mudra,* special edition, February 1993, 128–36.

Sudnow, David. 1978. *Ways of the Hand: The Organization of Improvised Conduct.* Cambridge, Mass.: Harvard University Press.

Sumarsam. 1995. *Gamelan: Cultural Interaction and Musical Development in Central Java.* Chicago: University of Chicago Press.

Suryakusuma, Julia I. 1996. "The State and Sexuality in New Order Indonesia." In Laurie Sears, ed., *Fantasizing the Feminine in Indonesia,* 92–119. Durham: Duke University Press.

Sutton, R. Anderson. 1984. "Who Is the *Pesindhen?* Notes on the Female Singing Tradition in Java." *Indonesia* 37:119–34.

———. 1986. "The Crystallization of a Marginal Tradition: Music in Banyumas, West Central Java." *Yearbook for Traditional Music* 18:115–32.

———. 1987. "Identity and Individuality in an Ensemble Tradition: The Female Vocalist in Java." In Ellen Koskoff, ed., *Women and Music in Cross-Cultural Perspective,* 111–30. New York: Greenwood.

———. 1991. *Traditions of Gamelan Music in Java: Musical Pluralism and Regional Identity.* New York: Cambridge University Press.

Tenzer, Michael. 1985. "KOKAR Den Pasar: An Annotated List of Gamelan on Campus." *Balungan* 1 (3): 12.

———. 1991. *Balinese Music.* Berkeley and Singapore: Periplus Editions.

Tétreault, Mary Ann, ed. 1994. *Women and Revolution in Africa, Asia, and the New World.* Columbia: University of South Carolina Press.

Thompson, Robert Farris. 1973. "An Aesthetic of the Cool." *African Arts* 7 (1): 40–43, 64–67, 89.

Titon, Jeff Todd. 1988. *Powerhouse for God: Speech, Chant, and Song in an Appalachian Baptist Church.* Austin: University of Texas Press.

———. 1993. "Knowing People Making Music: Toward a New Epistemology for Ethnomusicology." Paper presented at the Annual Meeting of the Society for Ethnomusicology, Oxford, Miss.

———. 1997. "Knowing Fieldwork." In Gregory F. Barz and Timothy J. Cooley, eds., *Shadows in the Field: New Perspectives for Fieldwork in Ethnomusicology,* 87–100. New York: Oxford University Press.

Toemenggoeng, Datoe. 1953. *Wanita di Indonesia.* Jakarta: Penerbit Chailan Sjamsoe.

Toth, Andrew. 1975. "The Gamelan Luang of Tangkas, Bali." *Selected Reports in Ethnomusicology* 2 (2): 65–79.

Turino, Thomas. 1993. *Moving Away from Silence.* Chicago: University of Chicago Press.

Turner, Victor W., and Edward M. Bruner, eds. 1986. *The Anthropology of Experience.* Urbana and Chicago: University of Illinois Press.

Van Esterik, Penny, ed. 1982. *Women of Southeast Asia.* Monograph Series on Southeast Asia, Occasional Paper No. 9. De Kalb: Northern Illinois University Center for Southeast Asian Studies.

Vetter, Roger. 1981. "Flexibility in the Performance Practice of Central Javanese Music." *Ethnomusicology* 25 (2): 199–215.

Vickers, Adrian. 1985. "The Realm of the Senses: Images of the Court Music of Pre-Colonial Bali." *Imago Musicae* 2:143–77.

———. 1989. *Bali: A Paradise Created.* Berkeley and Singapore: Periplus Editions.

Vitale, Wayne. 1990. "Kotekan: The Technique of Interlocking Parts in Balinese Music." *Balungan* 4 (2): 2–15.

———. 1996. *Music of the Gamelan Gong Kebyar.* Vol. 1. Booklet accompanying the compact disc recording. El Cerrito, Calif.: Vital Records.

Wallis, Richard. 1980. "The Voice as a Mode of Cultural Expression in Bali." Ph.D. diss., University of Michigan.

Warren, Carol. 1993. Adat *and* Dinas: *Balinese Communities in the Indonesian State.* Kuala Lumpur: Oxford University Press.

Waterman, Christopher. 1990. *Juju: A Social History and Ethnography of an African Popular Music.* Chicago: University of Chicago Press.

Weiss, Sarah. 1993. "Gender and *Gender:* Gender Ideology and the Female *Gender* Player in

Central Java." In Kimberly Marshall, ed., *Rediscovering the Muses: Women's Musical Traditions,* 21–48. Boston: Northeastern University Press.

Wiener, Margaret. 1995a. "Doors of Perception: Power and Representation in Bali." *Cultural Anthropology* 10 (4): 472–508.

———. 1995b. *Visible and Invisible Realms: Power, Magic, and Colonial Conquest in Bali.* Chicago: University of Chicago Press.

Wikan, Unni. 1990. *Managing Turbulent Hearts: A Balinese Formula for Living.* Chicago: University of Chicago Press.

Williams, Sean. 1995. "Female Performers and the Politics of Sexuality in West Java, Indonesia." Paper presented at the Annual Meeting of the Society for Ethnomusicology, Los Angeles.

———. 1997. "Gendered Space—Onstage and Offstage—in West Java." Paper presented at the Southeast Asian Studies Conference, Tempe, Ariz.

Williams, Walter. 1991. *Javanese Lives: Women and Men in Modern Indonesian Society.* New Brunswick, N.J.: Rutgers University Press.

Willner, Ann Ruth. 1980. "Expanding Women's Horizons in Indonesia: Toward Maximum Equality with Minimum Conflict." In Sylvia A. Chipp and Justin J. Green, eds., *Asian Women in Transition,* 182–93. University Park and London: Pennsylvania State University Press.

Willner, Sarah. [1992] 1996. "Kebyar Wanita: A Look at Women's Gamelan Groups in Bali." Revised version of a paper presented at the meeting of the Society for Balinese Studies, Denpasar, August 1992.

Yasa, I Ketut, with I Nyoman Sukerna, I Wayan Sadra, I Nengah Muliana, and I Gusti Gedé Putra. 1993. *Kehidupan dan Repertoire Gending Gong Kebyar Wanita di Denpasar.* Laporan Penelitian Kelompok. Surakarta: Sekolah Tinggi Seni Indonesia.

Zurbuchen, Mary Sabina. 1987. *The Language of Balinese Shadow Theater.* Princeton: Princeton University Press.

Index